Information Literacy Programs in the Digital Age:
Educating College and University Students Online

Compiled by

Alice Daugherty and Michael F. Russo
Louisiana State University

Association of College and Research Libraries
A division of the American Library Association
Chicago 2007

The paper used in this publication meets the minimum requirements of American National Standard for Information Sciences–Permanence of Paper for Printed Library Materials, ANSI Z39.48-1992. ∞

Library of Congress Cataloging-in-Publication Data

Information literacy programs in the digital age : educating college and university students online / compiled by Alice Daugherty and Michael F. Russo.
    p. cm.
  ISBN 978-0-8389-8444-4 (pbk. : alk. paper)
  1. Information literacy–Study and teaching (Higher)–Case studies. 2. Information literacy--Web-based instruction–Case studies. 3. Library orientation for college students–Web-based instruction–Case studies. 4. Libraries and distance education–Case studies. I. Daugherty, Alice. II. Russo, Michael F.

  ZA3075.I538 2007
  028.7071'1–dc22
  2007031204

Printed in the United States of America.

11 10 09 08 07   5 4 3 2 1

Table of Contents

Information Literacy Instruction Embedded into Discipline Courses and Programs

Information Literacy Instruction Tutorials (General and Subject-Specific)

1. Introduction

Alice Daugherty and Michael F. Russo

There is more than one way to skin a cat.

As library educators, we are always concerned with the efficiency and effectiveness of our instruction. Though philosophy and theory inform what happens in the class, ultimately this concern for efficacy focuses on the technique of instruction delivery—the "how to."

Of course, some methods of conveying information are better than others. Circumstances such as learning style and institutional support weigh heavily on the method we choose. Increasingly, because of burgeoning need and the recognition by institutions of higher education of the importance of information literacy, library instruction programs are looking to online instruction as the solution.

Just as cats don't come in one size and color, neither do online instruction programs. The varieties of these programs have been compelled and shaped by the circumstances of the individual institutions that have brought them into being. Our goal in this book is to showcase the array of online information literacy programs that have cropped up across the country. Readers will discover a spectrum of program types, starting with the broad breakdown of tutorials and credit courses. Some of these programs are general in nature, and some have a specific subject focus. In some cases the instruction is required, in other cases it is optional. The genetics of each institution—its individual needs, desires, mandates, and facilities—

contribute to the final form of the end product. Chances are that readers will find their own institutions to be similar to one or more of those described here.

For example, in chapter 2 Badke discusses the maturation of a graduate-level Web-based information literacy course where the emphasis of instruction is placed on the understanding of information systems and the use of "information as a means." Chapman, Landis, and Smith (chapter 3) discuss the development of a graduate-level information literacy course designed for the Department of Curriculum, Leadership and Technology, with particular emphasis placed on motivating and engaging students in the online environment and preparing students for writing their masters' theses.

Kinnie (chapter 4) discusses his experience of transforming an undergraduate three-credit information literacy course from the traditional classroom to the virtual world of teaching using WebCT. He presents the challenges encountered, such as keeping students motivated and deciding on how much and which technology to use. Similarly, in chapter 5 Lindsay, Scales, and Cummings discuss the transformation of a distance education information literacy course from a time when mailing videotapes was apropos to the use of a course management system including discussion board communications, interactive quizzes, and a virtual class lounge. Likewise, Colburn and Shan (chapter 6) write about the development of an information literacy course derived from its face-to-face counterpart; the online course is complete with fifteen instruction modules, homework assignments, and regular graded communication, meeting the needs of distance learners.

The one-credit information literacy course is discussed in chapter 7. With particular focus is on ACRL's Information Literacy Competency Standards for Higher Education, Ridlen and Theissen provide readers with examples of the alignment of those standards and student learning objectives.

In chapter 8, Salela, Green, and Chapman discuss the development of a credit-bearing information literacy course developed for graduate and undergraduate students, with different requirements for each group. Sample assignments and rubrics are included.

McManus and Lankford's chapter 9 reviews the development of an online information literacy course while providing readers with practical advice such as creating a sense of community in the course and realizing that online teaching is very different from face-to-face teaching.

Not all information literacy virtual instruction takes form as a credit-bearing course. In chapter 10, Allenbach Schmidt writes of an embedded library instruction program in a community college. The librarian is part of the instructional team and collaborates with the professors of record in Writing for Business and Adolescent Psychology.

In chapter 11, a different kind of example comes from a former librarian turned full-time lecturer: D'Angelo explains the integration of information literacy standards into a Multimedia Writing and Technical Communication Program curriculum and the importance of building in extra information literacy initiatives at every given opportunity.

Kennedy (chapter 12) provides an example of a librarian embedding information literacy instruction into a graduate engineering program in an unobtrusive yet thoroughly successful way. She presents examples of needs assessment surveys and works through the variety of effective methods of information literacy instruction incorporated into the program.

Other technological approaches also address distance learning and teaching of information literacy. Tutorials are valuable teaching tools. There are several software applications for the creation of multiple tutorials, and pedagogical implications are widespread. In chapter, 13, Resnis and Yu write about the development of a new tutorial customized to meet the needs of life sciences courses and engineering courses. The tutorial was developed as a shared resource, and librarians can adjust the programming to meet the needs of other disciplines.

The librarians from the Library of the Health Sciences–Chicago deliver effective online instruction to third-year medical students using interactive tutorials that mimic clinical scenarios. Wallis, Appelt, Pendell, and Pappas (chapter 14) provide information literacy instruction in a format that enhances student education and the practice of evidence-based medicine.

Sult and Greenfield use chapter 15 to present a newly piloted tutorial created for an upper-division education course, Children's Literature in the Classroom, for which they also provide faculty instructional guides with background information and teaching suggestions for using the tutorial.

In chapter 16, Prorak, Hill, and Hunter explore embedding Flash movie tutorials into an English 101 course through the course management system. They consider characteristics of the learning styles of Generation Y along with the collaborative efforts of the library and English Department to work together successfully. Wassenich (chapter 17) discusses the development of the Info Game, created to introduce community college students to general information literacy concepts and skills, and explains how to maximize the instructional outreach potential of a general purpose tutorial. In chapter 18, Murphy, Hightower, and Lyons write about a self-paced, self-assessing tutorial created for instructing undergraduate research concepts. This tutorial was redesigned to include, among other highlights, a section on information ethics, which proved to be most utilized by faculty and students.

Also, targeting first-year students, Oakleaf (chapter 19) addresses the benefits of incorporating an information literacy tutorial into the curriculum of a required first-year writing course from the perspectives of all stakeholders involved: faculty, students, and librarians. Similarly, McBride (chapter 20) discusses the redesign of an information literacy tutorial for Freshman Seminar and English 1000 courses for which the purpose is to provide a basic foundation of knowledge of library services and information literacy skills. Sinkinson and Knievel (chapter 21) present the success of a collaborative effort incorporating a four-module tutorial into the required first-year writing course in the Program for Writing and Rhetoric.

In chapter 22, Hayden, Rutherford, and Pival explain an information literacy tutorial designed with a "holistic framework" that incorporates Kuhlthau's theoretical work, explains the complexities of the information-seeking process, and is supportive of a university trend toward an inquiry-based learning environment.

In some cases, information literacy programs evolve into virtual programs. Mohanty, Norberg, and Vassiliadis (chapter 23) provide a synopsis of a virtual information literacy program starting with the creation of a tutorial for first-year and transfer students and progressing toward subject-specific tutorials in Exercise and Sport Science, Researching Art and Artists, Psychology Research, and more. In chapter 24, Rice, Crowe, Harris, and Leininger provide a summation of their university's general information literacy tutorial, nursing tutorials, an online information literacy game, and brief video tutorials for point-of-need instruction. Also, in the progression of building a virtual information literacy program, Gremmels and Mashek (chapter 25) present the virtual instruction of information literacy as a tool for enhancing classroom instruction. Not only do they serve their students through an enhanced instructional library home page, but they also meet educational needs with information literacy tutorials for Oral Communication, Biology, and Biblical Commentaries.

This book will be useful to those just now contemplating an online program for their institution. The examples included in this book provide the practical food for thought that should precede and stoke strategic planning. For further information on a particular program, the authors have generously included their e-mail addresses with their biographical information.

We hope the programs described in this book provide some modicum of inspiration and guidance as you travel into the realm of online information literacy instruction.

Information Literacy Credit Courses
and Programs

2. Graduate Online Information Literacy: The ACTS Experience

William Badke

Introduction

Associated Canadian Theological Schools (ACTS) is a graduate seminary consortium that is a division of Trinity Western University. The seminary educates pastors, missionaries, counselors, and religious workers at the master's degree level as well as serving, for a few students, as a feeder to doctoral studies. Academic requirements are rigorous and research papers are a common feature in most courses.

When ACTS formed in the late 1980s, it inherited three features from one of its founding members: a library, its librarian (me), and a one-credit information literacy course taught in a classroom setting only. The latter became a required prerequisite for all academic programs in ACTS almost by default, having been developed in 1985 through my lobbying of a sympathetic academic dean who agreed with me that "graduate students don't know how to do research." Unlike many other institutions, there simply was no barrier to creating the course; once the need was perceived, the course was created. Its implementation within ACTS as a prerequisite for all programs, however, likely would not have succeeded if that same dean had not become academic director of the fledgling ACTS. Such are the vagaries that sometimes occur within academia—a course is implemented because the right people to support it are on site at the right time. In the ACTS setting, there was no debate over putting the course, still taught in the classroom, into the curriculum.

Rationale and Content

The online version of the course, now serving some 130 students per year in sections of fifteen to thirty students, was built upon the foundation of the original classroom version, so I begin by looking at the philosophy and structure of the classroom course. Research Strategies (RES) 500 was established on the premise that graduate students did not need merely instruction in library skills but a course in which library skills training was a component of the comprehensive informational research method. From the beginning, the classroom course was based on a model for research that asked students to develop a research question or thesis based on a working knowledge of the topic. The course then went through the various steps of research, involving instruction in a strategies approach to enable students to gather relevant materials in a variety of formats, evaluate those materials, and present the research effectively within the bounds of the research question (though the actual mechanics of essay writing have never been a significant instructional element).

All of this was based upon the premise that research is not merely the gathering of information but the effective use of information to address a problem. *Information as end,* though a philosophy that students commonly bring with them from their undergraduate studies, was replaced by *information as means.* Thus an understanding of information systems and the development of critical thinking/critical evaluation skills were key components of instruction.

The classroom course was heavily assignment based, with at least ten of the twelve class sessions requiring that the results of actual research tasks be handed in. Here, the potential problem of students doing assignments not relevant to the actual requirements of their programs had to be resolved. Thus we decided to encourage students to identify research paper assignments for other courses they were taking and allow the Research Strategies course to be the vehicle within which they completed those other courses' projects. Professors have been cooperative, recognizing that students may be "double-dipping" but knowing that a better and more interesting research paper will come out of the process.

Development of the Online Information Literacy Course at ACTS

After an initial intake of about twenty-five students ACTS grew rapidly, soon reaching several hundred students and now serving four hundred to five hundred, many of whom are part-time students, but all of whom need to take the Research Strategies course. This demanded the creation of more sections of RES 500. Two difficulties emerged. First,

I did not have the time in my schedule to teach more classroom sections of the course. Second, some students felt it would be better to take the course before they started their first semester. This would obviously demand a summer section, but getting a class physically together in summer was nearly impossible. Compounding the problem was the fact that many of our students were taking their programs part-time and found it difficult to come to campus for a one-hour-per-week class even during a regular semester.

The World Wide Web had been active for a few years, so mounting the course on a Web site and teaching it online emerged as a potential solution. Thus, in 1999, I began investigating our options for creation of an online section of RES 500. I had no real mandate from the administration at ACTS, which appeared to take the attitude that, if I could pull it off, it might be a good idea, but if I could not, little harm would be done. Unfortunately, those who lack a mandate also lack support. I knew nothing of creating Web pages, nor was there any courseware (Blackboard, etc.) available to me.

Two students came to my aid. They let me know that, if I could provide them with con-

Figure 2.1 Basic course page with links

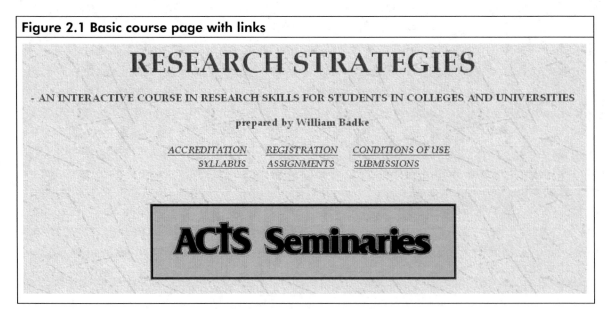

tent, they could create and mount the Web site. The initial product was useful, but the benign assistance of students soon became problematic. Though willing, they were not nearly as committed to the project as I was, and I found it increasingly difficult to get prompt updating of the site when I needed it. Lacking a mandate from administration, and struggling to create and maintain the site with student help, I decided to go it alone. I asked for and received access to my own space in the institutional Web site within which I built the next version of the course myself.

It soon became apparent that I was hopeless, even though I was using Web page-creation software, at creating or even understanding hierarchical page structures, advanced bells and whistles, and so on. So, the first product was a fairly basic set of Web pages hard-linked to each other, each doing part of the task.[1] (See figure 2.1.)

The administrators of ACTS, to their credit, saw the fledgling online course as experimental but worth trying. They gave it the green light, and the first class of six students began in June 2000. Enrollments for following course sections would soon grow to an average of twenty. By the end of 2006, close to five hundred students have taken the course.

An initial consideration was whether to protect the course content with a password. I used a password for the first year, but I could find little reason to justify it, since other course syllabi were publicly available. Thus the password requirement was removed, and the course remains open to anyone who wants to view it.

The platform for the course emerged as another potential difficulty. Once the institution acquired a courseware system (Jenzabar), I came under some pressure to move the research course into it. This would not have been an insurmountable problem, but I found the new courseware in its early versions cumbersome, especially for navigation among course pages and for quick revision. Thus, I have continued to resist the use of courseware despite the advantages that it could afford for assignment submission, forums, testing, and grading. Clearly, although courseware is beneficial in some situations, online courses can also be run successfully as Web pages, thus making them feasible even for institutions with limited technological resources. To this day, the research course is on the open Web, available to anyone with a current browser (http://www.acts.twu.ca/lbr/research500.htm).

Even with my rather limited initial understanding of Web-based course design, I was well aware that students prefer to feel like a community, even if the online environment makes it a far-flung one. Initially I tried to engender a virtual community with discussions and opportunities for students to interact directly regarding challenges they were experiencing. This turned out to be a wasted effort. These graduate students, doing daily battle to prioritize their complicated lives, were interested only in getting through the course and had no taste for spending extra time communicating with each other, participating in forums, and so on. To this day, therefore, student interaction is primarily between student and professor.

Technical difficulties such as downtime, broken links, and e-mail not received have been surprisingly few and are usually identified and resolved quickly. Initially administrators were concerned that the weight of technical troubleshooting would consume too much of my time, but that has not been the case. The major challenge technologically has been with the few students who have limited computer experience and struggle to accomplish their assignment tasks, sometimes misunderstanding even basic computer operations. Yet, as graduate students, they are quick learners and are usually doing much better by mid-semester.

A new challenge has come from the seminary's introduction of a Korean Worldview Program at the master's level, intended to enable Korean professionals to integrate their work with an understanding of their faith. The program is taught primarily in Korean (not one of my languages), and its students have little or no experience with Western education, though they have master's degrees and even doctorates in a wide variety of disciplines. Very early it became clear that if Korean Worldview students were to succeed with the Research Strategies course in its online form, taken in English, they would need an introduction to Western academic library skills and education philosophy, as well as to the nature and construction of research papers in the North American setting. These students thus receive ten hours in classroom instruction before they begin the online course.

Even with this level of assistance, it has become clear that students from non-Western countries do not do nearly as well at the online research course as do Western students. This has nothing to do with their intelligence and little to do with their English language skills but rather with their understanding of the research task in our setting (research as problem solving) as opposed to theirs (research as compilation). After several years of including international students in the online course, I have concluded that they would do better with classroom instruction, where they can interact more directly with the research philosophy I am teaching.

Faculty reaction to the course has ranged from neutral to enthusiastic, though it is not always clear how well some faculty members understand the nature of RES 500 OL. Students have been positive about their learning experience in the course, and their research projects have been generally better than one would expect of the average graduate student.[2] Thus, faculty have taken the approach "If it ain't broke, don't fix it."

This does not mean, however, that faculty members understand that the course is neither library skills training nor instruction in the mechanics of research papers. In the past year, an administrative decision to have a non-librarian teach one section of the classroom version of the course led to a renewed dialogue among administrators, faculty, and myself about what is being taught and the expertise required to teach it. I have begun doing ten- to fifteen-minute sessions during faculty meetings in which I demonstrate aspects of the research course content and take feedback. Faculty appreciate the opportunity to upgrade their own knowledge of information systems, databases, and research design, and I have been able to give the course more prominence to ensure that support for it continues.

Course Content

The original classroom Research Strategies course was premised on the following:

1. Students need more than library skills and an introduction to research paper construction. We must teach them strategic skills built around a sound informational research methodology. They need to come away with a clear understanding of research and the information cycle.

2. Students need to conceptualize research as more than an information-compil-

ing exercise. Thus "information as problem-solving tool" is an emphasis throughout.

3. The course needs to be a combination of knowledge and skill development. Thus we must provide students with frequent assignments based on the instruction they are receiving.

4. Students must take a hands-on approach to learning through practice with development of research questions, as well as exercises in using databases and doing evaluation tasks.

Translating these premises and the features of the classroom version into an online environment proved both challenging and surprisingly easy. The challenge came from the need to preserve the best features of classroom interaction in a online setting. The easy transition resulted from the fact that the classroom course was already in a modular format with a heavy emphasis on student assignments. Had this been a high content–low skill development course, the online environment would not have worked nearly as well.

I built the entire online course around its assignments, cutting the number of them from ten in the classroom version to six but broadening each assignment so that the workload was similar to that of ten assignments. The thinking here, based on published research related to online course dropout rates, was that, for those students who would struggle with self-discipline in the online environment, six assignments was psychologically less daunting than ten and could be broken down to two assignments per month over a three-month semester.

With the assignments creating the structure, the biggest difficulty was developing materials that could simulate the interactive nature of the classroom. Informational content came from the textbook I had written, *Research Strategies: Finding Your Way through the Information Fog,* currently in its second edition.[3] The book had been written with a view to being a self-teaching tool, if that were necessary. I also injected an online "backgrounder" into each online assignment, in which I summarized the most crucial infor-

Figure 2.2. Sample online backgrounder

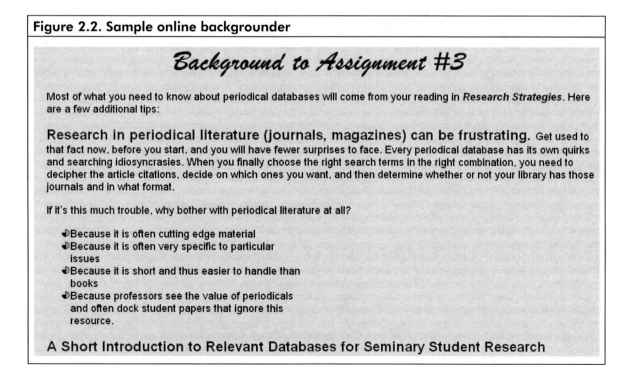

Background to Assignment #3

Most of what you need to know about periodical databases will come from your reading in *Research Strategies*. Here are a few additional tips:

Research in periodical literature (journals, magazines) can be frustrating. Get used to that fact now, before you start, and you will have fewer surprises to face. Every periodical database has its own quirks and searching idiosyncrasies. When you finally choose the right search terms in the right combination, you need to decipher the article citations, decide on which ones you want, and then determine whether or not your library has those journals and in what format.

If it's this much trouble, why bother with periodical literature at all?

    ↵Because it is often cutting edge material
    ↵Because it is often very specific to particular
      issues
    ↵Because it is short and thus easier to handle than
      books
    ↵Because professors see the value of periodicals
      and often dock student papers that ignore this
      resource.

A Short Introduction to Relevant Databases for Seminary Student Research

mation required by the student to complete the assignment. For example, figure 2.2 is a portion of a backgrounder for the third assignment.

The interactive components of the classroom were more difficult to reproduce in the online environment. As a first step, I increased the number of topics the student had to work with from one in the classroom course to two in the online. The rationale here was that online students had no classes to attend and thus could use those hours for additional practice, allowing me to combine the extra practice with my feedback to their assignments to simulate what could be gained from classroom interaction. In an effort to avoid making the online course overly heavy, I abandoned the original classroom course's requirement for a full research paper at the end and, instead, asked for two sets of research questions, expanded outlines, and final bibliographies. I also added links to online tutorials for some of the major databases.

The six assignments encompass the following:

1. Choice of two topics (preferably from other current courses), use of reference sources for a working knowledge, development of several possible research questions, selection of one of these for each topic, and creation of preliminary outlines.

2. Searches for potential reference information (related to their research questions) on the Web; then keyword (Boolean) and controlled vocabulary (Subject Heading) searches in the library catalog.

3. Searches in four periodical databases for material relevant to their research questions, using advanced features wherever possible.

4. Exploration of the potential of Google Scholar for research, as well as searches in ERIC.

5. Exploration of "Hidden Internet" databases and evaluation of selected sources.

6. Presentation of two final research questions, annotated outlines, and bibliographies.

This list does not, however, describe all of the course content. The students must read the textbook (which provides the intellectual background for the skills demonstrated in the assignments) as well as the online background information at the beginning of each assignment. This separation of study content from assignments is deliberately intended to keep the assignments clear, without the baggage of an interpolated knowledge base.

Instruction

At first glance one could assume that most of the "instruction" was completed when the course was written. This, however, is far from the case. The online Research Strategies course demands as much as, and often more than, the classroom version in instructor time, both just before the course and when assignments are graded.

As students begin the course, they are provided with an online set of instructions explaining where the course is, what is expected of them, what due dates are set, and how they can contact me. I follow this up with a direct e-mail that asks students to respond so that I know we are communicating. Students take a pre-test, which is sent to me for grading.

Even with all of this introductory support, many students regularly e-mail questions about assignments or the tasks required so that they can be sure they understand what is required of them. At times, such questions point out ambiguities in instructions and appropriate corrections are made. Strangely, an assignment instruction can be in place for years with no problems, then suddenly one-third of a class is confused by it. The process of keeping instructions clear seems ever nearing perfection but never attaining it.

Some students with limited computer skills or lack of background in research method want to run initial versions of assignments by me before they submit the final version. This is a problem, since it may be unfair to students who submit only once, but I do offer some guidance and redirection to students who go to the trouble of sending me trial runs.

The major active instruction, however, comes through the grading process after assignments are submitted. Since later assignments build upon earlier ones, students expect to receive detailed feedback that corrects false steps, helps them sharpen research questions, guides them to better use of search terminology or choice of databases, and helps them develop their evaluative skills. Normally an assignment takes twenty minutes to grade, but some can take up to an hour. I may suggest several alternatives to the research question or point out options in approaching relevant search terminology. Regularly I repeat searches that students have tried, attempting variations of those searches and trying out other databases in order to provide guidance to better ways of searching.

Here is an example from recent grading related to a library catalog search on the challenges of communication in a counseling situation with an Asian client:

> Your title keyword search terms look good with good results considering the limited resources in this area, but I would drop the word "culture," which screens out possibly good results.

"Asian" is already a culture, so you don't need "culture."

> For your first subject heading search, unfortunately there is no subject heading *Communication and counseling.* Don't forget that you cannot create or alter subject headings. *Communication and culture* is an authorized subject heading. Possibly *Nonverbal communication* would be useful. Also *Cross-cultural counseling,* as well as *Intercultural communication.*

Students, once they have received my comments, sometimes ask for further clarification or try out other options and send me the results for evaluation. Clearly the grading process is a significant plank in the educational value of the course.

I have considered more immediate forms of communication with students beyond e-mail, but telephone contact tends to turn into communication between voicemail systems, and instant messaging would make me too much a slave of the communication demands of the moment. Since the average online student may well be a local person who prefers the online format, I do have my online students drop in personally for help. Overall, though, most communication remains in the medium of e-mail, which works quite well as long as I monitor and respond to it promptly.

Program Assessment

Finding good assessment tools has always been a challenge for the Research Strategies course. One clear measure is student progress through the assignments, especially the final one, which asks students to put the results of their semester together into a research question, annotated outline, and bibliography for each topic. This, however, does not ensure that all skills will be retained.

Recently I have been using a pre-test and post-test. The pre/post-test method does not, however, measure ongoing information literacy beyond the course completion date, though it does show initial dramatic improvement in understanding of research method and search skills. In this regard, the relatively small size of this graduate school is a benefit. I remain in contact with many of the students, encouraging them to contact me with research problems. I regularly observe quite strong retention of skills learned in the research course as I work with these students. Professors also tend to maintain high expectations of student research, so there is little opportunity for skills to grow rusty.

One useful measure of the ongoing success of the course is the graduating essay required of all students near the end of the largest program. To ensure that the research proposal process is a happy one, academic administration has asked me to evaluate all proposals, which include a research question or thesis, a rationale for the project, an outline, and a preliminary bibliography. Most students have put a reasonably sophisticated proposal together before they come to me (thus providing me a measure of their ongoing research skills), and I have the opportunity to provide further information literacy instruction related to their topic areas.

Still, assessment is a challenge. How, for example, does one measure research ability for students who take the course as opposed to those who do not take it, when the course is required of all students? One option for assessment might be to administer further post-tests in succeeding years, though a mechanism would need to be found to make such post-testing possible.

Lessons Learned

Several key lessons have been learned: Situating the research course as a program prerequisite that does not consume program hours proved to be a valuable move. Many of our graduate programs have prerequisites, so the concept is not foreign to the developers of the ACTS curriculum. A side benefit is the fact that we did not have to subject the course to program curriculum review, which could make it vulnerable to removal (though it has been reviewed by academic administration).

Though students are aware that the course is actually more work than its one credit billing, they are grateful that they are not being charged additional tuition for more credit hours. The ability to use research assignments from actual courses in programs has served to make the same prerequisite relevant to each program without the need for specialized sections, and it is a timesaver for students who would have had to do the research anyway.

The course actually appears to be working extremely well, with students showing evidence of genuine learning, as seen in assignment results and anecdotal reports from faculty, and the popularity of the course remains high. I entered the process with significant doubts about the effectiveness of providing information literacy instruction in the online environment where so much is left to student learning and so little to direct professorial instruction. Yet, year after year, students complete the course with my expectations met and often surpassed.

Another lesson is simply that you cannot wind up an online course like a clock and let it run. Online instruction is a hands-on enterprise with the professor on one side and highly dependent students on the other. Students need rapid response to problems, quick turnaround on assignment grading (generally 24–36 hours), and a confidence that, when they need you, you are there. While an online course is running, I cannot afford to stop monitoring my e-mail at 5:00 P.M. or take weekends off. If I have to be offline for any length of time, I must inform my students several days in advance. This puts a great demand on me, but the immediacy of an online environment makes it difficult to avoid monitoring student needs constantly. I must, as well, be prepared to fix links and resolve ambiguities in the course material as soon as I learn of them.

Once a proper course structure is found, it is wise not to alter it unless it is showing signs of not working. Online courses in a Web environment can easily become rather complex so that changes made to one page require changes to other pages. Thus, once the basic course is in place, small revisions are safer than large and dramatic ones. Through the years, I have dropped the password protection, abandoned an option that allowed students not near a library to do a fully Web-based version of the course (since almost everything can now be done through the Internet anyway), and updated what seems like a thousand links. One assignment now makes more use of the invisible Web than was true in the past, and I now have students doing searches in Google Scholar. But the basic structure of six assignments prefaced by six backgrounders has remained. The key is to start with something that has

a good chance of being successful and then revise it only as needed.

Actual glitches in the course have been surprisingly few and are usually correctible with small revisions. The worst kind of problem is one that prevents students from being able to complete part of an assignment or creates some sort of ambiguity. Students tend to take a "just in time" approach to deadlines, and challenges because of typos, bad links, changes in databases, or unclear instructions are usually intense sources of frustration. When such problems occur, I generally do a rapid revision of the Web site and e-mail the students to inform them of the changes made, along with the reasons for those changes.

Conclusion

Research Strategies 500 OL continues to meet the needs of well over half the students at Associated Canadian Theological Schools, and the rest take the classroom version. Is one format better than the other? That depends. For students who value personal interactions and are available to take the course on campus, the classroom is the preferred option. But for students who can handle the self-discipline and occasional feelings of isolation that are part of the online environment, the Web-based course continues to be a popular choice. Educationally, student outcomes appear to be the same whether the classroom or online version is taken. In those terms, the online course may be deemed a success.

Notes

1. See these pages at http://web.archive.org/web/20000511155543/http://www.acts.twu.ca/lbr/research.htm.

2. This observation is supported by a recent report of the National Survey of Student Engagement that found online students to be experiencing a greater level of engagement with learning and a more positive learning experience than are in-class learners: *National Survey of Student Engagement,*

Engaged Learning: Fostering Success for All Students: Annual Report 2006. Available online at http://nsse. iub.edu/NSSE_2006_Annual_Report/docs/NSSE_2006_Annual_Report.pdf.

3. *Research Strategies: Finding Your Way through the Information Fog,* 2d ed. (Lincoln, NE: iUniverse, 2004).

3. The Development of a Library Research Methods Course for Online Graduate Students in Education

Julie Chapman, Cliff Landis, and Shilo Smith

Introduction

The librarians at Valdosta State University (VSU) believe information literacy education, which encourages lifelong learning skills, is critical to the educational achievement of their library users. In the distance education field, it is necessary to extend this information literacy education beyond the walls of the library and to reach out to library users we may never see face-to-face. Extending library services to graduate students, who may be taking online courses for the first time and have varying comfort levels with technology, is especially important. For the past five years, librarians at VSU have been teaching the course ITED7900: Library Research Methods for Online Students. This course was developed in summer 2001 by VSU librarian Julie Chapman in collaboration with the Department of Curriculum, Leadership and Technology (CLT). In more recent years, the course has been taught by librarians Cliff Landis and Shilo Smith. Because of the constantly changing information landscape, ITED7900 course content has been revised each year and sometimes while the course is being taught. Conversations with CLT professors have shown them to notice a marked difference in the research skills of students who have taken the course.

Rationale

Since the 1970s the librarians at VSU have taught a one-credit, undergraduate level, face-to-face Introduction to Library Services course (LIBS1000). By early 2001, with the explosion of online resources and information literacy issues, the librarians began discussing ways to expand the course into a three-credit upper-level course with online components. At the same time, CLT contacted librarian Julie Chapman about developing a Library Research Methods course for CLT graduate students enrolled in EdD, EdS, and MEd programs. CLT faculty had begun to notice that their students were not prepared to do high-quality library research for their courses or in their master's thesis and doctoral dissertation work. CLT requested that the course be offered online during the eight-week summer semester, which would allow the majority of students who were not local and not taking classes on campus the opportunity to enroll. WebCT was the university-wide course management system used to develop and deploy the course.

Development

Chapman used the LIBS1000 syllabus as the frame for the new course. She expanded the topics and concepts introduced, increased the number and types of library resources covered, explored education-related databases, and adjusted assignment demands to elevate the new course to the graduate level.

Several challenges arose during the planning process. First, although Chapman had originally intended to incorporate synchronous components, such as a required weekly online chat session, she learned from CLT faculty that it would be difficult, if not impossible, to schedule a common time when a majority of students were available. She decided to make the course entirely asynchronous, while at the same time designing multiple ways for students and the instructor to communicate: announcements, discussion boards, WebCT e-mail, VSU e-mail, and phone.

A second challenge was fitting all the topics, resources, and assignments into an eight-week summer course. Chapman decided to group the topics by week and leave one week at the end for catching up, addressing problems, and allowing the students time to complete the final drafts of their annotated bibliographies. The skills and resources covered each week built on the lessons of the previous week. She also chose to post all seven weeks of course content by the first day of class and to allow students to work ahead at their own pace, which was made possible by the asynchronous aspect of the course.

Third, there was the issue of the diversity of students' existing library research abilities and experiences. Chapman knew the students could range from the computer-savvy who had used a variety of library resources during their master's thesis research to those whose experience with the library was limited to card catalogs and the print version of *Readers' Guide to Periodical Literature.* To help address this issue, she decided to administer a pre-test to gauge each student's library research level and help predict where an individual student might need additional instruction. In addition, she was determined to take the time to make extensive personalized comments on the weekly assignments. Finally, keeping in mind the advanced students, she prepared a set of tips for advanced database searching and a list of additional resources.

Chapman had originally planned to use Camtasia to record live tutorials on developing search strategies and searching databases, which could then be integrated into lectures posted on WebCT for students to view. Through a casual conversation with a CLT faculty member, however, she learned that many students did not own computers with enough memory to allow them to view such tutorials. Chapman decided to adapt by incorporating screen captures into written lectures.

As she prepared lectures and tutorials with screen captures, Chapman also realized that links, database features, and resource availability could change monthly, if not more often. To prevent the inclusion in the course of outdated material and incorrect directions, she scheduled time to double-check each week's lectures and links each Sunday evening and Wednesday afternoon.

Once these challenges were addressed, Chapman finalized the course format. The eight-week, asynchronous, WebCT summer course consisted of weekly topics: an introduction to the course; information types, selecting and narrowing a topic, and developing a search strategy; searching online catalogs for books and theses; using online databases to search for scholarly articles, ERIC documents, and dissertations (two weeks); finding scholarly Internet resources; and searching for other types of resources, including government documents and tests and measurements. Each week students completed two to three assignments, which were submitted electronically through WebCT, as well as at least one discussion board posting. Each assignment covered the week's topics and incorporated information evaluation and APA citation style exercises, including practice annotations for books, articles, theses, and Internet resources.

Each week's lessons were personalized in that every student chose a general topic during the first week and developed it through the weekly exercises (see appendix). In many cases these topics coincided with the students' thesis or dissertation topics, allowing them to further their research. One ongoing assignment was the keeping of a search log, in which students tracked which databases they searched, which search statements they used, and what results were obtained (see table 3.1). The search log included an evaluative component: students were asked to analyze the results of each search briefly and indicate if they decided to revise their search statements. The weekly assignments and search log culminated in a twenty-item annotated bibliography on the student's narrowed-down research question. The final assignment was an analysis of the research process, in which students discussed what they learned during the course.

The course, titled ITED7900: Library Research Methods for Online Students, was first offered during summer semester 2002 and enrolled the maximum of twenty students.

Content

ITED7900 was a highly skill-based course requiring students to master specific skill sets and build on them as the course progressed. In ITED7900, students learned how to

• identify and articulate an information need

• develop and revise a search strategy

• access library resources from remote sites

• retrieve information from online catalogs, periodical databases, full-text journals, and the Internet

• understand and use GALILEO[1]

• evaluate information sources

• use document delivery services

These goals were based on the Information Literacy Competency Standards for Higher Education as developed by the American Library Association.[2]

Students were initially introduced to the basics of research, including information types, search strategy construction, and controlled vocabulary versus keyword. Advanced searching, however, is a skill that is learned through experience. The students were given the tools to perform advanced research (using Boolean operators, truncation, wild-

Table 3.1. Search Log for GALILEO and Subscription Databases

Database Searched	Search Statement and Any Limiters	Number of Results	Comments
ERIC	Educat* and (leadership or administration) and (elementary or primary)	31748	My search is too broad.
ERIC	"Leadership effectiveness" and "elementary education"	15	I performed this search for descriptors, and got better results.
Professional Development Collection	educational leadership and elementary schools	131	These results were pretty good.

card, and database-specific tools) and then supervised through the use of worksheets and search logs. This method allowed the instructor to point out errors in logic and to suggest alternative search strategies.

Each weekly module progressed in complexity, as students learned how to search library catalogs, online databases, and the Internet. Students were required to find, utilize, and properly cite a variety of resources, including peer-reviewed articles, ERIC documents, theses and dissertations, Web sites, government resources, and educational tests and measurements. Education doctoral students often use standardized tests in their research, so it was vital to teach the students how to negotiate the (often confusing) information resources available to them on psychological/educational tests and measurements.

In addition to search skills, students had to learn proper information retrieval skills. Students learned about the variety of document delivery methods available to them as distance education students and discovered how to navigate through a variety of content types and services such as e-books, e-journals, interlibrary loan, document delivery, and various formats of full-text.

Beginning in 2006, to support the instructional course content students were required to purchase a copy of the *Publication Manual of the American Psychological Association* (APA). Over the years this course has been taught, it became apparent that many students had difficulty with higher writing skills and proper citation. The instructor's strict adherence to APA citation style ensured that students learned proper citation methods, which would prepare them for their theses or dissertations. In addition, because some resources (such as ERIC) have changed since the latest edition of the APA manual,

it became necessary to explain the rationale behind the APA style so that students could make educated decisions regarding their citations.

This attention to citation detail, coupled with lessons on information evaluation, ensured that students were properly educated about avoiding academic dishonesty. In academe, reports continue to surface about dishonesty and plagiarism. Students who have been taught to evaluate information are able to discover instances of poor research and academic dishonesty, as well as avoid these mistakes in their own work. The instructor emphasized this process of evaluation throughout the course.

The graduate students in ITED7900 put their citation and evaluation skills to work in their final project—an annotated bibliography. They are often working on theses and dissertations, so by completing an annotated bibliography they are analyzing and evaluating the resources for those works.

Communicating with Students and Creating a Sense of Community

WebCT was the course management software selected for teaching ITED7900 at VSU. ITED7900 took place in a virtual classroom with no traditional face-to-face instruction; it was imperative that the instructor establish various methods of communication to create an online environment that promoted learning and the exchange of ideas. Discussion boards, e-mail, announcements, and telephone calls were among the methods of communication used.

The first week's topic was an introduction from the instructor to the students. Each student was then asked to write a short biographical introduction of himself or herself and post it to the discussion board. This assignment served as an icebreaker and allowed students an opportunity to get acquainted with the instructor and their peers.

The instructor established a research topic discussion board to help students articulate and develop their research topics with input from the instructor and fellow classmates. The students' primary assignment was to develop an annotated bibliography using the APA manual; the research topic discussion board was the designated area to discuss issues regarding this assignment. This discussion board allowed students to refine their research topics, and many students discovered they were researching similar topics, which led to a cooperative exchange of information sources, such as journal articles and educational-related Web sites.

The instructor monitored the discussion boards, answered students' questions, and commented on class discussions when appropriate. She e-mailed students weekly to remind them of the week's topics and of upcoming due dates. Changes in due dates or assignments and additions to course materials were announced via WebCT in conjunction with an e-mail to ensure that all students were notified. If a student had a complex question, the instructor telephoned the student at a prearranged time to discuss the specific issue.

Teaching and Assessing Students

A separate learning module for each week covered designated topics. Each learning module consisted of assigned readings, topics for the week's discussion board, and worksheet assignments. Readings included assigned sections from the APA manual, education Web sites, journal articles, and subject guides created by librarians at VSU. The discussion board topic for each week was related to the subject material covered by the readings. Finally, students completed research

worksheets designed to guide them through various topics such as constructing a search strategy or searching a specific database. When the worksheet dealt with searching in a database and retrieving a book, article, or master's thesis, the student was required to write an APA citation and annotation for the document cited. The instructor commented extensively on the students' worksheets, paying particular attention to the thought processes and strategies the students used when documenting their searches within a database. A strong emphasis was placed on accurate APA citation; feedback was provided on errors in the citations, and students with extensive errors—more than two within a citation—were required to correct their citation and resubmit their assignment. At the beginning of the semester, students were instructed to keep a search log to record their citations. If students kept up with their weekly readings and worksheets, when it came time to submit the final assignment, an annotated bibliography, they would already have their citations and annotations ready to complete the assignment.

Course communications were structured around a series of subject-specific discussion boards directly related to the course's weekly topic. For example, week six's learning objective was to search the Web for scholarly resources, evaluate these resources, and write APA citations for these resources. On week six's discussion board, students were asked to discuss one Web site and provide the URL for the Web site they felt provided scholarly information about their current research topic. They were also asked to explain why they believed the information presented on the Web site was scholarly.

Participation in the discussion boards was mandatory. Students earned a significant number of points for active participation, defined as at least one original statement and two responses to classmates' statements. Students did not receive full participation points for the week if they simply stated "I agree" or "I disagree"; a thoughtful exchange of ideas and comments was the primary goal. Because the summer session is only eight weeks long, the instructor wanted to ensure students did not fall behind in their weekly readings or online discussion; therefore, each of the weekly topic discussion boards was closed at the end of the week to prevent late postings. This encouraged students to stay focused and engaged with the current week's topic. The instructor monitored the discussion boards and commented extensively on the students' posts. The discussion boards were used to share ideas about the research process, discuss issues students encountered when completing the week's assignments, and provide additional guidance on the week's topic.

Students were required to submit a draft of their annotated bibliography two weeks prior to the final due date. The instructor reviewed each draft and provided detailed feedback on the annotations and APA citations. This process allowed evaluations of how well students had progressed through the course materials and were able to apply what they learned in class to their annotated bibliography. Each draft was returned to the student with comments from the instructor. The student was required to make corrections and to include additional annotations and citations if necessary before submitting a final draft to the instructor.

To assess the students' understanding of the course material effectively, the instructor needed to evaluate each student's research skills at the beginning and end of the semester. Students completed a preassessment of research techniques at the beginning of the course—a short essay on how they approached the research process. At the end of the semester, students wrote a final research analysis essay, reflecting on research skills they had learned throughout the semester along with successes and failures encountered in using the various electronic resources. Students submitted this assignment with a search log documenting the databases they had used and searches conducted within each database for each assignment completed. The instructor compared each student's final research analysis with the initial preassessment of research techniques assignment to determine the progress each student made.

Many students were taking ITED 7900 along with an additional graduate-level course. Students with a research assignment for another course or working on their master's thesis were permitted to focus their ITED 7900 assignments on their existing research topics. These students had a vested interest in learning the material in ITED 7900, since acquiring new research skills not only affected their success in ITED 7900 but also impacted an existing project for another class. This gave each student an opportunity to complete a literature review while gaining a better understanding of the research process.

Program Assessment

ITED 7900 is offered at VSU each summer through CLT as a component of its Education Specialist (EdS) graduate program. Several librarians from the university's Odum Library have taught the course online, and its success has been measured in various ways. Instructors Julie Chapman, Cliff Landis, and Shilo Smith have solicited feedback from students and faculty in the CLT and have reviewed the course evaluation reports provided by VSU's College of Education.

Based on positive feedback from faculty and students, Smith has been invited to teach two sections of ITED7900 during the summer 2007 semester. One section will be offered to all incoming students in the EdS program; students will complete ITED7900 prior to enrolling in courses for their EdS program. The second section is for students who have already taken courses within the EdS or MEd programs. ITED7900 will prepare both incoming and existing students with the research skills they need to succeed in graduate programs. CLT will monitor the progress of these new students after they have completed ITED7900.

Two students completed course evaluation reports after the summer 2006 session. Both strongly agreed that, "Overall, this was an excellent course." At the end of the survey students were asked what aspects of ITED7900 were most valuable to them. They stated that "annotated bibliography and feedback" and "the practice worksheets for the research tools and techniques were the most valuable." These responses indicate that the overall structure and instruction of the course is challenging and fosters a positive learning environment for students.[3]

Problems Identified and Solved, Changes Made

The course content and design are reviewed annually to ensure the best possible learning environment for students. Previous course instructors are often consulted to help identify problems and help create solutions. For the summer 2006 iteration of ITED7900, the following issues were identified:

• There was too much material to present in the course of an eight-week semester.

• Students were not always motivated to participate in discussion boards and submit assignments on time.

• Students continually made the same mistakes in their APA citations.

• The final annotated bibliography assignment had to be reduced while still maintaining the learning objectives.

Taking these issues into consideration, the instructor implemented several changes in the course content of ITED7900. Students were required to purchase the *Publication Manual of the American Psychological Association*. Previous instructors had not listed this text as a required reading, but it appeared that students had to read specific sections of the manual to acquire a solid understanding of this writing style. It was important for students to learn how to use the APA manual to complete writing assignments not only for ITED7900 but for their other courses in the EdS graduate program. The manual was supplemented with additional examples of citing various sources, including the APA Style Web site, paying particular attention to the section devoted to electronic resources. The most up-to-date citation information concerning electronic resources is available from this Web site, and the instructor emphasized that students should refer to it rather than the older print version of the APA manual.

Every week students taking ITED7900 were required to complete worksheets and submit them through WebCT. These worksheets were carefully designed to help students learn specific skill sets, such as conducting a search in a database. They also gave students the opportunity to show their understanding of the course content. The instructor changed the due dates of these worksheets to Sunday evenings, giving students the entire weekend to complete worksheet assignments and allowing the instructor time to devote Mondays to grading worksheets and submit grades to students on Tuesdays and Wednesdays. When students received their graded worksheets with comments, they had plenty of time to make corrections and apply what they had learned to the next set of worksheets due the next Sunday evening.

The final annotated bibliography assignment needed revision. First, the number of required citations and annotations was reduced from twenty to fifteen, allowing students the opportunity to spend more time evaluating and writing about their sources rather than simply compiling an extensive list. Even with fewer examples, students were still exposed to a diverse selection of APA citation samples. Students were expected to complete citations and annotations for at least two books, one thesis or dissertation, one popular magazine, two scholarly journal articles, one ERIC document, and one Web page. The draft annotated bibliography assignment was due at the beginning of week six, the final annotated bibliography at the end of week seven. Previously, the final annotated bibliography and research analysis writing assignments were due at the same time. The instructor decided it would benefit students to have the final annotated bibliography due the week before the research analysis, allowing students time to write a more developed final analysis of the research process. The goal was to prevent students' feeling rushed in having to complete both assignments at once and, as a result, submitting substandard work.

Each of the seventeen students in the class was required to complete on average three worksheets a week. Writing extensive comments on every student's worksheet, especially the APA citations, was extremely time consuming; however, if the instructor simply told students what was wrong with their APA citations and corrected citations

for them, students continued to make the same mistakes. By week three, the instructor saw the need for a different approach and implemented new grading criteria for APA citations. If a citation had one or two minor errors, such as a missing comma or missing italics, the instructor would remind the student of the correct citation format and provide a sample citation, for a source other than the one the student was citing. This method forced students to review the weekly readings covering a specific type of APA citation, critically review their APA citation, compare it to the given sample, and finally correct their own work.

When students' citations had more than two minor mistakes, they did not receive full credit for their worksheet. A student was permitted and encouraged to correct and resubmit the citations. If all mistakes were corrected, the student received full credit for the worksheet. This method of revising mistakes encouraged an active exchange between students and instructor. The instructor emphasized that she was not expecting perfection, but that she wanted students to understand and learn from their mistakes. This approach to grading students' APA citations multiple times was still time consuming, but was more effective in helping students learn how to use the proper citation style. This process fostered a significant amount of individual instruction between each student and the instructor.

Keeping students motivated and involved in class discussions throughout the semester was accomplished by requiring weekly participation in discussion boards, as established by previous instructors. The instructor believed students would be motivated to keep up with discussion if they knew that each week's discussion board would be closed the day after the corresponding week had ended. Any student who did not participate in a week's discussion board was permitted to write a two- or three-paragraph summary of the week's discussion and submitted it for review. If the instructor was satisfied with the student's understanding of the week's topic, the student was given participation points for that week.

Covering a significant amount of information in an eight-week session required the instructor to be focused, motivated, and current with grading worksheets and answering discussion board questions. Students seemed to appreciate quick feedback. The instructor sets the tone for the class; active participation with students has a direct impact on the student interest and participation levels in both coursework and group discussions.

Conclusion

Since 2001, ITED7900: Library Research Methods for Online Students, has given graduate students in the Education program the opportunity to enhance their research skills in a constantly shifting information environment. Throughout its existence, the instructors have made a point of using the lessons learned to help design a more effective course. ITED7900 helps students gain the practical skills necessary to succeed in both their graduate education and their futures as educators. By consistently revising the course content and design, paying close attention to detail, and communicating effectively with students, the instructors have implemented a course that is exceedingly successful. This is demonstrated by the positive response of students and faculty as well as the requests for additional sections of the course.

Appendix.
ITED 7900: Finding Government Documents on My Topic Worksheet

1. Use GIL or the Catalog of U.S. Government Publications to find government documents on your topic.

    A. Which resource did you use?

       GIL—the library's catalog

    B. What, exactly, did you type in? What, if any, limiters did you use?

       Educational leadership, as a keyword search

    C. How many results did you get?

       422

2. Write down the title of one of the documents.

Effective leaders for today's schools: Synthesis of a policy forum on educational leadership.

    A. Which government agency is responsible for this document?

       U.S. Dept. of Education

    B. Is this document available full-text online? If so, write down the URL.

       No

    C. What sort of document is it—annual report, pamphlet, statistical digest, etc.?

       Policy brief

    D. Cite the document using APA format.

       National Institute on Educational Governance, Finance, Policymaking, and Management. (1999). *Effective leaders for today's schools: Synthesis of a policy forum on educational leadership. Perspectives on education policy research. Policy brief* (Report No. GFI 1999 9501). Washington, DC: U.S. Government Printing Office.

3. How well do government documents seem to cover your topic?

This covers my topic very well. It gives excellent case studies.

Notes

    1.　GALILEO (GeorgiA LIbrary LEarning Online) is an initiative of the Board of Regents of the University System of Georgia. A Web-based virtual library, GALILEO provides access to multiple information resources, including secured access to licensed products. See http://www.usg.edu/galileo/about/.

    2.　Association of College and Research Libraries, *Information Literacy Competency Standards for Higher Education* (Chicago: ACRL, 2000). Available online at http://www.ala.org/ala/acrl/acrlstandards/informationliteracycompetency.htm.

    3.　Student surveys responses are from VSU unpublished data.

4. LIB120: Introduction to Information Literacy

Jim Kinnie

Introduction

Converting a face-to-face credit-bearing course into one taught asynchronously on WebCT took lots of planning and even more time to build and implement successfully. Since creating the online version of the course, I have adjusted the original design over the past six years to deliver effectively course content equivalent to that of the face-to-face class and to address University Libraries' information literacy goals. This is the story of my experience transforming traditional classroom materials for an online environment and using them to teach LIB120: Introduction to Information Literacy, a three-credit course for undergraduates at the University of Rhode Island (URI).

Rationale

In early 2001, I was working as a lecturer on a one-year appointment at the URI Libraries when Joanna Burkhardt from the Providence campus library asked if I would be interested in teaching LIB120 online over the next summer. Like any lecturer looking for experience and a permanent job, I readily agreed. But after thinking about it for a minute, I began to have my doubts. I was just out of library school; I had taught a few college courses in a former career, but never online. Joanna said none of the instructors had online experience, and she expressed confidence in me. Besides, it was an experiment, and I could limit the number of students.

Of course, I had never taught LIB120 either. It is a three-credit course for undergraduates, first offered face-to-face in 1999. Since 2001 it has been included as one of two options within the English Communication area in the URI general education program. We generally fill six to eight face-to-face sections each semester with twenty-five students in each section. LIB120's goals parallel those of the ACRL Information Literacy Competency Standards for Higher Education.[1] LIB120 is an important part of the URI Libraries' Plan for Information Literacy,[2] and offering the course online would support the outreach goals of the plan. The plan calls for a wide range of information literacy instruction in different delivery modes to reach the widest range of students, and having an online section of the comprehensive credit course would be an important step toward that goal.

Asynchronous WebCT courses were also becoming popular at URI, especially during the summer session. Out-of-state students could work from home over the summer; Rhode Island students liked the idea of not having to drive to campus. The URI campus is in the rural southern part of the state, which is "way too fah" for many residents of the smallest state to drive. Distance is relative. Rhode Island lore has it that if you plan to drive more than ten miles, you should pack a toothbrush and a change of clothes.

At the time, URI's College of Continuing Education (CCE) in Providence administered the asynchronous courses delivered on WebCT. CCE marketed the summer session with a photo of a student sitting on the beach with his laptop, which made me wonder about the type of students I would get.

Development

In developing the online version of LIB120 I had to start from scratch, learning not only how to teach the course but also how to be an online course designer and WebCT user. I had heard and read that teaching online took lots of time and, looking ahead, I could see that was going to be the case.

LIB120 is a skills course that leads students through the research process to learn how to find, evaluate, and use information on a topic of their choice. As far as the course material went, the three instructors at the time graciously turned over all their syllabi, exercises, and handouts. In fact, they kept binders full of material they created and shared with each other, and now with me. All of it

was geared toward a traditional thirteen-week semester. One section met for three hours once a week, one for seventy minutes twice a week, the third for fifty minutes three times a week. The summer session runs for ten weeks. I learned everything about the course by synthesizing all the material and organizing it into ten session-friendly topic areas to fit the summer schedule.

I also saw a pattern that would fit a weekly schedule. Each week students would read lecture notes on a topic, complete a related exercise, and submit a homework assignment. (See figure 4.1.) Most of the homework assignments were annotated bibliographies that made up a large part of the semester project. I decided to concentrate on the lecture notes and build the modules around them.[3]

I was familiar enough with WebCT to know that HTML files were native to the version the university was using. I wanted to keep things as simple as possible, designing for the lowest common denominator—the student with a 12-inch monitor and a dial-up connection. I also wanted to make it easy to read online. I had strained my eyes too often trying to read small-font word-processed files that are best read on paper. I turned to Sarah Horton's *Web Teaching Guide* for page design ideas.[4] I followed her techniques of constraining page width and chunking information, keeping to one page with easy navigation rather than building multiple click-throughs. My colleagues' course materials lent them-

Figure 4.1 LIB120 course topics

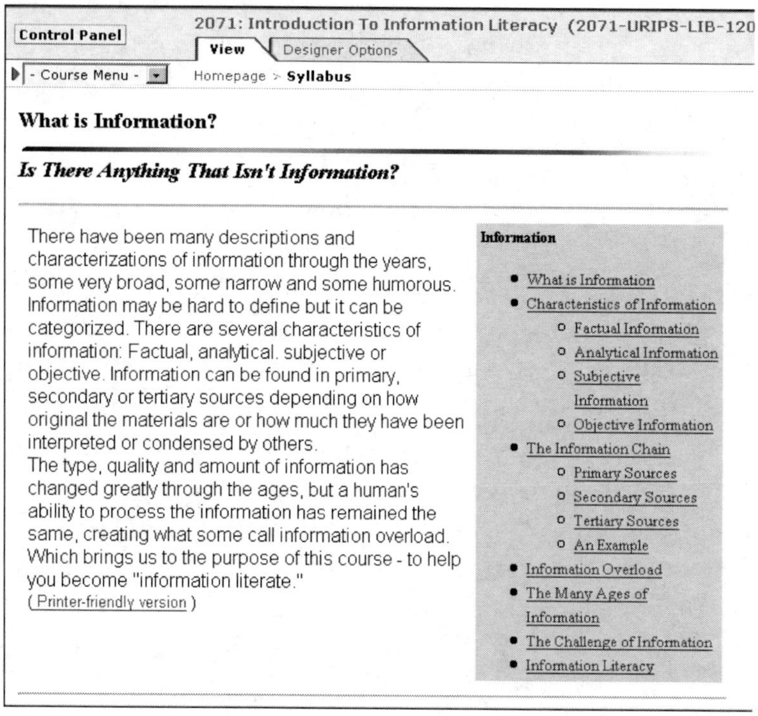

Control Panel   2071: Introduction To Information Literacy (2071-URIPS-LIB-120
View   Designer Options
- Course Menu -   Homepage > **Syllabus**

What is Information?

Is There Anything That Isn't Information?

There have been many descriptions and characterizations of information through the years, some very broad, some narrow and some humorous. Information may be hard to define but it can be categorized. There are several characteristics of information: Factual, analytical. subjective or objective. Information can be found in primary, secondary or tertiary sources depending on how original the materials are or how much they have been interpreted or condensed by others.
The type, quality and amount of information has changed greatly through the ages, but a human's ability to process the information has remained the same, creating what some call information overload. Which brings us to the purpose of this course - to help you become "information literate."
(Printer-friendly version)

Information
- What is Information
- Characteristics of Information
  - Factual Information
  - Analytical Information
  - Subjective Information
  - Objective Information
- The Information Chain
  - Primary Sources
  - Secondary Sources
  - Tertiary Sources
  - An Example
- Information Overload
- The Many Ages of Information
- The Challenge of Information
- Information Literacy

selves to chunking: Mary MacDonald's PowerPoint slides and Andrée Rathemacher's overhead transparencies translated easily; Joanna's handouts filled in a lot of the textual information. I wasn't ready for multimedia in the modules, let alone multimedia creation. (See figure 4.2.)

I wish I had known about the WebCT design workshop offered by the URI Informational and Instructional Technology Services department. I had used WebCT a little in library school but never in any great depth. I was assigned a course shell and started from scratch. After seeing other courses in school and helping patrons log in at the reference desk, I had some idea of what worked and what didn't. I wanted the home page to have all the links accessible without scrolling, and I wasn't crazy about the default icons. I rummaged around WebCT and found a folder full of alternate graphics including a set of small, stylized text icons, for E-mail, Content, Calendar, and so forth. I fit twelve of them on the home page along with the course title and my contact information, all accessible without scrolling (see figure 4.3). With the text icons I was locked into WebCT's terminology, but I could live with that.

That first summer I used as many tools as I could, but over time I dropped a few. Of course there were the Syllabus, Course Content, E-mail, Discussion Board, and Assignment tools to deliver the essentials, but I tried just about every other tool WebCT had to offer. I found that Calendar, Whiteboard, and Homepages were not used and dropped them after the first summer. I dropped the Presentation tool, thinking it was too difficult for students to learn, but I have since brought it back to help with a group project. I also found the Assignment tool confusing for students and had the students submit homework and exercises by e-mail. That system isn't perfect either, and I am thinking of bringing the Assignment tool back as well. Asynchronous

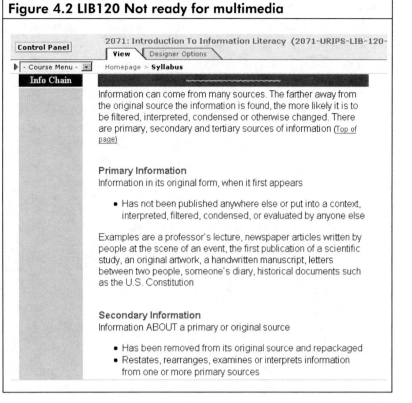

Figure 4.2 LIB120 Not ready for multimedia

Control Panel

View | Designer Options

- Course Menu - | Homepage > **Syllabus**

Info Chain

Information can come from many sources. The farther away from the original source the information is found, the more likely it is to be filtered, interpreted, condensed or otherwise changed. There are primary, secondary and tertiary sources of information (Top of page)

Primary Information
Information in its original form, when it first appears

- Has not been published anywhere else or put into a context, interpreted, filtered, condensed, or evaluated by anyone else

Examples are a professor's lecture, newspaper articles written by people at the scene of an event, the first publication of a scientific study, an original artwork, a handwritten manuscript, letters between two people, someone's diary, historical documents such as the U.S. Constitution

Secondary Information
Information ABOUT a primary or original source

- Has been removed from its original source and repackaged
- Restates, rearranges, examines or interprets information from one or more primary sources

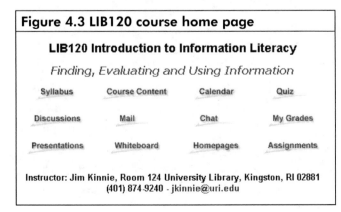

Figure 4.3 LIB120 course home page

LIB120 Introduction to Information Literacy

Finding, Evaluating and Using Information

Syllabus	Course Content	Calendar	Quiz
Discussions	Mail	Chat	My Grades
Presentations	Whiteboard	Homepages	Assignments

Instructor: Jim Kinnie, Room 124 University Library, Kingston, RI 02881
(401) 874-9240 - jkinnie@uri.edu

really means asynchronous, so I gave up on regularly scheduled chats. Only a few could attend, and there was not much discussion of course content with those who could.

I would have said that the face-to-face quizzes were easy to convert to WebCT if I didn't have to learn to use the tool to create the quizzes at the same time. The learning curve was steep, but the multiple-choice and short-answer questions I had fit the WebCT formats, and ultimately the quizzes were easy to grade. I was able to use existing quizzes, converting them from paper, and I wrote questions of my own as I gained more experience teaching the course online and in the classroom.

After my first summer, I saw a conference presenter who suggested using the WebCT Quiz tool to deliver exercises. I furiously converted paper exercises into the quiz format and greatly reduced the number of e-mailed attachments. It made it easier to grade and give feedback, and I could control deadlines. Since they showed up on the same list with the actual quizzes, I identified the exercises by following each title with (EX). The exercises, along with the discussion postings, contribute to the class participation part of the final grade.

It is pretty obvious that I am still working at URI Libraries. A continuing faculty position opened that first summer and my interview was scheduled the day the grades were due. I like to think my efforts in creating an online version of LIB120 contributed to my successful candidacy. I have since been teaching LIB120 in a classroom every semester in addition to the online summer sessions.

Content

LIB120 addresses all five information literacy competency standards and is designed to lead students through the process of researching a topic for an eight- to twelve-page paper—up to the point of writing the paper. Ideally, a student who has to write a paper in another course can plan it in LIB120. Through exercises and assignments students learn to use tools and strategies to create the Paper Trail, a summary portfolio of their research. The Paper Trail includes a detailed outline of their proposed paper, annotated bibliographies of sources they find useful and those they would not use, a reflective research journal, and miscellaneous classwork that demonstrates their research strategy. They keep track of non-useful sources to demonstrate their evaluation process.

The course content, divided into ten weekly lessons, has a logical flow starting with the theoretical aspects of information and moving through the practical exercise of finding, evaluating, and using information sources. The ten lecture note topics are as follows:

- What is Information/Information Literacy?
- Information Organization
- The Research Process
- The Quality of Information
- Finding Periodical Information
- Electronic Databases
- The Internet
- Facts, Statistics and Bias
- Information Packaging
- Issues of the Information Age

After an overview of information and its organization, students begin the research process by picking a topic and gathering background information in encyclopedias and books. They evaluate what they find and create annotated bibliographies, keeping track not only of the sources they would use but also those they wouldn't find useful as part of the evaluation process.

They then focus their research in periodicals and Web sites, creating bibliographies that will all become part of the Paper Trail. For each assignment students keep a journal of their experiences. All of the entries make up a reflective research journal, which becomes part of the Paper Trail. The Paper Trail also includes a detailed outline of the paper they would write to show how they would apply the information they found to their hypothetical (or real) research paper. Issues of the ethical uses of information are explored through guided discussions throughout the summer session.

Instruction

The ten-week schedule does not exactly fit the lecture note topics. The beginning of the summer session usually starts out slowly because of technical problems or students not remembering to log in. I knew the students would need the final two weeks to assemble the Paper Trails, so I decided to use the discussion board to spread out the Issues of the Information Age over the session rather than dedicate a week to them. After a few summers of trial and error, I was able to make effective use of the discussion board. Even the Information Packaging lessons were spread over the session as students learned about authorship, plagiarism, and citation styles as they conducted their research (see figure 4.4).

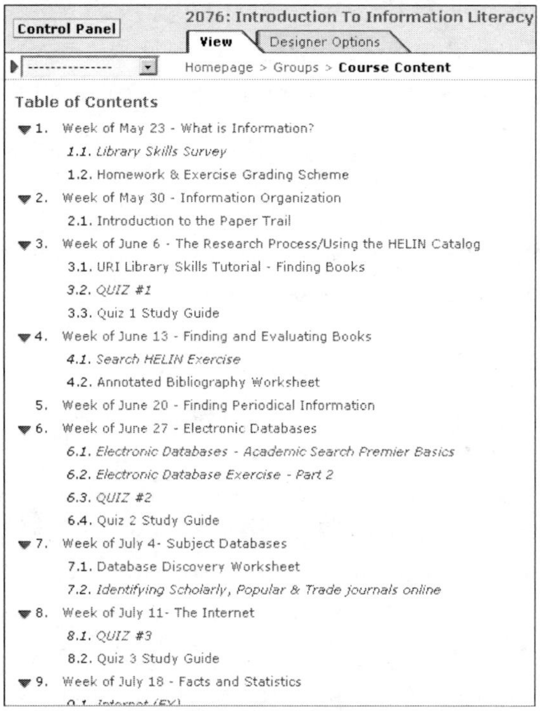

For me, e-mail is the major communication tool. Students have been using it to submit assignments, but also each week I send a message to all students summarizing the upcoming week and tying new knowledge to what they have learned. I use e-mail for this practice to make it seem more important and personal than a posting on the discussion board. I try to keep students on the weekly schedule and remind them of exercises and assignments coming up.

The weekly routine requires students to read the lecture notes and postings, com-

Figure 4.4 LIB 120 course content page

2076: Introduction To Information Literacy

Control Panel — View | Designer Options

Homepage > Groups > **Course Content**

Table of Contents

1. Week of May 23 - What is Information?
   - 1.1. *Library Skills Survey*
   - 1.2. Homework & Exercise Grading Scheme
2. Week of May 30 - Information Organization
   - 2.1. Introduction to the Paper Trail
3. Week of June 6 - The Research Process/Using the HELIN Catalog
   - 3.1. URI Library Skills Tutorial - Finding Books
   - 3.2. *QUIZ #1*
   - 3.3. Quiz 1 Study Guide
4. Week of June 13 - Finding and Evaluating Books
   - 4.1. *Search HELIN Exercise*
   - 4.2. Annotated Bibliography Worksheet
5. Week of June 20 - Finding Periodical Information
6. Week of June 27 - Electronic Databases
   - 6.1. *Electronic Databases - Academic Search Premier Basics*
   - 6.2. *Electronic Database Exercise - Part 2*
   - 6.3. *QUIZ #2*
   - 6.4. Quiz 2 Study Guide
7. Week of July 4- Subject Databases
   - 7.1. Database Discovery Worksheet
   - 7.2. *Identifying Scholarly, Popular & Trade journals online*
8. Week of July 11- The Internet
   - 8.1. *QUIZ #3*
   - 8.2. Quiz 3 Study Guide
9. Week of July 18 - Facts and Statistics
   - 9.1. *Internet (EX)*

plete an exercise, and use what they learn to find information on their Paper Trail topic. Three quizzes during the session are based on the readings; many of the exercises are electronic worksheets designed to practice using a search tool or method; most homework assignments are annotated bibliographies that become part of the Paper Trail.

Throughout each week I check e-mail for assignments and questions and the discussion board for postings. I respond as soon as I can to any questions, and I grade the exercises and assignments when I get enough free time for it. To discourage the conception that instructors are online twenty-four hours a day, I make sure everyone knows that it may be up to a full day before I can respond. I give feedback for the exercise results within the Quiz tool, and I reply by e-mail with grades and comments for the homework assignments. Grading for the weekly assignments is on a check-minus/check/check-plus scale that translates to a grade of 1, 2, or 3. Any assignment with a 1 or 2 (check-minus or check) can be revised and resubmitted for full credit. If students keep up with the work, most of the pieces of the Paper Trail have been vetted before they become part of the project.

The discussion board substitutes for traditional classroom participation. At the beginning of the session students introduce themselves and I post orientation information for the course. Students post the results of the first couple of exercises on the board. It took a few summers to make good use of the discussion board for, well, discussion. Five or six times throughout the session I posed a few discussion questions that related to course concepts or qualified as issues.

In a face-to-face section during the regular semester, I address Information Literacy Standard Five by devoting a class period or two to case studies or requiring attendance at on-campus information forums to "raise consciousness" about current information issues. Online, the Discussion tool is the obvious and perfect way to engage students in thinking about information issues in their lives. What seems to work best for me is to pose questions on two or three topics based on news reports or other current cultural phenomenon that will get a rise out of students and start them posting. Since many students do not keep up with the news, some are surprised to hear that famous historians are accused of plagiarism or that there are restrictions on civil liberties they thought were sacred or didn't know we had. One rather unexpected and heated thread followed in response to my question, "Should *A Million Little Pieces* by James Frey be shelved in the fiction or nonfiction section of the library?" Of course, part of the final grade is based on participation in the discussions, which also keeps students posting.

I make it clear from the beginning in initial e-mail, in assignment reminders, and even in the Welcome Page students see before they enroll that they will have to visit an actual academic or large public library to complete some assignments. In particular, they must actually get their hands on the books they use in their bibliographies so they can properly evaluate them. Although LIB120 instructors are emphasizing them less, print indexes are still part of our research process since many libraries still have to use them. Students are asked to find articles on their topics using a subject index in print as a conceptual exercise to show how articles are indexed and retrieved.

There is one group project, arguably the hardest part of the course to coordinate. Groups are hard enough to manage in a face-to-face class, and online it seems more difficult, even with the twelve to fifteen students enrolled in each summer section of the course. Not only is it sometimes difficult to motivate students and get them to work together online, there is the technical hurdle of learning to use the Presentation tool to present their results. It takes careful explanations and often some mediation to make it all work. Each group is assigned a subject-specific database to explore, and, using the Presentation tool, they report back to the rest of the class, posting information on the database's authority, coverage, features, and ease of use. Some create fancy reports with screenshots in PowerPoint slides and some present basic text files. Students learn to use subject databases for their research and for motivation's sake. I also include questions about the databases in the quiz. ("You have to find articles on using marketing a new educational product. Which two databases would you use?")

There are three quizzes throughout the session, all multiple-choice and self-grading based on the readings. The final exam asks students for an essay that tells me what they did in class over the summer; they choose one of three topics and tell me in two or three pages how they would conduct their research for a ten-page paper just as they had with that session's Paper Trail.

Program Assessment

Students are assessed through exercises, homework assignments, the group project, class participation (discussion board activity), the Paper Trail, and the final exam. The Paper Trail and the homework assignments that contribute to it make up a large percentage of the grade because they reflect how well students understood and used the research process.

Comparing the content of the Paper Trails of face-to-face students and those online, I see little difference. I receive word-processed files instead of binders full of printouts, but the annotations, outlines, and journals compare quite well. The only major difference in the semester project is not seeing actual proof that online students found the material. In the binders, face-to-face students include photocopies of title pages and first pages of articles. For the online class, I can check to see if the students can actually access full-text articles, but I have to rely on the strength of the annotations to determine if they had the books in their hands. The annotations must briefly summarize the ideas in the source, indicate why the author is credible, and explain why it will or will not be useful for their topic. Students who address these issues in a comprehensive way get full credit for the assignment. The detailed paper outline included in the Paper Trail shows how students would apply the information literacy skills they have learned.

Without following up on students in subsequent semesters, knowing if they continue to use their new skills is difficult. I usually see my former face-to-face students working on coursework in the library, so I know they are applying what they learn, but since I actually see very few of my online students, it's hard to tell if they continue to use the library for their research.

Effectiveness depends a lot on the self-motivation of the students in an online course. Not having to be in a classroom at the same time every week may sound great to summer students, but they must have the discipline to organize their time and "attend" class on a consistent basis. Summer session brings its own problems—with students working and taking other courses and seniors who have already participated in their graduation ceremony and need just three more credits to receive their diplomas. Just like traditional students, those who fall behind early in the session have a difficult time catching up.

There are also advantages to the online environment. Students who might be too shy to join a discussion in a classroom or who need to give their responses more thought may be more comfortable contributing to a threaded discussion. Since many of my students are out of state and cannot use the URI library, they have to apply their new skills to their local public or academic library and, I hope, realize those skills are transferable to any research situation.

The pre/post surveys students take show that most students learn to use library resources instead of Web sites for their research and that many had not realized the extent and worth of what the library has to offer. The Student Evaluation of Teaching surveys that are used in regular semesters have been administered to summer students in the past two years, and my results have been similar to traditional semesters. LIB120 instructors have worked closely with the URI Instructional Development program to design a student survey that allows for written comments. These, too, reflect results for the summer online session quite similar to those in the regular semesters.

LIB120 has been recognized by the URI Faculty Senate Curriculum Affairs Committee under new guidelines requiring online versions of existing courses be approved as a new teaching method. A second online section of the course has been added to the summer schedule, and I have gladly turned over my course shell to the instructor, Joanna Burkhardt, thus returning much of her original material in a different form. I have also been sharing the hybrid version of the shell with a few other instructors, who use it as a supplement to classroom instruction as I do. (There are now six to eight sections of LIB120 taught during the regular semesters.)

Lessons Learned

In adapting and running an online information literacy credit course, I have learned many lessons both in course design and online teaching methods. As stated above, I used far too many tools when designing the course. I whittled them down to the essentials, which created less confusion for students and left them with more time to concentrate on course content.

I learned a couple of lessons in asynchronous delivery. In trying to schedule a guest "speaker" using the Chat tool, I was not able to schedule a time when everyone was available. I used Chat for office hours the first couple of summers, but not all students could be around during the times I was available. Now I leave the Chat tool in the course for students to use; I communicate with them by

e-mail, unless a student wants to schedule a synchronous online appointment.

LIB120 is not the kind of course that allows students to work at their own pace, so I have learned to prod students to keep up with the weekly schedule. As my mother would say, it's for their own good. In communicating with students, I have found that it is important to be as clear as possible with instructions on how to work with the content. Just as face-to-face students learn to adjust to individual instructors' procedures, online students need to understand clearly how the course is run and what is expected of them.

Group projects are often difficult in an online classroom, and having geographically diverse students who rely exclusively on technology to communicate in an online course makes them even more of a challenge. I have to admit that it took a few sessions for groups to really work well together. I found that starting the project early enough and keeping on top of their project was essential in making them work. I will probably add a second, less-involved group project early in the semester to get students into a routine of working together.

Recent literature about pedagogy and the millennials has me thinking of adding multimedia learning objects to the course—but it's a fine balance between keeping it simple and adding bells and whistles just because I can. Besides, creating a podcast of my recitation of the lecture notes puts the students right back in a boring lecture hall, listening (or not) to their instructor drone on. I know there are much more creative uses of podcasts, but, as a former television producer, I know the time and effort needed to create an effective multimedia lesson, and that just hasn't been in my workload. Future versions of the course may, however, include some form of problem-based learning to get students more actively involved in the content. Again, designing effective problem-based lessons is not something I can accomplish in the near future.

It took a few summer sessions to learn these lessons, and each year brings new challenges to running an online course effectively. Although the basic structure of the course has been stable, there are always new ideas to try or problem areas to revise for better instruction. I don't see that changing for the life of the course.

Notes

1. University of Rhode Island Libraries, *Plan for Information Literacy*. Available online at http://www.uri.edu/library/instruction_services/infolitplan.html.

2. Association of College and Research Libraries, *Information Literacy Competency Standards for Higher Education* (Chicago: ACRL, 2000). Available online at http://www.ala.org/ala/acrl/acrlstandards/informationliteracycompetency.htm.

3. LIB120 Instructors, *LIB120 Lecture Notes*. Available online at http://www.uri.edu/library/staff_pages/kinnie/#notes.

4. Sarah Horton, *Web Teaching Guide* (New Haven: Yale University Press, 2000), chap. 3.

5. Integrating Information Literacy into Distance Education: The Progression of an Online Course

Elizabeth Blakesley Lindsay, B. Jane Scales, and Lara Ursin Cummings

Rationale

The mid-1990s was an expansive time for Washington State University's (WSU) distance program. Several academic departments at the Pullman campus, particularly in the social sciences, were interested in developing their own degree program for nonresident students. This environment promoted a more serious look at how this population received library services in terms of reference, document delivery, and research instruction.

General Education 300 (Gen Ed 300) was originally a partner project between the WSU Libraries and its Distance Degree program (DDP), the department responsible for organizing and facilitating the delivery of courses for distance students.[1] Developed to help undergraduates at a distance access online databases and organize information for academic projects, the course was first offered in 1995. The course, formally titled "Accessing Information for Research," has remained a one-credit course.

Development

Perhaps more than anything, the maturation of the Internet during the 1990s drove the development of our one-credit course. The Internet of the early and mid-1990s was not conducive to the delivery of course content. In 1995, distance students who enrolled in the course received a set of fifteen video tapes and a thin "course book" that outlined assignments, introduced each unit, and contained a glossary of terms relevant to the course

content.[2] As they worked through the course, students watched lectures on research concepts, interviews with professors about their research, and visual aids such as computer screenshots. To practice their developing research skills, students could access a handful of text-based online databases from the WSU Libraries. Assignments were required to be mailed in to the Pullman campus and were returned to the student with a grade. Students communicated with the instructor and their classmates over a listserv.

The theoretical basis of the course has changed little since first implemented. Students are still encouraged to think in terms of "research scenarios" and speculate as to what types of information formats and producers might be useful to them. Other elements of the curriculum remaining constant through the years are an overview of academic disciplines and discourse, the use of question analysis to focus and clarify the research topic, and an increased familiarity with database structure and search techniques. In contrast, technical aspects of the course, such as methods of accessing databases, communication between students and instructor, and the means of submitting graded assignments have all changed. Some of these changes have affected the topics covered within the course—most notably the importance of evaluating the information that is so readily available to everyone with the explosion of the Web.

As the Internet became more conducive to the delivery of course material, the

Libraries transferred the content from the videos to a set of online modules. Some of the video material was streamed from these modules. By the late 1990s, however, the original videos were too outdated to continue using. The DDP was willing to reshoot a set of videos for the course, but given the rapid pace of change and updates to the course we decided it better to migrate away from this medium. In 2006, Gen Ed 300 is offered via a well-known commercial course space, WebCT-Blackboard. Assignments are submitted in the form of "discussion posts," and students are graded on the basis of a formal set of evaluation criteria, which are also contained within the course space. These criteria vary from assignment to assignment, but they give the students clear direction on what is expected of them. The quality of their assignments and the level of their course participation comprise the most significant portion of students' grades. These changes, including a more formalized pedagogical approach, were introduced around 2001 as a result of collaboration between the Libraries and WSU's Center for Teaching, Learning and Technology.[3] The Center's renowned "Critical Thinking Rubric" served as a useful tool during this transition and provided a framework that fit well with the Libraries' learning objectives for the students.[4]

During the course of the semester, the library instructors have always had access to the DDP offices on campus. The DDP offices are always available to assist facilitation with students who might be having problems within the course, such as technology problems or issues dealing with disabilities. Courseware training and assistance are also offered generously, as well as access to tutorials and other courseware guidance.

Content

The online Gen Ed 300 course is divided into four modules with various threaded discussions within the activities. Students proceed through four modules that contain distinct, graded activities conducted as threaded discussions in the online course space. The topics of the four modules are Information Environments and Needs, Defining Information Needs, Searching and Gathering Information, and Evaluating Information. Each module contains both higher-level and lower-level tasks for students to accomplish, paralleling the ACRL information literacy standards. For example, in preparation for the first threaded discussion, students identify a general topic of interest to research during the entire semester. Students often select a topic related to another course they are taking, ideally one in which they must prepare a research paper or project. Students then begin to learn about the characteristics of information, including how information looks, how it is stored, and who produces it. These readings, coupled with some interactive quizzes, prepare students for the first threaded discussion, in which they are asked to describe what kinds of information might be useful for the topic they have chosen—brainstorming about their needs for statistics, research data, theoretical analyses, or other sources. By focusing on more abstract concepts such as "information types" (bibliographic, textual, graphic, multimedia, numeric, audio) and "information producers" (scholars, corporations, organizations, U.S. Government, private citizens), students gain the ability to think more critically about and anticipate what kind of information they may encounter in their research endeavors.

These activities take students through the research process, from defining an information need, to planning the steps the research will take, to actually performing the research and evaluating and citing the materials located. The final activity has students write about information literacy, its definitions, and their learning experiences throughout the course. Throughout the semester the various threaded discussions take on a library instruction role, per se, with point of need instruction. Detailed exchanges often arise involving evaluating or citing sources or choosing subject specific databases related to particular fields of study. These threads often give students the opportunity to share research tips and tricks learned during the course of their education and allow the librarian to direct the conversation toward other "hot topics" such as plagiarism and general or subject specific databases as compared to Web content.

Instruction

Gen Ed 300: Accessing Information for Research is taught online and on the campuses by library faculty. On-campus sections at Pullman focus on particular disciplines and are designed and taught by various librarians. Although there is a core set of goals and librarians readily share activities and teaching ideas, no uniform course design is mandated. The online version of Gen Ed 300 has a standard curriculum that focuses more generally on the research process, allowing students in the particular disciplines to learn basic skills and concepts that can be applied to specific resources and tools. Although not required, DDP students are strongly encouraged to take the course.

Gen Ed 300 is limited to twenty students per section, which falls into the typically recommended range for asynchronous online instruction. Among other experts, Donald Hanna states that for asynchronous online education where student interaction is important, class size should not exceed thirty

students.[5] In Gen Ed 300, all activities are done as threaded discussion, and a substantial portion of the students' final grade is based on their interaction with each other. Students are required to read and comment on other students' postings in a constructive way. The threaded discussion format allows all information to be available to all students and enhances communication and feedback, but the format can be problematic for students. Some students have difficulty reconciling the need to describe their search process with the more formal writing style they feel is necessary for a discussion posting. For example, they may assume that they should not provide a list of keywords or a list of databases they tried, and they write extensive, repetitive sentences about their search process. It is sometimes difficult for them to describe or replicate their search process and results into a traditional narrative format.

The curriculum is based on ACRL information literacy standards. For example, the first standard deals with the determination of the "nature and extent" of the information needed and offers four specific performance indicators. Assignments in Gen Ed 300 directly address each of those four indicators, asking students to answer questions about all aspects of the standard. Gen Ed 300 assignments address all five performance indicators within the second standard as well, with assignments related to the search and retrieval process.

The third standard deals with evaluating information sources, and the course covers evaluation techniques and requires students to write evaluative statements about the sources they choose to collect for their annotated bibliography projects. The fourth standard relates to how effectively the student uses the selected information sources. Gen Ed 300 has students report on their process and plans for future research in their annotated bibliography assignment.

The course also addresses the fifth ACRL standard, related to plagiarism and citation. Other aspects of this standard, such as Netiquette, using passwords, and following institutional policies, are obviously met by students who successfully participate in the course, although those issues may not be explicitly taught.

Program Assessment

Student assessment is a key feature of our program assessment. Gen Ed 300 measures a student's overall grasp of information literacy with a final essay and an annotated bibliography project. In the essay, students are asked to define information literacy, giving specific examples of what they learned and drawing upon their own experiences to demonstrate further their understanding. The annotated bibliography project is also one that can be worked on throughout the course, as students learn about different types of information tools and resources throughout the modules. Figure 5.1 shows the assignment explanation and grading criteria.

Figure 5.1. Final project, assignment explanation and grading criteria

Welcome to Unit 4—"Citing and Evaluating Information," the final Unit of the GenEd300 course. This semester, you've worked fairly intensively to define and focus a research topic. You've learned how databases are set up and how to efficiently and effectively search them to pinpoint needed information. Along the way, you've learned about the WSU Library system and the services it offers you as a DDP student. In Unit 3, you identified information resources you deemed useful for your project.

In the first Threaded Discussion of Unit 4 ("Citing and Evaluating Resources"), you will practice citing your sources according to a standard bibliographic style. You will also collect a number of these resources to evaluate according to criteria set up in the Web Resource "Evaluate Information Resources," which you first viewed during Unit 3 Discussion 3.

In addition, as the final Threaded Discussion ("Final Project") of the course, you will need to carefully and thoughtfully consider what you learned this semester about research and research strategies. The instructors of GenEd300 are interested in learning what you found valuable about the course, what useful terminology you learned and how this will influence your research in the future.

Goals
• Use examples from an appropriate bibliographic style manual (APA, Chicago, MLA or other) to correctly cite resources. Thoroughly evaluate information resources according to structured criteria. Create an annotated bibliography of 5 sources.
• Review course and discuss properties of information literacy and how to apply course concepts in the future.

Evaluation Criteria:
Threaded Discussion 1: Citing and Evaluating Information

75 points
Overall, demonstrate superior skills in evaluating information and citing resources according to an appropriate bibliographic style manual.

50 points
Overall, demonstrate some skill in evaluating information and citing resources according to an appropriate bibliographic style manual.

25 points
Overall, demonstrate little skill in evaluating information and citing resources according to an appropriate bibliographic style manual.

In Gen Ed 300, the students choose their own topic, usually matching a research paper assignment they have for another course. In rare cases when students have no research paper assignments in the semester, they can choose any topic, but it must be approved by the librarian teaching the course to ensure that they will be able to perform all the research functions required throughout the class. Throughout earlier modules, the students gather ten sources of various types that relate to their research paper. In the final project, they cite and annotate those ten items. As a part of this assignment students are also required to get access to these items, whether printing them from an online database, utilizing interlibrary loan, or using WSU's DDP book delivery service. After completing this portion of the assignment, many students comment on the ease of the latter service, often admitting that they had never used the delivery services before because they had heard the process was too complex.

Along assessing the students' work, we can also gather information collectively about how well students have learned the concepts and identify areas that appear to be problematic for many students. The essays in particular provide us a good deal of qualitative information.[6] The data we gathered from the qualitative analysis of seventy-six responses to the capstone assignment differ greatly from those generated from the use of a rubric or assignment evaluation criteria and provide a snapshot of attitudes and impressions of information literacy expressed by a group of distance education undergraduate students after a semester-long course in research strategies.

In that study, we learned that attitudes toward information literacy are complex and varied, but also measurable and perhaps useful to further the development of information literacy pedagogy. The most significant finding was that students had distinct and identifiable attitudes toward information literacy—which fell into seven categories. We did not devise these categories but simply identified, isolated, tagged, and grouped similar answers from the text of students' responses.

These categories presented themselves in the analysis in several ways. For example, within a student's response it was readily apparent whether the individual perceived the pursuit of information literacy as a task driven by inner needs and motivation or by external requirements placed by society. It is noteworthy that of these seventy-six students, less than 12 percent relate information literacy to a specific academic project or to the library as a place or entity. The overwhelming majority of students think more globally about information literacy, connecting it to broader concepts including human development, curiosity, and a need for knowledge. In contrast to those who answered the question more obliquely, we found that a larger number of students whose responses were coded as early-life-oriented and question-oriented considered information literacy as a lifelong process. The fact that these students identify personally with information literacy—connecting it to the life cycle or viewing it as a means to deal with questions that come up in their personal lives—possibly influences this result. We would like to think that these students might be more earnest and persistent and become adept in their future use of information and libraries. Further research on student attitudes toward information literacy might examine such an effect. Understanding the range of attitudes people possess may also facilitate more effective marketing strategies to promote information literacy as a lifelong pursuit.

Another point for consideration is whether individuals who think of information literacy or information skills in a more abstract or dissociated way tend to more readily dismiss the consideration of those skill sets as a lifelong pursuit? If we look at the library-oriented, need-oriented, and project-oriented response categories, we see students expressing the idea that information literacy is something one needs when confronted with some external and finite requirement to find information. Coincidentally, we see that these students express less interest in information literacy as a lifelong pursuit. Not surprisingly, students who fell into the "none" category follow this trend. One might suggest that this correlation is even stronger than our data show because students may have felt a bit compelled to endorse lifelong learning at all to please the instructor and possibly improve their grade.

Lessons Learned

The lessons we have learned from our experiences fall into three categories: fostering collaborative relationships, building enrollment, and facilitating communication.

Collaboration

Collaborative relationships with partners outside of the Libraries have been integral in shaping Gen Ed 300. Partners on campus have included WSU's DDP, general education program, and Center for Teaching, Learning and Technology. For a period of time, the course was offered to students at Oregon State University and the University of Idaho as well—an arrangement that involved our librarian counterparts at these institutions as well as their administrators.

The collaborative efforts have been effective and productive, yet the process of forming collaborative relationships, developing ef-

fective communication practices, and negotiating priorities with our partners takes work. Successful collaboration, we have found, is an intensive exercise that can challenge the participants in unexpected ways. The root of the issues addressed here revolve around group assumptions, authority over collaborative projects, and the difficulty of establishing a shared language that all collaborative members can utilize to build a vision together. We have outlined these challenges and analyzed our experience through the collaborative learning theories of Kenneth Bruffee.[7]

Enrollment

As many colleagues can attest, a one-credit elective information literacy course requires strong marketing, and enrollment levels can fluctuate greatly. In earlier years, the course enrollments were higher because of miscommunication from advisors that led students to believe the course was required of them. We market the course, along with other library services, in several ways, including contributing to the program's newsletter, attending an annual event where the students visit the Pullman campus, and getting our content and links into students' online course spaces. The latter became more difficult to accomplish after the university switched from a home-grown course management system to WebCT, but we recently succeeded in having a library link added to all WebCT courses that allows us to provide a wide array of information to students and faculty. Also, WSU has a strong writing program, including a required junior portfolio and required "writing in the major" courses, which gives us a valuable "hook" for marketing Gen Ed 300.

Communication

Communication facilitation really stands as a two pronged issue: communication within the course (student to student and student to instructor) and communication with the DDP offices regarding the course. The course overview states clearly that Gen Ed 300 is a collaborative learning environment and that students will be interacting and communicating with each other frequently within the activities and in the process of reviewing each other's work. It also states clearly that participation does account for a portion of the grade and is critical in the success of the class. Each DDP class, with Gen Ed 300 being no exception, also has access to a "virtual facilitator" (VF). A VF is a paid upperclassman (often a senior) who has experienced several online courses through DDP and has been trained to assist with the flow of course discussion, help students focus on the evaluation criteria for the assignments, and other services. The VF's job is to assist with the flow of the class by questioning students on important aspects of the threaded discussion, offering suggestions, and sometimes prompting students on missing portions of the assignment. This assistance is particularly valuable in the beginning of the semester, when students are generally a little more timid and reserved and may not be completely at home yet in the virtual environment.

Throughout the semester, students are required to respond to each other's postings. The first threaded discussions are based around the students introducing themselves and stating their information need. As is probably the case with the beginnings of many online courses, the students' responses to each other generally include friendly greetings and positive remarks and personal experiences about various aspects of projects and coursework. As the semester progresses, students often have a difficult time transitioning out of this type of communication (friendly and agreeing with everything

the author states), and often it takes a little work, with the VF or instructor demonstrating a more critical or evaluative response, which students then exhibit in their own threaded discussion responses.

Because distance students often report feeling a disconnect from campus and even their fellow classmates, there is ample room for them to interact with each other and the instructor within the course space. Besides the threaded discussion areas there is a space for "Announcements," "Questions for the Instructor," and a "Class Lounge"— a space where students are encouraged to discuss information related to their projects and papers that might not necessarily relate to the class (e.g., sick pets, political viewpoints, and health issues). Students are also given complete instructor contact information for any course-related communication. One idea that was attempted with success during two separate semesters was an "online picnic." Besides the threaded discussion areas, the course space also includes a chat room area. The online picnics were advertised to students within the lounge area as a time to get to know their classmates and "hang out" outside of class, as students in an on-campus environment would. Meeting times were suggested and agreed upon, at which times students met in the chat space. These online picnics were not graded or counted in any way toward final grades; they simply offered as a time and space to socialize, something distance students generally don't have.

Conclusion

We have undertaken several course revisions over the past years, including one grant-funded revision in which we incorporated several newly built Web-based tutorials. We collaborate as appropriate with colleagues who teach the on-campus version of Gen Ed 300. Although there is much common ground, we have primarily adult students in the distance course, and this difference in audience keeps the online course distinct from the version tailored for typical undergraduates.

With more than ten years of the online course under our belts now, new plans are being considered. In particular, in its next incarnation the course may be more modular, giving students the option to complete it on their own time without assignment due dates (called a "flex" course at WSU).

Regardless of changes in format, pedagogy, or technology used to deliver this course, Gen Ed 300 will remain a cornerstone of our library services to the distance degree program students.

Notes

1. At the time, this program was known as the "Extended Degree program."

2. Read Craig Gibson, "Going the Distance (and Back Again): A Distance Education Course Comes Home," *Reference Librarian* 69/70 (2000): 233–44.

3. For a more detailed account of this process, read J. Scales et al., "Compliance, Cooperation, Collaboration and Information Literacy," *Journal of Academic Librarianship* 31 no. 3 (2005): 229–35.

4. Washington State University, *Critical Thinking Rubric*. Available online at http://wsuctproject. wsu.edu/ctr.htm.

5. Donald Hanna, *147 Practical Tips for Teaching Online Groups* (Madison, WI: Atwood, 2000), 23–27.

6. For more information on one of our assessment projects, read B. J. Scales and E. B. Lindsay, "Qualitative Assessment of Student Attitudes toward Information Literacy," *Portal: Libraries and the Academy* 5, no. 4 (2005): 513–26.

7. For a more detailed account of this process, read Scales et al., "Compliance," 229–35.

6. Making it Available 24/7: Developing an Online Version of the One-Credit Class

Nancy Wootton Colborn and Feng Shan

Rationale

Web-based learning has become increasingly popular because of its accessibility and flexibility. Students can control their own pace of study and need not depend on a teacher's presence or on rigid classroom schedules. Indiana University–South Bend (IUSB) has taught a one-credit library skills course since 1996. Because of the success of this face-to-face course, the Office of Distributed Education at Indiana University requested that we transform this course from a traditional classroom instruction model to an online learning model. The course was envisioned as a way to meet the needs of distance learners throughout Indiana University. In addition, this course was designed to benefit the large number of commuter students on the IUSB campus.

Development

From the time we began planning the online course to the first course offering, the process took eighteen months and was divided into two phases: brainstorming and course structure design, and module development and programming.

Brainstorming and Course Structure Design

A core group of librarians began the task of planning the course content and structure. This group included the library director, the library instruction coordinator, another instruction librarian, and the Web librarian. This group examined the existing Library Skills & Resources course and envisioned how a completely online course might differ from the existing face-to-face class. The team then turned to the Internet to gather ideas from other online courses that were freely available on the Web. After initial discussions, all of the librarians were given a draft course outline and asked to comment on it. A final course outline was approved. At that time, both the library instruction coordinator and the Web librarian left the university to take other jobs. The instruction librarian became the library instruction coordinator, and the new Web librarian joined the online course planning team. Continuing work was coordinated by these two librarians, with input from the library director.

The design of the computing structure of the course was a little more complicated. The Web librarian and a student programming assistant examined other Web courses that were freely available on the Internet and researched a variety of Web programming languages. They also analyzed Oncourse, the university's existing course management system, to determine how an online class could best be integrated with it. Through meetings and discussions via e-mail and in person, the design team reached a consensus that a highly dynamic multimedia program was desirable. It was also deemed important to make the student learning process as interactive as possible. The course modules would ideally contain graphics, sound, and voiceovers in order to mimic face-to-face teaching. Short quizzes and questions would include instant feedback when a student clicked on an answer button.

Once the goals for basic course content and structure were in place, the Web librarian worked to find the tools that would best deliver the course through a user interface. ASP (Active Server Page) was chosen as the programming language, and the Microsoft Access database and SQL (Structured Query Language) database were selected for the dynamic Web program. At the time, the campus IT department did not support these Web services, so the library purchased a Microsoft Windows Web server. The IT librarian installed the server with SQL database software in readiness for program development.

Module Development and Web Programming

Two teams then began work on module development and Web programming. The Web design group consisted of a Web librarian and a student Web programmer. The group responsible for module development consisted mostly of reference and instruction librarians, although the library director and cataloging librarian also elected to participate in the process by designing course modules. The instruction coordinator was the team leader and coordinated the work of both groups.

On the computing side, the user interface structure was envisioned as an easily maneuverable, self-paced program, which required basic computer knowledge by the student and minimum instructor assistance. The Web librarian and programming student assistant presented their prototype design model to the course planning team for feedback. The prototype was approved on its third revision.

Module development was concurrent with prototype design. During the process, each librarian was responsible for the content of one or two modules. Some librarians created hand-written prototypes of their page outlines; others used Microsoft's Word, PowerPoint, or FrontPage. Some librarians included ideas for graphics, Web links, sound, or interactive exercises; others primarily presented the text of the lesson. The library instruction coordinator reviewed the modules initially for succinctness, overlap, and exclusion. Some module editing involved making the content consistent in writing style and tone (since many librarians were involved in writing the modules) and editing the assignments so that they were relatively equal in expectations and weight throughout the semester.

After the initial content was created, the Web librarian and programmer entered the content into the Microsoft Access database, writing Java scripts to activate the Web applications. Initially an ODBC (Open DataBase Connectivity) connection was set up between the Web database server and the Web librarian's desktop computer so that the Web librarian and programmer could edit the Access database. ODBC is a standard database access method that enables access of data from any application, regardless of database management system. This proved difficult logistically, however, so a Web administration interface with password protection was created. This interface made it possible for the design team to update the content from literally anywhere.

Once the initial programming of a particular module was complete, the librarian who wrote the module and the library instruction coordinator worked together to revise the content to better fit the existing course structure and objectives of the module. It was at this point that many of the librarians could completely visualize the best way to deliver their particular content. Because of the nature of writing content for online learning, the learning curve was rather steep for the librarians. Framing concepts in learning blocks and being succinct required considerable rewriting and editing.

After a few revisions, the library instruction coordinator and Web programming team took over the completion of the modules, increasing their visual appeal by adding graphics, interactive activities, and multimedia demonstrations.

One example of an added feature is from the Periodicals module. To demonstrate using the EBSCO*host* database to construct a successful search and retrieve a periodical article, a series of screenshots with voiceovers was created. Each time a student clicks on the "next" button and proceeds to a different database search screenshot, a .wav file automatically plays the related voiceover. In addition, to ensure that students can access the voiceover content regardless of technical limitations or hearing impairment, a script display option is available on each page of the module.

After the completion of the course modules as a whole, the Web programming team distributed the modules to the librarians for feedback. The order in which to present the subject modules was one of the most controversial issues discussed. The course modules were reconfigured several times before a consensus was reached on the current organization. The next step was to solicit feedback from the potential users—students. Library student assistants were asked to navigate through the course modules and provide their opinions or suggestions. After these two final sources of feedback, the interface appearance and content were finalized. The first official course offering was in the spring semester of 2003.

Content

The course, now titled "Introduction to Information Literacy," was originally designed as an "online sources only" course, called "Research and the Virtual Library." As noted earlier, the Indiana University Office of Distributed Education had requested that we design the course, and it was included in the Distance Education listing for the university from 2003 to 2005. No students from outside IUSB ever enrolled in the course. When the campus general education curriculum was changed in 2005 to include the one-credit information literacy course as a requirement, we restricted enrollment to IUSB students. At that time, both the face-to-face course and the online course were redesigned to cover exactly the same content, differing only in delivery methods. The course number for both courses is Q110. The course description reads as follows: "This course examines information structure and organization as well as teaching techniques and skills for effectively identifying, acquiring, evaluating, using and communicating information in various formats."

The course consists of fifteen modules that students must complete on their own. Each module covers either a research concept (search strategy) or a typical research tool (online catalogs) and is some combination of text, graphics, and sound, depending on the individual module. The modules are housed on a library Web server, and students access them via a link in the university's course management system, Oncourse. All auxiliary features of an online course (discussion forums, e-mail, grading, and chat rooms) are conveniently located within the Oncourse system. Each module was designed with specific course objectives in mind. One example is the Periodicals module, shown in the table 6.1. The course outline is included as an appendix for an overview of other course content.

Instruction

Because there are several instructors, the course modules are available on a library server. The modules are password-protected and available only to students currently enrolled in the course. Each week, students connect to the appropriate course module through a link in the course management system. The students interact with the course module in an asynchronous manner. Students read and view the content and then complete homework assignments designed by the individual instructors. Typically instructors communicate with students throughout the week to enhance the learning experience. An instructor might select one or two points in the weekly module that they wish to underscore or emphasize and send a message to all of the students via the Oncourse Course Announcements about it. If students have questions, they are encouraged to contact the instructor via Oncourse e-mail, personal e-mail, instant messaging, or phone, or during office hours. In addition, they can post questions or comments about the course content to a discussion forum housed within the Oncourse system framework. If one student raises a question that may be relevant to the entire class, the instructor shares that information via an all-class e-mail or course announcement in order to clarify issues for all.

Course enrollment for both online and face-to-face classes is set at twenty-four students. Some administrators have questioned

Table 6.1. Periodical module objectives and tools		
Objective	**How Met**	**Video Planned?**
The student will understand what a periodical is and be able to differentiate between a popular and scholarly publication.	To meet this objective, a page with definitions and photographs of a variety of periodicals is available to the students with accompanying text. In addition, there is a chart that delineates the difference between popular and scholarly publications.	yes
The student will understand the nature of periodicals in terms of the information cycle.	To meet this objective, a page with an ungraded, interactive quiz is available that tests student knowledge of periodicals and their use in terms of currency and format.	no
The student will understand that periodicals are available in print and electronic format, be able to determine if the Schurz Library owns a journal in either format, and be able to retrieve articles in either format.	To meet this objective, a narrative page explains this information.	yes, on two aspects: print/electronic comparison and physical location/retrieval
The student will be able to use one interdisciplinary database, EBSCOhost's Academic Search Premier, to conduct a successful periodical search.	To meet this objective, a series of screenshots with voiceover explain the database functions and demonstrate a simple search and retrieval of a full-text article.	no
The student will be able to order journal articles that are now owned by the Schurz Library through our Interlibrary Loan service.	To meet this objective, a narrative page explains this information.	no

the cap on the online class. When the online course was first offered, the online instructors kept detailed records of the time spent interacting with students and other course-related tasks. The results showed that online instructors spent at least as much time as face-to-face instructors in teaching the course; interaction with students and increased time in correcting papers electronically seem to balance the time that face-to-face instructors spend in class time and preparation.

Individual students are assessed on the basis of their completion of homework requirements, which, as noted, vary with instructor. Homework includes, but is not limited to, written responses to relevant videos or tutorials; research assignments with specific answers found in reference books; research logs in which students complete research and reflect on their search strategy, use of terminology, results found, and subsequent revision of the search process; and written evaluations of sources.

The term project for the course is an annotated bibliography that requires students to find material in specific formats (reference sources, books, journal articles, Web sites, government publications) on a topic, write an introduction to the topic, and cite and annotate each source. In addition to brief summaries of the source, the annotations include the relevant search strategy employed to find the item and commentary

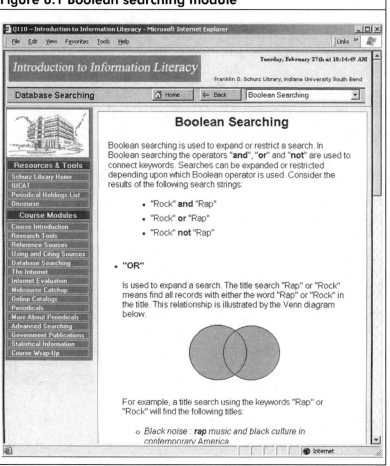

Figure 6.1 Boolean searching module

on how the source would be useful in a more complete research project.

Despite our best efforts to make our technological and self-motivation expectations clear to students, many of them have difficulty with these issues. One of the initial course requirements is completion of the Readiness Index for Learning Online (RILO), a self-administered survey that assesses the student's comfort with technology, the level of personal interaction in an online course, and self-motivation.[1] In addition, clear expectations for the use of specific browsers and word-processing software are outlined in the initial course module. Regardless of these measures, there are always some students who do not succeed in the course because they don't have the proper technology at home or aren't motivated to complete the course modules within the specified period.

Creating a sense of community in the online classroom is difficult. As previously mentioned, the Oncourse course management system includes an e-mail system and a discussion forum for both students and teachers. In addition, all faculty and student photos and personal profiles are available to class members on the system so that students can "see" and learn about each other on a more personal basis. There is also a chat room feature on Oncourse. Because the students are taking the course asynchronously, however, there is usually no good time for all students to participate in a chat room gathering. Individual instructors encourage the use of the discussion forum in various ways, but all make it openly available to the students for discussing their work together.

Program Assessment

Q110: Introduction to Information Literacy is now in its second academic year as a required course. Pre- and post-tests are administered to students in both the face-to-face and online versions of the course in order to gauge student learning. Among other variables, the analysis compares face-to-face and online learning. The results have been analyzed through December 2006. In both face-to-face and online courses, students are scoring better on the post-test than the pre-test, at a significant level. Online student learning in the Q110 course is comparable to face-to-face learning.

Yearly, the entire Q110 faculty meets to analyze the assessment findings and discuss relevant curricular changes or necessary changes in the tests. In addition, the online course instructors (currently three of the librarians) meet at least twice a year to analyze the course modules for currency in relation to database offerings and research trends and the effectiveness of the modules for teaching the relevant material. We then make necessary changes in the course modules themselves, the homework requirements, or our supplemental communications to the students.

We don't yet know if students who successfully complete Q110 are incorporating their new-found information literacy skills throughout the curriculum and thereby enhancing their college experience. The Q110 course in the general education curriculum falls in the category of "Fundamental Literacies," which also includes writing, quantitative reasoning, oral communications, critical thinking, visual literacy, and computer literacy. The general education committee's intent for the fundamental literacies was to introduce the skills and abilities as part of the shared general education curriculum and then build upon them throughout the student's college curriculum. Anecdotally, some professors report seeing a difference in the bibliographies of students who have taken the course, but further assessment as the class of 2009 nears graduation would be advantageous. The library instruction coordinator and the campus general education committee are investigating appropriate assessment tools to measure information literacy skills at the upper-class level.

Lessons Learned

Though the online course was well conceived and initiated in 2003, it is in need of some revision. As mentioned above, the online instructors routinely make changes in individual modules based on changes in vendor interfaces, available databases, or library practices. In addition, based on pre- and post-test comparisons conducted annually, all of the Q110 instructors have input into overall curricular changes. Still, the modules are beginning to look somewhat dated. In particular, we are investigating ways to make the content more dynamic and interactive, with an eye toward video content and tutorials. In the example module for Periodicals (table 6.1), we've identified a few segments that will be enhanced by further visual content. Since two of the online instructors also teach the face-to-face course, we are aware of which concepts and skills are more easily explained by demonstration than by narrative text. In addition, we hope to explore additional ASP and Java functionalities in order to add more dynamic hands-on exercises about important concepts. At the present time, all online instructors must use the same course modules. Making the modules more easily adaptable for individual instructors is another issue we would take into consideration if we were to rebuild or revise the program.

Conclusion

Designing an online course for the first time was a challenging but rewarding task. We faced challenges of staff turnover, lack of support from the campus IT department, and steep learning curves in terms of technological expertise. The initial design, though, is a good one and has stood the test of time rather well. The course modules are easily updated when necessary, and there are now three librarians who are comfortable with the basics of the database structure and have access to it via password. As noted above, we are always actively seeking ways to improve the course modules and will continue to do so in order to stay abreast of current technology. Student comments such as this one tell us we're on the right track: "I have taken three internet classes so far in my college career, and this one was by far the easiest to maneuver. I did not have trouble doing the assignments and really enjoyed the way the class was run."

Appendix. Q110 Course Outline	
Course Introduction	Overview of syllabus and schedule, RILO (Readiness Inventory for Online Learning) test, pre-test, term project overview
Research Tools	Types of materials in libraries, search strategy, the timeline of information, topic selection and modification, the importance of terminology
Reference Sources	The types of reference sources and their uses
Using & Citing Sources	Ethical use of information, plagiarism and academic honesty, MLA & APA style, Refworks
Database Searching	The structure of a database, search strings, keyword searching, controlled vocabulary, known item searching, stop words, Boolean searching
The Internet	Historical and technical overview, ownership and control, fee vs. free, uniform resources locaters, access tools (search engines, meta-search engines, directories), the deep Web
Internet Evaluation	Evaluation of Internet sources
Online Catalogs	Online catalogs in general/IUCAT specifically, types of searches, reading a citation, call numbers and classification systems (including LC, SuDocs and Dewey), subject headings, lateral searching, Boolean searching, advanced search techniques, request delivery option for ILL
Periodicals	Definitions and benefits of use, popular vs. scholarly, print vs. electronic, journal databases (focus on EBSCOhost Academic Search Premier), locating print journals, using IU-Link and ILL
More about Periodicals	Advanced searching techniques, introduction to a wider array of databases, controlled vocabulary, thesaurus searching
Advanced Searching	Field limiters, truncation, nesting, phrase searching, proximity searching, table of contents searching, saved searches, search histories and alert services
Government Publications	U. S. federal government structure, federal depository system, SuDocs classification system, government publications on the Web
Statistical Information	How statistics are gathered (census data, sampling, surveys), how polling works, evaluation and use of statistics and poll figures
Course Wrap-Up	Course overview, term project due, post-test administration, course evaluation

Note

1.   Serena Novosel, "Readiness Index for Online Learning (RILO)," Indiana University School of Nursing. Available online at http://nursing.iupui.edu/About/default.asp?/About/CTLL/Online/rilo.htm.

7. An Ever-Evolving Experience: Teaching Information Literacy as a General Education Requirement

Peggy Ridlen and Jane Theissen

Rationale

Several currents converged at Fontbonne University in 2000 that sparked the creation of an information literacy course. First, technology finally caught up with the university. Fontbonne installed the first fifteen computers in the library, initiated several database subscriptions with OCLC and Oxford among others, and automated its holdings for inclusion in the online union catalog of the Missouri Bibliographic Information User System (MOBIUS), the statewide consortium of academic libraries. Second, on June 7, 2000, the Coordinating Board for Higher Education of the State of Missouri adopted "Credit Transfer: Guidelines for Student Transfer and Articulation among Missouri Colleges and Universities."[1] Under the leadership of the dean of academic affairs at that time, Fontbonne University became a signatory institution of these guidelines. Third, faculty members recognized the urgent need to teach students to access and evaluate information in this new learning environment and verbalized this concern: "Rhetoric instructors have traditionally taught library research skills. However, as electronic resources have become more pervasive, teachers of rhetoric find themselves increasingly lacking in expertise, even as teachers and students alike devote more and more time to keeping up with the rapidly changing virtual landscape."[2]

The original idea was to add a one-hour information literacy component to Rhetoric II (ENG 102), making ENG 102 a four-hour course. However, Fontbonne's library director at that time wisely seized the opportunity to submit a proposal to the curriculum committee for a separate, free-standing information literacy course as a part of the Interdisciplinary Studies program.

The Faculty General Assembly approved the course, and in fall 2002, Information Literacy (INT 108), became a one-hour online general education requirement with a mandatory face-to-face orientation session. Fontbonne University had recently implemented Blackboard as the Web tool to deliver online courses; the online format was chosen for INT 108 because it conveniently delivered course content to many students simultaneously and eliminated the need for physical classroom space. Incidentally, one unique aspect of online instruction at Fontbonne, introduced during this time, was a prerequisite, FOC 101 (Fontbonne Online Course), a self-guided online tutorial designed to familiarize students with the Blackboard interface. Administered by an Information Technology staff member, FOC 101 was required for all students taking an online course for the first time. It consisted of five interactive modules graded on a pass/fail basis. This prerequisite currently remains in place.

As it was originally conceived, INT 108 began with a test-out examination. If students scored a B or lower on the test, they were required to complete the course. Coursework included required readings, six research assignments, eleven quizzes, and a final exam. Periodic workshops were provided by the instructors to assist students with the assignments.

Because INT 108 addressed several of the "Information Management" competencies listed in the university's transfer credit guidelines, it was eventually identified as one of the courses in which students are required to demonstrate proficiency in using electronic tools to access and generate information and to examine the legal and ethical issues involved with the use of information technology. These are two core competencies of Fontbonne's own general education requirements for managing information.

Development

In fall 2004, INT 108 was handed off to four newly hired librarians. The course they inherited was sound in structure, content, and instructional theory. It had, however, evolved to require only regurgitation of material students read from the textbook and did not utilize many of the Blackboard components designed to engage online learners. Various textbooks were used and course design was not consistent from section to section. The new library faculty faced challenges; the static content and poor student perception of the course eventually led to major revisions and continuous updates. With input from all librarians, the instruction librarian revised the curriculum to ensure consistency of content and to avoid divergent development of the course by multiple instructors. Short, interactive, rigorous practice drills utilizing periodical databases and virtual reference tools replaced multiple-choice quizzes. Higher levels of learning, following Bloom's taxonomy, were incorporated into lessons to improve critical thinking. Discussion board forums,

blog entries, and writing assignments were added to enable students to express opinions and to reflect on their own learning.

Over the next few semesters, several factors combined to alter student perception and improve the image of the course. Librarians emphasized concepts such as the value of intrinsic learning and delayed gratification in hopes of inspiring students to put forth more effort in a one-hour course to learn skills that would be beneficial in future courses. A library liaison program initiated by the university librarian and a comprehensive information literacy plan implemented by the dean helped faculty to understand information literacy and to reinforce skills taught in the course. Individual tutorial support from the university's Center for Academic Resources alleviated problems in dealing with the broad range of student technological expertise. Currently, INT 108 is offered in two slightly different formats: online with one mandatory orientation, or blended with several class meetings. Since the term "information literacy" was confusing to students and their advisors, the course was renamed "Libraries and Information Research."

Content

INT 108: Libraries and Information Research (figure 7.1) "is an introduction to basic skills and concepts for using diverse information sources and search strategies to locate, evaluate, and use information. Topics include classification and organization of information, information search tools and strategies, online search techniques, evaluation and analysis of information, and responsible and ethical use of information."[3]

Students are expected to use the Fontbonne University Library resources to successfully

Figure 7.1 INT 108 opening screenshot

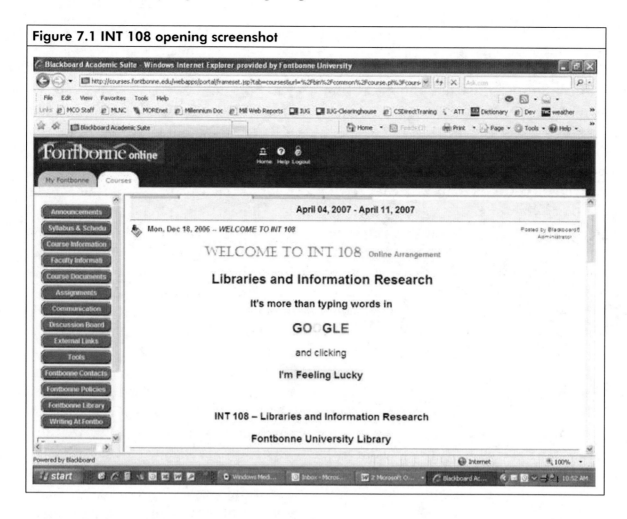

- locate books from the Fontbonne Online Catalog and MOBIUS Union Catalog
- navigate the Fontbonne Library Web site to access electronic resources such as virtual reference tools and periodical databases
- select appropriate multidisciplinary and subject-specific databases
- construct search strategies that retrieve manageable results
- identify academic, scholarly, and peer-reviewed sources
- locate and retrieve a full-text journal article from a bibliographic citation
- request material through interlibrary loan
- evaluate Web site content for authority, accuracy, currency, and objectivity
- paraphrase and cite information to avoid plagiarism

The ACRL Information Literacy Competency Standards provide the basis for what students are expected to learn. But these standards become meaningful only when students understand the skills and concepts associated with them. Therefore, alignment of the standards with learning objectives is crucial to engage students. Organizing content by weekly themes and linking standards with specified activities stated in the student learning objectives are an attempt to move students from the "twilight zone"[4] of educational jargon to the real world of information literacy. Figure 7.2 illustrates the alignment of INT 108 Student Learning Objectives with ACRL information literacy standards.

Figure 7.2. ACRL Information Literacy Competency Standards and INT 108 student learning objectives

Week Five: WEB 2.0: Blogs, Wikis, & Internet Websites
ACRL Standard Three: The information-literate student evaluates information and its source critically and incorporates selected information into his or her knowledge base and value system.

Student Learning Objectives
1. After reading Ch. 8 in *College Student's Research Companion* and the designated tutorials, INT 108 students will utilize the criteria of Accuracy, Authority, Objectivity, Validity, and Currency to analyze and evaluate selected Web sites by responding to fill-in-the-blank and short- answer essay questions.

2. After viewing a PowerPoint presentation, students will demonstration their knowledge of the WEB 2.0 by taking a short objective quiz.

3. After reading an ABC News transcript titled *Blogging 101* and listening to an NPR podcast about Wikipedia, students will express opinions and ideas about the future of the Internet through participation in a discussion board forum.

Week Six: Plagiarism
ACRL Standard Five: The information-literate student understands many of the economic, legal, and social issues surrounding the use of information and accesses and uses information ethically and legally.

Student Learning Objectives
1. After reading the instructor''s lecture posted in this forum, INT 108 students will demonstrate the ability to avoid plagiarism by discussing three ways to paraphrase properly.

2. After reading and studying designed handouts on APA and MLA citation styles, INT 108 students will demonstrate the ability to cite sources correctly by completing part one of the final project.

3. After completing the tutorial, Plagiarism Court, INT 108 students will demonstrate the ability to recognize plagiarism by completing part two of the final project.

Week Seven: Final Project
ACRL Standard One: The information-literate student determines the nature and extent of the information needed.

ACRL Standard Two: The information-literate student accesses needed information effectively and efficiently.

ACRL Standard Three: The information-literate student evaluates information and its source critically and incorporates selected information into his or her knowledge base and value system.

ACRL Standard Four: The information-literate student, individually or as a member of a group, uses information effectively to accomplish a specific purpose.

ACRL Standard Five: The information-literate student understands many of the economic, legal, and social issues surrounding the use of information and accesses and uses information ethically and legally.

Student Learning Objective
After completing INT 108, students will demonstrate the ability to access various resources to find, retrieve, analyze, evaluate, and use information by successfully completing part one of a final project, which will require
- selecting a topic and writing a thesis statement
- selecting appropriate resources
- planning a search strategy
- executing the planned search strategy
- explaining the steps involved with executing the search
- evaluating the results

Instruction

INT 108 has evolved into an interactive, student-centered virtual classroom. Multimedia content, current textbooks, updated tutorials, and ongoing assessment keep the course current. For example, video streams, podcasts, and transcripts of television and radio programs from CBS and NPR engage students as online learners. In the discussion board forum—the class participation component of the course—students voice opinions on pertinent topics such as the library as place, blogs and wikis, and plagiarism. Instructors creatively liven up the course by displaying colorful graphics; inserting humor, wit, and wisdom; and offering extra credit activities via Blackboard announcements (see figure 7.3).

In writing assignments, students are expected to reflect on the research process and contemplate the importance of being information literate. Course rubrics that enumerate specific qualitative criteria are used to evaluate written responses. These can also be helpful in clarifying expectations for the quality of writing. In addition, students receive direct feedback in the comments field of Blackboard assignments.

The College Student's Research Companion, by Arlene Rodda Quaratiello, provides the basic framework for skills learned in INT 108.[5] It is important that students be held accountable for reading it and for appreciating its worth as a reference source. Consequently, students are required to submit journal entries summarizing what they have learned from reading the textbook, chapter by chapter. Performance-based assessment activities also reinforce concepts presented in the textbook and in tutorials. Figure 7.4 illustrates the structure and organization of the course.

Students must also compose reflective responses to process-based assignments. Writing becomes a self-assessment tool for student learning when students ask themselves questions such as "What did I do?" "What did I find?" "What can I change to retrieve more relevant results?" "What have I learned in completing this project?" and "How will it help me in the future?"[6]

The final project (figure 7.5), completed in the final week of INT 108, is the culminating assessment activity. It requires students to utilize the skills and techniques they have acquired during the course: developing a strong thesis statement, formatting and evaluating a

Figure 7.3. Blackboard announcement space

Hello Class. Welcome to Week Three: The Virtual Library
Can any of you identify with the scenario in this comic? The first person to respond to me by e-mail explaining the irony in this comic will receive 3 extra percentage points! (It is very apropos for this week's theme.)

Scott, J., and Borgman, J. Zits. (2006, October 17). Retrieved October 27, 2006, from http/seattlepi.nwsource.com fun /zits.asp.

Figure 7.4. INT 108: Required assignments and grading	
DISCUSSION BOARD – Forum Topics	**Points**
The Library as Place – week 1	20
Wikipedia Wins Users and Critics – week 5	20
Preventing Plagiarism – week 6	20
WRITING ASSIGNMENTS	
Course Journal Entries: Chapter Readings: Reflections from The College Student's Research Companion, Chaps. 1–9	100
What Is Information Literacy? – week 1	30
Can the Internet Replace the Library? – week 4	30
PERFORMANCE-BASED ASSESSMENT ACTIVITIES	
Syllabus Quiz – week 1	10
Reference Room Treasure Hunt – week 2	15
Periodicals Quiz – week 3	15
Database Drill – week 3	15
Virtual Reference Workout – week 4	15
Web 2.0 Quiz – week 5	15
Evaluating Websites Assignment – week 5	15
CULMINATING FINAL PROJECT:	
Database Research – week 7	150
Plagiarism – weeks 6 and 7	50
Total	520

search strategy, selecting appropriate database and other resources, and then reflecting on the entire process with an eye toward improving it. "Helpful Hints" are provided to assist students in completing the assignment. Students have been allowed to select their own topic, but many struggle even at this step. Providing some parameters such as a list of suggested topics makes the process easier for them. The final project is typed in an outline format and submitted through Blackboard's Digital Dropbox. Students who successfully complete the final project have demonstrated proficiency in the ACRL standards and the INT 108 student learning objectives.

Program Assessment

A formal course assessment such as a survey of students or controlled case study has yet to be conducted and will certainly be necessary in the future to determine the success of INT 108 accurately. Substantial empirical evidence does, however, indicate that the course is effective in improving student performance in regard to meeting the course objectives and building information literacy. Feedback has come from four main sources: instructor appraisal of final grades, student evaluation forms, responses in student writings, and comments from classroom faculty. These informal methods of assessment provide insight that has been useful in various course revisions. For example, dissatisfaction with student performance on the cumulative final project prompted an optional face-to-face help session in which librarians demonstrated an effective search strategy on a sample topic using electronic databases. A comparison of grades by the instructor on the final project between students who attended the face-to-face session and those who did not indicated an increased grade of 10 percent on the final project for the attendees.

Student evaluation forms offer further evidence that students are learning information literacy skills and appreciate the course. Reflective students realize that what they learn in INT 108 is valuable, not only in future courses but as a life skill. The following comments are typical of those that were listed as strengths during 2005:

This course helped me with my computer and information literacy skills. I learned a lot of new tricks and it was interesting.

Figure 7.5. INT 108: Final project

Database Final Project: INT 108 Information Literacy
The assignment is to select a topic, conduct research on that topic, and formulate a working thesis. Use one of the databases found on library Web site under <u>Electronic Resources</u>.

Database Research (150 points)
I. Topic Formation. (30 points)
(Select an academic topic. An issue connected to your major might be a good choice, or a topic that you are interested in learning more about.)
    A. Topic _____
    B. To which subject discipline does the topic belong?
    C. Write a working thesis statement based on this topic. (Read Writing a Good Thesis Sentence.)
    D. List at least 3 keywords from the working thesis statement that might be used to find information on the selected topic.
II. Knowledge of the selected database. (20 points)
From the Electronic Resources link on Fontbonne University Library's Web site, select a periodical index database that is appropriate for researching your selected topic.
    A. Name of selected database:
    B. Is the database multi-disciplinary or subject specific? (If subject specific, what subject is it?)
    C. Is this a citation or a full-text database? How do you know? What is the difference?
    D. List the scope of coverage for this database—number of journal titles indexed, number of peer-reviewed titles, date coverage begins and ends, etc.
III. Demonstration of information literacy skills. (70 points)
Use the database selected above for this activity.
    A. Perform an Advanced Search using at least two of the search terms you listed above in section I.D. Briefly summarize your results, including the number of results. *Are these results useful for researching your thesis? Is there something you can do to make them more useful?*
    B. Explain how to limit or expand the search.
      • What options are available for limiting the search?
      • For expanding the search?
    C. Define a "field" search. Identify various field search options available in this database. Explain why they are useful in conducting searches.
    D. Briefly define "controlled vocabulary."
    E. Perform a "subject" field search in the Advanced Search screen using a subject term or descriptor relevant to your thesis. Discuss how you discovered the appropriate subject term, how subject field searching is different from a random or default keyword search, and how it helped to retrieve more relevant results.
IV. Citation of sources. (15 points)
    A. Cite one source you located on your topic using MLA format.
    B. Cite the same source using APA format.
V. Evaluation. (15 points)
    A. What did you like about this database? Be specific.
    B. Briefly reflect on what you learned in completing this project. How will it help you in the future?

The course forced me to learn how to access the library from my computer at home. I used to be afraid of this, but now I am quite comfortable with the idea.

Course was challenging, but not too difficult. The instructor made it fun and rewarding.

Good updated and related information; asset to continuous learning.

The course is very useful and needed. All of the information can be used throughout my education, work, and everyday life. I wish I had taken this class earlier.

Figure 7.6. Fontbonne University Comprehensive Information Literacy Plan

Drafted at the Council of Independent Colleges/National Institute for Technology & Liberal Education Library Transformation Workshop

1. THE PROGRAM

    a. Nature: *We will continue to provide quality library instruction and to integrate information literacy concepts into the Fontbonne University curriculum.*

        Currently in existence:

- INT108 – 1 credit required for General Education (Proficiency Exam → can test out)
- Cooperative teaching efforts with faculty
- Information Commons
- Initial conversations with faculty about embedding information literacy in capstone courses
- Performance-based assessment of competencies

    b. Mission:

Fontbonne University is a coeducational institution of higher learning dedicated to the discovery, understanding, preservation and dissemination of truth. Fontbonne seeks to educate students to think critically, to act ethically and to assume responsibility as citizens and leaders. Fontbonne offers both undergraduate and graduate programs in an atmosphere characterized by inclusion, open communication and personal concern. The undergraduate programs provide a synthesis of liberal and professional education. As a Catholic university sponsored by the Sisters of St. Joseph of Carondelet, Fontbonne is rooted in the Judaeo-Christian tradition.

    c. Goals:

Information literacy correlates with the institutional mission:

- Information literacy facilitates discovery and understanding of truth
- Information literacy facilitates critical thinking and ethical actions

Proposed additions (goals):

- Develop online module → integrate into Rhetoric I & II
- Strengthen library liaison – faculty relationship → infuse information literacy in the curriculum
- Embedded Web pages → for select programs / courses
- Investigate the viability of multi-media production

    d. Outcomes:

- Performance-based assessment of INT108 as part of Gen Ed assessment
- Performance-based assessment of capstone courses in program / major
- Senior survey (student satisfaction) and Alumni survey (lifelong learning)
- Assessment of ethical use of information

2. IMPLEMENTATION CHART

Step	What	Who	How	When
1	Develop online modules	Reference/ Instruction Librarian	Using various models	2007 (in process)
2	Infuse info lit. throughout curriculum	Liaisons & faculty	Liaisons attend department meetings	2006
			Designing course pages	Ongoing
			Participating in capstones	2007
3	Outcomes assessment	University Librarian	Embed questions in senior survey	2006
		Assessment Committee	Create alumni survey	2007-2008
		Liaisons	Performance-based capstone assessment	2006-2007
		Assessment Committee	Performance-based assessment of ethical use of information literacy	2007-2008
4	Improve INT108	Librarians	Evaluate and revise INT108	2007-2008

Unsolicited comments from classroom faculty such as the following indicate emphatically that the research skill levels of students who have completed INT 108 stand out from those who have not:

I met one of the English faculty members this morning and mentioned how important it is for the library to work with faculty from all departments across campus, and she in turn said that it is clear to her which students have been in INT 108 and how much it helps in her work for them to have had the course. That's just anecdotal evidence, but I thought I'd pass along the compliment—you are obviously doing a good job.[7]

Certainly, more formal surveys are needed to determine students' ability to transfer skills learned in INT 108 to research assignments in core classes, but empirical evidence indicates progress.

Fontbonne began campus-wide assessment of general education requirements in summer 2006. The INT 108 final project is used to assess student proficiency in two previously mentioned core competencies for Managing Information. A team of evaluators rate the artifact from 5 to 1, using a rubric developed by the university. Students scoring a 3 or above demonstrate proficiency in each competency. The forthcoming compilation and analysis of this data will be crucial in determining the nature of the course in the future.

Fortunately, Fontbonne University has administrative leadership that realizes that a dedicated course is only one part of a larger picture. In 2006 the university librarian, the vice president and dean of academic affairs, and an English faculty member attended the Council of Independent Colleges' Library Transformation Workshop and drafted a comprehensive information literacy plan intended to relate the nature of information literacy to the mission of the university and set measurable outcomes for its achievement. The Implementation Chart included in the plan sets a timeframe for the accomplishment of specific goals (figure 7.6).

As Fontbonne's new information literacy plan is implemented, the results of senior/alumni surveys as well as performance-based assessment in capstone courses will be used to chart the future of information literacy.

Lessons Learned

Many lessons that the librarians at Fontbonne University have learned in the ever-evolving nature of teaching an information literacy course are common ones reported widely by librarians everywhere:

- Don't reinvent wheel.
- Keep the course content current.
- Be aware that course assignments can heavily increase the workload of reference librarians.
- Take risks/try new things.

These are all lessons well-learned. However, the most important lessons learned at Fontbonne were ones of a broader, more abstract nature. Here is the countdown of the top three.

Number 3. Make No Assumptions about Technology Expertise

Computer literacy should precede information literacy. Students who have to learn computer literacy skills and information literacy skills at the same time face a double challenge. These students need more faculty-student interaction, demonstration, and guided hands-on practice to do well in the course. Although adding the optional face-

---

Figure 7.7. Blackboard buttons: Virtual tour

Take a virtual tour of Blackboard using the navigational buttons on the left-hand side of the screen. Use the following explanations as a guide.

ANNOUNCEMENTS -– The top button will lead to the page that automatically appears after you log in to the course. Pay close attention to all announcements. Important updates and weekly assignments are posted frequently.

COURSE INFORMATION- – This button contains the course syllabus and a schedule that will be your survival guide. Read them both carefully. Links that explain the course rationale and provide an opportunity for feedback are here.

FACULTY- – This button includes the instructor''s contact information. Be sure your Fontbonne email is working. Only Fontbonne email will be used to communicate with students for this course. Instructors will respond to email within 48 hours.

COURSE DOCUMENTS – -Clicking on this button will display instructional documents needed to complete assignments. Read, listen to, and study these documents carefully.

ASSIGNMENTS – -This button is crucial. It gives access to writing assignments and performance-based assessment activities. It also contains week-by-week instructions for completing and submitting assignments.

COMMUNICATION – -Use this button to access Discussion Board forum topics and to send email.

EXTERNAL LINKS – -This button contains links to upload programs, podcasts, video streams, and Web sites.

TOOLS – -This button contains the Course Journal, Digital Dropbox, My Grades, and the User's Manual.

FONTBONNE CONTACTS – -This button provides contact information for Information Technology, the Kinkel Center for Academic Resources, and the Library.

---

to-face help session has somewhat diminished this dilemma, a student who becomes lost even before interacting with the online course content loses the opportunity for learning.[8] Consequently, no assumptions should be made about a student's ability to intuit how to navigate Blackboard. Occasionally students drop the online course rather than admit that they could not find the components needed to complete assignments. Navigational strategies can be incorporated through self-guided virtual tours posted in the first announcement (see figure 7.7). These tours help students understand how to navigate Blackboard and find information.

Number 2. Put Salt in the Horse's Mouth

Motivating students to take responsibility for their own learning as online students is the first challenge faced in each new section of the course. As the old saying goes, "You can lead a horse to water, but you can't make him drink." On the other hand, farmers have developed a corollary to this maxim that we should take to heart: putting salt in the horse's mouth can make him thirsty. It has also been said that "motivation is caught, not taught."[9] In other words, real motivation is intrinsic, not extrinsic. Emphasizing both the value of intrinsic learning and the concept of delayed gratification is, perhaps, one way to put salt in the horse's mouth. Students already in upper-level subject area classes "often understand more immediately the need to become information literate."[10] For others, especially freshmen, the connection does not come until these skills are needed for another course. The value of intrinsic learning is emphasized by convincing students to accept short-term pain for long-term gain, by asking them to make an honest attempt at working hard in the class even though it is only one hour and by explaining that this hard work will pay off in upper-level classes. Furthermore, most students admit that the first place they start when searching for information is Google. Why? Because it is human nature to settle for the fastest and easiest way to a mediocre solution instead of doing all the extra work required for a better one. This inclination has been labeled as "satisficing,"[11] and it is exactly what happens when students accept the first one or two results from a poorly constructed Google search as the best possible information on a topic. Helping students understand that improving the quality of research is worth the time and effort can be the impetus to entice a thirsty horse to drink from the water trough.

Number 1. Perception Is Everything

Perception can become reality. It seems that even after completing FOC 101, some students are still unprepared for the online learning environment. As a result, the simple matter of informing students about the details of the online course can sometimes be incredibly complicated. The following excerpt from an article in the student newspaper illustrates just how baffling students found the course during the first year the current library faculty taught it.

Information Literacy: A Student's Guide to Surviving

Information Literacy was one of the many courses I was told was required in order to graduate. The catch: I had never heard of it. I would soon learn all of the dark secrets that are housed in the course... . I assumed that my fellow freshmen would be able to offer me some advice; after all, some of them were in INT 108. Yet the only real information they could give me was that it involved the library and was pretty easy. Could information literacy be a highly secretive subject? ... The teacher did send me two very nice e-mails. The first one was reminding me about the course [mandatory orientation] and the second one was asking me why I had not attended. Sadly, my lack of e-mail at home had kept me from reading them, so by the time I found the very nice e-mails, it was too late. Life does go on though, and I informed the teacher that I would take the class next semester. Sign up I did and ... all of my fantasies about Information Literacy were destroyed. It ended up being a class that teaches how to take full advantage of the library resources. At the end of six weeks a project is due. Information Literacy really is just information about literacy and FOC 101 [its prerequisite] still does not have a full name.[12]

Clearly this article was written to entertain, but for the sake of future INT 108 students, the enumeration of a few facts was in order. So, in the spirit of good fun, a letter to the editor, published in the next edition of the student newspaper, unveiled some of the "dark secrets" associated with INT 108. Of course, the irony that many students seemed so clueless about the purpose of information literacy reiterates the wisdom of the university administration in making such a course a general education requirement. The point is that if students perceive the course to be of little or no value, they are not interested in learning the skills that lead to information literacy. This perception was impeding student motivation as well as affecting the overall success of the course. The following action plan alleviated this communication problem. It is ongoing and includes

• working with the faculty advisors to make sure that details about the course are disseminated to the students during the advisory period

• offering transfer students the opportunity to take a proficiency test (aligned with course objectives) as an alternative method to fulfill the general education requirement

• mailing a letter via U.S. mail to inform students about the course

• emphasizing the value of intrinsic learning and delayed gratification

• renaming the course with a title meaningful to students.

These days, most students no longer find INT 108 so baffling.

Despite many growing pains, information literacy at Fontbonne has found its focus as a general education requirement, and INT 108 has become part of the campus culture. Students and faculty accept it as a valuable course that provides the basics of library and information research to undergraduate students. It has been and will continue to be an ever-evolving and rewarding experience. Implementing a successful information literacy program takes more than a burning desire on the part of librarians to teach a course. The course lays the foundation, but the skills must be reinforced throughout the curriculum at all levels. It seems that even when students can perform tasks in isolation, the application of skills in a new or different situation does not happen automatically without this reinforcement. It takes both—the course and the embedded reinforcement—to really bring about information literacy.

Notes

1. Coordinating Board for Higher Education of the State of Missouri, *Credit Transfer: Guidelines for Student Transfer and Articulation among Missouri Colleges and Universities.* Available online at http://www.dhe.mo.gov/mdhecentralgenedtransferpolicy.shtml.

2. Chair, English Department, Fontbonne University, e-mail message to Chair, Curriculum Committee, Fontbonne University, March 31, 2000 and to authors, December 12, 2006.

3. *New Course Proposal for INT 108*, submitted to Curriculum Committee, Fontbonne University, 2001.

4. Lynn Lampert, *The Role of the Librarian in Combating Student Plagiarism*, webcast, ACRL Learning Times Community, July 7, 2006, slide 40.

5. Arlene Rodda Quaratiello, *The College Student's Research Companion*, 4th ed. (New York: Neal-Schuman, 2007).

6. Ilene F. Rockman, "Successful Strategies for Integrating Information Literacy into the Curriculum," in *Integrating Information Literacy into the Higher Education Curriculum: Practical Models for Transformation,* edited by Ilene F. Rockman and associates (San Francisco, CA: John Wiley and Sons, 2004), 57.

7.   University Librarian, Fontbonne University, e-mail message to authors, April 2006.

8.   Patrick Sullivan, "Developing Freshman-Level Tutorials to Promote Information Literacy," in Rockman, *Integrating Information Literacy,* 77.

9.   Dennis E. Mannering, "Salting the Oats: What It Takes to Create a Motivating Environment," *AutoInc. Magazine,* January 2004. Available online at http://www.asashop.org/autoinc/jan2004/manage.cfm.

10.   Trudi E. Jacobson, "Meeting Literacy Needs in a Research Setting," in Rockman, *Integrating Information Literacy,* 156.

11.   Stephen J. Bell, "Submit or Resist: Librarianship in the Age of Google," *American Libraries,* October 2005, 68.

12.   "Information Literacy: A Student's Guide to Surviving," *Fontbanner: A Student Publication of Fontbonne University,* October 25, 2005, 7.

8. Online Information Literacy Course at UIS: Standing the Test of Time

Pamela M. Salela, Denise D. Green, and Julie Chapman

Introduction

Brookens Library at the University of Illinois at Springfield (UIS) (formerly Sangamon State University) has a long history of teaching full-credit library research methods courses. In fall 1975, a course titled "Library Lab: Basic Sources of Information" (UNI301) was offered for two credits. Over the next two decades the course would be called "Library Research" or "Library Research Methods" and become a 400-level course in the mid-1990s so that it could become a "swing course"—a credit course in which both graduate and undergraduate students can enroll, with different requirements for each group. The teaching and curriculum development has always been collaborative, with all instructional services librarians teaching the course in rotation and jointly developing, revising, and teaching the curriculum.

Rationale

This course evolved over the years to reflect changes in the growth of information technology and access, as well as information literacy needs in the constantly changing sociopolitical climate of media formation and dissemination. In fall 1998, UIS began to offer courses online. It was not long before we considered adding the then two-credit UNI401: Library Research Methods to our burgeoning online curriculum offerings.

The changing nature of library resources made it a natural for the online, asynchronous format since, increasingly, all major resources such as the OPAC and article databases were online via the Web. Also, enrollment had been slipping in the on-campus course to as low as three to five students a semester. This seemed like an inefficient use of library faculty time when online courses, including electives like UNI401, were routinely filling the twenty students per semester maximum. Students wanted a more flexible schedule than meeting in Brookens Library for two hours a week on a specific day. And, most important, the objectives of the face-to-face version of the course would still be relevant in the online learning environment and would reach the increasingly dispersed student body. The learning objectives, which included increasing critical thinking and information literacy skills and improving student research and writing abilities, were a good fit to the UIS approach to high-quality online teaching and learning. By 2007 our online student population had grown to 25.9 percent of our student body, so putting the course online has been a major step toward addressing the library instructional needs of these students. Currently, 46.3 percent of all UIS students take at least one online course.[1]

Development

The first online version of UNI401 was offered by former UIS librarian Ielleen Miller in fall 1999.[2] She worked with the campus Office of Technology Enhanced Learning (OTEL) to move the course into a completely online format utilizing a course management system. Perhaps one of the greatest concerns about moving to an online environment was the fear of losing the cohesion of a learning community. The discussion board component of our learning management system was put to full use and became an integral part of the course. Discussion questions were posted every week and students were required to respond to these questions as well as to at least one of their classmates, nurturing the dialog with substantive ideas. And just as in a face-to-face course, this participation aspect of the class was to be graded.

In addition to the discussion board, e-mail and chat could be put to full use to maintain a constant interface between instructor and students. In many ways, this had distinct advantages over the face-to-face class sense of community, because postings are public and transcripts are maintained. Of course, the dynamic of a live discussion and getting to know one's classmates would not be quite the same. To address that issue, Miller incorporated a biographical question into the first discussion board posting of the semester. Over time we have learned that these biographies, which include information on why students are taking the course, along with any personal information they care to share, definitely add to creating a sense of community and put students at ease with each other. Finally, the option of meeting with the instructor one-on-one via telephone or synchronous iChat was also offered as a way for students to get to know the professor and to ensure that students have all the requisite technical tools at hand to take the course online. We find that many students take advantage of this option.

Teaching visual material in the online, asynchronous environment was another major challenge to the course. In the face-to-face classroom it was easy to do a demonstration of a database search. Such demonstrations were considered critical, so Miller developed scripted demonstrations written with step-by-step instructions. Sometimes these would include filmed screenshots, and since bandwidth was a serious issue in those early days of teaching online these were placed on compact discs and mailed to students through the U.S. postal system. This proved to be a useful pedagogical technique, but one we had to abandon over time for reasons discussed later in this chapter.

The course content, components, and pedagogical approaches continued to evolve as different librarians contributed to this collaborative process. And, over time, the content of the course grew to include more and more material and assignments. Students were increasingly beginning to complain that it seemed there was far more work than a two-credit course should require. As we examined the content and evolution of the course, we had to agree. So in spring 2006 the library faculty successfully requested that the campus curriculum committee make the course three credits effective in the fall 2006 semester.

Content

As with any academic class, UNI401 begins the semester with a roadmap to academic expectations, course requirements, and ground rules for ethical and courteous conduct in the online classroom. For most of its history the textbook used has been successive editions of Bolner and Poirier's *The Research Process: Books and Beyond*.[3] In addition to the textbook we include readings that are accessible through the e-reserves portion of our learning management system (currently Blackboard). The course is designed to introduce the student to the foundations of doing research and then slowly build the skills and knowledge base necessary for approaching academic research assignments in a systematic and methodical manner. The following is a typical semester-long topic agenda:

Week 1: Introduction & Overview of Organization of Academic Libraries

Week 2: Research Topics & Types of Information Sources (Books, Articles, Web sites)

Week 3: Importance of Evaluation!

Week 4: Citation, Plagiarism, and Annotated Bibliography

Week 5: How to Think Like a Librarian: Controlled Vocabulary vs. Keywords

Week 6: Finding Background Information & Facts

Week 7: Finding Books

Week 8: Finding Magazine & Newspaper Articles

Week 9: Finding Scholarly Articles

Week 10: Finding Federal & State Government Information

Week 11: Finding Statistics

Week 12: Finding Web sites

Week 13: Other Information Sources —Biographies, Book Reviews, Literary Criticism, Tests

Week 14: Thanksgiving Break

Week 15: Recap—Annotated bibliography due.

Week 16: Research Summary due

The syllabus provides a complete map of the entire course with readings and due dates clearly listed. There is also a calendar utility attached to the course where instructors can simultaneously list major due dates. The menu structure we have devised includes a "Weekly Lessons" folder that makes it possible to incorporate the components necessary for completing that week's requirements in one place. Each week's folder includes pointers to the lecture, assignments (if any for that week), readings, a quiz, as well as the discussion board. If there are

Figure 8.1. Sample weekly schedule

Week 9 - Finding (Mainly) Scholarly Articles

To do Week 9

- **Read this lecture.**
- **Review chapter 8** of Bolner's *The Research Process*.
- **Read the article,** "In the Public Interest"
- **Respond to the discussion questions** in the **Discussion Board**. Postings are due Monday, October 23rd and responses are due by Friday, October 27th.
- **Take the Week 9 Quiz.** Due by Monday, October 23rd.
- **Do the Week 9 assignment** (located under the button **Assignments**) – You are explore finding articles on your topic. You can complete the assignment entirely online, though if you want to "get your hands on" some of the articles immediately that aren't available full text, you will want to physically go to a library. The assignment is due by midnight, October 23rd.

RESEARCH PROJECT

- **Research Journal #4:** Post the results on finding articles on your topic. **Due Wednesday, October 25th**
- **Thesis Paragaraph:** First draft – post to research journal. **Due Wednesday, October 25th**

any extra components to that week's activities, they can be placed in this folder as well (e-reserves, PowerPoint presentation, etc.). Each week's activities are designed to create a holistic approach to learning the topic at hand. Figure 8.1 provides a sample of how this is structured.

The first few weeks are spent establishing some basic building blocks. In week one, we ask the students to read chapter 3 of Kuhlthau's *Seeking Meaning: A Process Approach to Library and Information Services*, "The Information Search Process." Here Kuhlthau presents a study that examined student approaches and responses to the research process, based on a perceptions questionnaire. She discovered that most students who have not had guidance on the research process experience a good deal of trepidation. In large part, this is because they have no clear plan on how to approach a research project, and so it is all a mystery to them. They have little if any understanding of how information is structured or how to find it.[4]

Our students have consistently responded to this reading positively. The following comment, an actual post to the discussion board, is a typical response to our posted question, "What is your reaction to the chapter from Kuhlthau's *Seeking Meaning*? How does her theory compare with your research experiences?"

The reading "Seeking Meaning" put into words everything I experience when conducting research and writing a paper. I found it comforting because I previously felt that the feelings were solely my own. Specifically my initial apprehension when learning of a research assignment and even the feeling that the project is threatening. I also, as briefly mentioned in the

"Emerging Model" segment, tend to focus more on the technical requirements of the paper (length, style, deadlines, etc.) than choosing a topic and developing a focus that I can really work with. I did not feel that there was an actual pattern that I followed when it comes to writing research papers, but this chapter outlined my pattern rather accurately (UNI401, fall 2006).

Students discover, not only from Kuhlthau's work but from their public postings to the class, that they are not alone in their feelings of anxiety toward the research process. This creates a sense of ease, and the learning community begins to congeal. Of course, there are also those who do have some experience and confidence in approaching the research process in a systematic way. We have found they become de facto online peers and contribute to the learning process in significant ways by offering their own insights.

From the very beginning we stress the importance of ethics in information use and formation. We talk about plagiarism and the construction of students' own research projects. Building their topic into a viable thesis statement (we actually ask for a paragraph, encouraging them to articulate in more detail what their objectives are) increasingly impresses upon them the importance of being selective in their choice of resources. Selectivity necessitates evaluating their resources. Thus, early on we provide assignments that require them to begin to think about and gradually refine their critical thinking skills in this arena. In their first assignment, when we discuss locating background information (reference sources), we ask them to look at some specific sources and then let them locate resources of their own choosing, encouraging them to find resources relevant to their research topic. As we go through the process of teaching them about different information types, how to locate them and when to consider using them, we simultaneously provide exercises on assessing the materials they are finding or have been given in the assignments. Through a series of guided questions, we ask them to evaluate their sources, setting up a model to make analysis of resources a habit. In some cases, such as when we ask them to assess periodical articles or Web sites, we also ask them if any of the sources would be useful for an academic research paper and ask them to support their answer. Thus, we are continuously building, through the assignments for the course (see appendices A and B), the need for source evaluation and assessment.

We are also seeking to build the ability for close reading and the ability to articulate what is being read. Writing annotations can be a tricky prospect, so we build exercises for doing so into the course. We recycle the readings students were required to use for assessment so that, at least in theory, this will be their second reading of the article (or Web site).

As we introduce students to different information types, we simultaneously introduce them to different search tools as well as searching techniques. We teach Boolean logic early on, as well as techniques for refining or limiting searches. By the time they begin to explore various databases, students have an entire toolchest of basic skills. We then introduce them to differentiating between newspapers, popular periodicals, and journal articles—which builds even further on their evaluation skills. They start out by searching large, overarching periodical indexes such as Academic Search Premier or Expanded Academic ASAP. We then lead them toward the discipline-specific databases.

In addition to teaching students how to locate and effectively use discipline-specific databases, the course is designed to provide a good overview of resources such areas as federal and state government documents. We incorporate statistics into these weekly lessons, since government sources provide a plethora of such resources. We spend at least two weeks on this topic and then incorporate both documents and statistics into the same homework assignment. Also, since government information is predominantly online now, this makes it easy to customize the course for our students in other states. For the part of the assignment that focuses on finding state resources, we offer links to all state document Web sites appropriate to where our students live. This keeps the course relevant for all of our students.

Toward the end of the course, students are introduced to the idea of Web searching. This topic is intentionally saved for the latter part of the course since, as we all know, students have a proclivity toward beginning their research on the open Web. When the week on Web searching arrives, they conceive of this as a sort of vacation and are eager to demonstrate their search acuity. By now they have learned some things about search accuracy and specificity, and we can incorporate these newly developed skills into their Web-searching knapsack. They learn the difference between search engines and search directories and also how to limit their search results to scholarly resources through the use of Google Scholar.

One of the distinct advantages of teaching online is that it enables us to add fresh readings related to the topics at hand. During the week when we discuss searching the

Web, there is a cautionary discussion about using Wikipedia for academic research. In the fall 2006 semester, an article came out in the *Chronicle of Higher Education* about the development of a new wiki called Citizendium, which is being developed as a challenge to the model of the completely open authoring system of Wikipedia.[5] Citizendium will be designed with the capability of shared, open authoring, but with more scholarly peer reviewing put into place and a cache of subject experts to guide the process. Being able to link current articles directly into the lecture and adding them to weekly readings helps keep the course contemporary and active.

In the final week, in which we introduce new content to the course, we show students a selection of other useful resources, such as how to locate biographical information, book reviews, literary criticism, and test instruments. We do not expect them to become experts at these resources, but we do want them to be aware of their existence. This quick look also helps give them the idea that this is all just the beginning and that there is a lot more out there in terms of information organization and access. The last couple of weeks are devoted to giving students time to complete their research projects. If they have been using their time and the homework assignments wisely throughout the semester, their annotated bibliographies should be well on their way to being developed.

Instruction

The course objectives, clearly stated in the syllabus, are to teach the students to formulate a research topic, identify a wide variety of information types, learn effective search techniques and strategies when using databases, evaluate information on a variety of levels, and use information in a legal and ethical manner. We teach them how to plan an effective research strategy and find books, journal articles, data, Internet resources, and other sources of information related to an academic research assignment and, finally, to integrate those research sources effectively into a cohesive literature review (annotated bibliography). Over time, the course has evolved to include greater emphasis on thesis development and documenting the process itself. We have encouraged students to take this course as a complement to other courses wherein they are required to write a research paper.

The course has five major components: lectures and readings, quizzes, discussion board, hands-on assignments in which they apply the skills described in the readings and on the discussion board, and a final cumulative research project. The course is paced like a face-to-face course; we have found that providing a solid structure with assignment due dates helps keep students on track. But also, to create a learning community, it is critical that students focus on the same material at the same time, or else they are not able to discuss it in a cogent manner. Every week students do readings from the textbooks as well as our customized written "lecture." These lectures have evolved and are the collaborative product of many librarians. The quizzes were formulated in part to encourage students to do all of the readings. The discussion board is guided with questions developed by the instructors to complement the readings and urge the students to ask questions of the material as well as add to their own knowledge. Each week the students are typically given three questions, based on the lecture and readings for that week. For instance, during the week when the focus is on locating newspaper and magazine articles, students are asked:

1. When are magazine/journal/newspaper articles useful to you? Not useful?

2. When was the last time you used a print index, if ever? Did you find information successfully or not? How does finding information using a print index compare to finding information using a digital index?

3. What are your thoughts or comments on the last part of the lecture about news or media bias?

Students are graded on their discussion board activities in much the same way that students in a face-to-face course would be graded on class participation. They are required to post and to respond to the postings of other students. The assignments are designed to provide a practical, hands-on application of the skill set that has been discussed. Throughout the span of sixteen weeks, there are typically eight assignments that address the major conceptual components of the course.

Finally there is the research project—a compilation of four graded components: thesis paragraph,[6] research journal, annotated bibliography, and research summary (see appendix C for summary of research project guidelines). Students are given several weeks over which to explore and develop their thesis. They post their suggested topics, talk about the evolution of the topic as they begin doing some preliminary exploration, and are encouraged to provide feedback to each other as well as receiving feedback from the instructor. The thesis, when well developed, provides a solid foundation upon which to build their research. The research journal is organized as a public posting to the class through the discussion board and nurtured through the use of pre-posted queries from the instructors, such as "What are you considering for your research topic for this class?" and "Comment on how your thesis topic is evolving." The instructor may post anonymous examples of journal postings from prior semesters in order to provide a model of what is expected. As the course progresses, the research journal is increasingly tied into the relevant syllabus topics, and students are encouraged to incorporate what they are learning in the course into their own research process. At present there are seven research journal entries required throughout the course of the semester.

The final major products of the research project are the annotated bibliography and the research process paper. The research process paper (or research summary) is assigned to be due the week after the annotated bibliography is handed in. The process paper provides a graded rationale for the student to keep the process in mind. It also serves the purpose of dissuading plagiarism, since content and process need to match.

Grading and Feedback

All assignments are submitted electronically through the learning management system and are automatically date-stamped, eliminating any questions regarding whether the assignment arrived on time. Most of the components of the final project (annotated bibliography and research process paper) are graded with the use of a predeveloped rubric (see appendix D for sample rubric). Students are provided copies of this rubric when they are given the instructions for the assignment. Since the thesis paragraph is a part of the final project and is developed over the course of many weeks in close consultation with the instructor, the need for a rubric is seen as less relevant. There is also a rubric for discussion board participation to encourage students to provide substantive input and to discourage comments like "me too" or "I used the same database" (see appendix E for a copy of this rubric). Finally, as with any course, all homework assignments are graded and each assignment has a preassigned weighted grade. The component breakdown in the last iteration of the class was (quizzes, 10 percent; assignments, 30 percent; discussion board postings, 20 percent; research project, 40 percent).

In addition to grades, instructors provide feedback in a variety of ways to encourage the learning process. More specific and critical feedback is typically provided privately via direct e-mail from the instructor to students. The discussion board, though guided through predetermined questions, is left predominantly to student discussion. But instructors also participate by posting feedback to assist students and provide instructive modeling. Some students also become very active and, in our experience, typically very constructive in this feedback process and contribute in significant ways as peer educators. The discussion board provides a forum where questions can be raised that take knowledge formation beyond the parameters of the syllabus. In a face-to-face classroom environment, this might create a situation where the teacher would have to limit responses because of time constraints. The online environment, though, makes it possible to provide a thorough and complete response along with added informational Web sites and pointers to other readings that can satisfy the intellectual curiosity of the individual asking the question, stimulating the interest of those so inclined but not adding to the requirements of the course. This technique provides an enhanced ability to meet the needs of varying types of learners.

Another major pedagogical tool is the use of critical feedback on homework assignments. Since these are designed to engage the students in utilizing the skills we are teaching them, it is vital that they are given not only grades but also clear guidance when

their comprehension is obviously lacking. In cases where students are engaging in very visual activities, such as database searching, we provide ample commentary as well as screenshots in step-by-step fashion to demonstrate good practices. In the online environment this is easy, since we can place the screenshots directly into their homework assignments and deliver them back. Unfortunately, we have had to do this more often than we would like, because the original idea of providing active demonstrations of search techniques and various database interfaces has grown too complex to keep up with. Vendors are constantly changing their products, and new products are continuously being added to our cache of search utilities. Even small changes in a database interface can mean remaking an entire demonstration "movie." So, the demonstrations that were once created and sent to our students on compact discs no longer exist. The fact that we are continually increasing the amount of feedback provided to our students indicates the value of those active demonstrations as a teaching tool, as well as our need to find a way to reincorporate some sort of demonstration tool.

Program Assessment

One section of UNI401 has been offered on Blackboard each fall and spring semester for the past six years. Several faculty librarians have taught the course, and its success has been measured in various ways. One indirect indicator of the course's success is the fact that this elective course fills close to the maximum twenty students every semester, whereas the on-ground sections rarely enrolls more than ten students.[7] At the same time, comments on official and unofficial student evaluations indicate that the workload is challenging. We can thus conclude that, although the course is perceived to be demanding and the weekly assignments are "a lot of work," the students find the class valuable and recommend it to classmates. Another anecdotal indicator is the number of students who contact the instructors during subsequent semesters to describe how they are applying the theories and skills learned in UNI401 to research projects in upper-level courses in their majors as well as in graduate courses.

The recent inclusion of the research process paper component of the final assignment also helps instructors judge whether and how students are using the information literacy skills they were taught during the semester. It is essential that the process of their research match the product of their research, and thus it serves as a critical tool for determining engagement. If a student has been developing his or her research throughout the semester with the assistance of the assignments and the research journals, this graded assignment will essentially have already been written and merely needs to be formatted for presentation to the instructor.

For the past eight years, instructors have used the discussion board to solicit feedback from the students. The class's final required discussion thread asks students to comment on what they found most and least useful about the course, as well as to analyze if and how the course has helped them become more information literate. In response to the question "Do you now feel that you are 'information literate' after taking this class?" one fall 2006 student replied: "I have taken a huge step forward. I feel that I have learned a great deal that will help me in my quest for my bachelor's degree. I know that in all future classes, I will reference knowledge gained in this course, and for that, I feel that I am 'information literate.'"

A review of the official course evaluation reports (2000–2006) provided by the UIS Provost's Office shows several interesting trends. First, more than 95 percent of students indicate that the course has increased their skills in critical thinking, and just over 90 percent feel that their interest in library research methods has increased as a result of taking the course. One recurring theme—that the course should be a requirement rather than an elective—is summed up by this fall 2006 student: "This has been by far one of the most useful classes I have ever taken. This should be a required course for all undergraduate students."

Future Directions

Most of our future directions involve steps to strengthen the online learning community and student engagement. Woven through all our future directions are the need and desire to incorporate new technologies.

We are troubled by those few students who seem to "disappear" around midterm. Inevitably, one or two students simply stop submitting assignments and posting to the discussion board. Blackboard activity statistics often show that these students are still logging in to read the course material and even observe discussion threads, while disengaging in all other ways. One way to reengage these students is to build in more one-on-one conferencing opportunities throughout the semester. Such conferencing, conducted in person, over the phone, or through synchronous online chat sessions, is currently scheduled during the first two weeks of class. (Student feedback on the conferences is overwhelmingly positive.) Requiring at least one additional one-on-one conference around the time students are developing their thesis statements and beginning to search for sources should help in keeping all students engaged and preventing them from feeling overwhelmed and frustrated and then drifting away from the course. One ambitious idea could include requiring students to confer with each other rather than just with the instructor.

Currently all weekly assignments, exclusive of the discussion board postings, are completed individually. Adding a carefully designed group project could facilitate individual engagement and community building in several ways. First, each group could use the Blackboard virtual classroom and group workspace to build a small learning community. Each group member would be required to contribute to the project, thus building in the engagement of each student. The class could utilize Elluminate (or similar synchronous, archival conferencing technology) to share each group project, including question-and-answer interaction.

In addition to incorporating new technologies into assignments, we also plan to create online course modules, using Camtasia and other software packages, which can then be placed within lectures. For example, the lecture on periodical databases could include several multimedia modules demonstrating keyword and controlled vocabulary searches in several databases. In addition, we are hopeful that our IT unit will soon have course capture hardware and software in place so that we can easily provide certain types of lectures and demonstrations without the need for complicated prestaging.

Now that bandwidth is no longer an issue, these new course capture tools will enable us to do demonstrations in much the same way we would in a face-to-face classroom and simply have it captured and archived for future streaming over the Web.

Conclusion

By examining the history of online information literacy instruction at UIS, we can assert that the success of UNI401 has been the result of a strong tradition of library faculty collaboration. This tradition has enabled us to adapt more easily to the world of online instruction by sharing ideas, building the course as a team, and even team teaching. The collaborative model of teaching also nurtures the community building that is so essential to a dynamic learning environment. As our student population becomes increasingly diverse, as well as dispersed across time, space, and cultural perspectives, it will become increasingly important to devise ways of enabling community building in the online classroom.

As our curriculum and approach to teaching information literacy evolves with developments in Web 2.0, we feel confident that we will be able to continue to adapt by maintaining the solid foundation that continues to support collaborative teaching, focuses on developing engaged learning communities online, and allows modification of the curriculum to reflect the changing information landscape and the needs of our students.

Appendix A.
Week 3: Importance of Evaluation [14 pts total]

For this assignment, we want you to re-peruse/skim the two Web sites and the two articles from last week and analyze them. Write up an evaluation of all four sources and answer the questions (in italic).

A. Web sites
- Homebirth Can Be An Option: http://www.umilta.net/midwife.html
- Why Homebirth?: http://www.midwiferytoday.com/articles/whyhomebirth.asp

1. Evaluate both Web sites based on the following general criteria. Some of the criteria may not be applicable to the site, so indicate that you have thought about it and the reason why you think it isn't applicable. [0.5 pt each/6 pts total]

1. Authority – Who wrote it? What makes the person qualified to write it? Who is sponsoring the information?
2. Audience – Who is the intended audience of the information?
3. Bias – Is the information presented objectively? Are the opinions balanced, or does the author have an agenda?
4. Credibility – Does the information seem credible? Does the author give sources or suggestions for further reading for the information? How comprehensive is the source list? If some of the other sources are Web sites, do the links work?
5. Factual – If facts or statistics are presented, are they accurate? (Try verifying the facts with another source.)
6. Up to Date – Is the information current? Is that important for the type of information presented?

2. Would you use either one as a source for a research paper on midwifery? Why or why not? [1 pt]

B. Articles
Go back and reread the articles from last week's assignment.
1. Hartocollis, A. (2005, June 2). Midwives Keep Busy Despite a Decline in Births Outside Hospitals. *New York Times*, p. B1. You will find this article in electronic reserves.
2. Johnson, K.C., & Daviss, B.A. (2005). Outcomes of planned home births with certified professional midwives. *British Medical Journal*, 330 (7505), 1416-1422. The article is freely available from the publisher at: http://bmj.bmjjournals.com/cgi/reprint/330/7505/1416.pdf.

3. Evaluate the two articles based on the same criteria. [0.5 pt each/6 pts total]
1. Authority – Who wrote it? What makes the person qualified to write it? Who is sponsoring the information?
2. Audience – Who is the intended audience of the information?

3. Bias – Is the information presented objectively? Are the opinions balanced, or does the author have an agenda?

4. Credibility – Does the information seem credible? Does the author give sources or suggestions for further reading for the information? How comprehensive is the source list? If some of the other sources are Web sites, do the links work?

5. Factual – If facts or statistics are presented, are they accurate? (Try verifying the facts with another source.)

6. Up to Date – Is the information current? Is that important for the type of information presented?

4. Would you use either one as a source for a research paper in midwifery? Why or why not? [1 pt]

Appendix B.
Week 5: Search Techniques [10 points total]

We will explore various subject headings and keyword searches in PrairieCat Online, the book catalog, for treating ADHD. PrairieCat Online offers a wide variety of search types, so it will be good practice for all kinds of searching. (If you need more help using PrairieCat Online beyond the hints, go to PrairieCat Help [this is the uppermost right menu inside the catalog] for more detailed information about searching PrairieCat Online. We will discuss PrairieCat Online in depth next week.

Please answer all the questions in italic. You'll be doing 4 different types of searches. There are 9 questions total.

Go to PrairieCat Online to look for items in the UIS library.

A. Browse Subject Headings [2 pts]

1. Is ADHD a valid Library of Congress (LC) subject heading? If not, what is it? [0.5 pt]
[Hint: Type in ADHD and click on "Subjects," then click the Search button. If the catalog lists 0 results for that subject heading, then be sure to check the green See Also buttons!]

2. How many records does the UIS library have that match that exact fully spelled-out subject heading you found for question #1? [0.5 pt]

3. What Library of Congress (LC) subject headings would be good for finding items specifically on treating ADHD? [1 pt]
[Hint: Scroll down and browse through the permutations of the valid subject heading.]

B. Keyword Searching [2 pts]
We want you to do a keyword search for the issue of treating ADHD.

4. What are the keywords we would want to use? Think of as many synonyms as you can. [0.5 pt]

5. What is the truncation symbol in PrairieCat Online? [0.5 pt]
[Hint: There are search examples at the bottom of the Quick Search screen.]

6. Using the answers above, how would you phrase a keyword search for treating ADHD using Boolean logic? How many results did you get? [1 pt]
[Hint: Type in your query in the "Quick Search" screen and highlight "Boolean Search," then click the Search button. Put phrases in quotation marks. PrairieCat Online expects each single word or phrase in quotation marks to have one of the connectors (AND, OR, NOT) between each term.]

C. Relevance Rank – Any Word Anywhere [2 pts]

7. How would you phrase the search for the relevance ranked "Any Word Anywhere?" How many results did you get? [1 pt]

[Hint: Put phrases in quotation marks. Do not type in AND, OR, or NOT. If you want to require a word be there, put a + sign in front of it.]

D. Field Searching [2 pts]

Now let's try a more focused keyword search, narrowing the keywords to a particular field. In PrairieCat Online, click on "Advanced." You should get a screen with 3 search boxes instead of 1. You may have to click on "New Search" in the green bar at the top to start over.

8. How would you phrase your search if you wanted to find your keywords anywhere (Search For field) in the subject field (Search by field)? How many results did you get? [1 pt]

[Hint: Do not type in AND, OR, or NOT. Use the radial buttons instead, and within each box use the corresponding pull-down menu and choose "any of these words" if you want to put an OR between each word, "all of these words" if you want to put an AND between each word, or "these words as a phrase" to keep the words together.]

E. Conclusions [2 pts]

9. Of the 4 methods of searching (browse subject, Boolean, relevance Any Word Anywhere, and keyword field searching), which one gave you the best results and why? For instance, which appeared to give you the most precise, on-target results? Or which gave you the most results?

Appendix C:
Research Project

The Research Project will make up 40% of your total grade and will be composed of four parts: the *research journal,* the *thesis paragraph,* the *annotated bibliography,* and the *research summary.* Whenever there is a specific action to be taken in conjunction with the Research Project, this will be noted in the syllabus. This will enable you to stay on track with your progress.

- Research Journal – The *research journal* is a written account of how you went about developing your thesis, finding information, and determining which sources to use (selectivity). You will keep a journal that answers specific questions about your research topic and about how you completed the part of the assignments where you are locating sources on your topic, or whenever you are researching your topic. Tell us how you are approaching the research process with the facts, your thoughtful reflections, and your feelings. In addition, you should feel free to offer constructive feedback to your classmates. You will post the entries to Blackboard in the *Discussion Board* on a periodic basis as stated in the syllabus. The research journal will be worth 7% of your final grade.

- Thesis Paragraph - In order to conduct research, you must first have a plan. You will be required to construct a coherent thesis paragraph that states clearly what you intend to research and what the objectives are. You will post drafts as well as the final thesis paragraph on the Research Journal Discussion Board. You MUST turn in a thesis paragraph or your project will be void (i.e., you will receive a zero for the entire Research Project). The thesis paragraph is worth 3% of your final grade.

- Annotated Bibliography – The *annotated bibliography* is a list of relevant resources for your specific topic, in MLA, APA, Turabian, or other citation style, with an annotation. Annotations are a summary of the resource plus an evaluation of it by you in relation to your research. (Citation style is up to you, but most of the time your professor will require a particular format, so use that. Typically the social sciences use APA (American Psychological Association), humanities use MLA (Modern Language Association), etc. You must use your own words and ideas to summarize the resource. *Copying an abstract from a database or the abstract provided by the author is plagiarism, which will be discussed further Week 4. Any student caught plagiarizing will be given a zero for that assignment or project and may also be subject to further disciplinary action.* Besides, an abstract is NOT the same as an annotation, and you are expected to do an annotation. We will discuss and provide sample annotations in Week 4. You will practice writing annotations during the semester as part of various assignments. If you are an undergraduate, you must have a minimum of *10 annotations,* and if you are a graduate student you must have a minimum of *15 annotations.* Guidelines will be provided regarding what your 10 or 15 annotations should consist of. However, you are not required to have a certain number of books, articles, etc. That's what the weekly assignments are covering. It's up to you to decide what sources are most relevant to your thesis. You may use sources that you find for your topic when completing the weekly assignments. And you can certainly use this in conjunction with a research project you are working on for another class. You can use the same topic and set of sources for a term paper and also for the annotated bibliography. You are strongly encouraged to "plant two flowers with one seed." The annotated bibliography must be typed and turned in via Blackboard by Friday, December 1st. The annotated bibliography will be worth 20% of your final grade.

- Research Summary – The final assignment will be a 3-5 page essay. The purpose of this paper will be to summarize your research findings and describe your process. Process means both the mechanics of what you did (i.e., what indexes and resources you found most useful & why) and, of course, your intellectual process. You can describe how you selected the sources that you did and why, how everything ties together into a coherent whole because of the selective process you engaged in as a response to your thesis paragraph. If you utilize the Research Journal wisely & comprehensively, this will provide you with a good foundation for proceeding with your research project.

Appendix D.
Annotated Bibliography [75 points]

Plagiarizing of a source will be given a zero for the annotated bibliography, and turning in a term paper instead of an annotated bibliography will result in a zero for the whole assignment.

I. Assignment Criteria	Points
Annotated bibliography contains 10 sources (if undergraduate) and 15 sources (if graduate student). Includes cover page & thesis paragraph.	15
Missing 1 of the required number of sources. Includes cover page & thesis paragraph.	10
Missing more than 2–3 of the required number of sources. Missing either cover page or thesis paragraph.	5
Missing more than 5 of the required number of sources. Missing cover page and thesis paragraph.	0
II. Citation Format	Points
Virtually all sources are accurately cited using one common citation style format. Sources are in alphabetical order.	14–15
All sources are cited using one common citation style format but have one or two minor errors. Sources are in alphabetical order.	12–13
All sources are cited using one common citation style format but have a few errors. Or sources are cited accurately, but do not use one common citation style. Sources are in alphabetical order.	10–11
All sources are cited using one common citation style format but have some errors. Sources are not in alphabetical order.	8–9
There are major problems with the citation formats.	0–7
III. Summaries of Sources	Points
Virtually all of the summaries are concise and well reasoned in describing what the source was about, in 4 to 8 sentences.	14–15
Most of the summaries are concise and well reasoned in describing what the source was about, in 4 to 8 sentences.	12–13
Most of the summaries are fairly concise and well reasoned in describing what the source was about.	10–11
Some of the summaries are vague in describing what the source was about.	8–9
Summaries are not helpful.	0–7
IV. Evaluations & Justifications	Points
Virtually all of the evaluations of the sources are thorough in describing why the source is a valid and credible one. Evaluations & Justifications address who is responsible for the source (who wrote or published it), what type of source it is (scholarly, non-scholarly), and what biases are evident.	14–15
Most of the evaluations of the sources are thorough in describing why the source is a valid and credible one. Evaluations & Justifications address who is responsible for the source (who wrote or published it), what type of source it is (scholarly, nonscholarly), and what biases are evident.	12–13

Most of the evaluations of the sources describe why the source is a valid and credible one. Evaluations & Justifications attempt to address who is responsible for the source (who wrote or published it), what type of source it is (scholarly, nonscholarly), and what biases are evident.	10–11
Some of the evaluations of the sources are vague in describing why the source is a valid and credible one. Evaluations & Justifications fail to address who is responsible for the source (who wrote or published it), what type of source it is (scholarly, nonscholarly), and what biases are evident.	8–9
Evaluations & Justifications are not helpful.	0–7
V. Writing Quality	Points
Words chosen are clear, precise, specific, and appropriate; writing is well organized and does not have awkward phrasing, wordiness, clichés, or vague or generalized language; is free from grammatical and spelling errors.	14–15
Words chosen are generally clear, precise, specific, and appropriate; usually organized and does not have awkward phrasing, wordiness, clichés, as well as or vague or generalized language; is free from grammatical and spelling errors.	12–13
Some words chosen are not clear, precise, specific, or appropriate; may contain awkward phrasing, wordiness, clichés, or vague or generalized language; may contain some grammatical and spelling errors or some disorganized writing.	10--11
Sometimes has unclear, vague, or inappropriate words; contains awkward phrasing, wordiness, clichés, vague or generalized language; contains distracting and disorganized writing with frequent grammatical and spelling errors.	8--9
Has unclear, vague, or inappropriate words; contains awkward phrasing, wordiness, clichés, vague or generalized language; contains distracting grammatical and spelling errors and is largely disorganized writing.	0--7

Appendix E.
Initial postings

4 points: You demonstrate through your responses that you have thoroughly read and considered the readings for that week. You provide an articulate response to the questions, demonstrating your own insights and stimulating discussion.

3 points: You demonstrate through your response that you have thoroughly read and considered the readings for that week. You offer your own insights in your response to the questions.

2 points: You demonstrate that you have perused the readings for that week. Your responses to the questions demonstrate some understanding of the material.

1 point: Your responses leave it apparent that, at best, you skimmed the readings and are not fully aware of the topics or issues at hand.

Please note: You will also lose points if you don't respond to all of the questions for the week at hand.

Response postings

2 points: You demonst+rate thoughtful consideration of the ideas and insights of your classmates.

1 point: You demonstrate thoughtful consideration of the ideas and insights of your classmates and add to the discussion.

Discussion Board Grading Rubric

The purpose of the discussion board is to stimulate class discussion about the topics we are focusing on each week, and this is the equivalent of class participation. You are to respond to all of the questions that are posted for each week and to respond to at least one of another individual. You can receive a maximum of 4 points for your initial postings and 2 points for your responses. You will be graded on your postings based on the following criteria:

Excellent (A range): You know the readings cold and have thought about the material to be discussed. You help keep discussion focused on the major points, ask key questions of other students, and generate discussion. You make connections between the readings and their application to the research process.

Good to very good (B range): You generate discussion among students on the major points and know the readings well. You offer a major contribution. You tell us your thoughtful perspectives and help others learn the material.

Average (C range): You speak (or type) up regularly but tend to offer just what is in the readings without your own insight (so we do not get to know what you think) or without a larger overview of how the readings fit together.

Fair (D range): You offer your own opinion without much connection to the readings. You have a pattern of repeating what other students have said, but it is hard to tell if you have actually read all the assignments.

Not so great (E range): You might be the disruptive type, coming in late to a discussion, making comments such as "I agree" with nothing further to explain your position, or making comments that have nothing to do with the topic at hand. Or you might be the silent type, not saying a word even after several weeks so that we miss out on your thoughts, suggestions, contributions, ideas, and different perspective. If you are one of these folks, talk to me in the first few weeks of the course.

Notes

1.   "UIS Enrollment Sets Record for Spring Semester," *UIS News Release,* February 16, 2007. Available online at http://www.uis.edu/newsreleases/feb07/20070216.html.

2.   Ielleen Miller is currently a librarian at Eastern Washington University.

3.   Myrtle Bolner and Gayle A. Poirier, *The Research Process: Books and Beyond,* 4th ed. (Dubuque, IA: Kendall/Hunt, 2006).

4.   Carol Collier Kuhlthau, *Seeking Meaning: A Process Approach to Library and Information Services,* 2d ed. (Westport, CT: Libraries Unlimited, 2004).

5.   Brock Read, "Co-Founder of Wikipedia, Now a Critic, Starts Spinoff with Academic Editors," *Chronicle of Higher Education,* October 27, 2006. Available online at http://chronicle.com/weekly/v53/i10/10a03501.htm.

6.   In the early stages of planning and developing the course, it was thought best to stay clear of making it seem like a writing course and focus strictly on learning search skills. Over time, however, we realized that students were acquiring the technical skills without fully comprehending their purpose or application. We found that students sometimes ended up doing search dumps that had minimal connection to each other, though they satisfied the technical requirements of conducting a search (locating proper database for subject area, proper use of Boolean logic, etc.). Research is, after all, an encompassing process, and one should be searching for information in a manner that is selective, based on a goal. This led to the addition of the thesis statement and process paper.

7.   Invariably the course starts out at full capacity, but as with most courses, after the dust settles, a few students drop. We have also found that there are always more students wanting to enroll during advance registration, so it is quite possible that we could fill more than one class.

9. A Mature Information Literacy Program: Which Way Forward?

Mark McManus and Shirley O. Lankford

Rationale

In 1996, Ingram Library faced a dilemma that frequently confronts academic library programs: we were ineffectively successful. Bibliographic instruction was publicized and offered on an ad hoc basis. Individual instructors (primarily of lower-division courses) could request instruction for their classes. These requests were often last-minute substitutes for faculty absences, and it was not uncommon for library faculty to see students' eyes glaze over as they attended their third or fourth session. Although these sessions/tours were intended to provide a basic introduction to the library and its services, the library was also undergoing the significant changes that would transform scholarly communications: many services and resources were being transitioned to electronic format; whole classes of research, indexing, and abstracting resources were being created; referencing formats were being changed to reflect new scholarly resources. At about the same time, the University of West Georgia (UWG) began participation in state and regional activities that placed new demands on library services. UWG was a participant in the Georgia GLOBE project (Web-based continuing education), was one of a few university system institutions that offered a Web-based MBA, and was one of five host institutions for Georgia E-Core, a system-wide, transferable Web-based program that provided core curriculum coursework to undergraduates. Thus, the library faced a cohort of new students who needed infor-mation literacy skills they would not have when entering the new electronic programs. With limited library classroom space and an inability to meet the information needs of students or faculty in the limited time available, we were in the midst of creating a library much different from the traditional academic institution.

In addressing these demands, we determined the following course of action. All library faculty were already assigned liaison responsibilities with academic, disciplinary departments, but ancillary budgets indexed to departmental allocations were added. Liaison responsibilities included scheduling and providing upper-division library instruction, primarily for particular or specialized resources, or for deeper disciplinary research techniques. Public services departments (reference, instruction) were reorganized as Instructional Services; faculty in this division would provide elementary orientation sessions to lower-division courses and offer instruction on particular base-level resources. They would also provide the core group of instructors for a new credit course, a course that library faculty and administrations had successfully shepherded through the university faculty senate committee for courses and programs that would directly provide information literacy instruction to students.

Three years later, in 1999, the University System of Georgia changed from the quarter system to the semester system. The course was upgraded, with approval from the appropriate faculty senate committee, to two semester hours and qualified for satisfaction of core curriculum requirements. At that time, the course was developed in tandem as an online course.

Development

In the late 1990s, distance education was receiving considerable attention. The (online) Western Governor's University was being highly touted. In 1998 the library administration sent a representative to the first Educause conference in Orlando, Florida, and in fall 1999 the associate director served on a panel on distance education at the Long Island Library Resource Council Conference with the president of Blackboard, Inc. In Orlando, classroom faculty from several institutions made presentations on experiences with distance learning classes. With the exposure to Blackboard and other course management software, the library administration determined to expand the offerings in information literacy through online instruction. WebCT was developed at the University of British Columbia as a shareware program; although rudimentary, it appeared to offer an affordable, flexible online platform for delivering instruction. When WebCT became a commercial company, the University of Georgia System negotiated a bulk contract, and the platform became the de facto standard for the system.

University administration was generally very supportive of moving the course to an online environment (the university president and vice-president both regularly teach courses with online content), since there was a campus push to enter that environment aggressively. Although there was a substantial learning curve for the technical development issues, the University Of-

fice of Distance and Distributed Education was fully engaged in the provision of technical support. The greatest difficulty was to determine a common format with content that could be taught by several instructors and have wide applicability for students at a basic level (e.g., all majors) and that was as effective in the teaching/learning process as the face-to-face class. Since the face-to-face course appeared to be a success, based on anecdotal and formal evaluation, the online course was patterned on face-to-face course content. Also, regional accrediting associations require that distance learning courses must be comparable to onsite courses.

Originally designed by one librarian, the plan was to integrate all instructors into online instruction, including review and modification of content. As instructors cycled into the online teaching pool, they worked as a committee-at-large in modifying and further refining course goals, expected outcomes, and assessment techniques. From the outset, targeted groups that could or should profitably benefit from the course were advised to enroll in the class. One such group, at-risk students, were identified by the Freshman Center. Another group were academically gifted, resident high school students enrolled in college courses, as college students, in the university's Advanced Academy. When the ACRL Information Literacy Competency Standards for Higher Education were approved in 2000, they were incorporated into the learning outcomes and assessment for the course.[1]

Content

Early on it was decided to provide instruction that directly assisted students in completing traditional academic assignments: conducting research, writing papers, citing references, and the primary academic tasks concomitant with scholarly communication. The title of the course—"Academic Research and the University Library"—reflected the emphases. The library was viewed as an active laboratory for students to learn *how* to do the work required of them. Content therefore closely paralleled traditional library instruction: primary, secondary, tertiary sources; abstracting and indexing literature; encyclopedias, books, periodical literature; evaluation of sources; plagiarism and attribution. As resources and services became electronic, the place of the library as laboratory became electronic also.

Course content, lesson objectives, exams, and glossary are consistent for all sections of the course. Individual instructors have freedom to develop unique worksheets and application assignments for their respective sections. All course content is evaluated and updated approximately every two years.

A fourteen-lesson, self-paced textbook that has evolved over time as the collaborative work of all instructional services faculty, past and present, was written to support the learning outcomes anticipated. Each lesson has accompanying stated objectives at the beginning of the section. Students may print the lessons and bind them in a notebook or read them online. Additionally, the *MLA Handbook for Writers of Research Papers* is a required text.[2] Optional, ungraded self-tests, which allow students to monitor their comprehension and progress, are available for several lessons. Comments are provided for all answers, correct and incorrect, submitted on self-tests.

Essentially, the content of the course is designed to conduct students through the process of writing a research paper, although the content of the paper is not part of the course. (Students can use the process to create a paper for other, disciplinary courses.)

Worksheets, through hands-on experience, reinforce concepts presented in lessons. The number of worksheets varies from section to section and generally reflects two lines of thought: each lesson should have an individual worksheet; or fewer worksheets that cover multiple lessons enable students to understand the overall research process better. Stated another way, if you have more worksheets, you can provide more experience with each concept. The counterargument is that more worksheets do indeed provide more experience, but in the process students fail to make the connection between concepts and the overall research process. Unfortunately, this is a conundrum for which we have no answer.

Worksheets are not timed. Students may work on them as they progress through the course. There is, however, a deadline associated with each worksheet, and once the deadline passes students are unable to access them. Through feedback from students, we know that most of them print off the worksheets so that they can work on them as time permits. There are two options for submitting worksheets: input answers as they are found, or complete the entire worksheet offline and then submit. In either case, students must *save* each answer and then *submit* at the time of their choice, but before the deadline. Worksheets are graded individually, with feedback provided for each question. Once graded, instructor comments and grades are available to students.

Exams include a midterm and comprehensive final. Both are timed, sixty to ninety minutes, include fifty multiple-choice questions, are "open book," and are computer graded. They are typically available for two to three days during which students may log in at any time and take the exam. Instructors have the option to release individual grades as the computer grades them or to wait until all exams are graded and then release all scores. The latter option is our preferred choice.

Currently there are three subject/discipline application assignments that cover business, social science, and arts/humanities. From the three, students must select and complete two of the assignments. The purposes of the application assignments are to introduce students to and illustrate the structure of subject/disciplinary literature and to provide experience in the use of these materials. In the future we would like to develop more application assignments, with at least one related to the natural/physical sciences.

The semester project, student selected and instructor approved, consists of a documented search strategy, a thesis statement, and an annotated bibliography on a topic. Our experience is that a topic of research in another class is the best topic choice for a student in the research class, since the student recognizes the immediate need for research and presumably, as a result of enrollment in the library class, should perform better research that translates into a better paper for the other class. Obviously this scenario is not always possible. In those instances, other good options are topic selection from a student's major or on something that interests the student. If all else fails, instructors work with students to develop manageable research topics.

There are instances where students ask to change their topics because of lack of information, desire to research a different topic, and a variety of other reasons. Our instructors view this as part of the research process and generally allow the topic change.

Instruction

The actual process of teaching in an online environment is a complicated affair. Every student is required to attend an orientation session at the beginning of the semester. This session is to familiarize them with the mechanics of WebCT, to go over the syllabus, to outline the calendar for the course, and to clarify what assignments are graded, and how. We have found that the early engagement is valuable in getting students "geared up" for the course. Students do not have to attend an orientation session with their instructor—the sessions are general. If a student cannot attend, he or she must make a private appointment to go over the material with the instructor. Part of the rationale for the environment is the asynchronous process involved. Students don't have to be at a certain place at a certain time; they don't have to work together as a group; assignments are generally due within a window of time, instead of *now;* it is difficult to address the class as a group, or to keep people on the same schedule. Generally, instruction follows two techniques: the instructor must keep in touch with students to ensure that they are following the schedule and are keeping up; and they must be available to address particular questions that arise as students work their way through the course materials.

Most course management software has a reporting function that allows an instructor to monitor how often and how long students log in, and to what assignments. Faculty must constantly monitor activity and encourage students to keep on task. The course at UWG is an online course rather than a distance course; faculty must keep office hours and be available for individual consultation with students. One of the surprises in teaching online is that students, on their own, often assume that assignments are more complicated than they actually are; posted examples of satisfactory work and close feedback to completed assignments are important.

Program Assessment

Every student completes a pre-test before coursework begins. A post-test is administered prior to final grades being released. Thus far, results indicate that students are absorbing the course content satisfactorily. We have conducted preliminary research measuring GPA and retention rates of students taking the course.[3] Results indicate that at-risk students who do well in the course are more likely to be retained and have slightly higher GPAs than students not taking the course. This research will be replicated in the coming year. We have conducted regression analysis on test question pools for final examinations to assure that the questions are actually measuring the outcomes we are seeking; questions have been eliminated and reformulated as a result.[4] Anecdotally, disciplinary faculty have expressed the wish that all their students take the course. The University's Office of Distance and Distributed Education independently administers student evaluations of online courses each semester. Results are returned to faculty and are the basis for adjusting teaching methods and styles.

Lessons Learned

It is possible that library faculty have learned more by teaching information literacy in an online environment than students have. Some basic conclusions follow:

It's a lot harder than it looks. If you can, create a sense of community as early as possible in the academic term since an online environment can be impersonal. We have had mixed success with optional online introductions at the beginning of the semester. As a general rule, the instructor begins by introducing him/herself and then inviting others to do so. It is interesting to note that, when optional online introductions are utilized, the instructor can almost draw a conclusion about group participation for the academic term. We have found from experience that, if several introductions are offered, the class itself remains fairly engaged throughout the academic term. If there are few introductions, it will probably be a long academic term.

Engage the class as quickly and as frequently as possible. If you have public discussion capability in your course management software, you might try using it for posing discussion questions, alerting students to problems several students are experiencing, or clarifying problem areas.

Online is not easier than teaching in a classroom, and doesn't take less time. Online interaction eliminates a great number of cues that are available in the classroom. You can't tell when students don't "get" what's going on, or when they're completely lost. Grading (and explaining the grading to students) is a terrific time expense; since you can't show the whole class at once, explanations must be repeated for each question, for each student, for each assignment. Cap class enrollment at a manageable number. For us, the magic number is twenty-four, but some recommend classes as small as fifteen. When the situation warrants, we do add one or two students per semester per class.

Software and machines don't always work the way they're supposed to. Schedules, deadlines, and expectations have to remain flexible. Murphy's law is always in operation. Students will have difficulty or their machines will die; assignments will have to be reopened; deadlines will have to be extended. You will lose your own work and have to start regrading an assignment over from scratch.

It's terrifically rewarding, but it's not for everyone. We continue to face-to-face classroom courses. Some students simply do not feel comfortable or competent to succeed in the relatively independent online environment.

Development never ends. With the changing environment in academe, course content and learning objectives are constantly under scrutiny and revision. How can new software or techniques be integrated to create a more engaged student? How can students be encouraged to become part of a learning community? How are new services or techniques reflected in the course content; for example, how does the availability of bibliographic software change the course structure?

Don't be afraid to try something new. Sometimes something truly wonderful can be the result of an experiment; other times, you may not achieve the desired results. During the fourth year of teaching online, some of our students were having problems in class. We decided to offer an optional lab during specified hours during the week and staffed by library faculty who taught the course. Attendance was abysmal. We discontinued the lab after one semester, but at least we tried.

It's not advisable to develop course content around specific databases. In Georgia, we have GALILEO, a database aggregator, which until a few years ago provided all of the databases we were able to offer students and faculty. Thus in the first few years of teaching the course, we placed heavy emphasis on GALILEO. GALILEO, like any aggregator, may add and drop databases while the library provides increasing numbers of databases. What we learned is that you should focus on skills, not specific research tools.

Never underestimate the value of luck and do not be shy about taking advantage of a lucky situation. In our case, luck played a role in upgrading our course from a one-hour to two-hour credit course that became part of the core curriculum. The realization came fairly soon for us that the library course should have more credit attached to it because of the amount of work involved. When the university moved from a quarter to a semester system, courses that emphasized critical thinking and integrated technology were needed. We were ready.

We have taught the course online for about seven years; we teach as many as sixteen sections per semester. We have received great support administratively but also learned that politics and finance are important parts of that success. We have been able to show our administration, based on FTE students in seats, that we generate considerable income in state formula funding and in tuition payments. The administration regularly funds adjuncts to supplement the teaching cadre within the library.

This summer, we will be assessing the entire content and structure of the course, again. We have younger, newer faculty who want to implement learning groups, provide animated instruction for particular topics, and provide group projects for students. Although we have a mature delivery mechanism for content, we don't quite yet know how to integrate new technology into the learning process itself.[5] We are not certain which direction we need to face to be heading forward.

Notes

1. Association of College and Research Libraries, *Information Literacy Competency Standards for Higher Education* (Chicago: ACRL, 2000). Available online at http://www.ala.org/ala/acrl/acrlstandards/informationliteracycompetency.htm.

2. Joseph Gibaldi, *MLA Handbook for Writers of Research Papers*, 6th ed. (New York: Modern Language Association, 2003).

3.   Michael H. Aldrich, "LIBR1101 GPA and Retention Data." Design and data available from the researcher (maldrich@westga.edu). The study is scheduled for replication this year.

4.   Michael H. Aldrich, "Picking the Correct Answer: Assessing Multiple Choice Final Exams in a Library Research Course," *Georgia Library Quarterly* 43, no.3 (2006): 13–18.

5.   "E-Learning: Successes and Failures," *Chronicle of Higher Education,* January 5, 2006, B20. In an exchange of views between Gene I. Maeroff, a senior fellow at the Hechinger Institute on Education and the Media at Columbia University's Teachers College, and Robert Zemsky, chairman of the Learning Alliance for Higher Education, Maeroff noted that the Internet is a "communications device, not a learning device." There is probably not a consensus on exactly what constitutes a learning device, although Maeroff proffers Blackboard and FaceBook.

Information Literacy Instruction Embedded into Discipline Courses and Programs

10. Library Research Instruction for Distance Learners at Prince George's Community College

Norma Allenbach Schmidt

Rationale

An integral part of the distance learning program at Prince George's Community College (PGCC) in Largo, Maryland, is the policy to monitor closely the quality of each course being offered, including course content, structure, resources, and assessment. The intention is to provide equivalent learning in an online course as would be experienced in the traditional face-to-face classroom environment. A key component of the English and psychology courses at PGCC is writing a research paper. In a face-to-face situation, the English and psychology classes are scheduled for one or more sessions in the library for instruction in conducting research. These sessions are taught by the librarians, all of whom have faculty status. Session coverage typically includes Boolean searches, search strategies, identification of appropriate print and online information sources, evaluation of materials, and correct citations. Participation in the information literacy program is left up to individual instructors. The college does not have in place a universal information literacy competency. As early as 2003, professors in the English and psychology departments who taught online courses with Blackboard course software or who were teaching at satellite campuses raised the issue of providing library research instruction to their students. The instructors in the off-campus English and psychology courses noted that their students encountered particular problems more frequently than students in the face-to-face sections of the course. These special difficulties included unfamiliarity with correct citation style, misunderstanding the nature of plagiarism, and being unable to differentiate a refereed journal article from other types of periodical articles.

In summer 2003, PGCC psychology professor Diane Finley came to the library with reasons for including instruction in library research methods in the online psychology classes. She pointed out that distance learners pay the same tuition as classroom students and are entitled to the same services. The online students have equal needs to gain information literacy skills that will prepare them to transfer from the community college to the four-year institution. Finley also observed that librarians have the experience, practice, and most up-to-date knowledge to explain research methods and library resources to students. In addition, the information from a specialist visiting the online course would carry extra credibility and more quickly capture the students' attention.

Concurrently and independently, Professor Robert Goldberg of the PGCC English department was dealing with a similar issue. The classroom of his Writing for Business composition course was located at a satellite campus of the college, University Town Center in Hyattsville, Maryland. This center does not have a library on site and is eleven miles from the main campus. Goldberg also envisioned the inclusion of information literacy as a course component via an online presentation, since Blackboard software was in use as a communication tool. Both instructors stated that library instruction in research methods and appropriate sources is a necessary component of the overall content of their courses and could be best achieved by the librarian "visiting" the online classroom. These concepts were developed by the two PGCC faculty members in discussions with a librarian. The ideas were conceived independently without prior research of the literature regarding the inclusion of library services to off-campus students. Once envisioned, the plans were enthusiastically supported and promoted by the director of the distance learning program at PGCC, Mary Wells.

Development

Finley and I began collaboration in the summer and early fall of 2003. She provided a description of the nature of a research assignment the students were to complete and the requirements of the assignment. Out of this collaboration came the pilot for online library instruction at PGCC. The online course selected as the pilot was the fall semester session of Adolescent Psychology.

Blackboard course software is used by the distance learning program of online courses at PGCC. In addition, with increasing frequency, professors teaching in traditional classrooms also utilize Blackboard as a tool for posting syllabi and handouts and as a means of communication between class meetings. The initial offering of library instruction via Blackboard in a course being taught face-to-face at a satellite campus was the spring 2004 Writing for Business course taught by Goldberg.

Since Blackboard courseware does not have the category of "librarian" as part of

an instructional team, it was decided to use the Blackboard category "teaching assistant" to provide the librarian with access to the course. Also, we decided that the library instruction to be offered would be posted as a forum in the discussion board portion of the course. The discussion board lends itself ideally to communication between the librarian and the students in the class. It was quickly agreed that in addition to the actual presentation of instruction, a librarian would visit the discussion board during a specified interval of days to provide virtual reference.

Microsoft FrontPage was chosen as the software to develop the lesson content. Much of the material to be included in the content already existed on our PGCC Library Web site (www.pgcc.edu/library/index.htm). The "Quick Research Library Tutorial" is of particular importance. This interactive tutorial covers the steps in the process of writing a research paper. Librarian Imogene Zachery and I developed this tutorial as well as online subject guides for the library's Web site as a part of the college's participation in the U.S. Department of Education's Title III Grant Project.

The library research instruction of the lessons developed is rich in hyperlinks to sections of the interactive research tutorial as well as other resources found on the library's Web site and the Web. When a presentation is completed in FrontPage, it is copied and pasted into the designated forum in the discussion board segment of the Blackboard course software. The learners are able to read the instructional module and follow the hyperlinks while remaining logged into Blackboard.

The inauguration of this service required that I incorporate new activities into my workload. In addition to learning the FrontPage software, I needed to become familiar with the Blackboard courseware. Initially I attended an all-day workshop offered on the PGCC campus to increase my familiarity with the features of FrontPage. I also attended faculty workshops provided by our distance learning staff to learn the basics of Blackboard.

Both the learning of computer software and the development of a lesson to be posted for a particular course are time intensive. Fortunately, I commenced these activities at the same time that my participation in the aforementioned Title III Grant Project was concluding. I was able to start a new major project just as another was nearing completion.

Content

The content of the instruction for the two pilot courses participating in the online library instruction was determined by what was already being taught in the traditional classroom. Library instruction at PGCC is specific to the course and to the assignment being addressed. Active learning and critical thinking skills are incorporated. Development of a search strategy and evaluation of documents and Web sites are also part of the lesson. In the Adolescent Psychology course chosen as the pilot, students are assigned a research project. Information from refereed journal articles is a requirement of the assignment. Suitable refereed articles are readily available in the library's collection of online databases. In the pilot course from the English department, Writing for Business, students are required to conduct research in preparation of a final project. The library's online databases as well as Web resources are the key sources of information. As stated above, the Writing for Business course was being taught in a traditional classroom at a satellite campus,

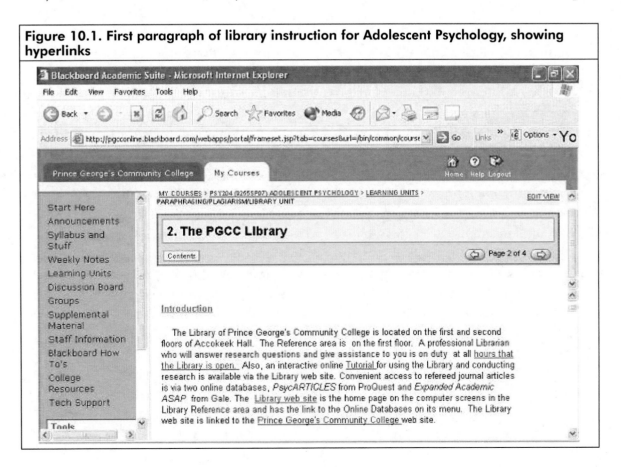

Figure 10.1. First paragraph of library instruction for Adolescent Psychology, showing hyperlinks

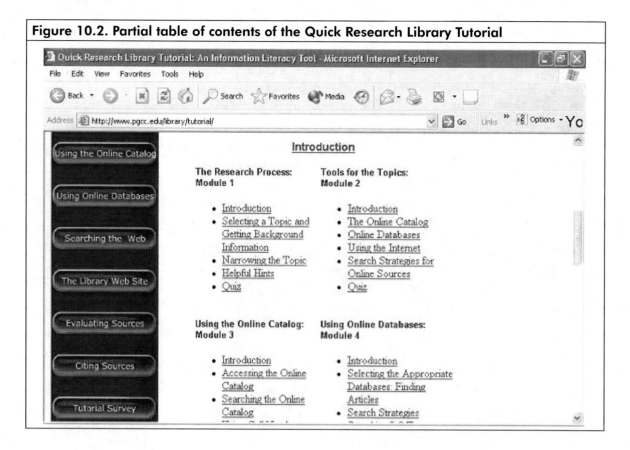

Figure 10.2. Partial table of contents of the Quick Research Library Tutorial

with Blackboard communication offered to enrich the face-to-face contact.

As developed, the library research instruction for the Adolescent Psychology course begins with an introduction to the PGCC Library Web site and the interactive Quick Research Library Tutorial there (figures 10.1 and 10.2).

The introduction is followed by a glossary of terms pertaining to research, guidelines on choosing and narrowing a research topic, and an explanation of Boolean searching with examples. Next is a thorough explanation of accessing, searching, evaluating, and managing refereed articles found in Proquest's PsychArticles and Gale's Expanded Academic ASAP. Hyperlinks are present throughout the text and lead the learner to the site being discussed. In this way, the student can do the assigned research within the Blackboard environment. Links to sites

that provide guidance on writing and citing in American Psychological Association style are also part of the lesson. In response to student requests in the pilot course, a link to a sample research paper in psychology correctly written in APA style has been added to the instruction (figure 10.3).

Content of the lesson for the Writing for Business course also included an introduction to the library Web site and the interactive research tutorial, a glossary of terms, and instruction in search strategies and Boolean operators. Again, the guidance in evaluation of materials and use of correct style was included. The featured online database for this course was Gale's Business and Company Resource Center.

The online databases that are recommended in the Blackboard library research instruction are available off-campus to all students enrolled at PGCC. Therefore, technical instruction in the procedure for accessing the online databases off-campus with a campus-provided user name and password is included in the library instruction module. Procedures regarding what to do if a student has forgotten his or her password and additional technical issues are incorporated at this point as well. Interlibrary loan procedures are also delineated. Typically, since the online databases contain both full-text articles and citations for which only an abstract is provided, information on obtaining a photocopy of the full-text article via interlibrary loan is necessary.

As the program expanded to include a wider variety of subjects and courses, coverage of a variety of additional resources was added. When appropriate to the course assignment and requirements, instruction in locating materials in the library's Web-based catalog of books, sound recordings,

and video recordings is offered. In some courses, there may be included bibliographies of print reference books in the PGCC library's collection. As in the case of journal articles, books not held in the collection of the PGCC library may also be obtained by the interlibrary loan service. A small but expanding collection of electronic reference books is available to our students. This is in the instruction as well.

Instruction

In the two pilot courses and all subsequent courses where online instruction in library research has been offered, the emphasis has been to use our own college library's Web site as a starting point to both Internet resources and the print materials in digital form that are contained in our thirty online databases and twenty-five electronic reference books. Specific learning outcomes include choos-

Figure 10.3. Hyperlinks lead to information on APA style and a sample research paper in APA style.

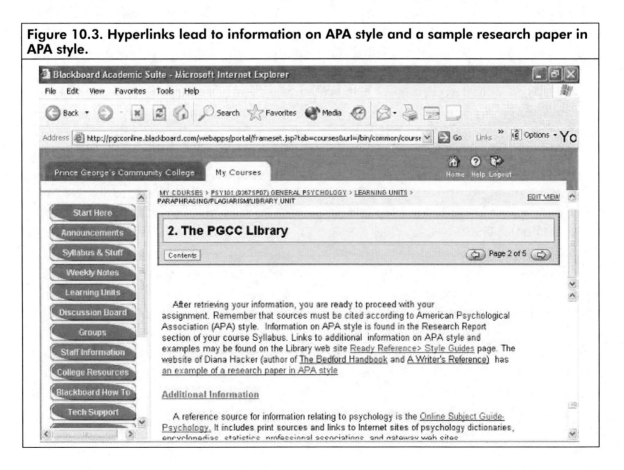

ing and narrowing a research topic; applying the basics of Boolean searching in a database search; differentiating between magazine, journal, and peer-reviewed journal articles; and critically evaluating articles. If finding and using Web material is also part of the assignment, coverage of search engines and evaluation of Web sites is included.

As previously mentioned, the distance learning program at PGCC is structured so that the course instructor requests the distance learning staff to add the librarian to a course as a teaching assistant. The librarian posts the instructional module on the Library Forum of the Blackboard discussion board before the semester actually begins or, alternatively, as soon as possible upon receiving a request from the course instructor. The instruction module is available to the students in the course as soon as it is posted and remains available for the entire semester.

When arranging for the library research instruction, the course instructor also specifies a period of seven to ten days during the semester when the librarian will visit the discussion board to answer any reference questions. As in the traditional classroom, where library research instruction is typically scheduled to coincide with the research assignment, the designated time for librarian visits to the discussion board in the Blackboard course also is coordinated with the research schedule. The librarian agrees to visit the discussion board at least once per day, though when students are visiting the discussion board frequently the librarian visits up to three times a day to answer the questions in a timely manner and facilitate any follow-up questions. This activity becomes a major part of the librarian's workload during the designated period.

It is the nature of online courses that students do their assignments on various days

of the week and any hour of the day. Therefore, the visiting librarian needs to visit the course evenings and weekends so that students may obtain answers and proceed to completion of their assignments. We have noticed that the weekend period from Friday night through Sunday evening has the heaviest usage by students of the reference question-and-answer feature of the library discussion board, and so the work schedule of the visiting librarian must be arranged to accommodate these hours. The hours are then considered to be telecommuting in terms of the librarian's work schedule. All students enrolled in a particular course, as well as the course instructor, may read all the postings on the library discussion board, both questions and answers.

The course instructors have various levels of involvement in the library module. The instructors often leave it up to the students to ask reference questions. In certain instances, the course instructor may decide that it is crucial for the student to understand a certain procedure, such as how to find a refereed journal article. In these cases, the students may be assigned to ask the librarian to verify that the search strategy being employed and results obtained fulfill the requirements of the assignment. In some instances, the course instructor may intervene in the question-and-answer exchange between student and librarian. A instructor who recognizes that a student is asking reference questions outside the parameters of the course may wish to steer the subject matter back on track.

Students are strongly encouraged to communicate exclusively on the discussion board when asking the librarian a question, primarily to allow all students in the class to see the question-and-answer exchange and benefit from it. A secondary reason is to give the course instructor the opportunity to check that each student is participating in the discussion, if participation is required.

Program Assessment

Assessment of student learning has been carried out by means of a pre-test and post-test on the material included in the library module, with multiple-choice questions such as this:

Which of the following best describes the contents of journal articles?

a. Scholarly and subject oriented

b. Popular topics with many photos

The questions and the answer key of these multiple-choice tests are developed by the librarian and supplied to the course instructor. The course instructor administers them via the standard Blackboard test administration and grading functions and then shares the results with the librarian. The results have consistently shown improved student scores on the post-tests.

The online library instruction program has grown from the initial pilot in fall 2003 to the recent high of seventeen courses in fall 2006. Subject disciplines have included anthropology, English, nutrition, psychology, speech communications, and women's studies. With the intense focus in psychology courses on learning the research process, the psychology department has been the most heavily represented of the academic departments. Eight specific courses within the psychology department have been a part of the program. Across the range of courses using Blackboard, instructors who have once included the visiting librarian and library research instruction have continued to do so each time they have taught the course.

Online library instruction is effective in that the student enrolled in the online course has constant access to the information and hyperlinks in the library module. In contrast, a student in a face-to-face class relies on handouts and whatever notes they happen to take while attending the class. In the online environment, the complete presentation is available for the entire semester. Students are able to complete the research while remaining logged into the Blackboard environment continuously. In the online classes that have had the library research instruction, instructors have reported an improvement in research papers in terms of students being able to identify scholarly refereed articles as specified in the assignment and in correct citation of sources.

The development of the program of offering library research instruction via Blackboard has proceeded smoothly since its inception. Faculty who teach courses that depend on research skills have been enthusiastic about including the library instruction module. Whether teaching an online course or using Blackboard as a communication tool in a face-to-face course, the instructors are appreciative of the customized library instruction modules and of the question-and-answer time when the participating librarian visits the discussion board. Often the librarian who answers a reference question in this circumstance has the luxury of devoting as much time as necessary to answering the question without the pressures of more patrons and ringing phones at the reference desk. The participating librarians have been able to adjust their work schedules to facilitate telecommuting evenings and weekends so that the students are best served by having their questions answered in a timely manner.

There are currently two librarians on staff trained in the process of answering reference questions on the Blackboard discussion boards. For this reason, when several instructors request visits from a librarian for the same time period, it is possible to divide the workload. As with traditional courses, the online faculties have been advised and have learned the habit of requesting the library instruction service a minimum of two weeks in advance of when it will be utilized. The instructors involved have expressed delight that librarians are offering this necessary service of library research instruction in the online Blackboard environment.

Lessons Learned

A few small glitches in the program have come to our attention. One, in the procedures, appears when students do not realize that the librarian's visits to the discussion board are asynchronous. This has led to students expecting an instant reply such as would be the case in virtual reference situations that take place in an Internet chat room. Although the participating librarian visits a heavily used board an average of three or more times per day, this is a periodic visit and not a continuous presence. To remedy this misconception, both the course instructors and the librarians have learned to remind students on numerous occasions about the nature of the librarian's participation. Another minor glitch is that students have occasionally asked reference questions on the discussion board that do not pertain to that particular course. Although the participating librarian may supply an answer, the course instructors do prefer to moderate the discussion and return it to pertinent topics. In a few courses, students have hesitated to ask reference questions on the discussion board. In order to encourage communication, the course instructor has at times opened up with a pertinent question or two to present an example of the communication process.

The initial development of the online module is a process requiring a large amount of time. Once the module is created, often minor adjustments are all that are needed for it to be used in the same course by the same instructor in a subsequent semester. Also, in developing a module for similar courses, such as two different courses in the psychology Department, it is often possible to copy and paste text and hyperlinks and then incorporate modifications to tailor the material to the course in development.

Marketing the program to faculty who use Blackboard in any capacity is a continuing project. Each semester, the number of faculty who utilize Blackboard increases, so there is an ongoing need to present this program of library instruction to them. I have composed articles for the in-house campus faculty journal, *Instructional Forum*. Also, all faculty receive a memorandum from the library prior to the start of the fall and spring semesters regarding planning and scheduling for library instruction, whether on Blackboard or in the classroom. The dean of learning resources is kept current on the growth of this program by means of monthly and annual reports. This is vital information to justify additional staffing requirements should the program experience significant expansion.

Ultimately, the service requires an adjustment in the arrangement of librarian staffing schedules. To date, this need has been met by rearranging the schedules of full-time and adjunct librarians who do not participate in online librarianship so that they cover additional hours at the library reference desk. This has enabled the librarian developing the online library instruction modules and the two librarians who participate in answering reference questions on the discussion boards to be scheduled fewer hours at the library reference desk. This arrangement has made it possible for the librarians who visit the discussion boards to telecommute evenings and weekends, when our online students are most active.

Our library research instruction offered in Blackboard to students off campus was conceived, developed, and implemented and is perpetuated with no additions to the library's budget. We have been able to do this without funds for several reasons. First, the developing librarian was able to incorporate the necessary activities into her workload. The software in use, Microsoft FrontPage, is already in place on the computers of PGCC as a part of the Microsoft Office Suite. A key source of instruction and information, the library's Web site and its Quick Research Library Tutorial, had been in place prior to the development of the online library instruction program. Also, the online databases and electronic reference books are already an integral part of the library's budget. Appropriate online databases as resources of information required in research assignments have been and will continue to be available. In order to offer reference service on the discussion boards of Blackboard, it has been possible for participating librarians' schedules to be arranged to facilitate telecommuting with nonparticipants covering the reference desk. In the future, if the number of courses significantly increases, attention will need to be directed to increasing staffing levels.

It is gratifying to note that the Library Forums of Blackboard discussion boards have postings that include not only reference questions from students and answers from librarians but also many expressions of thanks from the student participants. From these communications, we have learned that we are making the research process quicker, easier, and more productive for these students. In this way, the students are able to proceed more efficiently to completion of their assignments. The students also will have learned research techniques and resources that may be applied to future courses as well as the information needs of their daily lives.

11. From Partnership to Program Development: Information Literacy in an Academic Curriculum

Barbara J. D'Angelo

Rationale

The Multimedia Writing and Technical Communication (MWTC) program is an undergraduate degree-granting applied writing program that emphasizes instruction in the production, design, management, and communication of information. The creation of the MWTC program's model for integrating information literacy has been an evolutionary one built on our theoretical and practical assumptions about information literacy and rhetoric/writing. Although rhetoric/writing and library/information science are distinct disciplines, both are concerned with the mediation of information within the context of communication. The most common connection between rhetoric/writing and library/information science is manifested pedagogically in research writing and bibliographic or library use instruction in freshman composition. However, for applied writing programs such as ours information literacy is equally important. Technical communicators, for example, are mediators and communicators of information. Graduates work in fields as wide ranging as Web development, graphic design, and instructional design as well as traditional technical writing and editing fields. Although diverse in specific nature, all of the careers our graduates enter have strong information components in common. The field has rapidly evolved into one that necessitates an understanding of information. Single sourcing, for example, requires a sophisticated understanding of how information can be chunked, organized, and classified for retrieval for multiple purposes.

We are attempting to realize what Rolf Norgaard has advocated for an approach in which rhetoric provides information literacy with a theoretical foundation that rescues it from the danger of becoming narrowly defined as a functional technology skill and in which information literacy returns rhetoric/writing to its traditional roots with social, civic, and intellectual relevance.[1] Our approach, or model, builds on both theoretical and practical perspectives that information literacy should be holistically integrated into programmatic learning outcomes. Further, this approach allows us to emphasize information literacy as a process; finding, using, evaluating, and communicating information is situated within a rhetorical context that cannot be separated from the writing or composing process. With this perspective, it is essential that information literacy be infused in pedagogical practices and assessment. Our model includes the development of outcomes that merge information literacy within the framework of overall program outcomes so that it is fully infused into teaching and learning rather than separated as discrete skills. Criteria and standards for assessment of outcomes, including information literacy, are then directly associated with outcomes to foster strategies to evaluate and advance instructional pedagogy and practice for both on-site and online courses.

Development

The MWTC program at Arizona State University (ASU) was established in 2000 as the only degree-granting technical communication program in Arizona. The undergraduate program is upper division, consisting of thirty-three hours of coursework beyond ASU's general studies requirements. The MWTC program also houses the required upper-division writing requirement courses for other majors. The program's mission and direction were articulated in the original program proposal approved by the Arizona Board of Regents: "In the Multimedia Writing and Technical Communication Program, students will learn how to produce, to design, and to manage information, using both traditional and developing technologies."[2]

The curriculum was developed around four main foci reflective of an applied writing program: technical communication, visual communication, writing with technology, and technical editing. Students are introduced to these four components in an introductory course followed by four core courses, each of which emphasizes one of the foci. For the remainder of required coursework, students enroll in genre courses, information-based courses, electives, courses from a related area of interest, and a capstone course in which they submit an electronic portfolio that is used to assess both their learning and the program itself. Program courses are taught both online and on campus; during the spring 2007 semester, for example, 53 percent of classes were taught online. All required courses and the majority of electives are offered either solely online or in multiple sections with at least one online so that it is possible for students to complete the degree online.

Our model to integrate information literacy has developed gradually since 2001, while I was librarian working in collaboration with the program, to fall 2004, when I was hired as a full-time lecturer. Partnership and collaboration with the MWTC program while I was a librarian from was valuable and essential to our work. This collaboration initially involved partnership with one of the MWTC program's faculty to develop a project in which students created a library portal for faculty and students using the MyLibrary software developed at North Carolina State University. At the time this project was in progress, I proposed a three-credit course—"InfoGlut: Deal with It"—which was accepted in principle by the vice provost for academic affairs. However, since the library is not a teaching department, a place had to be found for it. After discussions with appropriate program directors, the course was placed in the MWTC program and included in the fall 2002 schedule as an elective offered onsite.

Designed as a course focusing on the impacts of technology on the production, dissemination, and use of information, InfoGlut reflected many information literacy outcomes. As an upper-division course, it emphasized ACRL Information Literacy Competency Standards Three, Four, and Five, reflecting the critical thinking aspects of incorporating new information with that previously known, selecting information to accomplish a specific purpose, and understanding the economic, legal, social, and ethical issues surrounding information.

One of the unexpected outcomes of housing the InfoGlut course in the MWTC program was student advocacy for the inclusion of information literacy in their program courses. Although research-related topics and assignments are included in other MWTC courses, InfoGlut was the first exposure to information literacy as a concept for the students. Students reacted positively to issues and concepts surrounding the organization and use of information, not only in class but also in discussions with other faculty and the program head. As a result, the program head and I integrated information literacy into program outcomes, and I was hired as a part-time instructor to revise and teach other MWTC courses to integrate information literacy further. In 2004 the program added a new lecturer position, for which I applied and was hired, with the responsibility of integrating information literacy into program curriculum and assessment. The benefit of this transition has been my ability to work full time to build our information literacy initiatives. I have also maintained my connection with the library to facilitate our attempts to teach students the full range of information literacy competencies.

The basis of our approach to creating an information literacy–infused curriculum has been the formalization of program outcomes merging rhetoric, information literacy, and technology. MWTC program outcomes are based on the Writing Program Administrators' Outcomes Statement for First Year Composition. In 2003 we finalized integration of information literacy into outcomes by merging ACRL information literacy standards (appendix A).[3] Once outcomes were finalized, we created a curriculum matrix to map each outcome to program courses. This matrix (appendix B) gives us a visual snapshot of the relationship between outcomes and courses. In addition, in fall 2006 we implemented a new assessment strategy that reflects a recursive approach in which assessment has two goals: it provides students a summative evaluation of their work in the program, and it provides us data with which to continually improve the program. By assessing student portfolios based on

program outcomes, we are able to identify strengths and weaknesses in courses and teaching strategies and use that information as evidence for curriculum improvement.

Content

TWC447: Business Reports is a required upper-level writing course for business administration majors as well as an elective genre course for MWTC majors. It is offered in multiple sections each semester and during summer sessions both onsite and online. Since it is the course with highest enrollment in our program, it was a logical choice for review and incorporation of information literacy. In addition, conversations with faculty in the business administration program regarding students' knowledge and use of business-related research sources and their writing abilities cemented our decision to target this course for revision soon after I joined the MWTC program as lecturer. One of the defined outcomes for this course is that students will learn to "find, access, retrieve, and use information from a variety of sources to analyze a problem and develop a solution" (see figure 11.1).

To strengthen this information literacy component of the course, we revised it to incorporate a sequence of assignments and in-class activities that emphasize the process of researching and writing a report. Three primary assignments facilitate learning this outcome. In a formal proposal, students identify a company-related problem to investigate and solve. Students then compose a progress report to provide an update on their research strategy, including an annotated bibliography. In this assignment, they are encouraged to analyze their strategy and discuss what has gone well, what has not worked, and their adjustments to develop other strategies. In this way, students are re-

Figure 11.1. Business Reports course syllabus

TWC4/547 Business Reports
Summer 8-Week
June 1 - July 23, 2004

Instructor:
Barbara J. D'Angelo
ASU East Library Services, Center 30A
Phone: 480-727-1160
Email: bdangelo@asu.edu

Office Hours:
Monday, 10:00-Noon
Wednesday,. 1:00-3:00
or by appointment

Course Description and Objectives

This course will introduce students to strategies, formats, and techniques of presenting information to business and other workplace audiences.

On completion of this course, students will be able to:

- Identify, organize, and communicate information to fit the audience, purpose, and situation
- Effectively use formats appropriate for business communication such as email, memos, letters, reports
- Find, access, retrieve, and use information from a variety of sources to analyze a problem and develop a solution
- Design effective business documents using appropriate style and visual elements
- Effectively use language, tone, and voice to fit the audience, purpose, and situation

Course Requirements

This is an Internet course. Because it is a summer course, you have much less time to complete work than you would during a regular semester. Read the Course Guidelines and Policies and Course Introduction. Review all information posted in Blackboard. Be sure you understand what will be expected of you.

All assignments are expected to be completed on time. See course evaluation section below for information on grading and Blackboard for information on assignments and due dates.

You will primarily be working on your own to complete assignments. However, you will be sharing a draft of your final report with another student in the class for peer editing and feedback.

Graduate Students: Students registered for graduate credit (TWC547) will complete an additional assignment.

Text

Locker, Kitty O. (2003) *Business and Administrative Communication*, 6th edition. New York: McGraw-Hill.

The text is available in the bookstore. **Be sure to purchase the 6th edition**.

Daily Schedule

Refer to the Schedule information in Blackboard.

Assignments

Refer to the Schedule information in Blackboard.

Course Evaluation

TWC447:

Assignment	Value
Email 1	5 points
Audience analysis	5 points
Proposal	10 points
Letter 1	5 points
Memo 1	5 points
Progress Report	10 points
Letter 2	5 points
Letter 3	5 points
Report draft/Peer response	5 points
Powerpoint	5 points
Memo 2	5 points
Job Application Materials	10 points
Problem-solving Report	25 points

Scale	Grade
90-100 points	A
80-89 points	B
70-79 points	C
60-69 points	D
0-59 points	E

TWC547:

In addition to the assignments/scale listed above, students registered for TWC547 will write an additional paper worth 20 points. The scale for final grade will be:

Scale	Grade
108-120 points	A
96-107 points	B
84-95 points	C
72-83 points	D
0-71 points	E

All assignments are to be completed and turned in by the due date listed in the Schedule section of Blackboard. **Late assignments will not be accepted for any reason other than family or medical emergency. If you cannot complete an assignment on time, contact me** in advance of the due date.

Throughout this course, you will be composing documents for a variety of audiences and purposes. Your writing should at all times be professional and consist of proper tone, style, formatting, language, and grammar.

Academic Integrity

As a student in this course you are expected to complete your own work and to properly cite work of others. Refer to the Student Academic Integrity Policy regarding students rights, responsibilities, and obligations.

Last modified: 24 May 2004

quired to engage in self-analysis and metacognitive thinking about their own work and processes so that research is, ideally, reflective and on-going rather than completed haphazardly the night before the report is due. Students then make recommendations to solve the problem in a formal report at the end of the semester, with evidence from their research in support of the credibility and viability of the recommendation. In addition to formal course assignments, students complete in-class activities to facilitate thinking about research as a strategy within the rhetorical situation (audience and purpose) rather than as an isolated concept. For example, brainstorming activities are used between the proposal and progress reports to help develop search strategies; peer review is used to help students work on identifying gaps in their information that require additional research.

I initially taught the revised course online during summer 2004 and later refined the assignments and activities for both online and onsite sections for spring 2005. This sequencing of assignments works well for course content that is taught in both online and onsite sections. Outcomes, assignments, and course activities are the same; they are simply delivered in different media. For the most part, activities that are done in the classroom during onsite sections are also assigned to the online sections. What differs is the use of technology for interaction between instructors and students and between students. Discussion boards, for example, are used in place of in-class discussions. Assignments such as brainstorming activities are posted in a Blackboard discussion board for feedback and comments from both students and instructor. Over time, I have revised the theme and assignments to allow for instructional flexibility. For fall 2006, instead of linked assignments students worked on a series of shorter assignments in a variety of genres while role playing as small business owners. Their final assignment was to write an annual report for their business. Outcomes for the course remain the same, and the role research plays in the course remains the same as students learn about and use business-related sources. These syllabi and sets of assignments now serve as templates for new instructors hired to teach the course.

In addition to revision of courses already included in the curriculum, development of new courses has been a cornerstone of our efforts. Our first information-related course, "InfoGlut: Deal with It" (now "Information in the Digital Age"), discussed earlier, was developed as an onsite course while I was a librarian collaborating with the MWTC program. Since transitioning into my current position as lecturer, I have moved the course online, where it has become the cornerstone of what we refer to as the information track of our curriculum. One of the challenges of

transferring the course from an in-person course to an online course has been the nature of instruction. Class discussion based on readings is a critical component of the course; transferring the enthusiasm and level of analysis necessary to the online environment has been challenging. One way I have dealt with this challenge is through the use of themes to facilitate understanding in an environment that requires a higher level of responsibility from students to manage their work and participate in course discussion. The use of themes and online instruction has also allowed for the incorporation of additional technologies beyond a course management system. For example, I taught the fall 2004 course using digital rights management as the central theme and asked students to keep blogs focusing on an issue of interest to them related to digital rights management. This theme provided a basis for concentrating on issues of production, dissemination, and use of intellectual property along with issues of access, privacy, and censorship—all topics consistent with ACRL standards included in this course's outcomes. The use of blogs provided students with a communication medium that was, at the time, new and unfamiliar to most of them, which facilitated teaching and learning of information literacy outcomes.

We have added several new courses to the information track to integrate information literacy concepts and standards beyond finding and accessing information. "Intellectual Property and Copyright in the Electronic Environment," "Information and Technology in American History," "Information Architecture," and "What Is Research in Technical Communication?" are all taught online and include components of information literacy, though not necessarily focused on research as their primary outcome. The "Intellectual

Figure 11.2. Intellectual Property and Copyright in the Electronic Environment course syllabus

TWC4/547 Business Reports
Summer 8-Week
June 1 - July 23, 2004

Instructor:
Barbara J. D'Angelo
ASU East Library Services, Center 30A
Phone: 480-727-1160
Email: bdangelo@asu.edu

Office Hours:
Monday. 10:00-Noon
Wednesday., 1:00-3:00
or by appointment

Course Description and Objectives

This course will introduce students to strategies, formats, and techniques of presenting information to business and other workplace audiences.

On completion of this course, students will be able to:

- Identify, organize, and communicate information to fit the audience, purpose, and situation
- Effectively use formats appropriate for business communication such as email, memos, letters, reports
- Find, access, retrieve, and use information from a variety of sources to analyze a problem and develop a solution
- Design effective business documents using appropriate style and visual elements
- Effectively use language, tone, and voice to fit the audience, purpose, and situation

Course Requirements

This is an Internet course. Because it is a summer course, you have much less time to complete work than you would during a regular semester. Read the Course Guidelines and Policies and Course Introduction. Review all information posted in Blackboard. Be sure you understand what will be expected of you.

All assignments are expected to be completed on time. See course evaluation section below for information on grading and Blackboard for information on assignments and due dates.

You will primarily be working on your own to complete assignments. However, you will be sharing a draft of your final report with another student in the class for peer editing and feedback.

Graduate Students: Students registered for graduate credit (TWC547) will complete an additional assignment.

Text

Locker, Kitty O. (2003) *Business and Administrative Communication*, 6th edition. New York: McGraw-Hill.

The text is available in the bookstore. **Be sure to purchase the 6th edition**

Daily Schedule

Refer to the Schedule information in Blackboard.

Assignments

Refer to the Schedule information in Blackboard.

Course Evaluation

TWC447:

Assignment	Value
Email 1	5 points
Audience analysis	5 points
Proposal	10 points
Letter 1	5 points
Memo 1	5 points
Progress Report	10 points
Letter 2	5 points
Letter 3	5 points
Report draft/Peer response	5 points
Powerpoint	5 points
Memo 2	5 points
Job Application Materials	10 points
Problem-solving Report	25 points

Scale	Grade
90-100 points	A
80-89 points	B
70-79 points	C
60-69 points	D
0-59 points	E

TWC547:

In addition to the assignments/scale listed above, students registered for TWC547 will write an additional paper worth 20 points. The scale for final grade will be:

Scale	Grade
108-120 points	A
96-107 points	B
84-95 points	C
72-83 points	D
0-71 points	E

All assignments are to be completed and turned in by the due date listed in the Schedule section of Blackboard. **Late assignments will not be accepted for any reason other than family or medical emergency. If you cannot complete an assignment on time, contact me in** advance of the due date.

Throughout this course, you will be composing documents for a variety of audiences and purposes. Your writing should at all times be professional and consist of proper tone, style, formatting, language, and grammar.

Academic Integrity

As a student in this course you are expected to complete your own work and to properly cite work of others. Refer to the Student Academic Integrity Policy regarding students rights, responsibilities, and obligations.

Last modified: 24 May 2004

Property" course, for example, focuses primarily on an understanding and learning of the legal and ethical use of information of ACRL Standard Five (see figure 11.2). "Information Architecture," on the other hand, focuses on the organization of information and incorporates competencies reflected in ACRL Standards Two and Four.

Instruction

At ASU online courses are taught using a variety of technologies. Blackboard is the standard course management system employed by the university for online courses, but the university also provides access to a wiki and blog service. Our online classes take advantage of the full range of technologies and applications available to us. For example, students enrolled in "What Is Research in Technical Communication?" use a wiki to maintain portfolios for their research projects to articulate and manage their research process, comment on each others' projects, and store documents. The use of a wiki for this purpose facilitates fulfillment of program outcomes in a holistic and integrative way, since students must demonstrate research and writing

Figure 11.3. What Is Research in Technical Communication? Portfolio Assignment Description

TWC494/598 What Is Research in Technical Communication?
Spring 2007

Research Project Portfolio

This semester you will keep a portfolio of all of the documents, tasks, and activities related to your course work and research project. Portfolios are more than mere collections of documents. When done well, they help us to both organize our work and focus on planning and process. The topic of this course--research--is a process. Portfolios, then, are an ideal way to manage our work, reflect upon it, and gather feedback. Instead of distinct assignments that have no relevance to one another, your portfolio should help you connect and integrate tasks and activities as you work on your project so that each is an integral part of completing it.

Project Requirements

Although not all workplace research is formal; by doing a project that requires planning, design, and implementation you will gain the experience and knowledge needed to conduct just about any research project. So, your research project should be one that is formal and substantive. That is, it should be a project of enough depth that it requires planning in order to choose appropriate methods, collect data/information, analyze the data, and prepare a presentation/report. During the first 5 weeks of class, your portfolios entries will include tasks to help you develop a topic/project.

Your project should also be workplace-related. That is, it should not be an academic research projec that results in an academic term paper with the only purpose of finding information about something that only you are interested in. Academic research is important but learning how to write a term paper is not the goal of this course. Your project should have a practical purpose and a real audience.

Alternatively, you may conduct a project which would result in the submission a grant proposal to the Society for Technical Communication. STC is the professional society for technical communicators; it awards research grants each year based on identified areas of concern and interest for the profession. Grant applications, however, must include preliminary research results in order to justify the request for funds. If you are interested in this option, contact me for a copy of the grant guidelines.

The length of your final presentation will depend on your topic, audience, and purpose. However, it should be thorough, demonstrate that you have conducted sound research using multiple methods to gather and/or analyze data, and a discussion that is based on your findings.

Final presentation of your completed project may be either a report, a narrated powerpoint, a video or another medium of your choice. However, the medium you select to submit your completed project must be appropriate for the audience and purpose of the project.

Portfolio Requirements

Your will use your portfolio to store your documents for this project. However, it should go beyond storage; your portfolio should include your reflection or articulation of your thinking about your project.

1. Each week, I will give you a portfolio prompt to guide your entries.
   Responses to prompts are due by **11:00pm on Thursday** of each week.
   Comments/feedback to a minimum of 2 other students' portfolio entries are due by **11:00pm on Sunday** of each week.

   You should consider prompts to be starting points only. You may want to include a section in your portfolio that you use as a journal or log in which you think critically about your own research process: how it's going, what is working well, what is frustrating, what hasn't worked, what questions you have that you need help with. Articulating your thinking and engaging in self-assessment is an important part of your portfolio; it assists with learning, it gives you the opportunity to consider whether or not your work is meeting your goals (and if not, to change before it is too late), and it gives you the chance to express frustrations and ask questions so that others can make suggestions and provide support.

2. You will also be responsible for responding/commenting/providing feedback on portfolio entries to other students. Unless otherwise indicated in the schedule or in course announcements, each week you must contribute to a **minimum of 2 other students' portfolios**. Contributions to other students must be constructive. Be constructive, think critically about your classmates' work, and provide help and assistance. You should consider your contributions to others as having 2 goals. First, it should be helpful. Contributions which state something along the lines of "thanks for the post, you do great work!" may be flattering and even encouraging but they do nothing to help the author improve his/her work. Instead, you should comment on their ideas, their planned methods, answer their questions if there are any, etc. Second, your contributions should at all times be polite and considerate. Telling someone that their ideas or work is wrong is not only rude, it is also insulting. Instead, tell them how they might try to improve it or alternatives to the approaches they are taking. The ultimate goal is to provide feedback that will improve the project. But remember, just like with all editing, reviews, feedback--the decision to accept and incorporate them or not is yours as the researcher.

   As you comment on each other's portfolios, please be sure that everyone has received comments and feedback.

Portfolio Logistics

I have set up a wiki for us to use for portfolios. Your names are posted on the main page of the wiki. Click on your name and it will take you to a new page. The design of your portfolio is up to you; however, consider how you want to both post your work and receive feedback.

I will be contributing my own portfolio as part of the class. In part, to give you a model for using a portfolio for a research project and in part so that you can see that even so-called "experts" struggle with research. Research always has limitations and frustrations; there are factors beyond your control and things happen. It is tempting, especially in a class where you are being evaluated, to present your work as problem-free and as perfect as possible. That is rarely the case, however.

You are welcome to use the same design or format for your own portfolios as I have; however, keep in mind that it is a sample only--you are free to format and design your wiki pages as you choose. You are also welcome to comment on my portfolio (I would, in fact, welcome it) but it will not count as one of your comments for 2 others.

Portfolio Evaluation and Grading

Above I've emphasized that process is an important aspect of using a portfolio. Therefore, you will receive two grades for your portfolio: one for product and one for process.

Product grade: research project (100 pts)
Outcomes measured: R1, R2, R4, C1, C2, K2, K3

- question/hypothesis (20 pts)
- selection, justification of methods (20 pts)
- final report/presentation (60 pts)

Process grade (100 pts)
Outcomes measured: All

Although I will comment on your portfolio entries each week, you will receive formal evaluations 3 times during the semester (weeks 5, 10, 14/15) via email.

Your responses to portfolio prompts and your feedback posts to other students should be thorough and thoughtful. Your process grade will be based on how substantial, thoughtful, and constructive your entries are. In addition, points will automatically be deducted based on the following:

- Failure to respond to a portfolio prompt by the deadline: -5 pts each
- Failure to respond to a minimum of 2 students' portfolio entries: -5 pts each
- Portfolio prompts that are submitted by the deadline but are superficial, contain little content or demonstrate little thought when responding to the question(s) or thinking about the project: -3 pts each
- Responses to other students' entries that are superficial, contain little content or demonstrate little thought and/or are unconstructive: -3 pts each
- Responses to other students' entries that are uncivil, rude, impolite or otherwise violate good citizenship: 0 pts

Last modified: 11 January 2007

Back to syllabus | Email the instructor

processes using a specific technology and within specific rhetorical contexts (see figure 11.3).

A Breeze server facilitates production of course videos that can be built into Blackboard or other course platforms to accommodate different learning styles. I have begun using short videos, for example, in most of my online courses to present short (less than fifteen minutes) lectures to introduce weekly topics. Students have the option of watching the video or reading through the transcript. Further, Wimba has been integrated into the Blackboard course management system so that instructors can now include voice announcements and send voice e-mail as well as text. Fall 2006 saw the introduction of the Sakai course management system as an alternative platform to Blackboard, as well as the introduction of iTunes University for podcasting.

Program Assessment

The MWTC program has used electronic portfolios for assessment since its inception. Portfolios are a well-recognized tool for conducting assessment within the field of rhetoric/writing because they are a direct and authentic measure of both the process and product of student composing. In addition, because students include work from multiple semesters, portfolios allow us to evaluate change and growth in learning. Portfolios are also being recognized and used as an effective way to assess information literacy outcomes related to research.[4]

Our initial evaluation procedures were informal because of our small size in terms of both graduating students and faculty evaluators. Although informal and without hard numbers to back it up, we were able to observe and draw general conclusions from student work, including those related to information literacy. These concerns revolved around the quantity and quality of student research demonstrated in artifacts included in portfolios and the ability of students to organize and use information. Course revisions and new course development described earlier in this chapter were intended and have begun to address concerns raised from this informal evaluation of portfolios.

Our current formalized assessment procedures were implemented in fall 2006 and continue our practice of using electronic portfolios to evaluate student performance based on outcomes including those related to information literacy. Students compose electronic portfolios prior to graduation to demonstrate application of their learning through a persuasive statement in which samples of their work from courses are cited as evidence to support their argument. Students are free to choose the application they believe most appropriate for their portfolio; in this way, their statement and their design of the portfolio are additional demonstrations of their learning.

To work on their portfolios, students enroll in a capstone course conducted online informally in workshop style; that is, students work through a series of tasks to help them think through the purpose of and audience for their portfolio within the context of outcomes and assessment. Students post tasks to a discussion board in Blackboard for feedback and comments from the instructor and other students. The discussion board is also used for posting draft portfolios so that students receive continual feedback and comments as they select their artifacts, write their statements, and complete their portfolio.

Faculty raters evaluate portfolios using a six-point scoring guide derived directly from program outcomes. In a final "showcase" event, students present their portfolios to faculty and fellow students. This presentation is not evaluated; rather, it is a celebration of student accomplishments and represents our way of welcoming them as professionals in our field. On the conclusion of this event, students receive a report consisting of their portfolio scores along with comments from raters. This summative feedback is intended to give students an idea of how well they have demonstrated application of their learning. We also use aggregated data for program improvement to identify which outcomes are strongly evident as well as which are not being met or not being met adequately.

Although we cannot generalize from one semester's results, evaluation of portfolios from the first semester of implementation has highlighted and reinforced some areas of concern from previous semesters' informal assessment. Our goal has been to take a holistic and integrative approach toward information literacy; therefore, we do not assess individual information literacy outcomes or standards. Still, using a holistic approach allows us to evaluate information literacy within a broader, rather than reductionist, context so that we are able to assess students' abilities within the context of direct measure of actual performance and application of learning. Some of our concerns, therefore, are broad in nature and relate specifically to enhancing awareness of outcomes and assessment procedures.

In the specific context of information literacy, however, the greatest concern raised by data generated from the fall 2006 semester is students' difficulty using their own work as evidence for their persuasive statement. Numerous rater comments focused on the lack of evidence presented by students for claims made in their statements. The persuasive statement is a form of argumentation that is a standard academic genre. The ability to support claims through citation of evidence is a key information literacy outcome demonstrated through the ability to integrate information and knowledge. One semester's data is not enough to conclude that there is a broad-based problem; many of the students in this group had not taken new or revised courses. It does, however, give us an awareness of a potential problem area to track over time, and in conjunction with less formal evaluations from previous semesters it provides us with a baseline for future comparison and assessment. One of the more immediate results of our assessment, though, has been the development of the research course referred to earlier to ensure that students are exposed to and applying research strategies and methodologies appropriate to the discipline. This course is currently being taught as a special topics course; we will, however, be proposing its addition as a required program course in the near future.

Lessons Learned

We are generally pleased with our progress to integrate information literacy into the out-

comes and instruction of the MWTC program and the use of online classes for teaching and learning. To date, none of the new information courses added to address information literacy outcomes and standards have been required. Students have multiple options for completing electives and graduation requirements; yet the information courses continue to generate healthy enrollment. In addition to MWTC program majors, we have also seen a steady rise in the number of students from other majors taking our information courses. Clearly the courses are fulfilling a need from the student perspective. We also believe the fact that information-related courses are offered online is a factor, since these courses accommodate students' busy schedules and lives and provides them with flexibility to earn their degrees.

One of the challenges of delivering course content in both online and onsite formats is ensuring consistency across sections taught by multiple instructors and communicating with part-time instructors who are geographically distant. We do not have the luxury of regular faculty meetings in which course goals and content can be discussed and shared. In addition, many of our instructors are practitioners in the technical communication industry rather than traditional tenure-line faculty. To facilitate an understanding of program outcomes, including those related to information literacy, and assessment we have created a program curriculum and assessment wiki (see figure 11.4). The wiki includes documents related to curriculum design and assessment and is open to faculty to post and contribute ideas and feedback. We hope to expand the wiki in coming semesters to include an assignment bank that allows instructors to contribute and share assignments. Assignments could, then, be tagged to indicate how they relate to program outcomes and information literacy. The wiki also serves as a repository and archive that we can refer faculty to when corresponding through e-mail.

In addition, we are using revised syllabi and assignments as templates when hiring new faculty to teach our courses. This accomplishes three goals. First, it encourages faculty to think about outcomes and how their course fits into the overall curriculum so that they are engaging in course design that reflects program goals. Second, it raises awareness of information literacy among faculty who may not be aware of it or have experience integrating it into their courses.

Third, by articulating outcomes on course documents, students are, we hope, better able to understand how courses and course content tie together. This effort has thus far met with some success; some instructors have developed grading rubrics that make explicit to students how their assignments are being evaluated based on assignment and course outcomes within the broader context of program outcomes.

As we have worked on this initiative, we are conscious that we have been learning as we go. We have been learning how best to integrate and implement information literacy within our curriculum, how best to

Figure 11.4. MWTC outcomes and assessment wiki

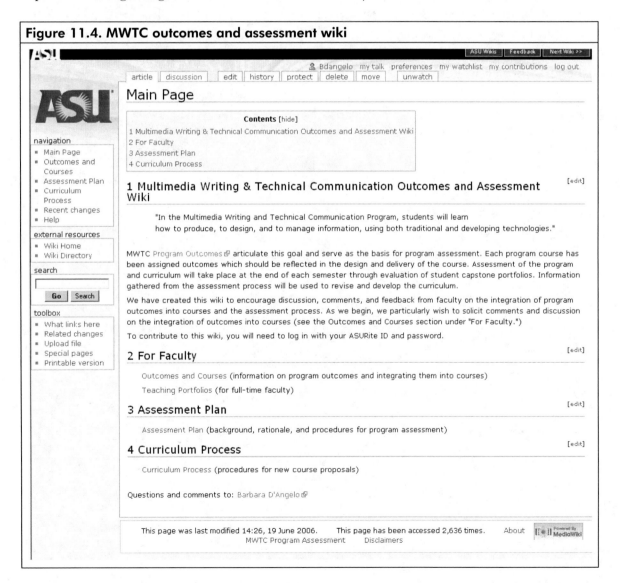

communicate what information literacy is within the context of broader programmatic outcomes, how best to teach it in both onsite and online classes, and how to assess it effectively using electronic portfolios. Over time, we have come to understand that the theoretical basis of integration of information literacy and rhetoric/writing is important to articulate because it facilitates our own understanding and allows us to reinvent teaching and learning in ways that we could not do when thinking of information literacy as a distinct and separate concept. This is best illustrated in the way we are beginning to approach teaching research—as a process that is intimately intertwined with the writing process and rhetorical situation.

Lessons learned do not come without challenges, however. Resources, both human and financial, continue to hamper our efforts, as they do other programs on a campus growing rapidly from the current 6,000 full-time students to a projected 15,000 by 2015. In addition, enhancing communication with distance faculty is a priority to increase awareness of program outcomes and familiarity with our approach to information literacy. E-mail and the curriculum and assessment wiki have facilitated communication; yet we also plan to add initiatives to raise faculty understanding of information literacy through online tutorials and guides.

We recognize, however, that patience may be our biggest lesson learned and biggest challenge. Clearly the momentum from our first information track course has contributed to its ongoing development. As new students enter the MWTC program and take courses, we hope to begin to see continual improvement demonstrated through assessment and research.

Appendix A.
Multimedia Writing and Technical Communication Program, Outcomes Statement
(revised 2000, 2003)

Incorporation of information and technology is in italics.

Rhetorical Knowledge
- Identify, articulate, and focus on a defined purpose
- Respond to the need of the appropriate audience
- Respond appropriately to different rhetorical situations
- Use conventions of format and structure appropriate to the rhetorical situation
- Adopt appropriate voice, tone, and level of formality
- Understand how each genre helps to shape the writing and how readers respond to it
- Write in multiple genres
- *Understand the role of a variety of technologies/media in accessing, retrieving, and communicating information*
- *Select and use appropriate technologies to organize, present, and communicate information to address a range of audiences, purposes, and genres*

Critical Thinking, Reading, and Writing
- Use *information,* writing, and reading for inquiry, learning, thinking, and communicating
- Understand that *research,* like writing, is a series of tasks, *including accessing, retrieving, evaluating, analyzing, and synthesizing appropriate information* from sources that vary in content, format, structure, and scope
- Understand the relationships among language, knowledge, and power including social, cultural, historical, and economic issues related to *information,* writing, and technology
- Recognize, understand, and analyze the context within which language, information, and knowledge are produced, managed, organized, and disseminated
- Integrate previously held beliefs, assumptions, and knowledge with new *information* and the ideas of others to accomplish a specific purpose within a context

Processes
- Be aware that it usually takes multiple drafts to create and complete a successful text
- Develop *research strategies* appropriate to the context and situation
- Develop flexible strategies for generating, revising, editing, and proofreading
- Understand *research* and writing as an open process that permits writers to use later invention and rethinking to revise their work
- Understand the collaborative and social aspects of *research* and writing processes
- Learn to critique their own and others' works
- Learn to balance the advantages of relying on others with the responsibility of doing their part
- Use appropriate technologies to manage information collected or generated for future use

Knowledge of Conventions

- Learn common formats for different genres
- Learn standard tools for accessing and retrieving information
- Learn and apply appropriate standards, laws, policies, and accepted practices for the use of information and communication technologies
- Develop knowledge of genre conventions ranging from structure and paragraphing to tone and mechanics
- Apply appropriate means of documenting their work
- Control such surface features as syntax, grammar, punctuation, and spelling
- Understand and apply legal and ethical uses of information and technology including copyright and intellectual property

Appendix B. MWTC Curriculum Matrix

TWC CURRICULUM MAP--November 2005
Core Outcomes for Each Program Course

	200	301	351	400	401	403	411	421	431	443	444	445	446	447	451	452	453	454	INFOARCH
Rhetorical Knowledge																			
R1: Identify, articulate, and focus on a defined purpose	X	X		X	X	X						X	X	X					X
R2: Respond to the need of the appropriate audience	X	X		X	X	X						X	X	X		X	X		X
R3: Respond appropriately to different rhetorical situations	X	X		X	X								X	X					X
R4: Use conventions of format and structure appropriate to the rhetorical situation		X	X	X	X						X	X	X	X					X
R5: Adopt appropriate voice, tone, and level of formality		X	X	X	X	X							X	X					X
R6: Understand how each genre helps to shape the writing and how readers respond to		X		X	X			X						X		X	X		
R7: Write in multiple genres		X		X	X									X					
R8: Understand the role of a variety of technologies/media in accessing, retrieving, and communicating information	X	X			X										X	X	X	X	X
R9: Use appropriate technologies to organize, present, and communicate information to address a range of audiences, purposes, and genres		X		X	X		X	X	X			X	X	X		X			X
Critical Thinking, Reading & Writing																			
CRW1: Use information, writing, and reading for inquiry, learning, thinking, and communicating	X	X		X	X					X	X	X			X	X	X	X	X
CRW2: Understand that research, like writing, is a series of tasks, including accessing, retrieving, evaluating, analyzing, and synthesizing appropriate information from sources that vary in content, format, structure, and scope					X					X			X	X		X	X	X	
CRW3: Understand the relationships among language, knowledge, and power including social, cultural, historical, and economic issues related to information, writing, and technology	X							X						X	X	X	X	X	
CRW4: Recognize, understand, and analyze the context within which language, information, and knowledge are produced, managed, organized, and disseminated							X	X							X	X	X	X	
CRW5: Integrate previously held beliefs, assumptions, and knowledge with new information and the ideas of others to accomplish a specific purpose within a context	X	X		X				X		X			X	X	X	X	X	X	
Processes																			
P1: Be aware that it usually takes multiple drafts to create and complete a successful text		X	X		X	X			X	X	X	X	X						X
P2: Develop research strategies appropriate to the context and situation				X		X				X			X	X		X	X	X	
P3: Develop flexible strategies for generating, revising, editing, and proof-reading		X	X		X				X	X	X	X	X			X	X	X	
P4: Understand research and writing as an open process that permits writers to use later invention and re-thinking to revise their work				X		X				X			X			X	X	X	
P5: Understand the collaborative and social aspects of research and writing processes	X	X		X					X							X			
P6: Learn to critique their own and others' works					X				X					X					
P7: Learn to balance the advantages of relying on others with the responsibility of doing their part					X				X					X					
P8: Use appropriate technologies to manage information collected or generated for future use		X		X					X				X						X
Knowledge of Conventions																			
KC1: Learn common formats for different genres		X			X				X					X					
KC2: Learn standard tools for accessing and retrieving information				X	X							X	X	X		X	X	X	
KC3: Learn and apply appropriate standards, laws, policies, and accepted practices for the use of a variety of technologies	X			X	X		X	X			X	X		X	X	X			X
KC4: Develop knowledge of genre conventions ranging from structure and paragraphing to tone and mechanics		X		X	X						X	X	X	X			X	X	X
KC5: Apply appropriate means of documenting their work	X			X		X				X	X			X	X	X			X
KC6: Control such surface features as syntax, grammar, punctuation, and spelling			X	X	X								X	X					
KC7: Understand and apply legal and ethical uses of information and technology including copyright and intellectual property	X		X				X	X	X					X	X	X	X	X	X
KC8: Understand and apply appropriate standards for use of technology including accessibility							X	X						X					X

Notes

1. Rolf Norgaard, "Writing Information Literacy in the Classroom: Pedagogical Enactments and Implications," *Reference & User Services Quarterly* 43, no. 3 (2004): 220–26.

2. Multimedia Writing and Technical Communication Program, Arizona University System Request for Implementation Authorization for New Academic Degree Program (Mesa, AZ: Arizona State University, 2000).

3. Barry M. Maid, "Using the Outcomes Statement for Technical Communication," in *The Outcomes Book: Debate and Consensus after the WPA Outcomes Statement,* edited by Susanmarie Harrington, Keith Rhodes, Ruth Overman Fischer, and Rita Malenczyk, 139–49 (Logan: Utah State University Press, 2005).

4. Margaret Fast and Jeanne Armstrong, "The Course Portfolio in a Library Setting," *Research Strategies* 19 (2003): 46–56; Claire McGuinness and Michelle Brien, "Using Reflective Journals to Assess the Research Process," *Reference Services Review* 35, no. 1 (2007): 21–40; Loanne L. Snavely and Carol A. Wright, "Research Portfolio Use in Undergraduate Honors Education: Assessment Tool and Model for Future Work," *Journal of Academic Librarianship* 29, no. 5 (2003): 298–303.

12. Providing Online Information Literacy Instruction to Nontraditional Distance Learning Engineering Students

Kathryn Kennedy

Rationale

The University of Florida (UF) educates more than 50,000 students and lays claim to $490 million in research and training grants per year. An estimated $90 million of this money goes to the College of Engineering, a powerhouse in innovation and technology. The College of Engineering's mission is to "provide world-class engineering education, research and service that enhance the economic and social well-being of the citizens of Florida, the nation and the world."[1] The college has eleven departments, six of which offer graduate degrees online through EDGE, the Electronic Delivery of Graduate Engineering. EDGE is the College of Engineering's distance learning program. It offers nine master of science degrees and two graduate credit-based certificates entirely online.

EDGE has unique dynamics because of the program's uniqueness, and there are challenges and opportunities in providing library services. Generally speaking, the UF Libraries offer the following services to distance learning students:

Interlibrary loan (ILL). Locates and borrows materials not owned by UF Libraries; sends UF-owned books directly to student/faculty members

Remote logon. Provides off-campus access to the UF Libraries' electronic resources

Ask-a-Librarian. Instant message/chat with a librarian

E-mail reference. E-mail a librarian

Subject specialist. Librarian who is knowledgeable about subject area and its resources

Subject guides. Guides designed by the subject specialist that emphasize the key resources in the subject area

Databases by subject. List of databases that provide the best coverage of the subject area

Library instruction. Class or part of a class that explains library resources

Web tutorials. Short videos/presentations demonstrating how to use library resources

Electronic reserves (Course reserves). Service that allows faculty to put articles and book chapters on the Web so students can access them easily

Aside from the services mentioned above, the UF Libraries pursue and acquire materials for the "instructional, research, and service needs of its faculty and students."[2] Because of a multitude of recent technological advances, collections, communications, and instructions are steadily migrating to electronic format. Consequently, online information literacy has become an effective way to reach distance learning students in the virtual classroom, and the UF Libraries' Instruction Committee is aware of this. They encourage all UF librarians to reach out to distance learning students through many technological means.

When I first joined the UF Libraries in August of 2005, I was assigned to the EDGE program. The first item on my agenda was to identify my users and their needs. To do this, I spoke with the College of Engineering; the information they provided, however, did not speak to the information needs of the students. I was also invited to give presentations about distance learning library services to the EDGE faculty during their fall 2005 and spring 2006 EDGE orientations. These orientations offered me a fifteen-minute time slot with no room for questions, so it was impossible to discuss the information needs of the students.

So, I decided to formulate and administer a needs assessment survey (using Survey Monkey, www.surveymonkey.com) to students and faculty during February 2006, asking the age-old question, "What do you know/not know about the library services we provide you?" (see appendices A and B for the full surveys). The results showed that 85 percent of faculty and 86 percent of students had no idea what resources were available. At this point, I knew I had my work cut out for me, so I started by fully defining my users, which eventually set the parameters for the development of the instruction plan.

Development

As mentioned above, when developing any type of instruction, it is good to get to know the users. I made appointments with EDGE staff and faculty to see what they thought would be most useful for students to know. The information attained from these informal discussions and the qualitative answers from the student and faculty surveys increased my understanding of EDGE users' needs. From the staff I received demographics. EDGE students are working professionals with full-time careers in engineering. They pursue their master's degrees part-time and take, on average, two-and-a-half years to complete their degrees. In spring 2006, 256 students were

enrolled in EDGE. They work at 78 different companies including Lockheed Martin, Boeing, Motorola, Microsoft, and all divisions of the U.S. military and reside in thirteen states with a majority (ca 70 percent) in Florida.

From the EDGE faculty I gained an understanding of the information-seeking behaviors of engineers. Engineers have a characteristic way of searching for information: they are practical, working to find solutions to problems. They are do-it-yourselfers who like to try things for themselves and tend to avoid asking others for help. If they ask for help, they do not want a stack of information to sift through; they want only what they asked for. Most of the time they are looking for datasets, which can be found in scientific handbooks, standards, and technical reports. Once they find information, they share it. Knowledge sharing in the field of engineering thrives via electronic technology; everyone shares for the betterment of the group. Students are technologically savvy but may not understand how to locate the best information, so they need to use subject-specific databases that provide proprietary scientific information. Most of these students have been out of school more than ten years and may not know the technologies now offered by university libraries. Because of this, some faculty suggested I help students find the most powerful and effective tools for retrieving exact information. They felt this assistance was crucial, considering EDGE students' distance from campus.

From the needs assessment surveys I found that most of the students have library services available through their place of employment but that, if they could not find the information they needed from their corporate library, they wanted to know how to use the UF Libraries' services. They especially wanted tutorials for every library service and subject-specific database, explaining how to navigate to and use the services and databases effectively. Faculty said they did not promote library services in their courses unless it was for an assignment. Since such assignments were rare, promotion of library services was also rare. They mentioned that students did not voice concerns about library services and that they felt students did not need to know about library services unless the library was needed for course purposes. At the same time, students reported that they wanted to know about library services even if they did not need them for their course(s). There was a disconnect between what the students wanted and what faculty thought the students wanted.

Another issue that surfaced in the survey was that both students and faculty are busy. As mentioned above, students are full-time professionals attending school part-time. They have multiple responsibilities outside of school, including family and other business. The faculty are also busy, teaching not only online courses but traditional campus courses, publishing papers, presenting at conferences, managing research groups, working with graduate students, serving on committees at the department, college, and university levels, and volunteering for community service. Needless to say, the students and faculty are highly motivated, extremely busy, sometimes to the point of overcommitment. Putting another task on their agendas would just add to their burden.

Besides being busy, EDGE patrons have the problem of information overload, which runs rampant in engineering. With the field's tendency to be cross-disciplinary, students not only have to look for information in their primary field, they also have to look at the research being published in related fields such as physics, chemistry, and envi-

ronmental sciences. One student shared his frustrations about information overload, noting the lack of standardization of terms. He explained that different disciplines may refer to the same process or research area with two different terms. This leads him and other graduate students to experience searcher anxiety, worrying if they have retrieved all relevant results. So my primary goal when developing the instruction plan was to avoid information overload by teaching students the most effective ways to search.

At this point in the process, I was feeling overloaded myself but also overjoyed, because I had all this helpful information to work with. I knew it was time to develop the instruction plan. So I met with the EDGE staff to determine the best way to approach the instruction development. The director was supportive about integrating me into the classes, but I explained to her the results of the survey in regard to the faculty not wanting library services included unless they were necessary to complete an assignment. Since faculty did not want to include library services in their virtual classroom in a course-integrated way, I told her that I needed another way to share library services. I also explained that I needed an instruction plan that was nonintrusive on the users' time and something that was easily accessible.

Since I still wanted to be integrated into the courses, the director outlined the EDGE course set up for me. The courses are managed in WebCT. The lectures are recorded, rendered as streaming video, and posted to WebCT, where students can access the course content. The course management system also has chat, e-mail, and bulletin board capabilities to enhance course communication. There are also folders in which the course instructor can organize documents. The faculty set up their courses in the EDGE template. The template is available so faculty do not have to worry about designing their courses. All they have to do is input their content.

After a few meetings with the director, we determined that the best approach would be to make a general library services course called the "Library Lounge." This course would be embedded in all EDGE courses at the start of each semester, beginning in fall 2006. The EDGE broadcasting coordinator suggested I take WebCT courses to become familiar with the WebCT interface and also learn how to design a course, so I took two WebCT courses during spring 2006 offered by UF's Center for Instructional Technology and Training. After taking the courses, I asked the WebCT coordinator if I could have a course set up within the EDGE template. Then I started designing the Library Lounge based on the content I wanted the EDGE students to learn.

Content

The content for the Library Lounge had to be general because students are in many different disciplines, including civil and coastal engineering, computer and information sciences and engineering, electrical and computer engineering, environmental engineering sciences, mechanical and aerospace engineering, and materials science and engineering. I decided that general engineering databases had to be included in addition to those that were discipline-specific. These included Web of Science, Compendex (Engineering Index), Cambridge Scientific Abstracts (CSA), IEEE/IEE Electronic Library (IEL), Knovel, ASM Handbooks Online, and SciFinder Scholar. I also wanted to include explanations of the library services. So as soon as I knew what content I wanted the students to learn, it was time to determine the methods to use to deliver the instruction.

Instruction

The instructional delivery methods could not be traditional when it came to the Library Lounge. The content I wanted to convey to students wasMsuitable for delivery through online tutorials. I made online tutorials for each of the engineering databases, including IEL, CSA, Compendex, and ASM Handbooks Online. Some are interactive and some didactic, and all were made using Camtasia. Tutorials for Knovel, Web of Science, and SciFinder Scholar already existed, so I added links to those. Figure 12.1 shows the engineering databases module.

These tutorials were designed to help students identify the best databases to use for their subject area and to learn the search strategies of the databases. For example, in the IEL tutorials viewers are shown how to access the database, what the database contains, and also how to search it effectively using Boolean operators, truncation symbols, and so forth. Figure 12.2 shows the tutorial for using alternate terms to maximize search results.

The different library services were explained during the most important tutorial for the students—a "how-to" video about getting started at UF Libraries. The EDGE broadcast coordinator also invited me to the EDGE studio to record a video of me presenting library services information. This fifteen-minute streaming video—"Getting to Know the Library Resources"—presents the purpose, location, and contents of the Library Lounge. It is also a way for students to make a personal connection between my name and my face. These two videos are available in the Getting Started folder within the Library Lounge, the layout of which is displayed in figure 12.3.

Figure 12.1. Library Lounge, engineering databases

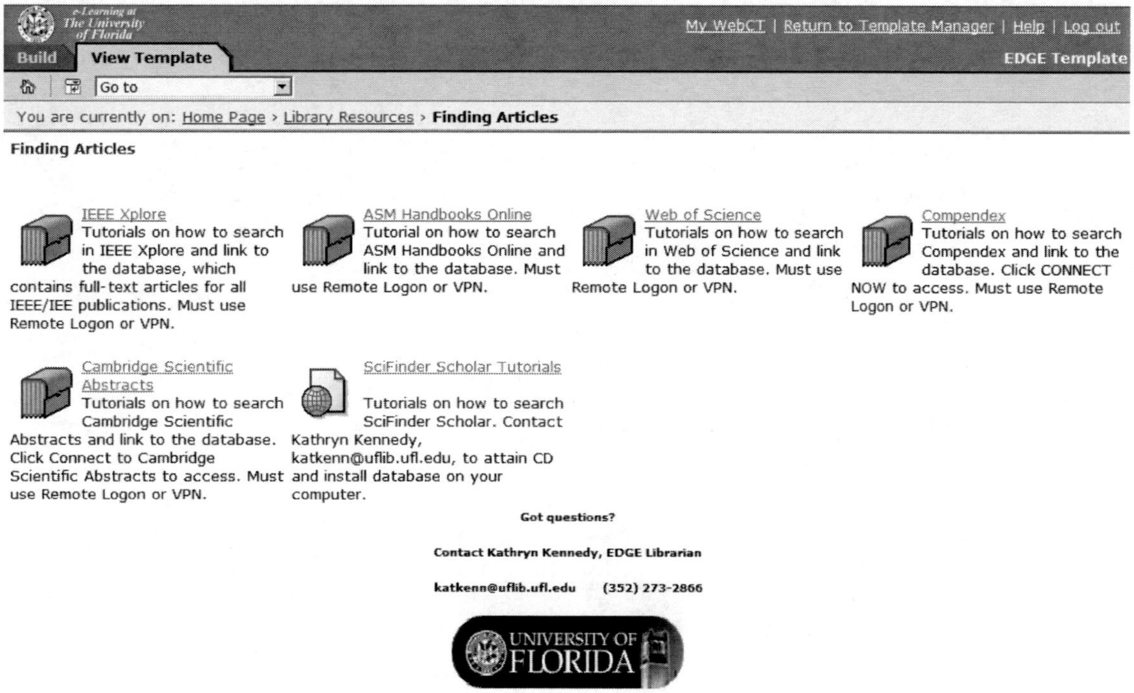

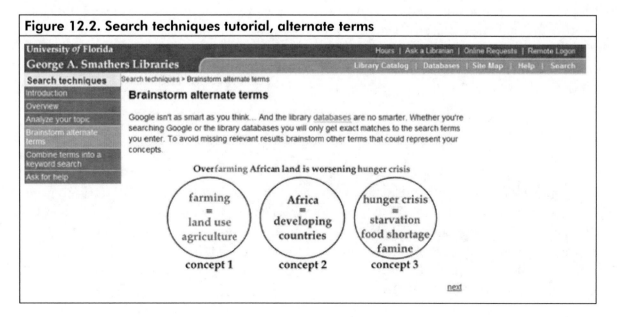

At the beginning of the fall 2006 semester, I sent EDGE students an introductory e-mail to tell them about the Library Lounge. In addition to e-mails, Web-based information on the EDGE site and printed brochures are also used to promote the Library Lounge.

Because these students are busy, I try to send a minimal amount of e-mail to them, about three to four a semester, including the introductory e-mail mentioned above. These provide a way to present new research tools. I also use e-mail to promote current awareness services, commonly known as alerting

Figure 12.2. Search techniques tutorial, alternate terms

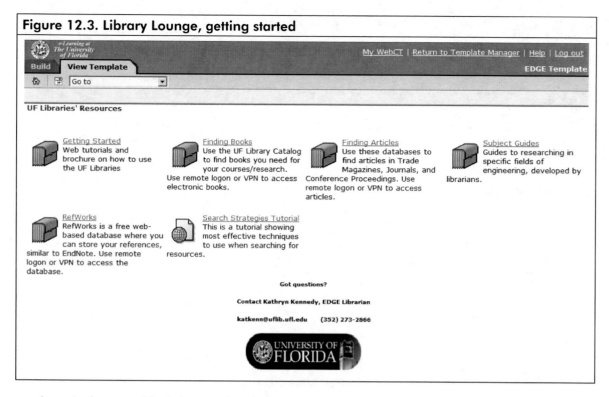

Figure 12.3. Library Lounge, getting started

services, in hopes of helping students keep information overload somewhat at bay. By creating the Library Lounge, I found a way to deliver library services in a noncredit-based way, allowing for easy information access.

Program Assessment

Now that it is complete, is the Library Lounge effective? EDGE patrons mainly use these tutorials to acclimate themselves with the databases in order to perform effective searches, rather than take a test or do an assignment. Do these tutorials meet the needs of these patrons?

Over the course of eight months, after collaborating with many people on campus, I have managed to make vast headway in reaching the EDGE students and faculty. The problems encountered thus far have been minimal, since I planned extensively ahead of time. Informally, I have received e-mail from a few students and faculty about the Library Lounge expressing its helpfulness.

I plan to run an assessment survey in May 2007 (using Survey Monkey) to assess the usefulness of this online information literacy program. This survey will include questions associated with the ACRL Information Literacy Competency Standards.[3] I use these standards to ensure that on-campus learners attain what they need to be successful at locating, evaluating, and using information effectively, and I would like to ensure the same for EDGE patrons.

Lessons Learned

The Library Lounge now serves as a portal, customized to cater to the needs of the EDGE students. The portal is convenient because everything—coursework and library resources—is accessed from the same place. During the development of the Library Lounge, I found a few roadblocks that needed to be fixed and detours that needed to be taken. In the future, I would like to have the opportunity to integrate myself into EDGE WebCT courses in a credit-based way, as I have been able to do in some of my on-campus courses. Looking at the EDGE courses' syllabi and analyzing the students' learning objectives might help me do this.

Currently, EDGE faculty can opt out if they do not want the Library Lounge in their courses. None of the faculty has done this yet, and I am hoping that is because the Lounge's presence has enticed students to use the libraries, which in turn has also signaled faculty to promote library services. If a faculty member ever asks to opt out of having the Library Lounge in his/her WebCT course, I can use ABET, the Accreditation Board for Engineering and Technology, as leverage, since information literacy is part of their accreditation standards. I think the faculty have chosen not to opt out because the link to the Library Lounge does not require them to do anything, and I am the one responsible for its upkeep. If I were to try to integrate myself into their course curriculum, that would be cause for faculty to become more involved, but to this point there has been no request for such involvement. For

library instruction services to be successful, approval is needed from departmental administration. The faculty are key in promoting the new tools.

In spring 2007, I plan to approach Library Lounge evaluation in a more formal way by adding page-hit statistics using Stat Counter, since WebCT did not provide usage statistics during the fall 2006 semester, and making all the tutorials more interactive so students can track their own learning. As of now, all the interactive tutorials are self-assessing only. If I do integrate myself into the course curriculum, I would modify the tutorials so that I can see and note students' progress.

In the future, I would like to collaborate with EDGE on a program-wide orientation that includes library services. Overall, it has been these collaborative efforts that have contributed to the making of the Library Lounge. The Libraries, EDGE, and Academic Technology helped to create the Library Lounge, and I count on the spring 2007 assessment survey demonstrating its goal of online information literacy to be a success.[4]

Appendix A.
UF EDGE Students, Library Survey

The purpose of this survey is to assess your thoughts on UF Libraries and our efforts to accommodate the UF EDGE Program. The answers will be used to evaluate and modify library services. These results may be used for future publications/presentations on the effectiveness of library services for distance learning programs.

1. Do you know what services the library provides distance learners?
   □ Yes
   □ No
   □ Not applicable
   □ I don't know

2. Below is a list of the services the library provides distance learners. Please indicate which services you have used:
   □ Remote Logon
   □ Interlibrary Loan/Document Delivery
   □ Ask-A-Librarian (Chat Reference Service)
   □ E-mail Reference
   □ Subject Specialist
   □ Subject Guides
   □ Databases by Subject
   □ Library Instruction
   □ Web Tutorials
   □ Electronic Reserves (Course Reserves)

3. In regard to the services you *have used,* what do you find most convenient? Most inconvenient? Please explain.

4. In regard to the services you have not used, what is the main reason for not using these services?

5. Below is a list of databases geared to engineering disciplines. Please indicate which databases you have used:
   □ Web of Science
   □ INSPEC
   □ Compendex (Engineering Index)
   □ Cambridge Scientific Abstracts
   □ IEEE/IEE Electronic Library (IEL)
   □ JCR Web—Journal Citation Reports on the Web
   □ SciFinder Scholar
   □ Kirk-Othmer Encyclopedia of Chemical Technology
   □ Crossfire

6. Which of the databases above would you like Web tutorials for?

7. Would you like to have library instruction sent to you via the Web as a component of your course(s)?
   □ Yes
   □ No
   □ Not applicable
   □ I don't know

8. Are you a working professional/non-traditional student?
   □ Yes
   □ No
   □ Not applicable
   □ I don't know

9. If so, do you use any of these resources in your work environment?
   □ Yes
   □ No
   □ Not applicable
   □ I don't know

10. Please discuss any other concerns you have in regard to library services.

Thank you for taking the time to fill this out!

Appendix B.
UF EDGE Faculty, Library Survey

The purpose of this survey is to assess your thoughts on UF Libraries and our efforts to accommodate the UF EDGE Program. The answers will be used to evaluate and modify library services. These results may be used for future publications/presentations on the effectiveness of library services for distance learning programs.

11. Do you know what services the library provides distance learners?
   ☐ Yes
   ☐ No

12. Below is a list of the services the library provides distance learners. Do you promote any of the following library services to your students? Check all boxes that apply.
   ☐ Interlibrary Loan/Document Delivery
   ☐ Remote Logon
   ☐ Ask-A-Librarian (Chat Reference Service)
   ☐ Email Reference
   ☐ Subject Specialist
   ☐ Subject Guides
   ☐ Databases by Subject
   ☐ Library Instruction
   ☐ Web Tutorials
   ☐ Electronic Reserves (Course Reserves)

13. Do your students ask you about library services?
   ☐ Yes
   ☐ No

14. Have any students voiced their concern to you about library services? If so, what were their concerns?
   ☐ Yes
   ☐ No

15. Would you be willing to place a link on your course(s) page(s) to the Library Distance Learning page?
   ☐ Yes
   ☐ No
   ☐ Not applicable
   ☐ I don't know

16. Would you be willing to have library instruction added to your course(s) (30 minutes per semester)?

☐ Yes
☐ No
☐ Not applicable
☐ I don't know

17. Please discuss any other concerns you have in regard to library services.

Thank you for taking the time to fill this out!

Notes

1.   University of Florida College of Engineering home page. Available online at http://www.eng.ufl.edu/about/index.php.

2.   George A. Smathers Libraries, *2005–2006 Library Goals*. Available online at http://web.uflib.ufl.edu/admin/toolbox/goals_obj_sum0506.pdf.

3.   Association of College and Research Libraries, *Information Literacy Competency Standards for Higher Education* (Chicago: ACRL, 2000). Available online at http://www.ala.org/ala/acrl/acrlstandards/informationliteracycompetency.htm.

4.   I wish to acknowledge explicitly the assistance received from the staff of the EDGE program, Director Mary Bonhomme, and coordinator Ruth Bryant, who provided statistics on the EDGE program.

Information Literacy Instruction Tutorials (General and Subject-Specific)

13. Smart Searching: An Easily Customizable Subject-Specific Online Information Literacy Tutorial

Eric Resnis and Jen-chien Yu

Rationale

Because of the popularity of online resources and search engines, Miami University Libraries (Oxford, Ohio) have developed various instructional materials for students to become skilled at navigating through the online world. In particular, the Libraries created E-learn, an online interactive information literacy tutorial for all first-year students.[1] E-learn was piloted in 2002 and completed in fall 2003, with five learning modules: Understanding Information, Finding Books, Finding Articles, Finding News Information, and Searching the Internet.

In 2003, the life sciences librarian (since retired) and an Electronic Information Services (EIS) librarian started developing a new online information literacy tutorial specifically for students in introductory-level science courses. The idea of the new science tutorial came from the life sciences librarian's participation in a task force formed by life sciences and writing center faculty. The task force was charged to revamp the laboratory component for multisection courses BMZ 115 (Biological Concepts: Ecology, Evolution, Genetics, and Diversity) and BMZ 116 (Biological Concepts: Structure, Function, Cellular, and Molecular Biology). The new laboratory components would not only "freshen" the experiment protocols but also include information to improve students' writing ability and lab report proficiency.

For most students, BMZ 115 and BMZ 116 are the first scientific courses they take in college. The courses have intense syllabi filled with labs and assignments almost every week. Additionally, the courses are considerably large: more than eight-hundred students and thirty to thirty-five lab sections. Therefore, it was clear to the life sciences librarian that delivering the instruction online would fit into the course design better. The BMZ 115/116 faculty could easily incorporate the tutorial as part of an assignment, and the students could take it independently outside of the class.

Why did we develop a new tutorial while there were E-learn and other online tutorials? E-learn introduces students to basic college-level information literacy skills, which can be utilized in any discipline or students' personal and professional lives. E-learn was, however, created with a "one size fits all" approach. Its content is extremely broad in scope, yet it does not cover specific resources or examples related to scientific research. E-learn is also limited by nature in terms of addressing the needs of a specific class or its assignments, which makes it difficult to be adopted by the faculty and students.

Through a new tutorial, we expected not only to fulfill the needs of BMZ 115/116 faculty and students but also to weave in new features. We envisioned that the new tutorial could be used as a template and foundation for science librarians to create subject-specific tutorials. For example, an engineering librarian should be able to adopt the tutorial and customize it for any engineering course. We also envisioned the tutorial to be a shared resource created and maintained by the entire user community, which includes students, faculty, and librarians.

The new tutorial—Smart Searching: Finding, Citing & Evaluating Information—created by the engineering librarian, EIS librarian, and former life sciences librarian, has three versions:

• BMZ 115: Biological Concepts: Ecology, Evolution, Genetics, and Diversity/ BMZ 116: Biological Concepts: Structure, Function, Cellular, and Molecular Biology (http://elearn.lib.muohio.edu/science/ bmz). These are cross-listed courses offered by the departments of botany, microbiology, and zoology. They are prerequisites for upper-level science courses. Each year thirty to thirty-five sections are offered with a total enrollment of approximately 800 students.

• EAS 101: Computing, Engineering & Society (http://elearn.lib.muohio.edu/science/eas). This first-year course is required for computer science and engineering students. There are eight sections each year (about 350 students), and the majority of the sections are offered in the fall semester.

• EAS 102: Problem Solving & Design (http://elearn.lib.muohio.edu/science/ eas102). This is a three-credit course for engineering students only; it is based on problem solving and design. It is also a multisection course with large enrollment (about 160 students).

Development

The entire development process of Smart Searching: Finding, Citing & Evaluating Information can be divided into three phases.

Phase I: BMZ 115/116

Beginning in the 2003/4 school year, the life sciences librarian and EIS librarian created the first version of the tutorial. As noted previously, the demand for the tutorial was generated by a task force with a mission of revamping the laboratory component of the course and, in so doing, strengthening students' writing abilities and improving the quality of their lab reports.

Students in BMZ 115/116 complete weekly labs, with lab reports due the following week. Often the assignments require students to conduct literature research and apply the literature to their own findings. The life sciences librarian and other librarians who worked with science students had observed that the students often had trouble finding peer-reviewed and relevant journal articles. The insufficient information often led to a lower-quality lab report. In addition, it was noted that the students were not clear about how to cite sources used in their lab reports.

The tutorial was first named "Information Resources Online Tutorial," a self-paced tutorial that was available 24/7 via the Web. It was launched in the fall semester of 2004. The tutorial consisted of two instructional modules: Finding Articles, and Citing Sources. The life sciences librarian identified these two modules because they covered the most essential skills that students needed (and lacked) to complete the lab report assignments. She wrote content for the two modules and the EIS librarian transformed them into HTML Web pages.

During this phase, librarians also looked at information literacy tutorials designed by other academic libraries for ideas to utilize in our tutorial. Research101, a U*Will* online tutorial designed by the University of Washington Libraries (www.lib.washington. edu/uwill/research101), was particularly inspiring. We found its way of demonstrating information literacy concepts through graphics and interactive Web-based games to be concise, effective, and user-friendly. The U*Will* team also graciously shared the source files with us, which jump-started our development process.

The librarians decided to create multimedia components, such as animation or interactive games, to help illustrate some information literacy concepts. We used Macromedia Fireworks to create an animated demonstration of how the Boolean operators make effective searches. To tie in with the BMZ lectures, the keywords we used in the demonstration were "*corn* AND *genetics*," "*daphnia* OR *water flea*," and "*plants* NOT *trees*."

We also used TechSmith's Camtasia Studio to create a screen recording of the steps to access research databases from the library's Web site. We then converted the screen recording to a QuickTime video clip and embedded it in the online tutorial. These multimedia components were tested on all browsers on both Mac and PC platforms. The components were light-weight and didn't take long to load or require an extra plug-in to view.

Phase II: Tutorial Refresh with an Administrative Interface

By the end of spring semester 2005, the first version of the tutorial had been running for approximately a year. We decided that a refresh was due. The refresh was in conjunction with the addition of the engineering librarian to the group. A new section of the tutorial was developed for EAS 101, a first-year course for computer sciences and engineering students.

EAS 101 is in many ways analogous to BMZ 115/116. It has high enrollment with multiple sections. Additionally, EAS 101 is only a one-credit course. Though faculty members were interested in integrating information literacy into the course, there just wasn't time for library instruction in a class that meets only fifty minutes a week.

Since the tutorial specifically for BMZ 115/116 was already in place, the engineering librarian presented the tutorial to EAS 101 faculty and pitched the idea of having an online tutorial instead of classroom instruction. He explained that the tutorial could be easily customized and retooled for EAS 101 faculty and students. The faculty was very supportive of the idea.

During this phase the expanded group first worked to refresh and revise the two learning modules that already existed. This involved improving wording and flow of the tutorial content as well as navigation of the content. We also identified portions of the tutorial that could be utilized for both the BMZ 115/116 and EAS 101 sections and portions that had to be revised significantly for engineering and computer sciences students. For example, we swapped keywords used to demonstrate the Boolean logic to "*emotional* AND *machine*," "*car* OR *automobile*," and "*saturn* NOT *car*."

At this point the volume of content in the tutorial increased significantly. The amount of time required for maintaining the tutorial also increased. In response, the EIS librarian created an administrative interface that allowed the life sciences librarian and engineering librarian to edit their own sections of the tutorial online. The administrative interface was created with PHP (scripting language) and MySQL (database management system). Though this administrative interface was simple and had minimal features, it helped distribute the workload among the librarians. In addition, we transformed the tutorial into a shareable resource that librarians could customize for any science course with minimal work, which was an initial goal of the project.

The tutorial was designed to be updated easily, but it, as most online tutorials, is more static than dynamic. A problem that came up with the BMZ 115/116 section of the tutorial was the variation in lab assignments each week. Search techniques in the tutorial could be applied to all lab reports, but it was impossible to include tips, such as suggestions for search terms, for each specific lab. The solution we came up with was to integrate a blog into the tutorial using WordPress (http://wordpress.org). We also used the blog to communicate real-time information, such as database outages, with faculty and students.

We also designed three more learning modules for EAS 101 after the refresh was complete: Finding Books, Finding Web Information, and Evaluating Information. We also gave the tutorial a new name, "Smart Searching: Finding, Citing & Evaluating Information."

Phase III: EAS 101 Final Quiz and EAS 102

One mistake we made during Phase II was being overly confident about the time we had to finish all the learning modules for the EAS 101 section. Though we worked feverishly, we didn't finish all of the modules before the fall semester of 2005, as we had planned. We changed the target deadline for the EAS 101 section to fall 2006 so that we could impact the majority of first-year engineering and computer science students. The extra year gave us time to complete all modules intended for EAS 101 and to incorporate other components that introduced library services and resources outside the scope of the tutorial.

One of the major tasks of this phase was the development of an online quiz for the EAS 101 section. As designed, the quiz consisted of five questions to assess students' learning outcomes and three questions to gather user feedback after using the tutorial. The students would need to log in with their unique university user IDs and passwords before taking the quiz.

The final quiz was designed with PHP and MySQL. Each student would be given different questions randomly selected from a set of questions developed by the engineering librarian. We stored all questions in a MySQL database and created a PHP script to randomize the questions. The display order of the questions was also randomized. We employed this mechanism specifically to prevent students from sharing quiz answers with each other. This was also a way to demonstrate the importance of academic integrity, as we had presented in the Citing Sources module. The quiz results of each student would be kept in the MySQL database for grading and assessment.

Development of the final quiz was finished in the fall semester of 2006. It received positive reviews from some engineering faculty, although some faculty didn't require students to take it, choosing instead to offer extra credit for those who completed the tutorial. This, however, sparked another conversation to make the tutorial part of the bibliographic instruction of EAS 102. Available in spring 2007, the EAS 102 section was designed to be used (and required) as a pre-lab in which students can learn basic information literacy skills before attending the formal library instruction session.

Content

The online tutorial is designed with a two-column Web page layout, with navigation on the left-hand side (figure 13.1). Below, we describe tutorial content by first going through the main content (center of each Web page) and then the content along with the navigation on the left.

Main Content

The tutorial content is based on the Smart Searching initiative created by several Miami University science librarians in late 2004. The purpose of the Smart Searching initiative was to create instruction materials to equip users with the information literacy skills needed to search the literature effectively. Results of the initiative include a set of handouts focused on topics such as Boolean logic and truncation and one-hour workshops that introduce library research and skills.

The tutorial currently consists of five learning modules: Finding Books, Finding Articles, Citing Sources, Searching for Web Information, and Evaluating Information. Each module is divided into four areas: Introduction, Tools, Techniques, and Practice.

The Introduction gives a brief overview of the module (including learning objectives)

and how a module connects to students' classes or assignments. As indicated in its title, the Tools area shows the tools (indexes, research databases, Web sites, etc.) that can be utilized for meeting the learning objectives of each module. Techniques shows effective and helpful methods for utilizing the tools presented previously in Tools. For example, the Finding Articles module features truncation and Boolean logic in the Techniques section, because they are essential for students to perform searches in EB-SCO*host*'s Academic Search Premier, which is introduced in Tools.[2] Meanwhile, in the Techniques section of the Evaluating Information module we give specific guidelines and hints for effectively examining Web pages. At the end of each module, a Practice area reinforces concepts presented in the other sections of the tutorial.

The Finding Articles module, used by BMZ 115/116, EAS 101, and EAS 102, is designed for students to learn how to search for scholarly, peer-reviewed journal articles. In this module we presented the differences between scholarly journals and popular magazines and showed students how to begin research by identifying the central concepts in a research question that can be used as keywords in searching research databases. We also explained that research databases are not designed to interpret natural language, so that putting an entire research question (which we observe the students do quite often) into the

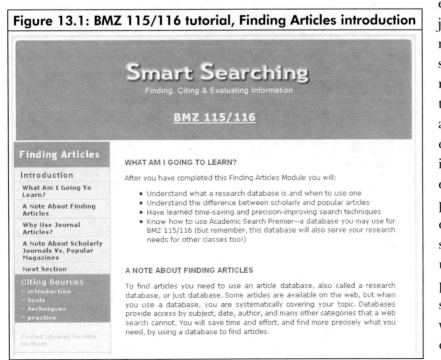

Figure 13.1: BMZ 115/116 tutorial, Finding Articles introduction

research databases won't retrieve good results. We also demonstrate Academic Search Premier, a general database suitable for introductory-level students.

The Citing Sources module begins by defining plagiarism and how documenting resources and citations helps one avoid plagiarism. Since American Psychological Association styles are utilized in BMZ 115/116, EAS 101, and EAS 102 assignments, we focused the module on the tools for creating APA citations and techniques for decoding an APA citation, which is helpful for students looking for full-text journal articles.

The focus of the Finding Books module is to teach users what is available in Miami University Libraries' catalog and how to search effectively for information in the catalog. Although the catalog does contain a lot more than books, we focused mainly on books so that students can begin to determine conceptually what sources to utilize, and when. The students also learn techniques for

searching effectively using truncation, limit/sorting capabilities, and the like. Finally, the students are exposed to collections outside of the Miami University Libraries by a brief explanation of what to do if the Libraries do not have a certain book—namely, request via OhioLINK, a consortium of eighty-five colleges and university libraries (including a few public libraries) in the state of Ohio (www.ohiolink.edu).

The Searching for Web Information module conveys the idea that, although Google is a good search tool, it indexes only part of what is available on the Web. We introduce the concept of the Invisible Web and tools for navigating through it. We also highlight OLinks, a link resolver supported by OhioLINK, for students to obtain full texts of entries they discover through Google Scholar.

The last module, Evaluating Information, concludes the tutorial by presenting guidelines for students to determine the quality and appropriateness of information

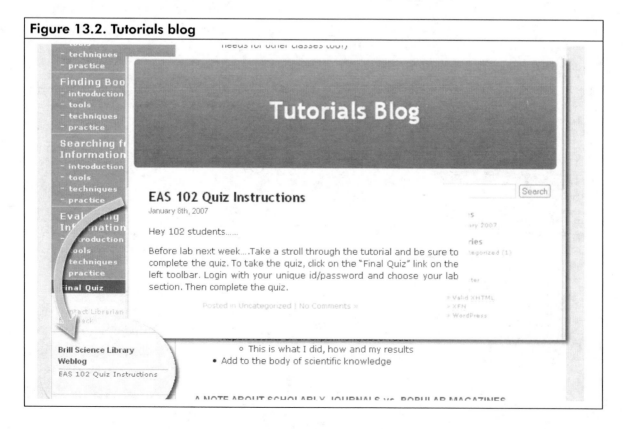

Figure 13.2. Tutorials blog

Figure 13.3. Tutorial "ads" promote resources. All slides are shown here, but only one is shown at a time in the tutorial (rotating every ten seconds)

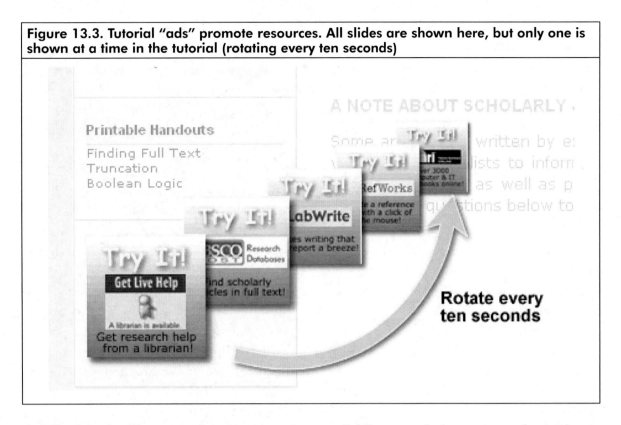

they find in the library catalog, in research databases, or on the Web. In this module, we revisit scholarly versus popular journals and discuss methods for effectively evaluating Web pages, such as determining authority and looking for objectivity. We also discuss how to utilize tools such as Academic Search Complete's limit option for finding only scholarly journals.

Additional Content on the Left

Besides tools (research databases, Web sites, etc.) highlighted in the main content, many other helpful resources for BMZ and EAS students are included in the tutorial. As librarians, we always try to make these resources known to faculty and students, but it can be quite difficult to get the word across. The Tutorials Blog is incorporated on each page under the navigation section. We apply a PHP script that parses and displays the blog's entries (RSS) on-the-fly (figure 13.2).

Oddly, one solution came to the engineering librarian's mind when he was getting annoyed by excessive ads on a certain Web page. Why not place "ads" on the tutorial? Although it seems contradictory, we thought that static ads might be helpful to expose students to resources they are not aware of, or perhaps have heard of but never used (figure 13.3).

The resources chosen for ads are those that can be utilized during students' first year majoring in science as well as throughout their studies at Miami University. Each ad is presented in an image in less than one hundred pixels in width and height. By clicking on the image, the student is redirected to the advertised resource. The images rotate every ten seconds. The resources that we chose to advertise include these:

* LabWrite
* NSF-funded project from North Carolina State University that provides excellent information on the fundamentals of a lab report

- RefWorks
- CSA's Web-based reference management system, to which Miami University Libraries subscribe
- EBSCO*host* databases
- Academic Search Premier and Business Source Premier are the databases we recommend for finding scholarly journal articles, so including them in the advertisement seemed natural.
- Safari E-Books
- ProQuest's collection of information technology e-books the Libraries subscribe to; these are heavily utilized by computer science and engineering students.
- Get Help Live
- Link to the Libraries' live chat and instant messaging service.

Instruction

Formal instruction varied between the courses the tutorial was targeting. Since the BMZ 115/116 and the EAS 101 sections of the tutorial were designed as a substitute to traditional classroom instruction, no formal instruction is required to use the tutorial. However, several methods were employed to introduce the tutorial to students. For example, since this project was initiated because of faculty's work revising the BMZ 115/116 lab manual, several parts of the manual direct BMZ 115/116 students to use the tutorial on the Libraries' Web site.

The EAS 101 curriculum consists of a culminating design project that involves literature searching. Since there is no classtime for instruction, the engineering librarian created a handout with pertinent information on literature searching and the link to the tutorial. The handout points students to the tutorial for further guidance, and faculty are encouraged to mention the tutorial in class as well. Several EAS 101 instructors also

have been giving extra credit to students who complete the tutorial and the final quiz. The database behind the quiz records the student's name, quiz results, and the time of entry; we use this information to let the faculty of each section know which student has taken the tutorial.

EAS 101 is primarily taught in the fall semester, but a spring section is offered for those unable to take the fall section. With only one section, EAS 101 faculty and the engineering librarian had more freedom to integrate the tutorial effectively into the class. As a result, in spring 2007 the tutorial was combined with an in-class library instruction session. The tutorial was assigned as a pre-assignment followed by the in-class instruction dedicated to library basics, such as recognizing the location of cataloged items and navigating the Libraries' Web site.

This setup was a great advantage for the in-class instruction because most students had basic knowledge of how to find books and articles, allowing the engineering librarian to focus more on tips and features. Students' initial knowledge of finding books and articles was notably better than in previous semesters, and it appears that the tutorial was in part responsible. Overall, a lot more could be accomplished during the fifty minutes of instruction in this session.

As of the spring semester of 2006, the engineering librarian has been conducting one of the weekly lab sessions for EAS 102. The librarian's lab session consists of an interactive instruction session with topics ranging from a catalog refresher to how to find and cite literature effectively and how to avoid plagiarism. After the instruction, students complete a graded worksheet that tests their knowledge on the topics presented.

As mentioned previously, a section of the tutorial created for EAS 102 and the final quiz became available in fall 2006. The engineering librarian then decided to make the tutorial a pre-lab for students in EAS 102. Students were required to complete the tutorial and take the final quiz. Again, the purpose was to release some classtime for more activities or discussion of each student's research interest.

In addition, the engineering librarian used ResponseCards (also known as "clickers") and Turning Point Software during the instruction to gauge students' knowledge of topics presented in the tutorial/pre-lab. The librarian also used this activity to assess students' prior knowledge and quickly adjusted the amount of coverage of different topics. As a result, there was more time for hands-on exercises and self-paced discovery time for the students who prefer learning independently.

Program Assessment

The BMZ 115/116 section of the tutorial does not have a built-in component for assessment, librarians have observed tangible improvement. For example, the science librarians have not seen a great influx of BMZ students to the reference desk, especially the night before a lab assignment is due. Even when students do seek reference assistance, their better understanding of research tools and techniques leads them to ask better questions.

The results of the final quiz taken by EAS 102 and some EAS 101 students were quite good. Nearly 76 percent of the students received a score of four (out of a total score five) or higher. Only two students (of 110) answered one or no questions correctly.

Many quiz questions were answered correctly by nearly everyone. These included

What do you do if Miami does not
have a copy of the book you need?

If you use an idea in your paper that is
not your own …
If you're looking for peer-reviewed
journal articles, you should be
looking in …

This is evidence that the students retained the information about OhioLINK, academic integrity, and peer-reviewed journals presented in the tutorial.

Results of some quiz questions were as we expected, with the majority of students answering correctly and about 15 percent choosing answers that seemed correct on the surface. A good example of the latter is the question "What is the JOURNAL TITLE in the following citation?" About 25 percent chose the article title instead of the journal title.

Only one question seemed to befuddle many students: "If you're looking for real-time information on a subject, the best place to look is …" This question was answered incorrectly by the majority of students (53 percent). The most frequent answer was "a research database," and a few chose "a magazine." The correct answer is the "Web," which is mentioned explicitly in the tutorial, although perhaps the concept of real-time information needs to be expanded. We did not provide concrete examples (traffic information, earthquake information) in the tutorial, but we plan to correct this in our next revision.

Three usability questions were included at the end of the quiz to test whether the tutorial was easy to use, whether it was helpful for locating design project information, and whether students will use it again in the future. More than 64 percent of students found the tutorial easy to use, whereas 27 percent did not have an opinion. Almost 70 percent said that the tutorial helped them find information for their class assignments. When asked if they would use the tutorial again, more than half of the students indicated that they weren't sure; only 37 percent said they would use the tutorial again.

In spring 2007 the engineering librarian invited EAS 101 students to share their tutorial experience via the class Blackboard discussion board. A few thought the tutorial was wordy and confusing, but most felt it was a valuable resource. One student commented, "I think it is very useful especially to me who used to think Google has everything. I just realize Google has so much but not everything."

As part the EAS 102 lab on library resources, the engineering librarian requires students to complete a worksheet to reinforce the resources or information literacy skills taught during the lab. This year was the first time students were required to complete a pre-lab assignment—the tutorial and the quiz. Initial data indicate that students who completed the tutorial performed better on the worksheet than those who did not have an opportunity to complete the tutorial. Students in spring 2007 sections of EAS 102 (when the tutorial was required) scored an average of 14.95 out of 15 (or of 16 with the possibility of extra credit). Students in other semesters (when the tutorial was not employed) scored averages ranging from 13.06 to 14.11.

Lessons Learned

Selling the tutorial to life sciences and engineering faculty has been easy. What gives it almost instant credibility is that the tutorial is tailored to the content, assignments, and projects of each class. Furthermore, faculty members are excited that the tutorial can be further developed to encompass information literacy problems they have faced in the past

with their own students. Last but not least, faculty do not have to give up classtime for library instruction. Although these tutorials were designed for introductory courses, they have opened up discussion for additional library instruction (and possible tutorials) in advanced courses.

Something else to remember when working with faculty is that they tend to forget about a project like this tutorial, sometimes quickly. Even though we initially had the buy-in for the tutorial from the faculty, they forgot about it while we were busy building it. In addition, when it came time to implement the tutorial, they had forgotten what it was about and had to be sold again. It would have been helpful to update interested faculty continually on what was happening during tutorial development or to ask faculty to test some capabilities. Some of our best feedback came from faculty who tested out tutorial before it was implemented in their classes.

Timing is important when working with faculty and classes to create an online information literacy tutorial. One important thing to recognize is that, although an online tutorial is often based on content from traditional classroom instruction or handouts, it still takes a lot of time to develop. Librarians must be prepared for that. We made a crucial mistake in estimating development time for the EAS 101 version and had to delay the formal rollout of the tutorial until the following academic year.

It is also important to be responsive to faculty needs. For example, although we created the Tutorials Blog to communicate with faculty and students, one faculty member felt it was confusing because the BMZ and EAS sections shared the same blog. In response, we temporarily disabled the blog during the time the tutorial was heavily used by this faculty member and his students. We consider this a chance occurrence and do not plan to change the nature of the blog. The common blog between all sections of the tutorial was meant to keep the tutorial simple, and our current way of posting items (with the class name at the front of the post) has generally worked well.

Generally it is easier to assume that students will see tutorial use as another assignment rather than as something that will affect the quality of their assignments and research. Although promoting the tutorial to faculty as a way to incorporate information literacy into curriculum was easy, we still have a long way to go to convince students. As the results of the usability questions indicate, half of the students weren't sure they would use the tutorial again for other classes. (Note that the results don't represent the feedback from BMZ 115/116 students, who didn't have a final quiz with the tutorial.) We do tell the students that "skills you learn here will also help you in your other classes and personal pursuits" in the beginning of each section of the tutorial, but reinforcement of this notion will be necessary in future tutorial revisions.

Appendix.
Final Quiz Questions

1. Which one of these is NOT a difference between a scholarly journal and a popular magazine?

    A. Scholarly journals contain articles that are reviewed by peer researchers in the field.

    B. Popular magazines contain many photographs and white space, while scholarly journals contain more tables/graphs and dense writing.

    C. Scholarly journals never cite references.

    D. Popular magazines are designed for the common man, while scholarly journals are for researchers in the field.

2. Why should I use journal articles?

    A. Google contains a lot of information, but not many journal articles are included.

    B. Journal articles are a quick way to keep up to date with the current literature.

    C. Journal articles are written by experts in the field.

    D. All of the above.

3. What is the name of a good general database to find journal articles?

    A. Find It

    B. Olinks

    C. Academic Search Premier

    D. Miami Libraries CatalogE.

4. If I search for *tadpoles* in Academic Search Premier, will the search find *tadpole*?

    A. Yes

    B. No

5. Which Boolean operator will expand our search results and is good for including a word and its synonyms?

    A. AND

    B. NOT

    C. OR

6. What can you do if Miami does not have a copy of the book you need, or the copy you need is checked out?

    A. Scream in horror and withdraw from college.

    B. Request a copy through OhioLINK.

    C. Get your friend at Ohio State to scan the pages you need and e-mail them to you.

    D. Call a library that owns the item and tell them to send it to you.E.

7. If you use an idea in your paper that is not your own, you ...

    A. don't have to do anything.

B. need to credit the idea to its author.

C. must quote the idea directly.

D. only need to stick in the page number next to the idea.

8. What is the JOURNAL TITLE in the following citation?

Troy, D. (1997). An approach for developing domain specific CASE tools and its application to manufacturing. Journal of Systems and Software, 38(2), 165.

A. An approach for developing domain specific CASE tools and its application to manufacturing

B. Journal of Systems and Software

C. Troy, D.

D. 38(2), 165

9. If you're looking real-time information on a subject, the best place to look is

A. the Web.

B. a research database.

C. a book.

D. a magazine.

10. If you're looking for peer-reviewed journal articles, you should be looking

A. in Google or Yahoo.

B. at some other Web site.

C. in a research database.

D. in the library catalog.

Notes

1.   E-learn, funded by the Ohio Board of Regents Grant (May 2003–August 2004). E-learn main site: http://elearn.lib.muohio.edu. E-learn with Macromedia Flash introduction: http://elearn.lib.muohio.edu/new.swf.

2.   While we were working on this chapter, Miami University Libraries upgraded the subscription to EBSCO*host*'s Academic Search Complete, which is built upon the Academic Search Premier with addition of access to more full-text articles. For the purpose of presenting the true process of this project, we continue to refer to the database as Academic Search Premier.

14. Giving Medical Students What They Want: Online Instruction at 11 p.m.

Lisa Wallis, Kristina Appelt, Kimberly Pendell, and Cleo Pappas

Introduction

Library of the Health Sciences–Chicago serves the health information needs of students, faculty, and staff of the University of Illinois at Chicago (UIC). The library is located in the heart of the Illinois Medical District, one of the world's largest medical districts. The University of Illinois College of Medicine is the largest medical school in the country, with four sites in Peoria, Rockford, Urbana, and Chicago, the largest of the sites. Providing instruction to more than two hundred medical students in a limited timeframe had become a challenge for the Information Services Department at the library, and a new instructional approach was needed. In 2006 we created an online tutorial for third year medical (M3) students. The M3 tutorial, Clinical Tools for Information at the Point of Care, identifies a variety of electronic resources for answering therapy, diagnosis, and drug information questions and finding credible health information to give to patients.

Rationale

Creating the M3 online tutorial was inspired by many factors, including an overall evaluation of library instruction across the career of UIC medical students. We recognized the need for a cohesive curricular sequence, and eliminating instructional redundancy was a particularly strong priority. The most frequent complaint from medical students about library instruction was that they had already attended library classes and knew how to search. We realized that different information resources were appropriate at different points in the students' training. After some success in sequencing the first and second years of medical student instruction, it became clear that the content of the third-year library instruction would lend itself to an online format. Also, scheduling the M3 courses had always proved difficult because of class size, which averages more than two hundred students, and staff turnover at both the medical school and the library.

Past attempts to provide M3 library instruction had involved hands-on small group instruction and demonstration to large lecture groups. The small group size was ideal; however, students were staggered throughout an entire academic year, meaning some students did not receive the library instruction until they had already completed clinical rotations. In addition, feedback from students on the large lecture format was that it was largely ineffective. We agreed with this assessment of the lecture format and were excited to build instruction in an online format, which would be more interactive and more flexible for both students and librarians.

Finally, we saw an opportunity to incorporate online instruction as part of the newly revised two-week course "Essentials of Clinical Practice & Professionalism" (ECP&P). ECP&P includes one week of lectures at the beginning of the M3 year, before M3 students begin a series of six clinical clerkships. Rather than teach the students in person during this week, the library liaison to the College of Medicine introduces the students to the new online tutorial. This approach neatly solved the dilemma of staggering instruction throughout the year or giving a demonstration to hundreds of students.

Instruction and Content

Students attend a face-to-face library instruction session in both the first and second years of medical school. The first year (M1) session is a basic introduction to the facilities and services of the UIC Library of the Health Sciences–Chicago, including the catalog and course reserves. The session in the second year (M2) complements an intensive series of plenary lectures in which students are introduced to evidence-based medicine. M2 students are taught to search the medical literature for primary and secondary studies using advanced PubMed search features. Since they already have a foundation in basic information seeking through the catalog and article databases, library instruction in the third year introduces students to clinical tools that can be used at the point of care. The library provides all of these tools through licensed subscriptions, and we believed many tools were underused because students and faculty demonstrated little awareness of them.

Previously, clinical tools were demonstrated to M3 students either in a large auditorium or small groups within the library classroom. In the online format, we wanted to shift the content away from basic demonstration of clinical tools to active learning exercises utilizing clinical tools in different scenarios. We looked to Florida State University's College of Medicine, which had developed several support resources for medical decision making. One resource of particular

interest focused on answering clinical questions and emphasized that finding the right clinical tool first starts with identifying the type of question being asked. We decided to use a similar approach by designing the tutorial so a student starts with a clinical question and then learns about the appropriate tools to answer that type of question. The online tutorial content was thus divided into learning modules based on four types of clinical information needs: diagnosis, therapy, drug information, and patient education.

In total, the M3 online instruction contained five learning modules, one practice scenario, and a tutorial evaluation (figure 14.1). In addition to the learning modules based on clinical questions, we created an introduction that provided an overview of basic information literacy skills needed to practice evidence-based medicine. When practicing evidence-based medicine it is important to understand different study designs and the varying levels of evidence these different designs show to support research findings. We found it important to discuss the difference between foreground and background information. Experience demonstrated that students were confused about when to consult PubMed, textbooks, or other clinical tools when looking for clinical information. A video demonstration in the introduction module taught them to navigate the Library of the Health Sciences Electronic Gateway Web page.

A crucial factor that influenced the content development of the M3 online tutorial was keeping the time to complete the tutorial to a minimum. A decision was made to keep the completion time for each module between ten and fifteen minutes. The time issue was influenced by the requirement that the library section of the ECP&P course remain close to the time allotted previously for

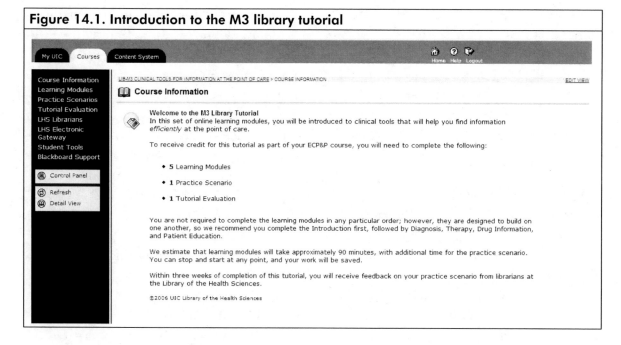

Figure 14.1. Introduction to the M3 library tutorial

classroom or lecture instruction. We also recognized that students' attention span would be relatively short and wanted to ensure that time would not be a barrier to completing the tutorial. Students were not required to complete the learning modules in any particular order; however, the clinical scenario used in each module was designed to be a cohesive diagnosis and treatment plan. We recommended that students complete the introduction first, followed by diagnosis, therapy, drug information, and patient education.

The format for diagnosis, therapy, drug information, and patient education learning modules followed a similar layout. The learning modules were divided into four main components, which included a learning module introduction, patient profile and scenario, preliminary questions on information seeking skills and preferences, and video demonstration (figure 14.2). First, students were asked to list possible search terms relevant to the patient scenario, the resource they would use to find information, and their reasons for choosing that particular resource. These questions were designed both to encourage reflection on the students' parts and to provide us with data on students' preferred information resources. For example, preliminary questions in the therapy learning module revealed that M3 students commonly use the resource Clinical Evidence. Another popular response, however, was PubMed, a resource that is not the most effective for quick access to point of care information.

We wanted the format for the videos to follow a similar layout, with each demonstration focusing on two clinical tools. Also, the clinical tools demonstrated in each video would not be replicated in the other learning modules. The tools taught were those that provide brief, digested information as opposed to traditional article databases, which require reading and synthesis on the part of the clinician. Limiting each learning module to two different clinical tools made for shorter module completion times while still allowing a wide range of clinical resources to be presented. The difficulty arose in selecting the best two clinical tools for each learning module (di-

Figure 14.2. Learning module, Patient Education

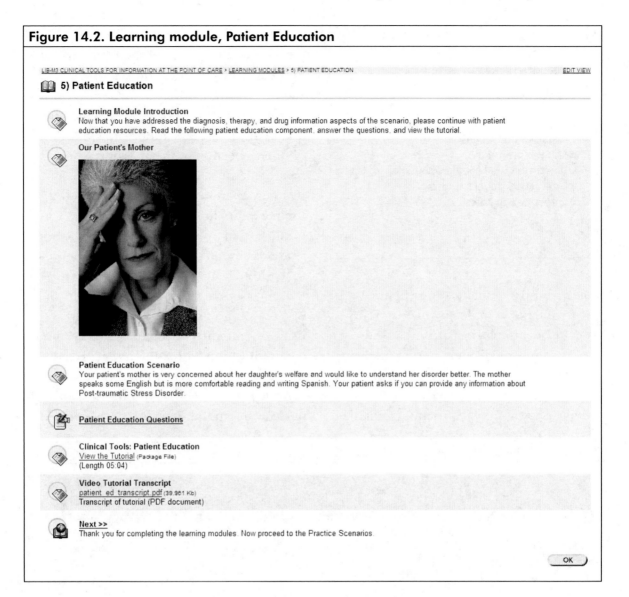

LIB-M3 CLINICAL TOOLS FOR INFORMATION AT THE POINT OF CARE > LEARNING MODULES > 5) PATIENT EDUCATION   EDIT VIEW

5) Patient Education

Learning Module Introduction
Now that you have addressed the diagnosis, therapy, and drug information aspects of the scenario, please continue with patient education resources. Read the following patient education component, answer the questions, and view the tutorial.

Our Patient's Mother

Patient Education Scenario
Your patient's mother is very concerned about her daughter's welfare and would like to understand her disorder better. The mother speaks some English but is more comfortable reading and writing Spanish. Your patient asks if you can provide any information about Post-traumatic Stress Disorder.

Patient Education Questions

Clinical Tools: Patient Education
View the Tutorial (Package File)
(Length 05:04)

Video Tutorial Transcript
patient_ed_transcript.pdf (39.961 Kb)
Transcript of tutorial (PDF document)

Next >>
Thank you for completing the learning modules. Now proceed to the Practice Scenarios.

OK

---

agnosis, therapy, drug information, and patient education), since some are appropriate resources for all clinical questions. We decided to outline the strengths of each clinical tool, then use the profile to determine which clinical tools best answered the four different types of clinical questions. Each clinical tool's strengths were then incorporated as an introduction to the clinical tool in the video (figure 14.3). All videos began with a patient profile and scenario that matched the scenario of the respective learning module, followed by a presentation of two clinical tools, and concluded with a list of additional resources.

We considered it important to demonstrate each clinical tool within the context of the learning module scenario. For example, in the patient education module the patient scenario asks about post-traumatic stress disorder, and within the video tutorial we demonstrated how to search for the condition in MedlinePlus (figure 14.4).

After completing the learning modules, students were required to select a practice scenario and apply their information-seeking skills to the clinical tools of their choice to develop a patient care plan, including diagnosis, therapy, drug therapy (if appli-

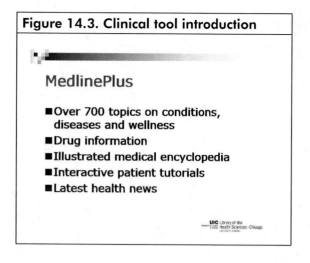

Figure 14.3. Clinical tool introduction

MedlinePlus

- Over 700 topics on conditions, diseases and wellness
- Drug information
- Illustrated medical encyclopedia
- Interactive patient tutorials
- Latest health news

students to choose one and use the tools to develop a care plan for their patient. This approach emphasized the relevance of the tutorial to the students' upcoming clinical practice. Students were not evaluated on the quality of their clinical decisions but rather on their selection of the appropriate tool for a particular information need and their ability to use search and browse features to find the necessary information.

cable), and patient education (figure 14.5). Since students completed this tutorial just prior to beginning one of six clinical rotations in family medicine, internal medicine, obstetrics and gynecology, pediatrics, psychiatry, or surgery, we developed a unique patient scenario for each rotation and asked

All lessons were asynchronous, meaning students completed the lessons on their own time within assigned days of the tutorial. This was an essential piece of this project, since one reason it was created was to address the issue of student convenience. Little direct communication with students occurred unless a problem arose with technology. We provided brief feedback on the students' final assessment, but it is unclear whether the

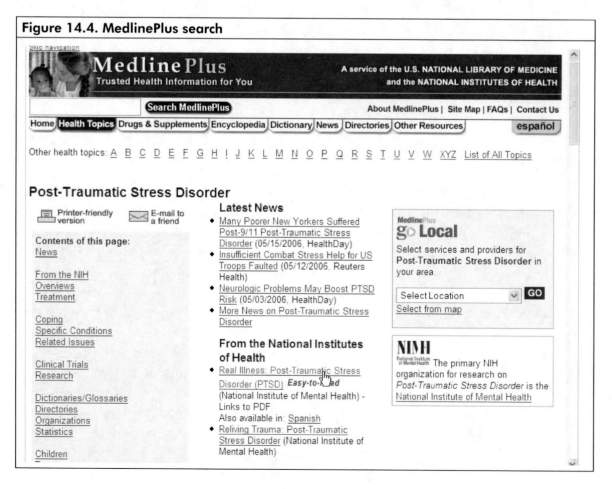

Figure 14.4. MedlinePlus search

students logged back in to Blackboard to retrieve our responses.

Because this was a new method for delivering ECP&P library instruction, the library liaison to the College of Medicine attended the first class lecture and briefly told students about the new tutorial. This was the only face-to-face interaction with the M3 students. The librarian had intended to demonstrate the login process and describe the sequence of the tutorial, but thanks to a scheduling error she was allotted less than five minutes to interact with students, which resulted in an initially poor response from the students. This event reinforced how important incorporating personal contact is when promoting virtual learning instruments. We felt that individual contact would make students take the tutorial seriously and realize that they would receive personalized feedback on their performance.

Development

From the start, the library liaison realized that buy-in from the medical school was going to be essential to the success of the project. Part of the challenge of library instruction for medical students has been the amount of staff turnover at both the library and the medical school. Without established relationships between the two units, library instruction had become somewhat haphazard and unstructured. With a new library liaison and new ECP&P course directors in place, communication had improved. The library liaison to the College of Medicine approached the ECP&P course directors, presented the idea for online instruction, and solicited their feedback. The course directors were enthusiastic about the idea for a new format and even emphasized the potential value of the resource for their own professional use. At the start of the project, only two full-time librarians were on staff. The librarian who was the liaison to the College of Pharmacy was a natural choice to develop the drug information module. The same librarian also developed

Figure 14.5. Practice scenario assessment

LIB-M3 CLINICAL TOOLS FOR INFORMATION AT THE POINT OF CARE > CONTROL PANEL > PRACTICE SCENARIOS > PREVIEW ASSESSMENT: PRACTICE SCENARIO ASSESSMENT

📖 **Preview Assessment: Practice Scenario Assessment**

Name	Practice Scenario Assessment
Instructions	Apply what you have learned in the modules to your chosen practice scenario. Search library resources to find information on the diagnosis, therapy options--including drug therapies, if applicable--and patient education. Summarize your treatment of the patient, addressing these factors. Please note: your choice of resources and search strategies are of primary importance. **Please note: In order to make sure your responses are submitted, please click the** *'Save'* **button to the right of each response after typing your answers.**
Multiple Attempts	This Test allows multiple attempts.
Force Completion	This Test can be saved and resumed later.

▾ Question Completion Status:

Question 1   0 points   Save

Diagnosis: What resource(s) did you search for diagnosis information?

| Normal ▾ | 3 ▾ | Times New Roman ▾ | **B** *I* U S | x₂ x² | ≡ ≡ ≡ | ≡ ≡ ≡ ≡ |

Path: body

the patient education module. The library liaison to the College of Medicine, who also was acting as the project coordinator, developed the diagnosis and therapy modules. A librarian with experience in online instructional design was hired shortly after the project began; her knowledge of required technologies and online project workflow made her indispensable for developing the structure of the overall tutorial.

With our production team in place, the first decision facing us was whether to develop the tutorial as an independent Web site or to use Blackboard, the course management software available from the university. We met with staff members of the university's Instructional Technology Lab and External Education department to discuss the tutorial project and development options. Creating an interactive tutorial was important, as was the ability to confirm the participation of students and provide students with feedback. Considering these factors, building the tutorial in Blackboard became the best option. Also, the Instructional Technology Lab offered design recommendations and Blackboard support. UIC medical students are frequent users of Blackboard for many of their courses, providing further support for this decision.

Course management software offers a high level of functionality in online course building. Though there are obvious design limitations, applications like Blackboard are customizable to some extent. For example, the team adapted the course menu system (see figure 14.1) to reflect the design of the tutorial and added direct links to the library resources and the tutorial development team for users' convenience. Other tools in Blackboard were also put to use, particularly the test creation tool, which the team used to add interactive assessment components

to the learning modules, as well as the larger practice scenario assignment at the end of the tutorial. The survey tool was also used to create a tutorial evaluation to better assess use and satisfaction of the online format.

Another major piece of tutorial development was the creation of the videos that discussed and demonstrated the various clinical tools. The team decided to use Camtasia to create the videos, primarily because of one librarian's experience with this software and the previous purchase of Camtasia by the library. The Instructional Technology Lab suggested very small dimensions for the videos, but the team discovered that a larger display dimension did not tangibly affect the uploading and downloading of videos in Blackboard. The librarians made every attempt to keep file sizes at a minimum while still creating visually intelligible videos. For example, the videos were produced as Flash (.swf) files with a .jpg compression quality of 75 percent, which was found to reduce file size without a noticeable decrease in video image quality. Also, the Camtasia files were compressed into a zip file, then uploaded to Blackboard and set to unpack the file on execution.

The tutorial videos developed in Camtasia include a video tour of selected clinical tools, accompanied by an audio track describing the various features, strengths, and weaknesses of the tools. We established a workflow process for video creation to help guide us in their production, including standards for file naming and Camtasia production. Each librarian creating a video demonstration first produced a script that was edited by the other librarians. We also decided to record the screen capture video first, guided by the timing of the finalized script. PowerPoint slides were also imported into the Camtasia project as part of the video (see figure 14.3). After the screen capture was successfully completed, the audio track was recorded by following the video playback. This approach to video creation was preferable to recording both screen capture video and audio tracks simultaneously, because editing the video and audio separately requires less skill and precision.

The most significant problem encountered in the production of the tutorial was recording audio for the Camtasia videos. We purchased a desktop microphone in hopes of producing high-quality audio tracks but had difficulty getting the microphone to work with the hardware and software effectively. After several troubleshooting attempts, the desktop microphone was finally abandoned for a standard headset with microphone. The audio quality was also compromised by the lack of a quiet, isolated room in which to record audio. Video transcripts were made available to students for broader accessibility and in case any user had difficulty playing the video or hearing the audio track.

Program Assessment

Library instruction for the M3 students has evolved and changed over the years. The structure of the course changed on the basis of student feedback but also because of reduction of librarians and changing leadership in the medical school. Because of the changing format of the course and how assessment was collected, past evaluations were inconsistent, and thus it is difficult to make direct comparisons between instructional formats. In the past, we learned from student comments that it was important to make the sessions interactive, that lecture format is boring, and that perceived usefulness and time constraints are important to students. Many students did comment positively on learning about new resources and being grateful that "this

wasn't another PubMed lecture." We thought that the online format would allow us to address students' complaints while highlighting resources unfamiliar to them.

Assessment of the new online course came from three directions: the practice scenario as an active learning exercise to assess whether students could incorporate content and resources covered in real life scenarios; the tutorial evaluation to assess whether students preferred learning this content online; and statistics from Blackboard that documented students' learning behaviors. As noted above, after completing the learning modules, students were required to select a practice scenario and apply their information-seeking skills to the clinical tools of their choice to develop a patient care plan.

We provided written feedback on each student's response to the practice scenarios. The two hundred plus students were divided alphabetically and feedback responsibilities were split accordingly. Our feedback focused on whether the students chose the appropriate tools to answer their clinical question and not on their clinical decisions. Most students took the exercise seriously and used a variety of clinical tools to answer different aspects of their practice scenario. There were, however, students who provided sarcastic responses or picked inappropriate tools. For example, several students said they used MedlinePlus as a resource to answer therapy or diagnosis questions. Though you can get therapy and diagnosis information from MedlinePlus, information in this resource is really tailored for the patient, not the physician. To the other extreme, some students said they would use PubMed to find information for their patients. While some patients may be sophisticated enough to understand the scientific literature, most patients need health information synthesized to a lower reading level. Providing feedback allowed us to correct any misconceptions students had about the different resources. Though it was announced that we would give feedback to the practice scenarios, students were not required to go into Blackboard to read it. Consequently, we are unsure how many students benefited from this approach.

In the past, we had a few requests from students to put the library section of ECP&P online. This feedback sparked our movement toward online instruction, but we still needed more feedback to assess students' learning preferences and layout of content. Blackboard allowed us to create a separate tutorial evaluation, which was a required section of the online course. We created four evaluation questions using the Likert scale or multiple-choice. Two questions focused on usability of the online tutorial, and the other two focused on interest of content and learning preferences. The responses to the tutorial evaluation questions were highly

positive. When asked whether "overall, the tutorial is interesting," 78 percent strongly agreed or agreed. Seventy-four percent of students preferred to learn this type of material "online, as I did in this tutorial" to learning in a computer classroom with a librarian (8 percent), in a lecture hall with a librarian (1 percent), or on their own reading handouts (16 percent).

In addition, Blackboard allowed us to look deeper into the learning behaviors of our students by providing extensive course statistics. One interesting trend was the date and time students completed the tutorial. The students had a week to complete the tutorial, starting Monday. Most students took the tutorial on the last day (figure 14.6), and throughout the week the most common time students complete the online tutorial was 9:00–11:00 P.M. (figure 14.7). We considered the feedback from the tutorial evaluation and course statistics an indicator that layout and delivery approach for this type of

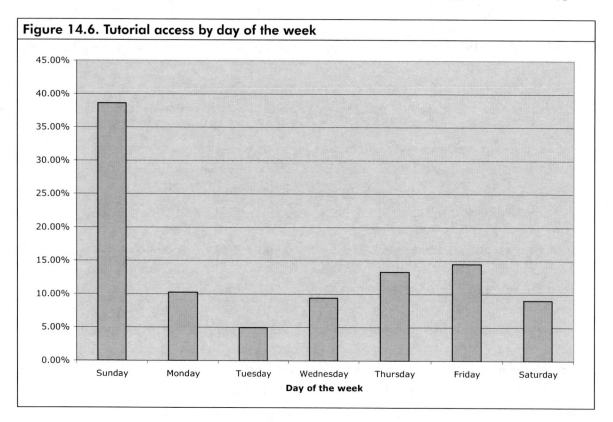

Figure 14.6. Tutorial access by day of the week

Figure 14.7. Tutorial access by hour of the day

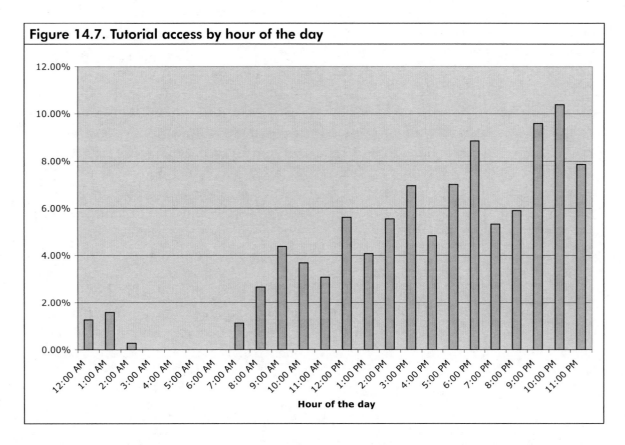

content was successful, and we will continue to support and revise the online tutorial for the ECP&P course.

Lessons Learned

This project was our first attempt to move library instruction to an online, asynchronous format. Though it is tempting to think of online instruction as less demanding than face-to-face instruction, building and maintaining online instruction can be time consuming and sometimes frustrating. Learning to use new software applications is always challenging, and it is best to provide some time for the creators to play and troubleshoot potential snags in the application. We also found it very helpful to establish a project workflow and deadlines for major components of the tutorial to keep us on track. A deadline was set for the completion of each video demonstration.

Online instruction also demands time and energy for maintenance. For example,

Blackboard was upgraded soon after the tutorial was to be completed by students; the upgrade altered the interface slightly, particularly within the practice scenario assessment where answers now had to be saved individually. Also, course management systems occasionally "lock" a student's work, requiring the instructors to "unlock" the student's account before the assignment can be submitted; this feature of the system or other user snags can lead to e-mail and phone calls from frustrated students. As software is updated and Web sites are revised, the tutorial must also be updated and revised. Within three months of producing Clinical Tools for Information at the Point of Care, we had to recreate the video demonstration of one featured clinical tool, since that resource had revised its Web site.

Online instruction does allow for better assessment practices that are harder to accomplish in the traditional classroom. Blackboard allowed us to keep track of practice scenario results, tutorial evaluations, and completed assignments. In the future, we plan to track usage statistics of the resources presented in the Clinical Tools tutorial in order to better assess the impact of the tutorial on student practices. Currently we do not have quantitative data on the use of presented clinical tools before and after the ECP&P course. Another project improvement idea is to follow up with the students at a later date to solicit their feedback on the tutorial and any impact it might have had on their information-seeking practices. Such feedback would include how often they use the tools taught in the learning modules, whether they have

developed preferences for one or more of them, and how proficient they think they are in searching for clinical information.

The work we put into the M3 tutorial was well rewarded by student satisfaction. Student evaluations were positive, expressing a preference for the online format. It is important to remember that the schedule M3 students experience is exceedingly heavy. Students liked being able to complete the library instruction requirement at their convenience. We consider the curriculum to be as rigorous as that presented in the face-to-face instruction. In addition, students were challenged more as individuals to think critically about the tools within the context of a cohesive diagnosis and treatment plan.

15. From Classroom to Computer: Collaboration, Integration, and Success

Leslie Sult and Louise Greenfield

Rationale

In fall 2005 the University of Arizona (UA) Libraries' public services team librarians were charged through our library strategic plan to identify foundational, gateway, and large enrollment courses on the UA campus that would enable our librarians to reach a maximum number of students in a minimum amount of time. The UA Libraries have been exploring scaleable instructional models for several years and have a mandate to develop and share sustainable, reusable materials. The UA Libraries also have a history of exploring innovative teaching modalities such as RIO (Research Instruction Online) and have done work in implementing usability studies. In the past few years, the Libraries have increased their efforts to scale instruction because of a combination of factors that include staff shortages brought on by shrinking budgets, questions of the efficacy of the one-shot instructional session, and a growing demand for library instruction thanks to past successes with librarian/faculty collaborations. Instructional design and technology skills are not pervasive among the library staff, but we do have an openness to trying new things and to taking pedagogical risks.

To meet the strategic goals identified above, we chose to work with the faculty in the College of Education who teach LRC480: Children's Literature in the Classroom. The fact that every elementary education major must take this class made it an excellent candidate for our scalable instruction efforts.

Also, all faculty who teach LRC480 are required to bring their students to the library for a class session. This requirement came about because one of us has established a very collaborative working relationship with the program supervisor and several of the faculty. Finally, all faculty in this class are required to integrate technology into their teaching, so our module gave both the education faculty and us an opportunity to experiment with using emerging technology to teach future teachers. Because the students and faculty in the College of Education are exposed to new forms of instruction and are expected to explore creative approaches to teaching, we had the opportunity to work with willing and knowledgeable partners.

Content

Fortunately, the class objectives, along with the skills faculty wanted students to master, had been developed and refined throughout years of collaboration between the librarian and the children's literature faculty. Our challenge was to translate the existing skills and objectives into an effective online model that would reach all students in the children's literature classes, be engaging and pedagogically sound, and require less library staff time than the existing in-person instructional model that was being used. We also wanted a sustainable model that could be updated and modified easily.

We began developing our online materials by identifying major objectives for the class. These included introducing students to the library and library services, providing them with hands-on experience in locating information about authors/illustrators, teaching them about subject guides to children's literature, and helping them identify and locate multicultural materials. In addition to the content, we wanted the tutorial to reflect the culture of the classroom. These classes are very participatory and include much student-to-student sharing, so we were challenged to develop an online learning environment that would facilitate hands-on experience and collaboration. We used the librarian/faculty-created goals and objectives to guide us as we considered which technologies to use to teach students the information literacy skills and sources listed below:

Personal Introduction to the Library and Library Services
  • Information commons help desk
  • reference consultation
  • children's literature collection

Locating Information about Authors/Illustrators
  • biography, bibliography
  • literature resource center
  • Something About the Author

Subject Guides to Children's Literature
  • subject headings for locating children's books
  • how to find children's books in our collection

Identifying and Locating Multicultural Materials
  • bibliographic sources
  • subject headings
  • Web sites
  • development

After a good deal of consideration and experimentation, we organized this outline into instructional chunks, in the hope that the teaching faculty would integrate the resulting instructional modules into different portions of their class curriculum. We set up a Web page to make the modules available and presented them in an order that we believed would facilitate integration. During the pilot, we also included an in-depth instructional guide for the teaching faculty. The instructional guide was designed to provide the teaching faculty with background information and teaching suggestions. We created the guide to provide faculty with flexibility as they planned their course syllabi. The guide describes the content, research skills, and concepts addressed through the tutorial. It gives instructors a timeframe for introducing each module and ideas for integrating the module into their curriculum. The outline below provides an overview of this first course design:

Introduction to the Library
  • Video Introduction to Library Resources
  • Introduction to the Library Gateway (printable exercise and quiz)
  • Evaluation of Introduction to the Library Module

Introduction to Literature Resource Center
  • Introduction to Literature Resource Center
  • Quick Guide to Using Literature Resource Center
  • Literature Resource Center—Independent Exercise
  • Evaluation of the Introduction to Literature Resource Center Module

Introduction to Something About the Author
  • Something About the Author—Description and Exercise
  • Evaluation of the Something About the Author Module

Introduction to How to Find Children's Literature (books) in the UA Library

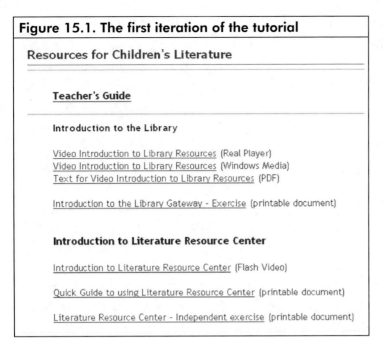

Figure 15.1. The first iteration of the tutorial

Resources for Children's Literature

Teacher's Guide

Introduction to the Library

Video Introduction to Library Resources (Real Player)
Video Introduction to Library Resources (Windows Media)
Text for Video Introduction to Library Resources (PDF)

Introduction to the Library Gateway - Exercise (printable document)

Introduction to Literature Resource Center

Introduction to Literature Resource Center (Flash Video)

Quick Guide to using Literature Resource Center (printable document)

Literature Resource Center - Independent exercise (printable document)

- Video Introduction to the UA Library's Main Juvenile Collection
- Guide to Finding Materials in the UA Library's Main Juvenile Collection (printable document)
- Guide to Using Subject Headings to Locate Resources for Children's Literature (printable document)

To see the complete version of the first tutorial, go to http://intranet.library.arizona.edu/users/sultl/instructor%20page.htm.

Instruction

The first instructional module of our pilot tutorial (Introduction to the Library) contained an eight-minute video presentation that introduced students to the education librarian as well as the children's literature collection (see figure 15.1). We opened the module with a streaming video because we believed that seeing the friendly face of the education librarian would help students feel connected to the library and encourage them to seek her if they needed assistance. To create the video, we collaborated with the UA Learning Technology Center, which records, edits, and hosts instructional videos for faculty; all we had to do was develop our talking points and practice speaking in front of a camera. (The video can be viewed in its entirety at www.library.arizona.edu/documents/ust/introlibgate.doc.) We also included a printable exercise on using the library gateway, which covered several topics including how to locate a book and how to find a subject librarian. The exercise, which was not required initially, was developed as a means of introducing students to the Library's Web site.

In the second instructional module (Introduction to Literature Resource Center), we moved into introducing students to the Literature Resource Center database. To teach students about the database, we developed an online tutorial using Captivate, chosen because of its screen capture and Flash editing abilities as well as for its ease of use. The tutorial demonstrates how to navigate the Literature Resource Center to locate information about children's authors the students are studying. As a part of this module, we also developed a printable exercise and a printable quick guide for students to use as they navigated the database. Finally, we included a blog to facilitate student, faculty, and librarian sharing and communication. We believed that this would be an important component of the tutorial because of the participatory nature of the LRC480 classes.

The third instructional module (Introduction to Something About the Author) introduced students to the print resource Something About the Author. For this section, we developed a printable guide and exercise for students to use when they came into the library. Interestingly, this was one of the modules that received some of the most positive feedback when we conducted our first round of follow-up interviews. Although the printable exercise lacked some of the bells and whistles of the other modules, the fact that it was directly related to the students' assignments made it a faculty and student favorite.

For the final instructional module (Introduction to How to Find Children's Literature [books] in the UA Library), we developed another video as well as a printable guide to help students find children's literature materials in the UA Library. The video introduced students to the UA Library's children's literature collection and showed them some of the reference resources they could use as they worked with children's books.

The first iteration of the tutorial was introduced to faculty and students during spring 2006. We presented an introductory session for all faculty who would be teaching the LRC480 course during that spring semester. We showed each component of the tutorial, offered to set up a personal interface for each faculty member's class, and encouraged them to contact us for any assistance in integrating the module into their curriculum. We explained that this was a pilot project and that we would be meeting with them again to assess the program.

Implementation

We did not receive a lot of communication from the LRC480 faculty during the spring 2006 semester, but in a follow-up interview conducted after the initial implementation period the faculty shared their thoughts as well as student evaluations and experiences. One of the first things we learned from the discussion was that classes did not use the blog because the faculty did not want to "learn one more thing." There were set-up and administrative tasks required of individual faculty members to implement the blog, so they chose not to activate it. The faculty teaching this course are PhD students in the midst of their own coursework and research. They are wearing many hats and juggling many obligations, so having to learn a new technology was not high on their list of priorities. As a result of their feedback we eliminated the blog in the next iteration of the tutorial. The faculty also found the instructional guide too detailed (figure 15.2); they preferred a simplified "grab and go" approach. Based on this discovery, we abandoned the instructional guide and replaced it with an easy to read "Why do this?" section for each instructional module, which was used to communicate the objective of the module to both faculty and students (figure 15.3).

Along with the feedback about the blog and the guide, the faculty requested that we add a printable self-tour of the library for any student who might want it, along with written scripts for the video presentations so that they could be used by deaf and hearing-impaired students. They also reported that the students did not grasp the importance or relevance of some of the exercises. In particular, the students did not like the printable exercise that introduced them to the library gateway because they felt that it took up too much time and did not provide them with useful information. The faculty asked that we modify this exercise so that it was more obviously tied to student assignments. Students could then directly apply what they learned. The faculty also shared that the students requested that the learning activities and assignments be more interactive.

In the revision of the first module, we recreated the printable exercise that follows

---

Figure 15.2. Example from the eliminated instructors guide

Introduction to the Library

Video Introduction to Library Resources

- Students will view a video that introduces them to the services and collections in the UA Library that are most relevant to their research needs.

Please ask students to view the 8 minute video. It is most helpful if you introduce the video at the very beginning of the semester so that students know how to use the library for this class, and know that there is library and research assistance available to them. Inform them that the video will introduce them to a variety of reference services including one-on-one consultations.

Introduction to the Library Gateway—Exercise

- Students will complete an exercise on the UA Library's Information Gateway. This is a document that can be printed out from the student page and completed by each student.

This should be assigned for the same day that students watch the video. Students can open the assignment as a Word document and print it out. Feel free to ask students to return the completed assignments for a grade or completion points or just for your own information.

---

the video introduction to the library by simplifying it and making it an interactive quiz. In this revised version, students are asked to answer two questions after viewing the video. The questions are online and immediately relevant to their classwork: identifying the e-mail address of their subject specialist, and identifying the various reference services available to them.

In the second module, we increased the interactivity of the Literature Resource Center lesson by adding playback controls that enable students to set the pace that they work through the lesson. We also capitalized

---

Figure 15.3. Example from the revised tutorial

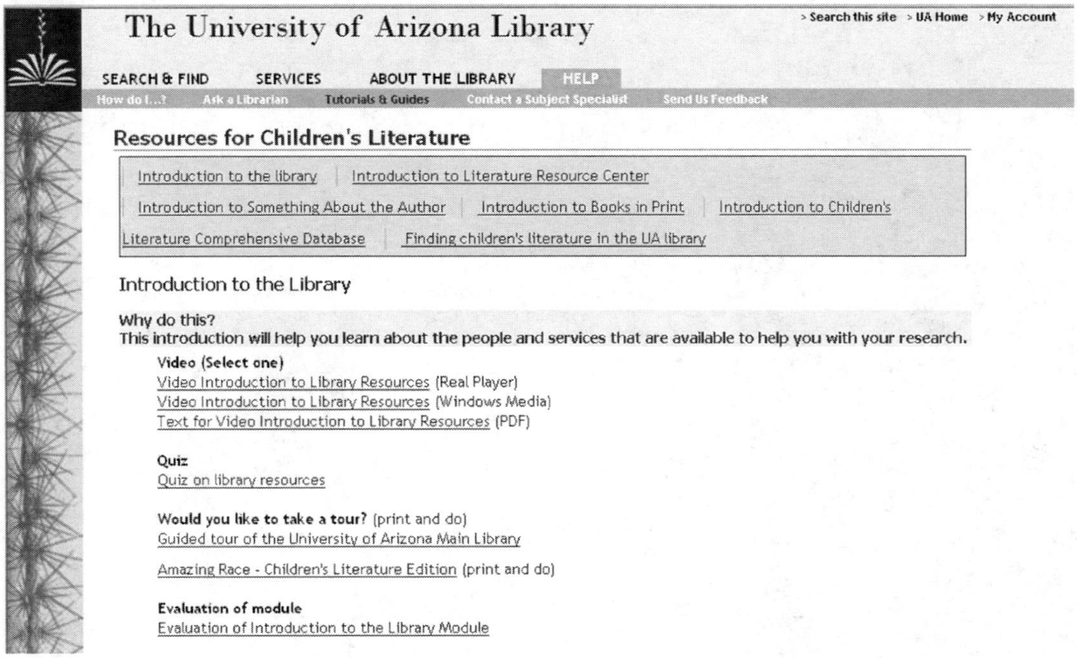

on the interactive features available in Captivate by adding opportunities for students to practice performing some of the searching and navigation functions within a demonstration version of the database (figure 15.4).

In the final section of the tutorial, we added an HTLM-based interactive guide (figure 15.5). This online guide was designed to teach students how to limit UA Library catalog searches to the children's literature collection. In this case we did not to use Captivate, because we wanted students to interact with the "live" catalog as they performed their searches. Our goal was to have them be able to retrieve materials as they went through the process of learning. We did this based on the assumption that students would want to complete the exercise and retrieve relevant materials in one session. This would increase the exercise's relevance in that students could use the search experience to identify and

retrieve materials for their assignment. Finally, we worked with the course director to ensure that the faculty integrated the modules throughout the semester rather than treating the set of modules as a "one-shot" session.

The revised tutorial was offered again in fall 2006. As in the past, all LRC480 faculty used the tutorial in their course. Because of other priorities in the department we were not invited to introduce the modules to the faculty. Though we viewed this as a lost opportunity, we did our best to encourage the faculty to meet with us if they had any questions or needed assistance in using the tutorial. We sent a variety of e-mail to each faculty member inviting them to meet with us at any point during the semester and reminding them that we had much experience in integrating library-related instruction into the curriculum. As it happened, the department supervisor assigned the most experienced faculty to work with four

Figure 15.4. Captivate tutorial

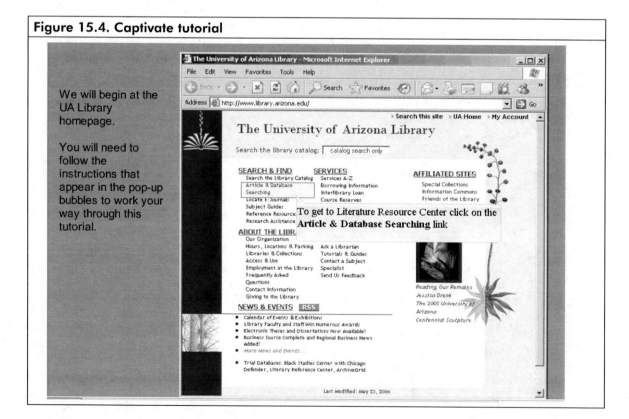

Figure 15.5. HTML-based interactive guide

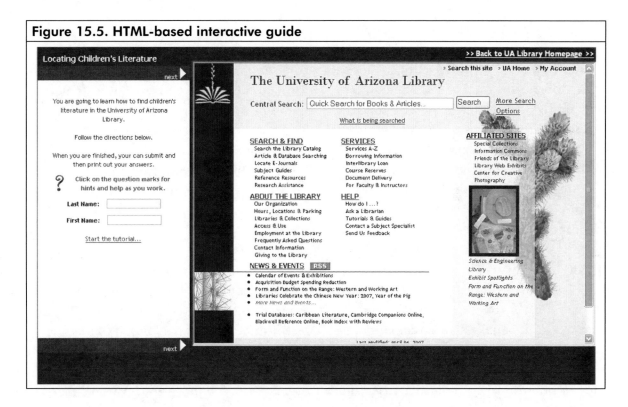

of the newer faculty on this project, and she was the person they went to with questions and concerns.

Program Assessment

Faculty Assessment of the Revised Tutorial

At the end of the fall 2006 semester, we met with the five faculty and their supervisor to assess our revisions. Before the meeting, we sent the faculty and supervisor a series of questions that we thought would help all of us assess the revised program. During our second round of assessment meetings with the faculty, they shared that students in the LRC480 classes had little library experience and that many had never actually checked a book out of the UA library. Since this is an upper-division class, this was an eye-opening revelation for all of us. This piece of information led the faculty to ask for a library tour, which we developed for the spring 2007 semester. The faculty also felt that they did not introduce the tutorial early enough in the semester

and that they did not take full advantage of the organization of the modules by having students do them one at a time, when they were most relevant to the in-class work they were doing. It appears that, although all agree that having distinct instructional segments is perhaps the tutorial's greatest feature, it takes more time and planning on the part of the faculty to present it in this way.

Overall, there was positive appreciation for the revised tutorial. The faculty were not at all bothered by the lack of a "real" librarian and felt that the video "welcome" was warm and inviting. They believed that the students who completed the series of modules had a deeper understanding of library reference tools and that their work was stronger as a result. They recognized that the tutorial helped to expand their students' worlds by allowing them to discover the "huge area of databases and reference sources" the library has to offer. It should be noted, however, that faculty and students did experience some difficulties in working with the technology. For example, two faculty members had technical trouble when they showed the video to their students at the college's instructional lab, and two others reported that the tutorial site was difficult to find and that their students wished it was more prominently displayed on the library Web site. Still, the faculty also indicated that students were able to take the technical issues in stride and approached the difficulties they encountered with the attitude, "If it doesn't fail at times, then it's not technology."

Our meeting ended with a firm agreement from the faculty to continue to use the tutorial during the spring 2007 semester. They made an equally firm agreement to assume definite responsibilities for its implementation. In an effort to achieve greater integration within the course curriculum, the faculty agreed that they would treat the exercises associated with the modules as required assignments. Although we had recommended that faculty make the assignments a required part of their courses at the outset, it took them a semester to realize that full integration would not be achieved until students received a grade for each of the assignments. They also agreed to try introducing the tutorials in segments. Finally, they committed to experimenting with working through some of the modules with students during class sessions as well as pairing students up to work through some of the modules outside of class. The faculty hope that pairing students up will reduce some of the intimidation that the students experience when they use the library and also encourage more student-to-student sharing. Both librarians and faculty agreed that these actions could increase students' information literacy skills and appreciation of the relevance of the library and its resources to their coursework and assignments.

Student Assessment

Along with the extensive information gleaned from the faculty, we gathered assessment information from students through an eleven-question survey (based on Survey Monkey). The questions used a five-point Likert scale to assess student opinions on the content and quality of the modules. We based our survey questions on those used by the University of Tennessee Library to assess their online instruction (www.lib.utk.edu/refs/teachinglib/tutorial-detailed.pdf). We surveyed students during the spring 2006 pilot and a second group during the fall 2006 semester. We were disappointed with the small number of students who responded to the survey (under 10 percent), which limits our student assessment information. In the future, we plan on exploring methods for ensuring that we receive a good survey response, including offering rewards for survey completion or asking faculty to assign the survey as homework.

Even though our response rate was low, the results we received were consistent with the faculty reports of student reactions and learning. For example, many of the faculty commented that their students did not find the original exercise in the Introduction to the Library module helpful. The student evaluations of this module bore this out. In the original module, 66 percent of respondents strongly agreed or agreed to the statement, "I feel more confident in doing library research as a result of this module." After revising the module, 75 percent of students strongly agreed or agreed with the statement. We saw a similar increase in affirmative responses to the question, "This module will be useful to me in successfully completing my class projects."

When our module covered search skills directly related to a class assignment, such as using the print volumes in Something About the Author, faculty and students clearly saw the relevance of the module and responded accordingly. Based on positive comments from faculty and students, we did not revise the Something About the Author module and, in both the spring and fall semesters, 100 percent of online survey respondents indicated that "the content of the module was clearly related to the class assignment."

Although faculty members have reported that their students have demonstrated stronger information literacy skills, we have found it difficult to prove objectively that their information literacy skills are the result of using our modules. Still, our faculty interview data as well as written comments from students lead us to believe that our modules are having a positive impact. The following comment is representative of the positive feedback: "I learned about the resources that the library has to offer. In these days I've become so dependent on the Internet and forget the valuable contributions that are available through the library system." At this writing, we do not have an objective assessment of the modules in place. We intend to remedy this lack by creating pre- and post-assessments to provide some concrete data.

Lessons Learned

We learned much while planning, creating, and implementing our program. One major finding was that, despite the electronic nature of most of our tutorial, many of the skills we needed to develop online instruction were similar to those needed to design face-to-face instruction. We were able to draw extensively from our teaching knowledge and experience.

We used many core teaching skills when developing our program. Our ability to develop learning objectives, organize information into meaningful instructional chunks, understand our audience, and build a cohesive learning experience were skills that proved essential to our project's effectiveness. We learned that collaboration skills are essential. Our success was due, to a large extent, on how well we listened to the faculty and students. Such a project demands continuous sharing of ideas, issues, and results. For example, based on the comments of faculty and students, we revised our modules to be more interactive. We also changed the questions and exercises that accompanied several of the modules so they would directly address the information literacy skills students needed to complete their coursework successfully.

A big lesson we learned throughout the collaboration was that we needed to draw upon the confidence that comes with our own expertise and experience. As equal partners in this collaboration, we had the ability to disagree with the teaching faculty, to identify problems, and to discuss barriers to the success of the project. For example, on the basis of our own experience in teaching information literacy, we emphasized to faculty the importance of tying the information literacy modules directly to the course curriculum and assignments. It took two semesters, but the faculty came to realize that introducing the tutorial module by module would increase student success in completing the research portions of their coursework.

Although such intensive collaborative efforts help to ensure success, they can be extremely time consuming. Although the online tutorial replaced six face-to-face sessions each semester, we did not save any librarian time. The initial creation and construction of the individual modules was labor intensive, but the continuous collaboration and revision took even more time. As we head into the future with this project, we see a continuing pattern of development, use, evaluation, and revision. Although we have not seen any savings in librarian time, we have heard from students that they appreciate "being able to access information on the computer without having to physically go to the library," and that they like being able to revisit the modules as needed. Being able to support students wherever they are and whenever they need help is a valuable outcome that may outweigh the time and cost this intensive type of partnering requires.

We also found that it is important to collaborate with experts in areas such as programming and graphic design. We are fortunate to have a programmer as well as a graphic designer on staff, so we did not have to seek out these skills from other campus units. Equally important was identifying the resources and partners available to us for assistance in using appropriate technology and pedagogy. We learned that we can no longer limit ourselves to what we alone can do.

We know that our experiences in this project are not necessarily unique and be- lieve that much of what we learned will be valuable to both our next project and to our colleagues who are beginning similar programs. We have already been asked to share our experiences with colleagues through a library forum and to consult with UA Library teams who are creating online instruction.

Conclusion

We have moved from a ninety-minute classroom instructional session to a four-module online tutorial that incorporates video, Flash video, interactive Web tutorials, and printable exercises. Such a transformation came primarily through strong partnerships between librarians and teaching faculty, clear instructional objectives, the instructional design and pedagogical skills needed to transform objectives into online content, and access to technology and technical assistance. We look forward to continuing this dynamic and rewarding partnership and to strengthening student information literacy skills through online instruction.

You can view the complete tutorial at www. library.arizona.edu/help/tutorials/cours- es/educ/childlit/LRC480resources.html.

16. Introducing Information Literacy in a WebCT-based Composition Course Using Streaming Media Tutorials

Diane Prorak, Beth Hill, and Ben Hunter

Rationale

The University of Idaho (UI) welcomes thousands of new students to campus every year. In the course of their studies, they must use electronic databases, online catalogs, and Web sites, but often they do not have the skills to use them effectively.[1] Realizing an information need, knowing where to find the information, accessing and synthesizing the information, and then applying it in a presentable form make up the skill base necessary for being information literate. Information literacy skills are important to acquire, and yet information literacy instruction has not been integrated into the majority of classes offered on campuses.

The majority of the new students are members of a cohort commonly named Generation Y. Gen Ys have been described as

> having a positive attitude toward new technologies, particularly computers, oriented more toward images rather than linear text, and viewing the Internet primarily as an access tool, a distribution mechanism for books, articles and music. Displaying a low threshold for boredom and resistance to memorization, Gen Y students show more willingness to engage in and better retention of peer-learning activities, as well as a preference for active, discovery learning opportunities. These students embrace active learning styles and an electronic learning environment.[2]

To address the learning styles of Gen Y, librarians may not need to change the content of library instruction, but the activities and delivery need to take this awareness into account. Adapting the lecture material to include interactive components can appeal to different learning styles. "Whereas lecture appeals to auditory learners, hands-on activities reach kinesthetic or experiential learners. Lecture may be very appropriate for older students; however, students in Gen Y may prefer hands-on activities."[3]

Like libraries in many other institutions, the UI Library has provided library instruction and orientation within freshman composition classes for many years. We have spent the most time and effort teaching sessions for the English 102 classes, the standard freshman composition class that includes a unit teaching the process of writing a research paper. Although this provides an orientation to about thirty-six sections of freshmen, many freshmen do not take that course in their first semester. An almost equal number are enrolled in English 101, a precursor to English 102, "intended to prepare students for the demands of student writing" according to the course description. This course does not assign a research paper so, for many years, the library did not provide any orientation for these students. English 101 is taught by graduate student teaching assistants (TAs), closely overseen by the director of writing.

As the enrollment in English 101 increased, we began to hear from students that they had to use the library for other courses but did not get any orientation until spring semester. UI librarians and the director of writing began to feel that perhaps a brief fall semester orientation for students in this course should be offered. In English 102, librarians teach an entire week's worth of sessions, teaching skills for finding library-based resources and evaluating sources. When possible, the sessions are taught at the time the students are doing research for their papers. For English 101, we decided to offer a one-shot session providing a brief physical tour of the library, an introduction to the library Web site, and a brief worksheet to provide hands-on reinforcement. These sessions were initially done in a block of about two to three weeks near the beginning of the fall semester.

Over the course of a few years, the library instruction coordinator worked closely with the director of writing to create assignments in which English 101 students had to access outside sources to give a greater sense of purpose and need to the sessions. Sometimes the search for outside sources seemed strained and lacked a clear purpose for the students. In addition, the scheduling of sessions was difficult for both the English instructors and the librarians. Since English 101 is a highly structured course, having library sessions for the different sections on different days made it difficult to keep the whole course schedule intact. At the same time, squeezing all the sessions into the shortest period possible (two to three weeks) created heavy teaching and reference schedules for librarians. We began to explore alternatives.

Content and Development

In 2005 we began to develop Flash movie tutorials that provided an introduction to the library's Web site and resources. Looking at our objectives for English 101, we realized that students could learn how to navigate the Web site using one of the tutorials. Using the tutorials, with the printed worksheets as follow up, we felt that students could learn much of what they needed to know; thus we proposed to substitute this method for the face-to-face version. The library building tour would not be included, but we had questioned its effectiveness.

In fall 2005 we launched this new version of the English 101 instruction, using two Flash movie tutorials. The first tutorial highlighted key resources and services for first-year students on the UI Library Web site. This covered roughly the same content as in-class demonstrations in the past, helping students become aware of how the Web site could be helpful to them for research. The second tutorial covered a specific skill, finding a required article by searching in an article database. This skill was needed to find an article for their writing assignment. After watching the tutorials, students completed a worksheet that checked their understanding of the tutorial content. The English 101 instructors assigned students to do these activities on their own. Worksheets were turned in to the instructors, so librarians were not directly involved. The instruction coordinator provided an answer key for the worksheet to the English instructors.

Though many English instructors and librarians were happy with the plan in general, it was difficult for librarians to monitor the program's use and effectiveness. We did not see the completed worksheets, so we could not assess student learning or compliance. Thus, for the next year, we searched for a better way to assess learning while allowing students to learn independently.

In fall 2006, when English 101 began using a blended method of teaching, incorpo-

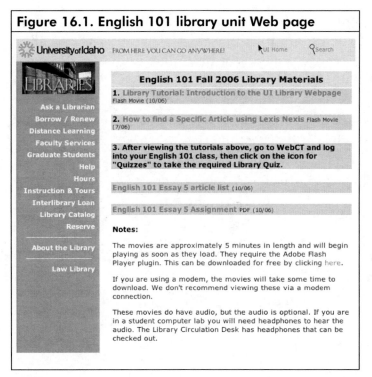

Figure 16.1. English 101 library unit Web page

rating WebCT courseware and face-to-face class sessions, we saw an opportunity. Working with the director of writing, the instruction coordinator was given WebCT designer access. We could develop a unit that fit into the syllabus, and the worksheet could be redesigned as a quiz that could be graded automatically. Then we could monitor both how many students took the quiz and their scores.

Next Steps

Research has shown that "the key to developing a successful Web-assisted library instructional module is to link it directly with the pedagogical objectives of the course and to use technology effectively to enhance and enrich students' learning experiences."[4] We worked with the director of writing to coordinate our unit with an appropriate writing assignment in the course. The best choice was an assignment in which students write a response to an argument. They were given a list of articles to choose from, but instead of

being provided links to the articles students were required to find their article using the library Web site to access the LexisNexis database. Based in WebCT, a thirty-point quiz (see appendix) asked students to answer ten questions similar in content to those on the former printed worksheet. The WebCT syllabus was updated to include a link to a library Web page for English 101 (figure 16.1) that gave them information for the assignment to (1) view the library tutorials, (2) take the quiz (linked from within WebCT), (3) find the full text of their article, and (4) write their summary. They were encouraged to view the library's Web site while they took the quiz, so we did not expect them to memorize information from the tutorials.

As library instruction continues to focus on digital services and resources, it becomes increasingly possible for library instruction to be adapted to an online format. This allows the curriculum content to be accessible to students at the "point of need" throughout the semester, not just for use with one assignment. Students are intimately familiar with electronics as communication tools. They may, however, come to the college environment with various levels of understanding of computer skills and of how to conduct library research. Being able to work through the tutorials at their own pace and review the content as needed allows students to match their information need to their learning style.[5]

Creating opportunities for students to have hands-on practice yields greater outcomes in the development of cognitive and psychomotor skills. Assignments should include an active learning component, which provides needed reinforcement of the skills taught. Web-based instruction has distinct advantages over other forms of instruction; specifically, it is more effective in teaching undergraduates how to access materials in the library. Students have stated a preference for Web-based instruction because it offers them the ability to work at an individual pace and to go back and review any sections that were more difficult for them.[6]

Streaming Media Tutorial development

Previous online tutorials used with English 101 classes had been created with Tech-Smith's Camtasia screencasting software. This software was chosen because of its low price and the speed with which one can learn the software and create a finished product. Camtasia creates a movie of everything that happens within a specified part of the screen with an accompanying soundtrack provided by input from a microphone. This software is a logical choice for library tutorials, for it allows the creator to explain and demonstrate

the use of library catalogs and databases. The finished movie can then be posted online and viewed by anyone with a Flash plug-in installed on their browser. This plug-in is free and installed on all the computers in our library and computer labs.

These tutorials were used successfully for a year, but there was general agreement that revisions were needed. The software performed as promised, but some felt that the final product left something to be desired. Many were of the opinion that the lecture format used in these tutorials, though effective in a classroom, was not very engaging in the online environment. Other librarians felt that their voices were not well suited for recording and broadcast. The problem with voiceovers was compounded by the fact that we do not have speakers on any computers in our library labs. We have headphones that can be checked out, but this created an additional barrier to students trying to use the tutorials.

Figure 16.2. Sample screenshot from the library's Web site introduction tutorial, created using Captivate

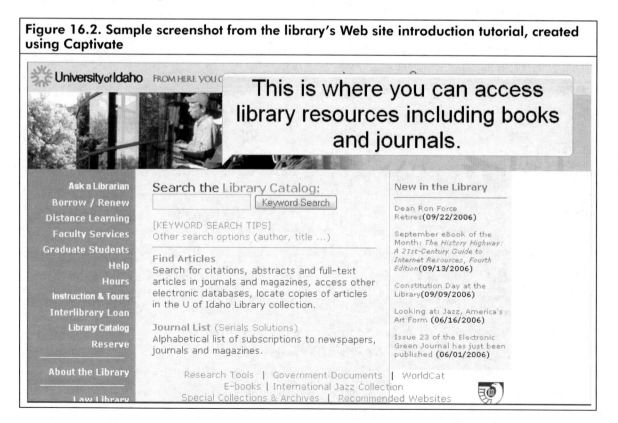

Figure 16.3. Sample screenshot from the library's Web site introduction tutorial, created using Captivate

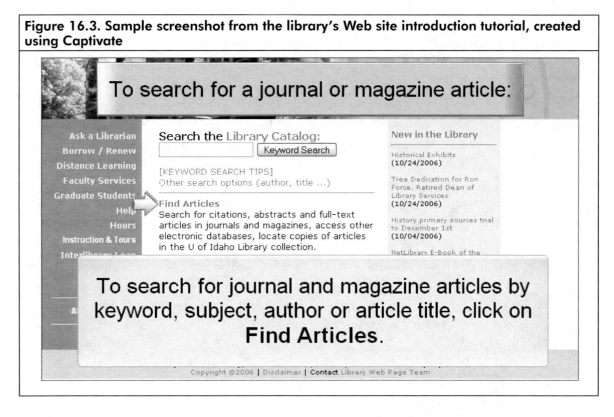

To gain some insight into how better to create a next generation of tutorials, we referred to literature on online tutorials and online learning. Dewald and Clark proved especially useful in providing practical guidance.[7] On the basis of this research, we decided that our next generation of tutorials should include active learning elements (interactivity), accommodation for multiple learning styles, shortened lessons, more control over lesson pacing by the user, concrete objectives, and elements of nonlinear learning.

To better accommodate our new teaching objectives we decided to use a different screencasting application, called Adobe Captivate. Captivate costs more than Camtasia and has a steeper learning curve, but it offers more opportunities for incorporating interactivity, visual learning, and nonlinear learning. Additionally, Captivate integrates well with Flash. Because one of our librarians had experience with Flash, the possibili-

ties for what we could do with Captivate were extended even further. Creating the content of the tutorials was a collaborative effort, but one librarian did the majority of the technical work (figures 16.2 and 16.3).

Our final design for the tutorials replaced the voiceover almost entirely with pop-up text boxes. Special care was taken to keep text as clear and succinct as possible. The only voiceovers are presented as optional elements that present additional information if clicked on. In an attempt to make the lessons more interactive and less passive, the learner is required to frequently click links on the screen to continue the lesson. This reinforces the learning by requiring the student to mimic steps that would be taken during the actual research process. Additionally, it allows the viewer to control the pace of the lesson to a large degree. After small sections of the tutorial have been viewed, there is a link that allows the learner to review the section if desired. This gives users an opportunity to reinforce their own learning when they feel it is appropriate.

The content of the redesigned tutorials is similar to the previous versions. One tutorial highlights services and resources on the library's Web site that are of use to the general user or freshmen students. This tutorial points out the links and gives tips for searching the library catalog and article databases, finding the magazines owned by the library, as well as showing where to renew books, how to get help or access interlibrary loan, and more. The second tutorial shows the specific steps for finding a known article using LexisNexis, which students apply to find the article for their writing assignment (figures 16.4 and 16.5).

Program Assessment

In the 1990s, accountability became more of an issue, with an expectation that assessment of outcomes would be conducted in library instruction programs.[8] Although library instruction assessment has been conducted in colleges, only a few institutions have done assessments on the program level. Over the past ten years, however, the number of research studies assessing the influence of library instruction on student learning outcomes and information competency has grown.

Only keeping a count of how many students complete the face-to-face one-shot library orientation sessions does not provide the level of evaluation necessary to determine student-learning outcomes. Quizzes, tests, and surveys offer the types of quantifiable data needed for assessment and provide instruction librarians with the ability to measure certain aspects of instruction.[9] Survey research is commonly used to evaluate forms of library instruction; survey methodology has been found to be "optimal for measuring changes in skill level, attitude, and behavior (level of use) as the result of library instruction."[10] Providing an online, machine-gradable quiz for students to access and submit gave us better feedback on the content of the online materials and the design of the Web-based instruction overall.

The start of the assignment was marred by a technical problem with one of the tutorials. Mozilla Firefox and Microsoft Internet Explorer require slightly different methods to embed a Flash movie in an HTML document. We had failed to test the final page in Internet Explorer and did not realize that the line of code intended for Internet Explorer had an error. The problem was fixed, though a little late in the process, and most students were able to complete the quiz and assignment in the time allotted. This problem had an effect on some of our evaluative comments.

We evaluated the unit in three different ways: instructor comments, student comments, and quiz score results.

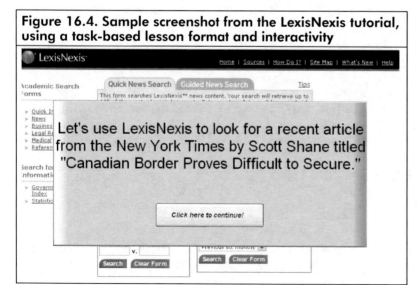

Figure 16.4. Sample screenshot from the LexisNexis tutorial, using a task-based lesson format and interactivity

Figure 16.5. Sample screenshot from the LexisNexis tutorial, using a task-based lesson format and interactivity

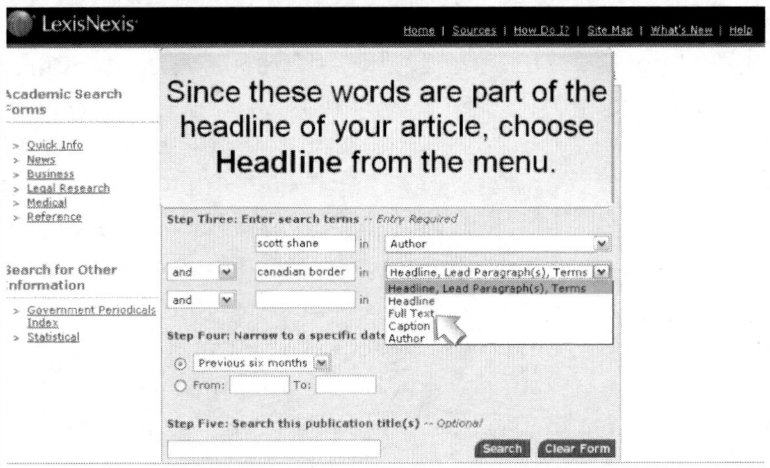

Instructor Comments

We met with many of the instructors during one of their graduate TA course sessions. In addition to talking with them, we asked them to fill out evaluation forms, which nine completed. The results indicated that overall they both liked the online library unit and felt it was useful. They felt the content of the tutorials was appropriate. All rated them from 3 to 5 (five-point scale, 5 very good). Comments stated that the tutorials were easy to use, and several really liked the independent and repeatable nature of the instruction. Most felt the quiz reinforced the learning and was appropriate. The overall content of the library instruction was rated 4 (good) and 5 (very good).

Because of the temporary technical problems with one tutorial, some TAs demonstrated the tutorial in class using Firefox to avoid the technical issue. Though they mentioned that this took class time, some were of the opinion that using the tutorials as a class activity might be a good approach in the future. One said, "My class loves movies." This approach may be one we suggest for the future; we had not previously considered our tutorial in the same category as class movies.

TAs commented that the short-answer questions in the quiz were problematic. Though the questions were designed to accept many variations of answer (including some different spellings), students seemed to feel some were marked wrong unfairly, because of different spellings or terms. It was suggested that all the questions should be multiple-choice. Some students resisted the quiz ("Do we have to take it?"), but most TAs felt it encouraged them to view the tutorials. Some commented that they felt students could take the quiz without viewing the tutorials. One final point was that, since the quiz counted for only a small portion of their grade, those who encountered difficulties sometimes skipped the entire library unit.

The last major area TAs commented on produced split results. Were the students successful at finding their article after the library unit? A couple felt technical problems limited success in this area. Another felt students did not necessarily use information or skills gleaned from the tutorials to find their articles. Another commented on problems related to the LexisNexis search interface itself. Despite these criticisms, the majority (in this case, five) felt that the library instruction met the goal of helping the students find the articles. As one instructor said, "Most of [the students] could find the articles now."

Student Comments

One instructor (one class, n=26) asked her students to write a few sentences expressing their thoughts about the online library instruction. These comments were therefore unstructured and wide ranging. We had to get past several comments that seem to pervade many evaluations about tutorials and quizzes: "boring," "already knew this," "not helpful." Some felt it was too simple or too slow, while others commented that it went too fast for them. However, even if their comments began negatively, some students went on to say that they now know what is available on the library Web site or that the instruction helped them in other classes. Some felt they had to revisit the tutorial to answer the questions on the quiz adequately. Since they were instructed to view the library Web site as they took the quiz, we found it a little surprising that some of them went back to the tutorial. Perhaps they preferred the tutorial method to finding the answer on the Web site. One student gave this response: "The library tutorial was good for me because I have already had to go back to Lexus Nexus [*sic*] for another class. It is a good reference to be able to use. It was nice to be able to look up news articles without any problems." This response made us feel that the tutorial and quiz, at least for this student and several others, successfully served the purpose of a general orientation to the library's resources.

Quiz Results

The quiz consisted of ten questions—seven multiple-choice, two short-answer, and one matching. The mean score was 83.22 percent. Mean scores were consistent across class sections; all mean scores were from 80 to 85 percent.

Mean scores on certain questions were consistently lower. One of these questions asked students what link (from the library homepage) they would click on to start looking for magazine articles on a topic. The exact right answer on our Web site is the link on the main page, "Find Articles," which links to our article databases page. Other answers such as EBSCO or LexisNexis were allowed. The mean score was 68.7 percent. This question was short-answer, and in their narrative evaluations students commented that the format of this question seemed problematic; they thought they were penalized for incorrect spellings. WebCT allows for accepting variations of answers, and we tried to allow for many spellings and combinations. Looking closely at the results for that question reveals that in some cases students were marked wrong for unexpected spellings, but, since they were allowed to look at the Web site, most answers marked wrong were incorrect choices. Thus the students had difficulty with this concept, perhaps because the tutorial did not teach them the concepts adequately, because they are confused by the Web site, or a combination of factors. Those who wrote "catalog" or "search" (referring to the library catalog search box on our main page) probably did not understand the difference between the library's catalog and the article databases. Those who wrote "journal list" had trouble differentiating between the list for accessing our periodical holdings and the indexes to articles. We need to revise both the tutorial and the questions to improve the results, as well as make changes to our Web site. It does seem that multiple-choice is preferable, since it appears that short-answer questions in this format are problematic. Another short-answer question had better results, but still some surprising answers.

Another question (this one multiple-choice) asked about the purpose of our Journal List, and results showed the same confusion mentioned above between the article indexes and the list for accessing periodical holdings. The mean score on this question was 53.5 percent. This is a difficult concept that many librarians and library Web sites struggle to make clear. The Journal List should primarily be used for searching for known items, either a specific article in a journal or a known journal in which to browse. The article indexes would be recommended for looking for items by subject, to see what articles are available. Though we expected this concept to be difficult, the number of students who answered "The Journal List is used for looking for the personal journals of historical people" was somewhat surprising. There may be a confusion of jargon in different disciplines at play here, but this also points to a change needed for our Web site as well as our instructional materials.

Another question that had one of the lower mean scores was a multiple-choice question that asked about the use of LexisNexis, with the correct answer reading "LexisNexis is a good database for finding newspaper articles." The mean score was 79.2 percent. The most frequently chosen wrong answer finished the statement above with "scholarly journal articles." Since our tutorials dealt little with the definitions of scholarly versus popular publications, this shows that these students need further instruction about this concept, which they generally get in our library instruction sessions in the next level of composition class.

Overall, the quiz results point to changes needed in the tutorials, quiz, and Web site. But they also show general competency of the basic concepts and skills we included in our instruction.

Lessons Learned

Our assessment results suggest that our virtual instruction unit was successful overall in meeting its learning objectives. Although we received some negative comments, we also received some solid praise and helpful constructive criticism. Between quiz results, student comments, and instructor evaluations we have a clear idea of where we need to make changes.

The results from the quizzes pointed to certain concepts in the tutorials that need extra emphasis. Important concepts such as the content of LexisNexis, where our article databases can be accessed from our homepage, and what our journal list does were some of the most frequently misunderstood topics. The LexisNexis tutorial is very task based, and adding a more thorough conceptual overview at the beginning of the tutorial could be a first step in clarifying the content of this database to students. Information about our journal list and article databases is contained in the tutorial that introduces the library Web site. Although these concepts are covered in the tutorial, it is possible that they were not given treatment proportional to their importance. Possible solutions include simply adding more information to those sections, scaling back other sections deemed less important, or breaking those concepts out into a separate tutorial. We also have considered working with the director of writing to change the assignment so students can search another database, such as EBSCO's Academic Search Premier, to see if a different database and search interface might help. We will continue to experiment and to monitor quiz scores.

One of the most interesting aspects of the student evaluations was the number of students who characterized the tutorial as being too slow or said they "already knew this," but with an almost equal number of students characterizing the tutorial as being too fast. This suggests a need for increased user control over pacing. To address this issue, we will present the "Click Here to Continue" buttons immediately rather than after a few seconds for each text box. An additional step we may try is to break the tutorial down into smaller, shorter chapters. This would help clarify the roles of the sections to students and allow for greater control over the order and pacing of the instruction.

In their evaluations, no student stated that the quiz was an enjoyable part of the unit. The primary goal of administering the quiz was, however, to ensure that the students watched the tutorials. TAs confirmed to us that this goal was met, and as a result we plan to keep the quiz. Because both TAs and students frequently cited WebCT's automated grading of short-answer questions as a problem, we plan to convert all questions to multiple-choice. A problem we have less control over is the very small number of points assigned to the quiz. Some TAs mentioned student apathy created by the negligible effect the quiz would have on their overall grade, causing students to skip the exercise altogether. Despite this, the vast majority of students did successfully complete the quiz. We may want to explore this issue with the director of writing, but given that this writing course does not include a research paper, we do feel fortunate for this

small opportunity to integrate information literacy into a course. We can now use this experience to work to include such mini-units in other WebCT-based courses. We can also use this now-established unit to create tiered information literacy instruction for those students who take both English 101 and 102.

We have found that using online tutorials as an alternative to classroom instruction is a convenient and effective method for teaching the skills needed for English 101 at UI. But online instruction is a complex, rapidly changing, and relatively new teaching method. We will continue to revise and rethink our tutorials, quizzes, and overall instruction method, in terms of both presentation and content. Certainly our most valuable asset is the full cooperation of the English department. We plan to continue assessing learning outcomes and soliciting responses from both instructors and students. Through this collaborative effort between departments we will be able to provide new students with a strong foundation of information literacy on which they can build throughout their college careers.

Appendix.
WebCT Quiz Questions

1. (Multiple choice) The Journal List is used for
   a. (correct) finding out if the UI Library owns a particular magazine or it can be accessed electronically.
   b. Finding our if the UI Library owns a book
   c. Finding articles on a subject for your research
   d. Looking for the personal journals of historical people

2. (Multiple choice) LexisNexis is a good database for finding
   a. (correct) Newspaper articles
   b. Books
   c. Web sites
   d. Scholarly journal articles

3. (Multiple choice) Your Vandal ID card is your library card. The number on your ID that you will need for many library transactions is your
   a. (correct) Barcode number
   b. Student ID number
   c. Social Security number
   d. Phone number

4. (Short answer) To start looking for magazine articles on a topic, click on _____.
(answer: find articles (best choice), EBSCO, LexisNexis, plus some variations)

5. (Matching) Links from the main library web page can take you to the resources below. Match the name of the correct link in the pulldown for each item on the left.
   a. WSU Library Catalog
   b. Research Assistance Program
   c. Information about library cards

   Choices (in correct order here):
      Other libraries and library catalogs
      Ask a Librarian
      Borrow/Renew

6. (Short answer) What link do you click on to see if anything is on Reserve for your English class?
   a. Answer: Reserve (spelling variations accepted)

7. The search box on the UI Library home page searches
   a. Magazine articles

b. The Internet

c. (correct) The UI Library catalog

d. Just items on Reserve for classes

8. To find out what library books you have checked out and if any are overdue, click on

a. Library catalog

b. Ask a librarian

c. (correct) Borrow/Renew

d. Faculty services

9. When you search the UI Library catalog, you may find

a. Books

b. Electronic books

c. DVDs

d. Music CDs

e. (correct) All of the above

10. EBSCOSearch is a good database for finding

a. (correct) Magazine and journal articles on a subject

b. DVDs for your class

c. Books on a subject

d. Recommended web sites

Notes

1. Jeff Rosen and Gina M. Castro, "From Workbook to Web: Building an Information Literacy Oasis," *Computers in Libraries* 22, no. 1 (2002): 30–35.

2. Carolyn N. Willis and Wm. Joseph Thomas, "Students as Audience: Identity and Information Literacy Instruction," *Portal: Libraries and the Academy* 6, no. 4 (2006): 432.

3. Ibid., 438.

4. Betty Ladner, Donald Beagle, James R. Steele, and Linda Steele, "Rethinking Online Instruction: From Content Transmission to Cognitive Immersion," *Reference and User Services Quarterly* 43, no. 4 (2004): 332.

5. Ibid.

6. Lucy Holman, "A Comparison of Computer-Assisted Instruction and Classroom Bibliographic Instruction," *Reference and User Services Quarterly* 40, no. 1 (2000): 53–60.

7. Nancy H. Dewald, "Transporting Good Library Instruction Practices into the Web Environment: An Analysis of Online Tutorials," *Journal of Academic Librarianship* 25, no. 1 (1999): 26–31; Nancy H. Dewald, "Web-Based Library Instruction: What Is Good Pedagogy?" *Information Technology and Libraries* 18, no. 1 (1999): 26–31; and Ruth Colvin Clark and Richard E. Mayer, *E-Learning and the Science of Instruction* (San Francisco: Pfeiffer, 2003).

8. Gabrielle Wong, Diana Chan, and Sam Chu, "Assessing the Enduring Impact of Library Instruction Programs," *Journal of Academic Librarianship* 32, no. 4 (2006): 384–95.

9.   Willis and Thomas, "Students as Audience."

10.   Chris A. Portmann and Adrienne Julius Roush, "Assessing the Effects of Library Instruction," *Journal of Academic Librarianship* 30, no. 6 (2004): 461.

17. Many Birds, One Stone: Benefits, Drawbacks, and the Process of Creating an Online Tutorial

Red Wassenich

Rationale

Thirty-two thousand students at seven campuses and fifty teaching sites versus eighteen public service librarians dedicated to information literacy. An unfair fight.

Given the impossibility of in-person presentations to more than a fraction of this number of students, the only teaching methods to deliver a large volume of library instruction we could see were training the faculty to present material, using paper or video resources, or having online tutorials. Although we have employed the former two methods to some extent, it is online instruction that has carried the great bulk of our teaching load. Our most widely used tutorial is the Info Game (http://library.austincc. edu/infogame.htm)—the focus of this chapter. The Info Game does not require a login (other than isolated times when accessing databases), including the quizzes. Dedicated readers may wish to explore it prior to wading through the following.

Library Services at Austin Community College has had course-integrated library instruction since the late 1970s and maintains a strong dedication to what is now called information literacy. Standardized information literacy projects are integrated into the curriculum of English Composition I, Introduction to Business, Chemistry I, and all developmental reading and writing courses. When combined with the many individual faculty throughout the academic disciplines who request instruction, approximately one thousand sections receive information literacy instruction, whether online, in person, or paper-based, per calendar year, totaling roughly 15,000 students. We maintain paper-based exercises for our developmental classes, but our Composition I and Introduction to Business classes do the general information literacy Info Game tutorial, and Chemistry has a separate subject-specific online tutorial. We are currently developing another online tutorial for Introduction to Public Speaking that is cowritten by Library and Speech faculty.

Our biggest single point of instruction, as is common with many colleges, is Composition I. This is the only course that is required for all degree plans, and students cannot test out of it. Since it requires a documented research paper, it is the obvious best place to reach the maximum number of students. In the fall semester of 2006 there were 199 classroom sections, seventeen distance learning sections (in three different formats—online, video, and correspondence, with online being predominant), and four separate semesters within the timeframe. The classroom sections were taught at seven campuses and thirteen other sites, usually high schools that offer college courses in the evening.

Given this volume and variety of course formats and locations and given the small number of librarians, not to mention the increasing number of distance learning classes, there is simply no way to employ in-person contact with hands-on activities by the students. A well-designed online tutorial provides the next best thing because it can provide consistent content and active learning. Indeed, in some cases it can be superior in those areas and can go into more depth than is usually the case with a one-shot presentation.

The alternative of having classroom faculty rather than librarians present information literacy in a standardized way is not seen as viable, largely because of the high number of adjuncts, who have a relatively high turnover rate. For example, in Composition I more than 60 percent of the sections are taught by adjunct faculty. We do offer in-person and online professional development workshops related to information literacy for faculty, but we reach a relative handful. Faculty are overworked (five sections is the full-time faculty load per semester) and unlikely to attend information literacy training in sufficient numbers.

Once we embarked on the road to developing an online tutorial, the big question was whether to adapt an existing one or develop our own—a difficult decision that we might make differently now.

At the time, 2000, there weren't as many open-source information literacy tutorials, of course. The Texas Information Literacy Tutorial (TILT) was the major one (and continues to be widely used and adapted, such as SearchPath). It was longer than we wanted, the graphics didn't appeal to us, and we wanted more interactivity, so considerable work would have been required to adapt TILT. Thus we came to the decision to create our own. Now that it's done and in place, I'm happy with the decision, but the amount of work should give one pause. Especially now that tutorials have become numerous and there are sites that collect and rate materials, such as PRIMO (Peer-Re-viewed Instructional Materials Online) and Merlot,[1] perhaps it would be wise to concentrate energies on creating new tutorials that are very discipline-specific (e.g., our current effort to create one aimed at a public speaking course).

Development

Austin Community College, as with many schools, has an internal grant project to encourage development of innovative coursework. In conjunction with the business department, in 2000, the library was granted funding to get partial release time for one librarian (me) and one business faculty member for a semester to develop the online tutorial and related research assignment. An instructional designer was also assigned to work with us.

The business faculty member's role was the development of the research assignment topics that the students would pursue after completion of the tutorial, which was my responsibility. The approximately three dozen topics offered to the business faculty range from local to international issues. An effort was made to have topics that clearly required research, as opposed to ones students could just opine about. Some examples: Franchising and Small Business Growth, Self-Regulation of the Advertising Industry, NAFTA and Texas.

One of the initial setbacks we encountered turned into a blessing. For obvious reasons, I was planning to have the content of the tutorial focus on resources and search techniques related to business. However, the internal grantors stipulated that the tutorial be useful to a general student audience. At first I fumed that this would water down the value of the project, but wiser heads prevailed and we proceeded with the production of a general tutorial, counting on the

Figure 17.1. The Info Game look

© Images courtesy of retroadart.com

actual assignment to get the focus on business-related matters. Having a general purpose tutorial led to its adoption by Composition I, our biggest prize, within a year. My advice to those considering the relative merits of creating or adapting a general information literacy tutorial or a subject-specific one, other factors aside, is to cannibalize and expand an existing general tutorial to create a specific one.

After creating a general outline of what the intellectual content would cover, the actual day-to-day process of developing the tutorial generally consisted of me writing many very short Word documents, bouncing them off other librarians who were on our information literacy committee, and giving them to one of the college's instructional designers, who turned them into individual Web pages. Learning to write as succinctly and jargon free as possible was an enjoyable challenge. The project had a serendipitous bit of fortune in that the instructional designer, Tina Buck, was also an adjunct instructor in Composition I (and a personal friend). We enjoyed many arguments over the content, with Tina reigning in my tendencies to include too much detail and forcing me to justify inclusion of all content. Any such project should build in an editor who has some independence and a nonlibrarian perspective.

As to the choice of the look and feel of the tutorial, we agreed we wanted something lighthearted to help offset the lack of enthusiasm students bring to the topic of information literacy. We decided a game show theme would have a funny quality, and passing the tutorial could be presented as winning. (It should be noted that, although the tutorial does have some superficial aspects of a game, it doesn't truly fall into the currently popular instructional gaming category. We are currently considering ways to insert more games within the tutorial as a way to increase student engagement.) Tina and I share a fondness for retro-style designs and went for a forties and fifties look (figure 17.1). We discussed how after even a few years you could look at a Web site and have a feel for when it was created. We hoped using a retro look would ironically undercut that problem and not require frequent major revisions to the design.

Since neither the instructional designer nor I were working exclusively on this, creating the Web-based tutorial took approximately two months, followed by testing and revision. Student library workers did the initial test run-throughs.

Our classroom faculty partner had one section of Introduction to Business pilot the project in the summer. We administered pre- and post-tests, which showed improvement in information skills. The instructor had his students write short papers commenting on the Info Game, and these were overall quite positive. I also visited the class to discuss it. Students gave useful suggestions and were generally supportive. The main objection was that portions covered areas they already knew, particularly the explanation of the Internet and basic use of a Web browser. The instructor said that the summer students tended to be more advanced—many of them were returning home for the summer and had more college credits than did the typical long-semester students—so we only did minor tweaking of the tutorial content but added a way to test out of the initial module. Thus one esoteric factor to consider in pilots: select a semester that matches the most likely ongoing audience you expect.

The instructor and I presented the product to the business department, and they voted unanimously to require it in the introductory course, although faculty members created their own research projects, with most using the topics developed as the bases for the assignments. As word spread within the college about this tutorial and given that the English Composition I course had a research component and a long tradition of involvement with the library, key individual faculty in that department pushed for adopting the Info Game, which happened in spring 2001.

But the work doesn't stop with adoption and initial implementation. A significant question to keep in mind in development is who is going to maintain the tutorial. Presumably a librarian will handle the intellectual content, but can he or she also address technical concerns? For example, if there are cascading style sheets or Java or Flash, will there need to be a technical specialist, and how dedicated to resolving issues will this person be?

Another factor to address from the beginning (we didn't, sadly) is accessibility, especially if these more complex formats are used. It is probably a good idea to create a text-only version as you go along.

Content

A major quandary for any teacher is what depth one should teach. There is the obvious struggle between wanting to cover all the material we know is important and what we can get students to absorb and how much time we have. This seems to be doubly true for information literacy, a topic often seen by students as marginal or irrelevant. Online tutorials bring a new angle and, possibly, some solutions.

The classic in-person information literacy session is the fifty-minute one-shot. Here the struggle to cover just the basics often forces us to spend too much time lecturing. Some avoid active learning portions because they take more time than we feel we can give up. The end result is a snorefest. Or we go for the active learning and settle for a "less is more" approach where students learn two or three things more thoroughly.

Online tutorials address this predicament. Since they are typically done independently, outside a classroom setting, the strict time factor is largely eliminated (however, to restate the obvious, keeping the content succinct and clear is paramount), and active learning activities can be included to immediately reinforce the content.

An additional virtue of tutorials is that students who don't understand something have the means to review material—unlike in-class sessions, where they typically don't want to interrupt to ask for clarification and don't often respond when asked if they have questions, presumably out of a desire not to appear ignorant.

I should claim I went through some sort of formal, scholarly process to develop the content for the initial tutorial, but to be honest I mainly applied my experience with our program's overall goals (which are based on the ACRL Information Literacy Competency Standards) in an intuitive way. The content was largely a reflection of what we taught in our in-person sessions, with a module at the beginning explaining the Internet and basic Web browser skills, which wasn't a normal portion of our presentations. The modules I, in consultation with fellow librarians, came up with did not directly correlate with the ACRL standards—that is, there wasn't a module on Standard One and another on Standard Two, and so on— but the Info Game did cover them to a large degree.

The original Info Game had these modules:

1. The Online World: What the Internet is and how to use Web browsers.

2. Questions and Answers: How to focus your topic and locate information.

3. The "Private" Web: Understanding subscription databases.

4. Who Do You Trust? How to evaluate the quality of the information.

As stated earlier, our pilot of the tutorial showed that many students thought the initial module covered material they already knew. Since it's really a bad move to have the opening section be something that puts off

users, we gave students the option to test out of the initial module of the tutorial.

There had been constant tweaking of the details of the content—databases come and go, statistics mentioned change, and so on— but in 2005 it was time for major revision. Objectives that led to this decision included addressing the results of an assessment of learning that indicated we should add more content on evaluation; a better alignment with the ACRL standards; improvements to make testing more rigorous (see the Assessment section for details); and a desire to add visual pizzazz and more interactivity. Again, I received release time to work on this with the same instructional designer, Tina Buck, and an additional multimedia designer, Cindy Yates. We went to cascading style sheets from straight HTML and added Java and Flash components. The tutorial went from four to five modules: The Basics, Topics, Search, Techniques, Variety of Sources, and Evaluation.

I created a page for each ACRL standard and its performance indicators and recorded where each one was addressed in the Info Game.[2] Table 17.1 is a truncated example. This exercise made me focus the content into the appropriate module and helped me spot gaps. It also let me monitor whether I had reinforced important concepts in later modules.

We created test banks for each module so every student didn't get the same test.

Table 17.1. Topics Module		
Standard One	Performance Indicator	
The information literate student determines the nature and extent of the information needed.	1. The information literate student defines and articulates the need for information.	2. The information literate student identifies a variety of types and formats of potential sources for information.
Page 1	x	
Page 2		x
Page 3	x	x
Page 4		x

Students have the option to test out of each module, although there is an exit quiz that is "comprehensive"—it has questions related to all five modules. For each of the first four quizzes, students get ten multiple-choice questions drawn from a pool of twenty. The fifth quiz has fifteen questions.

Instruction

Community college students lead stressed, fractured lives. More than 72 percent of our students are part-time. Eight percent take only distance learning classes, and another 11 percent are enrolled in both on-campus and distance courses. A large percentage of all students are also employed. Students welcome projects they can do independently and remotely.

The Info Game is a traditional online tutorial: content is explained, and examples—interactive ones as much as possible—illustrate it, followed by testing to prove mastery. Students work at their own pace and can start and stop as they wish and may retake the tests.

The Info Game stresses use of our online databases, because we feel many students do not understand either what these are or why they are generally more credible than the public Web. In the Variety of Sources module, after a couple of interactive exercises that demonstrate the basics of accessing and using some general databases, such as Academic Search Complete, students choose databases to explore in any of six subject areas.

This is the only time the Info Game branches to allow students to self-select where to go. With this minor exception we gave a strictly linear structure to the tutorial. The students only see a menu at the beginning or when they are ready to move to the next module; it is not a routine part of the navigation, as is common; TILT, for example, always has the menu on the left margin. We thought that our content built in a logical path, so being able to maneuver within the overall tutorial wasn't needed. We also thought that being able to go only forward or back one screen at a time discouraged users from simply clicking on the next module after going through a few screens. They at least have to click through the entire section to get to the end. We chose not to display the address bar in the browser to prevent users from picking up on our sequence (p1.htm, p2.htm, etc.) and inputting guesses of which page might be the end.

These decisions go against standard practices of tutorials, where giving users more control is seen as beneficial. We are in the process of reconsidering this arrangement. The latest revision we are just beginning to talk about will most likely include a menu so students can return to specific sections for review. Other features we are considering, in addition to the previously mentioned insertion of gaming, is a way to have students create, as they go through the tutorial, a document that collects information they will use to write their papers. We hope this can be used to replace or shorten some of the quizzes. We do like our current testing process wherein the fifth and final quiz "proves" mastery. It has questions from all four previous modules, and to even get to it students have to complete the prior modules successfully.

Students do not communicate with each other or a librarian as a standard part of the tutorial. Their only mandated contact with their instructor is when they send the results of the final quiz, and even that is optional since they can print off a certificate instead. An e-mail contact for a librarian is given at the very beginning of the Info Game and is used, but not frequently. Having some sort of required interaction would be nice to show students the value of a librarian's skills, but the sheer number of students and their schedules preclude it.

Testing

For each module of the Info Game, students can try placing out with a pre-test. In the original version, for each module successfully completed, students sent their instructor an e-mail or printed off a certificate, for a total of four. In the revision we reduced the need for documenting completion to one, at the end of the final module. Since students had to complete each module successfully before they could go on, they had proved mastery. The final module's quiz is longer (fifteen vs. ten questions) and also includes questions from the previous modules to test whether students have really understood those areas. A survey after the revision showed this approach to be highly popular with faculty, since they had 75 percent less e-mail or paper certificates to deal with. Somewhat disappointing, they also asked the passing score to be decreased from 80 percent correct to 70 percent, which matches a passing grade in the other portions of coursework.

The Info Game is not done in a secure location or via a student login, so undoubtedly some students bring in help on the quizzes. We live with this since the options involving secure testing are too daunting. (Not all students are enrolled in our course management system, Blackboard, for instance.) But one of the inspirations for our revision of the tutorial was to address faculty concerns that the quizzes were being passed around. Originally, every student received the same quizzes for each module. For the revision, we created a test bank where at least a third of the questions are new each time the test

is taken. Since students can retake the tests, this feature discourages simple guessing.

A feature of our testing that is a bit out of the ordinary is that the students do not get feedback on their answers. Both the instructional designer and I thought this added rigor; given that they can retake tests, if students got feedback they could adjust the results. The lack of feedback is, however, a consistent complaint.

Another feature was added in the revision to discourage cheating by having someone else take the quizzes. This clever creation by Cindy Yates, the multimedia designer, gives the illusion of a database that tracks the students' progress. In fact, scores are not recorded anywhere, although students assume they are and act more honestly out of fear. As long as students receive a sufficient score, they get what appears to be a computer-generated "token code" (e.g., R4U57W) that they use, along with their last names, to gain access to the next module. In fact there are only four codes per module and any letters will be recognized as a legitimate last name. We maintain the appearance of a process that keeps students honest without actually having to have a huge database running behind the scenes. Don't tell anybody about this.

Program Assessment

Our major program assessment came in 2003. We had eighty-three students in five sections of Composition I do a pre-test early in a summer semester, go through the Info Game during the middle of the semester, then take a post-test with the same questions at the end of the semester. A statistician from our institutional effectiveness department applied a McNemar test to gauge the significance of the results. There were only six information literacy questions, plus one in which students ranked their confidence in doing college-level research. All questions except one (related to judging objectivity of sources) showed statistically significant improvement. This result was one piece of evidence indicating a need for more emphasis to the evaluation portion of the tutorial. Since our results are in agreement with the literature in general, which indicates that online instruction is effective,[3] we felt assured enough to develop online tutorials for Chemistry and (in development) Public Speaking.

An additional assessment has been done twice by me. Our Composition I faculty assemble once a year to have a group review of their grading criteria to assure reasonably uniform standards. They use a sample of the required research papers. Each one is graded by two instructors, and their grades are compared. I horned in on this process and reviewed papers using my own rubric to judge the research elements—as opposed to the rhetorical elements. I used the criteria given below to rate them on a one-to-three point scale. The criteria related to evaluation and the value of using background information and building to the specific came in lower than the others, again stressing the need to emphasize these in instruction. For example, the January 2003 review gave the following scores:

- used multiple sources, 2.9
- used a variety of sources (e.g., web, book, periodicals), 2.3
- used both background and specific information, 2.2
- used appropriate sources (on topic, not outdated), 2.7
- used apparently credible sources, 2.5
- articulated evaluation of sources within text of paper, 1.2
- documented sources (judged only whether the concept was there and whether

it was possible to identify sources, not strict accuracy of citations), 2.4

I must admit that both times I've done this there has not been a dramatic correlation between high scores on my rubric and the quality of the writing, which surprises me.

We had never before done a formal assessment of any of our large information literacy projects, only those done by individual faculty, so it's impossible to tell if the move to online instruction has been an improvement. It certainly feels like it is, and faculty, in two surveys, indicate satisfaction with it. (Sample question: Generally, did you notice any change in students' work on the research paper from previous semesters? Better work \ Same work \ Worse work \ Not applicable if new faculty.) In truth, this survey largely asked about technical and procedural issues, which were a major concern to an overworked faculty.

It is possible to say objectively that in Composition I a uniform level of instruction has occurred that was previously lacking: individual classroom faculty with widely varied research skills handled explaining the research process to students who, prior to the Info Game, were armed only with a three-page guide to the basics about the library and search techniques.

Lessons Learned

The Info Game has been a success, in my view, and several other colleges have either linked to it or actually asked for the coding so they can modify it for their own. It has either solidified or increased the library's profile within the college. I have never regretted doing it. Some practical advice from a grizzled instruction librarian:

1. Work with a small team and include someone who is not a librarian. As much as possible have one person write the text so it

has some personality rather than the drone of a committee.

2. Align the content with what is asked on quizzes. This should be obvious, but I did a poor job of this when we revised the Info Game and students had a very hard time, not surprisingly. It was an amateur's mistake on my part.

3. There will most likely be a need for frequent tweaks, both in content and technical. Make sure a process is in place to handle them rapidly, including when someone is out of the office.

4. Take advantage of existing open-source materials as much as possible and cannibalize your own work to create new products. For example, we use the Info Game as the basis of a faculty development opportunity, coupling it with additional information on how information literacy can be integrated within the curriculum.

5. You will hear complaints. Take them seriously the *second* time you hear them.

6. Students aren't going to get everything you want them to, so don't despair too much. You really are helping them learn.

Notes

1. PRIMO, http://www.ala.org/ala/acrlbucket/is/iscommittees/webpages/emergingtech/site/index.htm); Merlot, http://www.merlot.org.

2. ACRL Standard Four: "The information literate student, individually or as a group, uses information effectively to accomplish a specific purpose." We felt this was the turf of the classroom faculty and their assignments rather than that of librarians, especially in the case of Composition I, so it was not included in our tutorial.

3. James Nichols, Barbara Shaffer, and Karen Shockey, "Changing the Face of Instruction: Is Online or In-class More Effective?" *College and Research Libraries* 64 (2003): 378–88; William Orme, "A Study of the Residual Impact of the Texas Information Literacy Tutorial on the Information-Seeking Ability of First Year College Students," *College and Research Libraries* 65 (2004): 205–15; Elizabeth Blakesley Lindsay, Lara Cummings, Corey M. Johnson, and B. Jane Scales, "If You Build It, Will They Learn? Assessing Online Information Literacy Tutorials," *College and Research Libraries* 67 (2006): 429–45.

18. NetTrail: The Evolution of an Interactive, Self-Guided Tutorial for Undergraduates

Deborah A. Murphy, Christy Hightower, and Ken Lyons

Rationale

In 1996 a University of California system-wide conference on undergraduate education brought together a self-selected group of University of California, Santa Cruz (UCSC), librarians, Computing and Technology Services staff, and faculty interested in developing a resource to provide students a solid grounding in basic online skills. It was evident to those involved that such skills had become fundamental to college students' academic success and needed to be taught, although it was not a university mandate to do so. The group decided that an online tutorial (a rather new format at that time) was the best approach since it could be delivered at point-of-need and would be taught in the very medium with which the students had to become adept. Additionally, it would introduce more specialized computer resources available at UCSC, eliminating the need for faculty to teach these competencies in their classrooms.

NetTrail was intended to meet the needs of the users of 1996—specifically incoming undergraduate and transfer students unfamiliar with the then-new environment of the Internet. Its original purpose was to introduce students to, and provide basic competency in, the various components of the Internet—the World Wide Web, electronic mail, and newsgroups/Usenet—and library-specific print and electronic resources as tools to aid their academic research. The development team, comprising UCSC li-

brarians, faculty, and programmers, began work on this initial version of "NetTrail: The UCSC Computer Literacy Course" in fall 1996, and it was released in fall 1997.

In 1998 the development team wrote a grant and competed for campus-wide IT funds. Based in part on the successful introduction of NetTrail, the team was awarded a $36,000 instructional improvement grant that made possible both upgraded server support and further development of the tutorial itself. For example, a portion of the funds was used to hire, during the summer of 1998, an editor to give a consistent voice to all of the NetTrail modules, and in 2003, a Web designer to aid in renovating the Web site.

Development

By 2002, NetTrail was beginning to show its age. As student knowledge and experience of the Internet, particularly in secondary schools, had become more widespread in the years following the tutorial's release, it became evident that NetTrail's introductory, computer-literacy approach had outlasted its usefulness. Web-based abstracting-and-indexing databases and library catalogs were now taken for granted, though students' increased familiarity with the Internet had not necessarily translated into skilled research techniques. NetTrail had to change—and change radically.

Given the amount of work that a revision of this scale would entail, remaining members of the development team recognized the need to review membership with a renewed level of commitment and expertise in mind. The recruitment effort resulted in a new team composed almost entirely of librarians, and the group began work on the new NetTrail in early 2003.

The team looked at everything from content, graphics, and interactivity to the quality of the "voice" of the tutorials. In determining overall design goals, this newly formed team decided (based on the Santa Cruz campus's natural forest-and-pasture environment) to retain the original NetTrail's map-and-trail motif, a metaphor for the students' journey in search of research skills and the destination of useful information. Keeping in mind the primary audience of first- and second-year undergraduates, the "voice" of the tutorial became more informal and conversational rather than pedantic, while taking care not to slip into colloquialism. As a result, the new version retained a similar feel and flow to the original design but incorporated changes in the librarians' approach to instruction as well as innovations in online technology to keep the modules current and fresh.

The revision focused on providing an introduction to print and electronic information useful for academic research, evaluation and ethical use of this information, and development of some key library-specific search skills (e.g., finding books based on Library of Congress call numbers, and retrieval of electronic article text) for retrieval of such information. NetTrail now covers the research process from beginning to end—selecting a topic, choosing appropriate resources, database search techniques, and concluding with an overview of plagiarism and academic ethics. NetTrail was redesigned as a resource available to UCSC students as well as members of the general public. Incorporating a consistent look and feel with modifiable content, the skills presented are in the context of UCSC, though they can be easily modified with updated content or for use at other institutions. No longer just a computer-literacy course, NetTrail was transformed into an *information-literacy* tutorial, which was launched in late 2003.

The redesign was not without its challenges, for example, the transition in the development team. A new group had been formed, including some original NetTrail developers but consisting mainly of newcomers to the project. The group spent what in retrospect was a very important period discussing goals and approaches and reaching a general consensus on a new outline before actually beginning work on the modules. Discussing and reaching agreement on these types of fundamental issues was an important part of the team-building process and gradually helped fashion a cohesive and enthusiastic group of developers.

Content

The current version of NetTrail now focuses on the six areas, as seen in figure 18.1. There were many hard decisions to make as the redesigned tutorial took shape. A vexing issue was the decision to eliminate live searching of external databases within some of the modules, opting instead for "canned" search examples and movies. This choice was necessary because of the increased licensing restrictions for off-campus and nonaffiliated student access. The entire subject of navigation both within and between modules was a major concern during development. How far could the outdoor trail metaphor be taken and still prove an effective way to move around the Web site? How could the user's path through the tutorial be reasonably anticipated if modules could be accessed in random order?

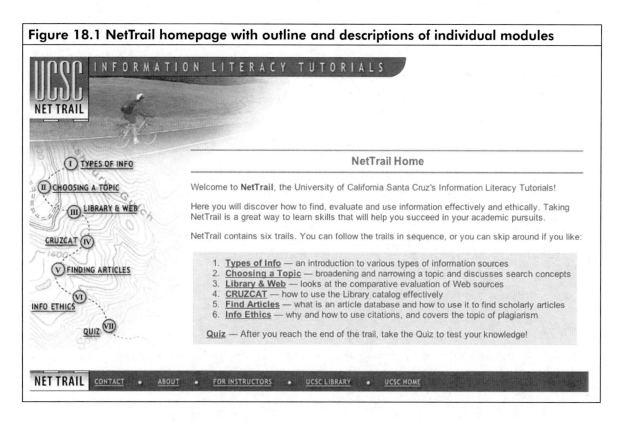

Figure 18.1 NetTrail homepage with outline and descriptions of individual modules

Later, on the basis of informal faculty comments, a final module was added that had not been considered previously, namely, the information ethics section that touches on issues of plagiarism. This inclusion, late in the development process, has turned out to be one of the most-used portions of the entire tutorial and certainly one of great interest to UCSC faculty and instructors, given the increased emphasis on copyright and issues of plagiarism in academia.

It is important to note that during the development process of the revised NetTrail creativity was primed by the willingness of other universities to allow the use and modification of their tutorials' text and software. The generosity of Colorado State University and the University of Texas System in sharing their Data Game and TILT content, respectively, was very helpful. When the time came to share NetTrail's content with other colleagues, the development team was delighted to discover the Creative Commons license. Creative Commons (http://creativecommons.org) is a nonprofit organization that offers "free tools for authors, artists, and educators to mark their creative work with the freedoms they want it to carry. Our tools change 'All Rights Reserved' into 'Some Rights Reserved'—as the creator chooses."

The Creative Commons license makes it easy to offer content such as text, software, music, and video as open source and provides choice as to the degree of openness of the license. It can also increase the visibility of the resource through the license metadata contained in the Web site. This metadata is utilized by Google (see the Usage Rights option on Google's advanced search page), Yahoo, and other search engines to steer developers to open-source content bearing a Creative Commons license.

Instruction

What Do NetTrail Users See?

The user experiences NetTrail as a friendly, approachable environment that offers six short modules for self-guided exploration. The modules are offered as links in a numbered sequence on the homepage and in a persistent navigation bar at the top of each screen within each module. This order arranges the topics in a progression that generally follows the research process. However, students also have the freedom to access the modules in whatever order most appeals to them or is most applicable to their immediate research needs, including the option to skip some modules altogether. So, though numbering indicates a suggested sequence, the modules can be accessed randomly and the content of each module assumes no prior NetTrail experience. This capability to unbundle the modules allows instructors the option of using a single module—say, the module on information ethics—as part of a class lecture. At the end of each module users are presented with a "trail head" sign that orients them to where

they are in the overall sequence, but it also suggests that they can choose any of the other modules, or "trails," in any order they wish.

The current appearance of the tutorial is the result of extensive discussion and user testing to determine how informal or cartoonish the graphics should be to encourage a sense of relaxation and informality within the target audience without detracting from the core lessons the tutorial was designed to impart. The modules teach through text, graphics (original cartoon figures and screenshots from online sources), interactive segments, and movies, as seen in figure 18.2. Users progress through the modules screen by screen, at their own pace. User testing indicates the entire tutorial is on average completed successfully in forty-five minutes to an hour.

NetTrail is designed to be a non-imposing portal or entrée to the real world of research. After taking the NetTrail tutorial, students

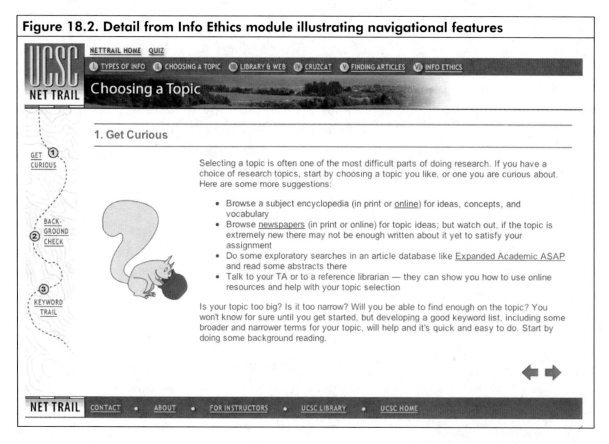

Figure 18.2. Detail from Info Ethics module illustrating navigational features

should be less intimidated by the actual library or by consulting with live librarians so that the research conversation can then move out of NetTrail to the reference desk or to the e-mail reference service.

Multimedia

Two of the modules end with interactive Flash segments that engage the user with hands-on decision making, asking them to apply the skills or information acquired while taking that particular module. These interactive tasks provide instant feedback to reinforce what was learned. In the Choose a Topic module, users type in their choice of keywords for a provided topic and receive an immediate response in which their words are compared to those selected by the tutorial's developers. In the Types of Info module, the multiple-choice Flash segment instantly informs students if their selection of the particular type of information (book, article, or Web site) is most appropriate for the research questions presented. The user must choose the correct answer (each incorrect choice is explained) before proceeding to the next question.

Several of NetTrail's modules contain one or more movies, for a total of three original movies (two for searching the catalog, one for linking to full text from a citation within an article database) and an open-source animated movie that explains the copyright implications of downloading music from the Internet. Each of these is helpful in conveying longer multiple-step processes, such as the mechanics of catalog searching, without being text-heavy and while holding the user's interest. User testing has shown that the movies are well liked by students, but their drawback is that they are time consuming to create and any specific database examples must be updated as changes occur. Although Camtasia software was initially used to create animated content, newer software such as Adobe Captivate has made it easier to create and update movies. Incorporating movies, however, still requires a significant investment of time and effort.

Feedback for Users

NetTrail provides two types of feedback for users: the self-assessments at the end of each module, which are included in the activity sections, and the optional multiple-choice quiz that covers material from the tutorial as a whole. The self-assessments within the modules are exclusively for the student's benefit and are not recorded. Students may also skip these assessments if they wish. The final page that confirms the successful completion of the quiz can be printed out and submitted to their instructor as proof of completion. If a student entered her name at the start of the quiz, the completion certificate includes the name.

The development team decided to make all of the NetTrail assessments pass-fail, and in all cases a perfect score is required to continue, including a perfect score on the final quiz. If a student scores less than 100 percent on the final quiz, the software informs him which questions he answered incorrectly and lets him try again. The quiz can be taken as many times as necessary to answer all the questions correctly. A 100 percent score for the overall quiz was made a requirement for several reasons. The tutorial as a whole is not long; it covers very basic core competencies, all of which are important for student success in future research; and it is advantageous to urge students to review their incorrect choices, reinforcing the correct ones.

Program Assessment

Assessment during Development

A modest amount of user testing was conducted during development of the revised NetTrail. For the initial assessment, two modules were chosen for focused usability testing: the Types of Information module, which includes an interactive section, and the longest module, Finding Articles, which includes a movie. These modules also differed in tone, the former being casual and the latter more formal. Five students were asked to navigate through the two modules and to "think aloud" as they did so. They were each observed by two NetTrail team members who kept track of start/stop times, thoughts expressed, body language, and links clicked. Two additional students were asked to take the entire tutorial (which took them each about forty-five minutes to complete). They were then asked a series of questions about the content and their perception of their experience.

These tests did not uncover anything startling and were reassuring overall; the casual tone of voice was not too juvenile, and all participants mentioned that they learned something new. Navigation between pages within modules was, however, refined as a result of test responses. Comments from user testing included these:

What's a database? I usually find articles on the Internet using Google.

I never thought about the difference between magazines and journals—that was helpful.

I like this [module] because it's like a game.

I thought [NetTrail] was good … broken into chunks so you don't have to read the whole thing at once. This stuff is a good start.

The final quiz underwent a larger-scale assessment. The quiz alone was administered to 150 undergraduates who had not seen the tutorial. This phase of user testing produced the most interesting development to arise prior to launching NetTrail: the discovery that the initial version of the final quiz was much too easy to be a good assessment of knowledge gained from the tutorial. Of the students tested, 78 percent answered all but one of the questions correctly. As a result of this assessment, the number and specificity of the quiz questions were increased.

Analyzing Usage

Anyone who has attempted to analyze Web usage statistics will be familiar with the difficulties the NetTrail team has encountered in this area. Ideally it would be most useful to know the number of unique visitors to the site and the sequential path those visitors took so that it could be determined where they entered the site, where they went page by page, how much time they spent on each page, and where they left the site. However, the current log-analysis software used by the UCSC campus tracks only hit counts for pages. The graphics on each page are not counted separately, a factor that can inflate usage statistics, so these numbers represent actual page hit counts. Although not ideal, these counts provide some sense of NetTrail's usage.

Usage of the NetTrail Web site has increased over time. The NetTrail homepage received 10,515 hits in 2006. Approximately 13 percent of hits to the entire Web site came from crawling by robots and search engines. Analysis of the page hit counts indicated that usage was spread throughout the site, not just concentrated on the homepage of each module.

Attention was also paid to weekly on-campus usage statistics throughout the 2005/6 academic year, and these were found to mirror the campus's activity pattern, with increased usage during the busy research weeks of each academic quarter and a corresponding decrease in usage during the quieter periods between quarters and over the summer. Of hits to the entire Web site (8,562 hits) in 2006, 12.5 percent originated from on-campus hosts, with the remaining majority of NetTrail users originating off-campus. The most-visited module in 2006 was Types of Information and the least used was Library & Web.

The team was frustrated in its attempt to determine how much off-campus use was by the target audience of student researchers. The university library is currently evaluating two examples of log analysis software, Sawmill and WebTrends, to replace an inadequate existing application. This not only will improve traffic analysis of the library's Web site but can also be employed for the same purpose by NetTrail.

As the development team attempted to interpret NetTrail's statistics, it became clear that it would be helpful to have a way to share usage statistics with developers of similar Web-based tutorials. Particularly useful would be a shared resource that collated these statistics using metrics standardized across tutorials (thereby assuring that everyone counted a "visitor" the same way)—admittedly a huge effort to initiate and maintain. Short of that, a resource providing an annotated list of Web-based information literacy tutorials that included links to the publicly available statistics of each would be of considerable use.

Faculty Feedback

Informal feedback from faculty indicates that NetTrail is helping to meet their needs in terms of both content and delivery mechanism. The tutorial helps bring their students who are new to the research process up to speed, and all the instructors who have contacted the team have been pleased to see the Information Ethics module included. NetTrail also addresses a need to efficiently reach the hundreds of students enrolled in their introductory classes, whose large numbers make individual hands-on instruction within the library unfeasible. Faculty are also pleased that the tutorial can be taken independently and thus doesn't impede classtime. The team noted that the For Instructors page that outlines how NetTrail can be used in classes was heavily used in 2006.

Although no evidence of plagiarism has been reported, the team received a request from an instructor to make the quiz more plagiarism-proof. As a first step toward plagiarism prevention, the order in which the questions appear will be randomized each time the quiz is generated, making it more difficult for students to develop their own "answer keys." Additionally, a request has been made for a module covering the Web of Science database of citation indexes. The design goal for phase one of the project was to avoid resource-specific instruction except in the case of the library OPAC, enabling the tutorial to be used by the widest possible audience. Subject-specific module development is on the agenda for the next phase. However, as database vendors increasingly provide their own movies highlighting the features of their products, any future modules need to be planned to complement, rather than duplicate, what the vendors already provide.

Librarian and Staff Feedback

Instruction librarians are particularly grateful to have NetTrail for very large classes that were previously underserved by library instruction. During the past two years in its current incarnation, NetTrail has also started to be used extensively and very effectively as a basic instructional tool for the training of student workers in the reference unit, and of staff at the library assistant level, known as "reference aides," who volunteer in an ongoing program to assist patrons at the reference desk. In December 2006, six reference aides and two student workers were formally interviewed using a set of uniform questions. The profiles of the interviewees are quite diverse—ranging in age from early twenties to early fifties, long-time library employees to students with less than two years' experience, undergraduate students with no special knowledge of library research to a library assistant with a master's degree in library science and another in the midst of an MLS program.

Of the eight employees interviewed, the majority said that NetTrail not only helped them better understand the concepts of library research but was also useful in helping them convey research concepts to patrons as well as in conducting their own library research. All respondents ranked the tutorial in the top two of five tiers of the survey for effectiveness at conveying research concepts; six gave it top marks. On the other hand, all but one respondent ranked NetTrail in the bottom two of five tiers for level of difficulty. When asked, however, if they thought Net-Trail could be more effective by making it easier or more difficult, many offered suggestions for improvements and additions but most felt the tutorial should probably remain at the same level of difficulty.

Overall, reaction to NetTrail in its current form was overwhelmingly positive among those interviewed, and, although there were many suggestions for additions to the tutorial, all seemed to indicate that the right balance of basic research concepts, level of dif-

ficulty, length, and mood or atmosphere in the interface had been struck. All of those interviewed would recommend NetTrail to others.

Lessons Learned

The NetTrail development team has grown over the years as interested and technologically innovative colleagues have joined the group. The success of the tutorial can be attributed to several key concepts and developmental decisions. Some of the recommendations the team feels are most important are listed below.

Create a development team with a range of skills and backgrounds, including Web development. Bringing together both science and social science/humanities librarians was a real plus in expanding the mindset of both groups about the level of research skills possessed by their respective patrons.

Actively seek funding, look for grant opportunities, and allocate time and energy to grant writing for current, as well as future, development. Securing adequate funding was a crucial factor in obtaining resources as they were needed. For example, funding allowed the incorporation of interactive features to replace text-heavy explanations—an expensive yet extremely well received change to several modules.

Share ideas and approaches with others via Creative Commons and open licensing. This can save much planning and development time, improve the quality of your final product, and build collegiality.

Dedicate time and resources for marketing. Turnover in faculty and student populations, as well as new features added to the tutorial, makes ongoing promotion an essential outreach activity.

Integrate user testing into the entire development process. Ideally, dedicate a portion of your team to user testing so that by a third of the way into the development process they are ready to conduct user testing in parallel during the remainder of development.

Communicate with library colleagues, keeping them informed and involved during all aspects of development and assessment. Concern over automated instruction replacing in-person instruction, though never NetTrail's intention, led to some misconceptions about the purpose of the tutorial. Keep all colleagues, especially those not involved in the project, continually informed and reminded of the goals of the tutorial.

Build flexibility into your tutorial. Keeping components modular within sections of the tutorial makes it possible to replace parts rather than a whole unit. On a larger scale, allowing users to experience the tutorial in a nonlinear manner and avoiding an inflexible, sequential path make it easier to incorporate changes without having to adjust the entire tutorial to preserve continuity.

Think of both short- and long-term development. Keep a wish list of future revisions and be prepared to take advantage of opportunities as they arise. Changes in technology may make some previously complex operations easier or cheaper to implement. But be sure to anticipate obsolescence, and think ahead to major reviews and revisions.

Conclusion

The information environment constantly changes, and NetTrail must continue to evolve to remain relevant. The development team maintains a wish list of potential revisions that are routinely assessed and prioritized, based on perceived need, expense, and effort required for implementation. Some examples from the current list include plans to better assess knowledge gained, the addition of pop-up glossaries and more interactive features to replace textual explanations, expanded statistics-gathering and -reporting capabilities, and targeted tutorials for specific audiences (e.g., graduate students, new faculty).

NetTrail has become an important and unique component of the UCSC Library's instruction and outreach programs. Developed ahead of the curve, it is now a featured resource whose success is the result of the team remaining focused on the concepts and developmental decisions presented in this chapter.

19. Planning, Building, and Assessing an Online Information Literacy Tutorial: The LOBO Experience

Megan Oakleaf

Introduction

Each fall, first-year students arrive at colleges across the country with widely varying abilities to complete library research assignments. Some students enter higher education as veterans of the information seeking process, armed with strong school library media preparation and ready to conquer any research assignment. Far more first-year students are over-reliant on Internet resources, confused about distinctions between scholarly and popular sources, daunted by scores of article databases, and mystified by the LC classification system. Academic librarians face the challenge of establishing baseline information literacy skills in all students, often with limited time and resources. One way to confront this challenge facing academic librarians is an online information literacy tutorial.

Setting

North Carolina State University (NCSU) is an urban, research-extensive university with an enrollment of 23,000 undergraduates. Typically, entering classes include 4,000 students. More than half are male, 80 percent are white, and 90 percent are in-state. Many first-year students at NCSU major in engineering, management, agriculture and life sciences, or humanities and social sciences.

Library Instruction for First-Year Students

NCSU librarians partner with faculty across the university to facilitate the integration of information literacy instruction into the undergraduate curriculum. One example of this information literacy integration occurs in ENG 101, a first-year writing course. ENG 101 is the only course required of all NCSU students. In ENG 101, instructors are required to teach and assess specific learning outcomes. One of these outcomes states that students should "demonstrate critical and evaluative thinking skills in locating, analyzing, synthesizing, and using information in writing or speaking activities."[1] To teach and assess this information literacy outcome, ENG 101 instructors look to their librarian colleagues for assistance.

NCSU librarians and first-year writing instructors are longtime partners in information literacy instruction. In the early 1990s, librarians created workbooks that encouraged first-year writing students to practice locating information in the library. Later that decade, librarians concluded that the face of library research changed faster than they could update the workbooks. As a result, they replaced the workbooks with an online tutorial that focused on broad information literacy concepts and required less maintenance. At first, this tutorial was well- received by ENG

Oakleaf, Megan (2008). "Planning, Building, and Assessing a Library Instruction Tutorial," in Elizabeth Connor (ed), *An Introduction to Instructional Services in Academic Libraries.* New York: Haworth Information Press. Article copies are available from The Haworth Document Delivery Service : 1-800-HAWORTH. E-mail address: docdelivery@haworthpress.com.

101 instructors. However, by 2001 this tutorial was deemed overly conceptual, linear, and text-heavy. As a result, ENG 101 instructors ceased to use the tutorial. Some instructors eliminated information literacy content from their courses entirely, other instructors attempted to teach library skills independently, and many instructors requested librarian-led workshops. Because there were more than 200 sections of ENG 101 each academic year, the librarian assigned to the first-year writing program was overwhelmed with requests. Even when additional librarians were enlisted to teach ENG 101 workshops, only 40 percent of the sections received library instruction. Librarians who taught information literacy workshops in other NCSU courses noted the impact of this uneven coverage. In these courses, students who had experienced library instruction in ENG 101 were bored, while those who had not were frustrated and confused. In late 2001, NCSU librarians acknowledged the need to develop a new information literacy tutorial for ENG 101.

Before starting work on a new tutorial, NCSU librarians searched the library literature to confirm the effectiveness of online approaches to information literacy instruction. The literature supplied adequate reassurance that online library instruction can be effective. According to Russell, no significant differences between learning outcomes from online and in-person lecture instruction can be documented.[2] Germain, Jacobson, and Kaczor concluded that there is "no difference in the effectiveness of the two types of instruction, Web and live,"[3] and both Holman[4] and Kaplowitz and Contini[5] supported this conclusion.

The review of the library literature also confirmed the value of online information literacy instruction. Online tutorials can be used whenever and wherever students find it convenient. They are accessible remotely and supply independent, self-paced instruction. Online tutorials also ease the burden of generalized, drop-in instruction.[6] Using online tutorials for first-year students allows librarians to "guarantee that freshmen are familiar with fundamental concepts and prepared for the more advanced research skills of their academic careers."[7]

In January 2002, NCSU librarians commenced development of a new information literacy tutorial called Library Online Basic Orientation (LOBO). They envisioned a tutorial that would balance conceptual and practical skills; be modular, interactive, and easily integrated into the ENG 101 curriculum; and be completed by August 2002.

Objectives

Development of the LOBO (www.lib.ncsu.edu/lobo2/) tutorial began with an analysis of the objectives of the three stakeholder groups impacted by the proposed online information literacy tool: ENG 101 students, ENG 101 instructors, and librarians.

Students

ENG 101 students face the challenge of completing college-level research papers and navigating a large academic library for the first time. For these students, an information literacy tutorial needs to fit limited attention spans and include accessible language. ENG 101 students also prefer interactive learning activities and modular designs that permit them to jump between areas of interest. ENG 101 students expected the new library tutorial to teach them to

- navigate the physical space of the library
- locate books in the catalog
- use LC call numbers

- obtain print and electronic journal articles

Instructors

Because ENG 101 instructors consider library research skills necessary for good writing, they seek ways to teach their students these skills efficiently and effectively. Instructors wanted the new library tutorial to address a number of objectives, including teaching students to

- observe the steps of the research process
- evaluate resources
- avoid plagiarism
- contact librarians for help

They also expected the tutorial to

- be accessible to all sections of ENG 101
- include resources provided by the NCSU Libraries
- accommodate different instructors' teaching styles
- show students "how to" accomplish common tasks
- integrate into the context of ENG 101 course content
- help students complete a real ENG 101 assignment

Librarians

All NCSU reference librarians teach classes and work at the physical and virtual reference desk. Although not all librarians teach ENG 101 students, they encounter these students when they teach library workshops in advanced courses and benefit from students gaining a baseline level of information literacy skills. As a result, reference librarians hoped the new tutorial would address a number of objectives, including teaching students to

- distinguish between scholarly and non-scholarly sources
- use databases to locate articles and the catalog to find books

- build keyword search strings using Boolean operators
- use subject headings

Librarians also wanted the tutorial to

- be available at students' point-of-need
- be useful for one-on-one instruction at the physical or virtual reference desk
- be interactive
- portray librarians as friendly and helpful
- encourage students to contact librarians for help, in-person or remotely

Learning Outcomes

In addition to considering the objectives of stakeholders, NCSU librarians used learning outcomes to guide the development of the LOBO tutorial. The outcomes addressed by the LOBO tutorial were derived from several sources. These sources include the Information Literacy Competency Standards for Higher Education,[8] Objectives for Information Literacy Instruction: A Model Statement for Academic Librarians,[9] previous information literacy instruction approaches used in ENG 101, and ENG 101 curriculum.

Methods

The development of the LOBO tutorial included six steps: (1) assessing needs; (2) building a framework; (3) creating content; (4) applying technology; (5) building, testing, and launching; and (6) assessing and planning for future development. These six steps were coordinated by the NCSU instruction librarian and accomplished by a team of five reference librarians and two systems librarians. As project manager, the instruction librarian orchestrated collaboration, facilitated communication, encouraged progress, and integrated the work of the LOBO team to build a cohesive tutorial. The entire LOBO team met weekly during tutorial development. As the project progressed, team members moved into a "work independently, see what another team member thinks of completed work, work some more independently, then present to the team" cycle. Over time, this cycle allowed librarians with different levels of experience, skills, and work styles to communicate effectively and balance workloads fairly. Individual librarians felt valued, developed a unified vision, and understood group expectations. Franks et al. note that this behavior is often exhibited by librarians working to create an online tutorial.[10]

Assessing Needs

The first step of LOBO development focused on identifying all stakeholders and determining the learning outcomes to be addressed by the tutorial. Stakeholders for the LOBO tutorial included students, instructors, and librarians; the needs of each group informed the tutorial development process. This stage of LOBO development also included careful consideration of the learning outcomes taught by the tutorial.

Building a Framework

According to Franks et al., most tutorials begin as an outline.[11] In January 2002, NCSU librarians developed a rough outline for the LOBO tutorial that organized the learning outcomes of the tutorial around the steps of the research process. This outline served as the planning structure and ensured that the tutorial would be driven by outcomes-focused content. Furthermore, the outline enabled librarians to share concrete plans with ENG 101 instructors and gain their commitment to the tutorial project.

Creating Content

Armed with a LOBO tutorial outline, librarians met with the director of first-year writ-

ing in April 2002 to ensure that the content of the proposed tutorial would support the ENG 101 curriculum. After agreeing that the LOBO tutorial would integrate well into the course, she decided to require instructors to incorporate the tutorial in their courses and volunteered ENG 101 instructors to contribute content to the tutorial. As a result of the director's decision, sections of the LOBO outline were assigned to individual librarians and instructors for content drafts. After initial drafts were created, instructors and librarians worked in tandem to make level of difficulty and tone revisions.

Applying Technology

After creating the content of the tutorial, NCSU librarians searched the library literature for guidelines governing technological aspects of tutorial creation. According to Franks et al., information literacy tutorials should include "consistent use of titles and headers"; "prominent use of navigational aids"; "availability of help links"; "proper use of white space, color, and fonts"; "appropriate use of graphics"; effort to make all pages ADA compliant"; "use of templates"; and testing in various browsers, platforms, and monitors.[12] Dewald delves beyond appearance and navigation to list components of successful online tutorials. She includes assignment-related instruction, active learning components, clear objectives, and focus on concepts rather than on mechanics only.[13] Dewald also notes the importance of creating an interactive, self-paced learning tool that capitalizes on the extrinsic and intrinsic motivations of students completing research-based assignments.[14] ACRL includes clear objectives, interactivity, and a focus on concepts in their guidelines for tutorial construction. ACRL also recommends that tutorials have clearly defined structure, contemporary language and topics, and strong relationships to course content.[15]

With these guidelines in mind, the LOBO team designed a tutorial that was outcome-focused, modular, interactive, and centered on students' motivation to complete course assignments. One librarian used Qarbon ViewletBuilder to create "movies" that demonstrated database and catalog searches. A second team member developed "wizards" to guide students through databases and the catalog using student-created search terms. A third LOBO team member developed a "keyword builder" to illustrate Boolean concepts and a "citation builder" to guide students through parsing database citations and generating works-cited citations in MLA, APA, and CSE formats. Finally, a link to the NCSU Libraries' virtual reference service was added to each page of the tutorial to ensure that students could easily access librarian assistance.

Building, Testing, and Launching

In July 2002, librarians inserted all of the LOBO components into the tutorial Web template. Next, the LOBO team revised the tutorial to improve the flow and unify the tone of the tutorial. Finally, all interactive elements were tested, and the tutorial was made available to library staff for experimentation and training.

In August 2002, LOBO launched and the team members presented the new tutorial to ENG 101 instructors and offered tips for inclusion of each module in their curriculum. Instructors were most excited by the interactive components—wizards, viewlets, and builders—as well as the practical focus on helping students complete actual research assignments. They also lauded the convenience of the Ask a Librarian link that encourages students to contact a librarian in real time while they move through the LOBO tutorial.

Since 2002, librarians continue to offer training to new ENG 101 instructors to ensure familiarity with LOBO and best practices for integrating the tutorial into ENG 101.

Assessing and Planning Future Development

Library literature emphasizes the importance of assessing the outcomes of library instruction. Lindauer states, "an increasingly important concern for academic librarians is how to document and measure the ways that the library, learning resources, and computer services units make a difference in the academic quality of life for students and faculty."[16] Franks et al. also underscore the significance of assessment in "meet[ing] accreditation standards, secur[ing] funding, maintain[ing] staffing levels, and achiev[ing] service and teaching excellence." Thus, tutorials must undergo assessment "to provide validation of our instructional effectiveness … [and] convince library and campus administrators to continue to support these activities."[17]

Assessment of the LOBO tutorial is based on open-ended questions included throughout the tutorial to help students advance through the research process. These assessment questions help students analyze, synthesize, and evaluate material. Many tutorial questions focus on students' specific research topics. By the conclusion of the tutorial, students have answered questions that help them

- identify and narrow a topic
- select keywords and extrapolate synonyms and variants
- search a database and the NCSU Libraries' catalog for articles and books on a topic
- use Google to search for related Web sites
- evaluate sources according to specified criteria

Figure 19.1. Instructional content before assessment revisions

Evaluate Web sites—Authority
Determining who created a Web site is critical in being able to judge its quality. Anonymous information should not be used for academic research.

1. *Can you tell who (person or institution) created the Web site?* Look at the very top or bottom of the Web page for a name, email address, or "About Us" or "Contact Us" link.

2. *Are the author's credentials listed on the site?* If you can't find these details on a Web site, try typing an author's name into a search engine to get biographical information.

- select appropriate support for arguments
- decide when to paraphrase, summarize, or quote directly from sources
- develop citations to avoid plagiarism

Students view their answers to the open-ended questions in the form of an online worksheet that they can print or email to their instructors. For instructors, the worksheets serve as self-checks, discussion starters, or as evidence that students have explored all sections of the tutorial.

For librarians, the database that stores student answers is a rich source of assessment data. However, because students' answers to the open-ended questions in LOBO are specific to each student's research process, they are not scorable as "right" or "wrong." Instead, NCSU librarians have developed "rubrics," or charts describing different levels of student performance, to aid in the assessment of answers. Each semester, librarians select one or two questions in the LOBO tutorial for assessment. Then, they score a random sample of student responses to the question using the rubric for that question. Assessment results are used to describe students' information literacy skill level, isolate areas for improvement, and celebrate successes.

Results

The assessment of the LOBO tutorial is an iterative process. Each semester, students' answers to new questions are assessed and

---

Figure 19.2. Instructional content after assessment revisions

Evaluate Web sites—Authority
The URL (Web address) and author information for a Web site reveal a lot about site reliability. Determining who created a Web site is critical in being able to judge its quality. Generally, anonymous information should not be used for academic research.
Consider the following questions when you're evaluating the authority of a Web site:
1. *What type of domain does the site come from?*
   Government sites use .gov and .mil domains. Educational sites use the .edu domain. Non-profit organizations use .org and business sites use .com. Generally, .gov and .edu sites are considered more trustworthy than .org and .com sites.
2. *Who "published" the site?*
   The name between http:// and the first / usually indicates what organization owns the server the Web site is housed on. Learning about the organization that hosts a site can give you important information about the site's credibility.
3. *Is it a personal Web site?*
   Look for the names of companies that sell Web space to individuals, like AOL or GeoCities. Also look for a tilde (~). Tildes are often used to signify a personal Web site. Personal sites are considered less reliable than sites supported by organizations.
4. *Can you tell who (person or institution) created the site?*
   Look at the very top or bottom of the Web page for a name, email address, or "About Us" or "Contact Us" link.

Figure 19.3. Writing prompt before assessment revisions

Answer the questions above for the Web site you're evaluating. Overall, does what you know about the authorship of the Web site indicate that it's a good resource?
---

changes made to improve instruction. For example, the LOBO question that elicits information about students' abilities to use authority as a criterion for evaluating a Web site has been assessed twice. The first time, librarians used a rubric to score fifty student responses to the question that asks students to answer to a series of questions about the authority of a Web site they are considering as a source for an academic paper or project. Librarians discovered that a majority of students were able to address the authority of a Web site (88 percent). Most students also demonstrated that they were able to refer to indicators of authority (90 percent). However, less than a third (32 percent) of students could give specific examples of authority indicators from the site they were evaluating. In addition, fewer than half (44 percent) could provide a rationale for accepting or rejecting the Web site for use in their assignment based on their assessment of the site's authority. The results of this first assessment were vital to the improvement of the rubric, the content of the tutorial (figures 19.1 and 19.2), and the open-ended questions that form the writing prompt (figures 19.3 and 19.4).

A year later, after both the tutorial and the assessment rubric were revised, librarians assessed the same LOBO question. This time, 100 percent of students addressed the authority of the site and 93 percent could give specific examples of authority indicators from a site they were evaluating. However, only 50 percent of students could provide a reason for accepting or rejecting a Web site for use in an assignment. Although this was an improvement over the previous year, students appeared to need additional instruction. In response, NCSU librarians designed a new lesson plan that ENG 101 instructors can use help students make final determinations about the usefulness and appropriateness of Web sites.

Conclusions

The effectiveness of LOBO as an information literacy instruction tool has been illustrated in multiple ways. The LOBO tutorial has been honored with the ALA Library of the Future Award and the PRIMO Site of the Month Award in 2003. In recent years, the tutorial has been the subject of conference presentations at EDUCAUSE, ACRL, and various

---
Figure 19.4. Writing prompt after assessment revisions

Respond to the following prompts in the space below, using complete sentences:
- Identify the "domain type" of the site you're evaluating and explain why that is acceptable or unacceptable for your needs.
- Identify the "publisher" or host of the site and tell what you know (or can find out) about it.
- State whether or not the site is a personal site and explain why that is acceptable or unacceptable for your needs.
- State who (name the person or institution) created the site and tell what you know (or can find out) about the creator.
- Look for the author's credentials on the site. List his/her credentials and draw conclusions based on those credentials. If there are no credentials listed, tell what conclusions you can draw from their absence.
- Using what you know about the AUTHORITY of this Web site, explain why it is or is not appropriate to use for your paper/project.
---

national assessment conferences. In the three years since its launch, the tutorial software has been copied and adapted by more than ten other libraries in higher education.

In addition to external benchmarks of success, NCSU librarians continue to improve the tutorial. Each semester, the assessment of student responses to LOBO questions allows NCSU librarians to improve the tutorial and ensure that it continues to support the ENG 101 curriculum. These assessment efforts have also given rise to a suite of lesson plans that support ENG 101 instructors who wish to extend LOBO content in their classrooms. Technical improvements continue. During the 2006/7 academic year, NCSU librarians plan to migrate LOBO from a HTML-based Web template to a content management system so that recommendations resulting from assessment can be followed quickly and easily. Under watchful eyes, LOBO has a promising future as a flagship of information literacy instruction at NCSU Libraries.

Notes

1.   NC State Academic Programs GER—Writing, Speaking, and Information Literacy Rationale. Available online from http://www.ncsu.edu/provost/academic_programs /ger/wrtspk/rat.htm.

2.   Thomas L. Russell, "The No Significant Difference Phenomenon as Reported in 355 Research Reports, Summary and Papers: A Comparative Research Annotated Bibliography on Technology for Distance Education" (Raleigh, NC: Office of Instructional Telecommunications, North Carolina State University, 1999).

3.   Carol A. Germain, Trudi E. Jacobson, and Susan A. Kaczor, "A Comparison of the Effectiveness of Presentation Formats for Instruction: Teaching First-Year Students," *College and Research Libraries* 61 (January 2000): 65–72.

4.   Lucy Holman, "A Comparison of Computer-Assisted Instruction and Classroom Bibliographic Instruction," *Reference and User Services Quarterly* 40 (Fall 2000): 53–65.

5.   Joan Kaplowitz and Janice Contini, "Computer-Assisted Instruction: Is It an Option for Bibliographic Instruction in Large Undergraduate Survey Classes?" *College and Research Libraries* 59 (January 1998): 19–28.

6.   May A. Tricarico, Susan von Daum Tholl, and Elena O'Malley, "Interactive Online Instruction for Library Research: The Small Academic Library Experience," *Journal of Academic Librarianship* 27 (May 2001): 220–23.

7.   Elizabeth A. Dupuis, "Automating Instruction," *School Library Journal Net Connect,* April 2001, 21–22.

8.   Association of College and Research Libraries, *Objectives for Information Literacy Instruction: A Model Statement for Academic Librarians* (Chicago: ACRL, 2001). Available online at http://www.ala. org/ala/acrl/acrlstandards/objectivesinformation.htm.

9.   Association of College and Research Libraries, *Information Literacy Competency Standards for Higher Education* (Chicago: ACRL, 2000). Available online at http://www.ala.org/ala/acrl/acrlstandards/informationliteracycompetency.htm.

10.   Jeffrey A. Franks, Robert S. Hackley, Joseph E. Straw, and Susan Direnzo, "Developing an Interactive Web Tutorial to Teach Information Competencies: The Planning Process at the University of Akron," *Journal of Educational Media and Library Services* 37 (March 2000): 235–55.

11. Ibid.

12. Ibid.

13. Nancy H. Dewald, "Transporting Good Library Instruction Practices into the Web Environment: An Analysis of Online Tutorials," *Journal of Academic Librarianship* 25 (January 1999): 26–31.

14. Nancy H. Dewald, "Web-Based Library Instruction: What Is Good Pedagogy?" *Information Technology and Libraries* 18 (March 1999): 26–31.

15. ACRL Instruction Section Teaching Methods Committee, *Tips for Developing Effective Web-based Library Instruction.* Available online at http://www.lib.vt.edu/istm/WebTutorials/Tips.html.

16. Bonnie G. Lindauer, "Defining and Measuring the Library's Impact on Campuswide Outcomes," *College and Research Libraries* 59 (November 1998): 546–63.

17. Franks, Hackley, Straw, and Direnzo, "Developing an Interactive Web Tutorial."

20. Redesigning a Library Research Tutorial: A View from the Trenches

Kelly Rhodes McBride

Introduction

Appalachian State University (ASU) is a public comprehensive university offering degree programs at the baccalaureate, master's, specialist, and doctoral levels. Founded in 1899 as Watauga Academy, Appalachian is one of sixteen constituent institutions in the University of North Carolina System. Located in the Blue Ridge Mountains of western North Carolina, ASU is primarily a residential campus with a current student enrollment of 15,117.

ASU has two libraries on its campus: the Belk Library and Information Commons, which serves as the main library for the campus, and the Erneston Music Library, which supports the curriculum of the Mariam Cannon Hayes School of Music.

Rationale

In 2003, Belk Library and Information Commons launched the ASU Library Research Tutorial, "a series of self-paced instructional modules designed to introduce important research concepts and guide students in the use of the ASU libraries."[1] The tutorial was developed for use with our freshman seminar program, which "offers first semester freshmen assistance with transitions to college, information about University resources and support, and opportunities to strengthen learning skills and to broaden personal and cultural horizons."[2] The tutorial comprises an overview "About the Tutorial" section, six main sections covering ASU libraries (Searching Basics, Finding Books, Finding Articles, Finding Reserves, and Citing Information), and a graded quiz that students complete at the end of the tutorial.

One of the overall goals of the Belk Library and Information Commons is to be a significant part of the academic success of ASU students. To this end, the library instruction program has always offered support to faculty in helping students learn about library research. Librarians provide instruction for freshman-through graduate-level classes. Statistics from fall 2004 through fall 2006 indicate that, of the 1,099 classes taught, 161 were for freshman seminar and 180 for English 1000, a required class for most incoming students. The remaining 758 instruction sessions represent all other instruction sessions taught by reference librarians for this period.

Prior to the development of the tutorial in 2003, instruction for freshman-level classes consisted primarily of one-shot sessions that provided a generic introduction to the basics of library research. Students in both freshman seminar and English 1000 often received identical instruction. The librarians had made attempts to design handouts and sessions that were unique to each class, but these efforts were not very satisfactory. In addition, the freshmen in these classes varied widely in their skill levels and knowledge of information resources. Unfortunately, our approach to teaching this specific segment of freshman-level classes was often to teach to the lowest common denominator.

In fall 2001 an instruction librarian conducted a session for an Instructional Technology faculty member who was interested in giving his students a pre-test that measured their library skills before their formal library session.[3] It often happens that informal collaboration can breed significant change, and such was the case in this instance. The outcome of this conversation was a decision by librarians to explore the possibility of creating a computer-based program that could introduce first-semester freshmen to the basic concepts of library research and test their current level of understanding before they attended a formal library instruction session. A tutorial seemed the best way to handle this, and a task force was developed to explore the possibilities.

The Library Research Tutorial Task Force looked at several tutorials and decided to use the Introduction to Library Research tutorial of the University of North Carolina at Chapel Hill (UNC–Chapel Hill) as a model (www.lib.unc.edu/instruct/tutorial/). Several features of the UNC–Chapel Hill tutorial appealed to us: it was designed in modules so that it could be completed in any order; each module contained questions that could be used to test the level of understanding of the concepts being introduced; a quiz at the end tested all the concepts covered throughout the tutorial; and content management of the tutorial did not require extensive technical expertise.[4] In addition, UNC–Chapel Hill gave us permission to adapt and use their tutorial, which meant we would not have to design one from scratch. That is not to say there was not quite a bit of work involved—quite the contrary. We had to revise UNC–Chapel Hill's content significantly to reflect our library's unique resources. One librarian, who has since left the university, was pretty much solely responsible for the creation, content, and maintenance of the tutorial.

When our Library Research Tutorial was rolled out in fall 2003, it was used primarily in a three-part library component in the freshman seminar program: students took the tutorial prior to their visit to the library, then received instruction in the library, and finally complete a library-related assignment. After three years in use, although it had met our initial goal of introducing students to the basics of library research, we felt it was time to revise the existing tutorial framework with a critical eye toward embedding information literacy throughout. Additionally, we hoped to redesign the tutorial to reflect the growth in our library instruction program since 2003.

In June 2006 a second tutorial task force was formed to facilitate this process. The redesigned version of the Library Research Tutorial was completed March 2007 and made available to the public that April.

Development

The Redesign Tutorial Task Force made up of one Web services librarian, two reference and instruction librarians, one distance learning librarian, one catalog librarian, and two computer consultants. In addition, several other individuals contributed to and provided valuable input on this endeavor.

Why did we decided to embark on a complete redesign of our existing tutorial? The tutorial was voluntarily included in a large number of freshman seminar classes, limited site statistics were being collected, and the tutorial had been kept current with updates each semester. By all accounts things seemed to be working just fine, and "if it ain't broke, don't fix it."

The success of our initial foray into the creation of an online tutorial was made easier by the fact that we used an existing framework, but we still had concerns. Although we did conduct some limited assessment during this period, the tutorial did not have a mechanism in place that allowed user feedback. In addition, extensive new updates were required, which would have been doable but very time consuming, and new instructional software had been developed (e.g., Adobe Captivate and Camtasia Studio) during the past three years that we were interested in incorporating into our tutorial. Finally, given our desired scope—build a tutorial from the ground up—we were concerned whether the payoff would be worth the time and effort. In other words, would it be an efficient use of our time to update the original tutorial if the effort proved to be as labor intensive as a complete redesign? Good question.

A review of library instruction statistics from fall 2004 to fall 2006 showed that freshman-level instruction continued to provide a high number of library instruction requests, and we saw no immediate change on the horizon. In January 2005, ASU created the General Education Task Force, charged with developing a new general education program that would outline educational goals and learning outcomes for undergraduate students (see www1.appstate.edu/orgs/gen_ed). The task force comprises faculty across disciplines and includes the associate university librarian. We anticipated an increase in the number of library instruction requests with the implementation of the task force recommendations. Suffice it to say, the need for a tutorial still existed. After much discussion, the Redesign Tutorial Task Force felt strongly that an online tutorial was still the best vehicle for introducing a large number of entry-level freshmen to the basic concepts of library research.

So, the new question on the table was not if we would embark on a redesign but what form it would take. Should we modify the framework of the existing tutorial and find individuals within the library willing to take on the long-term responsibility of maintenance, or scrap our current model and design something completely different? We decided to go with door number two and our work began in earnest.

We developed a timeline for the project and began meeting during summer 2006. Our projected completion date was February 2007. We thought this timeline would provide enough time to chose software, work out technical and accessibility issues, develop content, and conduct usability tests. Since our existing tutorial was modular, we did not need to change all the components at once. By completing the redesign project in early spring, we would still have the summer months to make final modifications if needed before the tutorial began to be heavily used in fall 2007.

Our task force began its review with a critical examination of the original tutorial. What would we keep and what would we change? There was a lot of good information in our first tutorial, but we wanted to do more than repackage the content. We viewed this redesign as an opportunity to incorporate core information literacy concepts and present them in a way that was more interactive and visual.

What would be the purpose of this new tutorial? Was it to be a review source, an introduction, or a source of in-depth knowledge? How much could we reasonably expect students to learn and retain? Would freshman seminar and English 1000 students still be our primary audience? Would the tutorial take the place of entry-level freshman library instruction? What would be our learning outcomes? How would we measure whether students had achieved these outcomes? Technological issues were also of great concern. Should the tutorial incorporate screen capture, audio, and other new technologies?

We decided that our target audience would be entry-level freshmen, primarily those enrolled in freshman seminar and English 1000 courses, and our focus would be on introducing students to the basic concepts involved in library research. Concepts tackled would include how information is organized, how one chooses appropriate information sources, how these resources are used most effectively, and how one evaluates the information found.

In thinking about how the tutorial would fit into our instruction program, we identified two objectives: information should focus on specific topics at the point of need, and base-level instruction for freshman seminar and English 1000 classes should be followed up with in-library instruction. To provide a basic foundation upon which to build, we decided that the redesigned tutorial would cover the following areas: library services, information sources, search basics, finding materials, evaluating information, and plagiarism. Our overall goal was to introduce the research process, reinforce information literacy skills, and help our students integrate research concepts and critical thinking.

The task force set up a focus group with ASU students using tutorials from other campuses to give us information about what features students preferred in online instruction. We choose two sample tutorials: Guide to Using UBC's Library Catalogue, available at the University of British Columbia (UBC);[5] and Introduction to Library Research Tutorial from UNC–Chapel Hill, which our original tutorial was based on.

We liked these examples because they represented two very different approaches—one a tutorial that presented screen capture with audio, the other more traditionally text-based.

We put together a focus group of student workers in Belk Library and another of Upward Bound students[6] and then compared the results. Upward Bound students would serve as our primary test group. Each group was asked to complete the finding books section of the UNC–Chapel Hill tutorial and the catalog introduction section of the UBC tutorial. We allotted ninety minutes for each focus group. The groups consisted of four Belk Library student workers and seven Upward Bound students. The format of the focus groups was as follows:

1. Students were welcomed and thanked for their time, then given an overview of our purpose, the goals of the session, and a timeline.

2. Students were given fifteen minutes to view UBC's tutorial and then given five minutes to discuss their first impressions (i.e., general comments, likes, dislikes).

3. Students were given fifteen minutes to view UNC–Chapel Hill's tutorial and then given five minutes to discuss their first impressions.

4. Students were given a fifteen-minute break with refreshments.

5. Students were brought together in a circle and asked a series of formal questions:
   • Which tutorial did you prefer?
   • Why?
   • What did you like best about the one you prefer?

Here is a selection of some of the students' comments:

Library student workers' impressions (4) of the UBC tutorial (screen capture with audio)

- Covered less, but explained more in-depth.
- Ease of following instruction was not a problem.
- The sound wasn't always good.
- Liked hearing and seeing.
- Visual appearance—some felt UBC was better laid out, others felt it was more cluttered than UNC–Chapel Hill.
- Pace—not a problem, loading time not an issue.
- No Flash control bar (for stop, pause, volume control); this was a weakness.

The most interesting comment made was about the Boolean search section: "I didn't have to explain all that, you can just use keywords."

Upward Bound student impressions (7) of the UBC tutorial

- Content issues
  "When I listen to someone talk I fall asleep."
  "Ignore it if you don't understand it, it just turns into droning."
  Sections not broken up into fine enough components.
  Searches repetitive.
- Technical issues
  Pacing—too fast.
  Liked the mouse in UBC. Really want it to be interactive.
  Would like a visual trail.

Library student workers' impressions of the UNC–Chapel Hill tutorial

- "This one explained more."
- Some of what it explained, like how to read an LC call number, was overkill—signs in the stacks would be more effective.
- "You have to read."
- Like the built in quizzes as you go.

Upward Bound student impressions of the UNC–Chapel Hill tutorial

- Do at your own pace.

- NOT very attractive.
- Didn't explain enough; it referred back to previous part.
- When it referred back to Boolean, didn't explain. Should be specific.
- "Liked reading better than listening, more engaging."
- Liked Citing information. Liked LC stuff.
- Quiz is interactive.

In general, these focus groups indicated that students prefer tutorials that are self-paced, interactive, graphic, and nonlinear. The students expressed a desire to "test their knowledge" with some type of quiz imbedded in various sections of the tutorial or at the end. Our student sample was small, but the results were significant for our purposes, and the information gained provided useful anecdotal evidence that could guide our future discussions on content.

Content

Our next step was to determine the content. What did we want our students to learn, and how would the tutorial's content facilitate this learning? A literature search revealed relevant articles. Nancy Dewald, outlining good instruction practices in the Web environment, noted that "traditional best practices in library instruction can provide a beginning guide for Web designers." As practicing professionals, we know that good library instruction is distinguished by several characteristics. It should include active learning, incorporate collaborative learning, be assignment related, facilitate various learning styles, outline clear objectives, focus on concepts rather than mechanics, and provide additional opportunities for assistance. According to Dewald, these traditional criteria can and should be applied to Web-based library instruction. Although our tutorial was designed to be used in conjunction with a library instruction session, we thought that including these "best practices" in the online environment would prove invaluable.[7]

Our first step toward developing content was to identify the core learning objectives. Our goal was to have the tutorial take approximately thirty minutes to complete. Within this timeframe, students had to be introduced to the key learning objectives. Although this seems like plenty of time, we felt the pressure to be selective. The librarians working on the project formed subgroups to focus on specific objectives. We used Debra Gilchrist's "Five Questions for Assessment Design" as a model to identify appropriate learning objectives:[8]

- Outcomes. What do I want the students to be able to do?
- Curriculum. What does the student need to know?
- Pedagogy. What is the learning activity?
- Assessment. How will the student demonstrate learning?
- Criteria. How will I know the student has done this well?

Using this model, we came up with a list of learning objectives: Students will be able to identify services offered within the library; learn types of information sources; develop a search strategy; find materials through the online catalog, reserves, and online databases; evaluate information; and avoid instances of plagiarism. The process of narrowing our learning objectives down to these six was laborious and time consuming, to say the least, and we went through quite a few variations before we felt we had a workable and achievable list of objectives. Many of the learning objectives do not neatly fall into one category. There is quite a bit of overlap between them, so we had to decide how to present the material in the tutorial without appearing overly repetitious.

Once we had identified the learning objectives, we began storyboarding sections of the tutorial to get an idea of flow and presentation of the concepts. Our approach was to go low-tech and utilize generic presentation software to input the information into PowerPoint slides. This made it easy to see and focus on the content and not concern ourselves at this point with the format or sequence of information. The idea was to get the information down and not spend too much time with the details. Looking back on the process, this was as important and useful step. It was one thing to think about the learning objectives but quite another to actually present them in visual form.

While the librarians were concentrating on the content, the computer consultant members of the task force were exploring various software options, which would be crucial to the look and feel of the tutorial. There is a wealth of literature that provides tips on design issues specific to the online environment. We incorporated Dewald's aforementioned best practices and took a multiple learning styles approach when addressing the instructional component. The redesigned tutorial includes interactivity, graphics, screen capture, video screen capture, and navigational tools. We also addressed computer requirements and issues of accessibility. The results of our focus groups indicated that students desire a combination of approaches, and we attempted to reflect this preference in our tutorial redesign. There was quite a bit of collaboration between the librarians and computer consultants in choosing software. After examining a variety of options, we decided to use Adobe Captivate and Flash.

Instruction

The purpose of the redesigned tutorial is to introduce students to the basic concepts involved in library research. The individual modules can be completed in any order, but the content of each module is linear, and a student cannot quit in the middle of a given module and come back to it later. Embedded within each modules are "test your knowledge" questions designed to allow students to check their understanding of the concepts covered. We designed these questions so that students would not only receive feedback when they got a question wrong (i.e., the correct answer) but also get additional information if they answered correctly (a reaffirmation of the learning objective).

Students must complete a quiz at the end of the tutorial and achieve a minimum score of 70. We set that score as a benchmark to indicate a base level of understanding of the concepts introduced. The final quiz utilizes a bank of questions that are randomized. Students who take the quiz more than once receive different questions each time. Since we had found with our previous tutorial that students often went straight to the quiz and then memorized the answers in order to meet the minimum score, we felt this was a significant improvement in the redesign.

Program Assessment

Development of our tutorial was now entering the final stages. Our earlier focus groups had been extremely informative, and we wanted another opportunity to get user feedback. We decided to test the effectiveness of the tutorial by administering a pre-test and post-test to several classes. The pre-test, consisting of ten questions addressing concepts introduced in the tutorial, was given to three English 1000 classes (41 students). The students then completed the tutorial and were asked to answer the same ten questions in the post-test. The average pre-test score was 5.7; the average post-test score 7.36.

To test the tutorial's usability we asked two students to complete it under controlled conditions in our usability lab using Tech-Smith Morae software. This screen capture software records the user's mouse movements and clicks and voice and provides video of the user via a Webcam. We observed the students as they moved through the modules, and they were given an evaluation questionnaire to record their impressions of each section of the tutorial. The results of the testing identified ongoing technical issues (e.g., screen images fading out before the student clicked the "next" button) and student preferences for content and design (e.g., students liked the drag-and-drop options quiz design but thought the plagiarism examples were too long).

The Redesign Tutorial Task Force has completed the final phase of the tutorial redesign. Our plans for ongoing assessment include pre-test and post-test sampling of freshman seminar and English 1000 students, individual testing in our usability lab, and analysis of statistical data gathered from reports generated by the tutorial itself. Our overall goals are to assure that the tutorial provides students with the basic knowledge they need to find, use, and evaluate information resources and a firm foundation on which to develop additional skills.

Lessons Learned

Assessment is an important step. We took the opportunity to gather information from students at two key intervals. Our focus groups were designed to gather information on the design elements and find out what students liked and disliked in online tutorials. The usability testing was conducted once the tutorial was in the finished form. The purpose of this testing was to have students rate their overall satisfaction with the content, design, and usability of the tutorial. The number of students we tested was small, but the feedback we received resulted in additional revisions and enhancements to the tutorial. Assessment (whatever form it takes) should be a fundamental component of successful online tutorial development.

Set a reasonable timeline. Our task force began its work in July 2006 and had the tutorial largely completed by March 2007. The tutorial debuted on the Belk Library home page in April. Librarians will use the summer months to make minor modifications, if needed. Heavy use of the tutorial is anticipated when classes reconvene in fall 2007. Building in allowances for flexibility is a good idea. This was a new experience for us, and so the learning curve was often very steep—so be prepared for things to take longer than you expect. The tutorial redesign was in addition to our regular job responsibilities, and there were times when all the members of the task force felt overwhelmed by the amount of time and work this project demanded.

Schedule regular meetings. Throughout the redesign we met on a regular basis. These regular meetings, more than anything else, helped keep us focused and on task. Much of the work was done individually or in subgroups, so it was imperative that we have some mechanism whereby we could all come together and report on our progress or any problems we might be encountering. Our initial design of the tutorial and the final product went through quite a few revisions. It was during the group meetings that we were able to hash out the details and come to consensus on the next step.

Don't reinvent the wheel. Whether you are developing a tutorial for the first time or embarking on a redesign, there is no need to reinvent the wheel. It is beneficial to explore what is already out there. We spent quite a bit of time looking at existing tutorials to try to figure out what form our final version might take. We examined everything from the technology used (audio, Flash, etc.) to the layout and design. This helped us identify not only elements we wanted to consider for inclusion in our own tutorial but also elements we did not want. There are some truly excellent online tutorials that embody tutorial design "best practices." If you see something you would like in one of them, then by all means contact the host library and ask if it is willing to allow you to use it. Our initial foray into tutorial development was a result of just this sort of collaboration. Make use of all the expertise available within your library and outside of it.

Keep your eyes on the prize. Remember that the end result of your efforts will be a product that adds value to your instruction program. Throughout the process you may encounter setbacks, revisions, and debates, but it is important to persevere. Success is often the result of persistence.

Perfection is not the goal. There were many moments throughout the process when we got bogged down in the minutia—in an effort to make each aspect of the tutorial perfect. Remember that, whatever you do, modifications will be needed to meet future developments in the library's instruction program. Go with your best effort and try not to sweat the small stuff.

Conclusion

Tutorial development is a tremendous learning opportunity. Our experience throughout this process was positive. As a task force we collectively felt that time spent on this project was well worth the effort, and that the redesigned tutorial would be a valuable addition to our library's instruction program. The redesigned Library Research Tutorial is now available at www.library.appstate.edu/tutorial/.

Notes

1. Appalachian State University Libraries, *Library Research Tutorial*. Available online at http://www.library.appstate.edu/tutorial.

2. Appalachian State University Freshman Seminar Program, *Welcome to Freshman Seminar*. Available online at http://www.freshmanseminar.appstate.edu/index.htm.

3. Joy Gambill and Kelly Rhodes, "Can You Hear Me Now? Integrating a Library Component into a Freshman Seminar Program," in *Library Instruction: Restating the Need, Refocusing the Response*, edited by Deb Biggs Thomas (Ann Arbor, MI: Pierian Press, 2005), 87–93.

4. Ibid., 88.

5. University of British Columbia Library, *Guide to Using UBC's Library Catalogue*. Available online at http://www.library.ubc.ca/scieng/videos/library_research.html.

6. The Upward Bound program "provides the necessary support for economically disadvantaged and/or first generation high school students to complete high school, enroll in college, and successfully obtain a four-year college degree." College Awareness Programs, Upward Bound. Available online at http://www.upwardbound.appstate.edu/.

7. Nancy H. Dewald, "Transporting Good Library Instruction Practices into the Web Environment: An Analysis of Online Tutorials," *Journal of Academic Librarianship* 25, no. 1 (1999), 26–32.

8. Debra Gilchrist, *Outcomes Assessment from the Inside Out*. Presentation at meeting of the Library Media Director's Council, Washington State, 1999.

21. Starting a RIOT: Information Literacy Instruction Online and in the Classroom

Caroline Sinkinson and Jennifer Knievel

Introduction

Not all libraries are fortunate enough to develop a strong relationship with a campus program, such as the writing program, that allows them to integrate information literacy instruction into a required course. Information literacy instruction can be delivered in many different ways; the University of Colorado (CU) at Boulder has experienced great success in integrating information literacy into the required first-year writing course, via the writing department on campus. The Program for Writing and Rhetoric (PWR) welcomes this ongoing collaboration, which includes a four-module online tutorial, an in-person seminar, and a drop-in research center. The successful structure of this collaborative endeavor is one that could work successfully on the campuses of many similar institutions.

Rationale

The University of Colorado at Boulder is a Research I institution with student enrollment totaling 31,068 (2005/6). The University Libraries have worked to develop strong instructional and information literacy programs. RIOT (Research Instruction Online Tutorial) was developed to encourage these goals, specifically for the first-year writing courses offered by PWR.

Information literacy can be delivered in many different ways: the ever popular one-shot session, online only, programs relying on voluntary sign-up from teachers, course-integrated programs, and credit courses. Although each of these kinds of instruction has its strengths and weaknesses, at CU the course-integrated approach seems to be most effective. A credit course in information literacy is listed in the CU course catalog, but it is rarely taught because it is not required for any major, and as a result it reaches far too few students. The first-year writing course is already a part of the required curriculum for the majority of students, and so it presents the best possible avenue to reach the highest number of students. Most writing courses assign large research projects, usually in the middle of the semester and again near finals. With thousands of students taking these writing courses, we face the specter of hundreds of students descending upon the reference desk as the due dates for these projects approach. Information literacy instruction that is integrated into the writing course allows us to control reference desk traffic by proactively offering research assistance to all students taking the course, diverting from the reference desk an overload of basic research questions associated with the course.

An extensive information literacy program existed at CU before the writing course was widely required of students. In that iteration, instruction was targeted to various courses in the College of Arts and Sciences, particularly the Communication department. Participation was, for most of these courses, voluntary. As is always the case with voluntary programs, some teaching faculty participated and others did not. Since the courses that routinely offered information literacy instruction may have been required for some majors, but not for the general curriculum, only some students were receiving instruction. There were large numbers of students who were completely missed, as well as wide overlap of students who received instruction many times in different Communication courses. The idea of multiple opportunities for instruction is positive, but the problem of missing many students while reaching others multiple times needed a solution.

In the late 1990s a writing department existed, but it taught almost exclusively upper-division courses and did not seek information literacy instruction for these courses. A lower-division writing course existed and was theoretically required of all students, but the vast majority of incoming students, nearly 90 percent, were exempted from the course based on SAT scores. As a result, the course had over time taken on the stigma of a remedial course that few students were forced to take. The course was almost exclusively literature based, and most instructors of that course were not responsive to solicitations for information literacy instruction.

Development

Leading up to 2000, a program review of the writing department triggered a campus-wide call to reevaluate the writing curriculum. As a result, PWR was created. The first-year writing courses were restructured to be more interdisciplinary and based on critical thinking, and to actively integrate research with writing. The long-term vision was to redesign the first-year writing course and eventually build it out until it was required of all incoming students in the College of Arts and Sciences, rather than only a small number.

A university committee was formed to create the overall curriculum of the course. A librarian was a member of that committee. She introduced to the other committee members the concepts of information literacy and the ways they tie so ideally to a critical thinking and writing course. The group successfully integrated a strong information literacy component.

The redesigned first-year writing course began with only seven sections. Participation in the information literacy component of the course was required of all instructors. The information literacy element was designed and redesigned as the course matured and expanded. The various elements of information literacy instruction were always based on ACRL standards. From the beginning, instruction included sections on keywords, searching, and evaluating. Another component of citing sources was added later. At first, instruction was a combination of paper assignments followed by a seminar. Librarians graded the assignments, which helped enormously with securing the support and willing participation of the writing instructors. With seven sections this was not a problem, but when the growing program burgeoned to sixty sections, grading became a major issue. As evidence of its strong commitment to this collaboration, PWR began paying for 0.5 FTE students to assist the librarians in providing information literacy instruction, including grading.

In summer 2002 a library position opened up and was written to incorporate instructional technology in hopes that the new librarian could write an online tutorial, developed from the paper assignments that had been refined over several years. The library hired a new librarian, who hired a programmer, who built a four-module tutorial. Content for the tutorial was developed primarily by two instruction librarians (a humanities reference librarian and the instruction co-ordinator) who had been working with the program for some time. The content was written in HTML, and the programmer created login and quizzing features. Shortly before the new tutorial was supposed to debut to almost eighty sections, an insurmountable compatibility flaw was discovered, and the entire quizzing sections of the tutorial had to be scrapped. There was not time to build a new one for the school year, so one more year of paper quizzes loomed, with huge piles of student assignments to be graded.

At that point, reference librarians brought in the systems department and began rebuilding a new online tutorial from scratch, with a great deal more attention to planning and development. An extraordinarily talented digital projects librarian redesigned and programmed the new tutorial, including a large number of extremely useful features for all the various users (students, faculty, and librarians). For example,

students can log into the tutorial and view the test questions again, including their own answers along with the correct answers. Faculty can log in to the tutorial and view all of their students' grades, organized by section, as well as individual quizzes for each student and each student's answer to every quiz question. Librarians can log in to the tutorial and quickly see a summary of each section, including how many students have completed each module of the tutorial and the average class score for each module. Librarians can also view each student's answer to individual quiz questions. The features for librarians are particularly helpful because they allow them to tailor in-person instruction based on student responses. The new tutorial was dubbed the Research Instruction Online Tutorial, or RIOT, in joking reference to the CU students' penchant at the time for couch-burning street parties. With the new tutorial, grading is objective and automated in three of four modules. Scores are e-mailed both to the students and, in bulk once a week, to professors. The one subjective, hand-graded module is graded by librarians online, and comments and scores are e-mailed to students as soon as a grade is recorded in the tutorial.

The PWR first-year writing course is now required of all incoming students enrolled in the College of Arts and Sciences: 3,808 freshmen in 2005/6 (of 4,905 freshman overall), or approximately one hundred sections per semester. The

Figure 21.1. Tutorial contents

Tutorial Contents

This tutorial includes four modules with **quiz questions** interspersed throughout. Quiz questions will be graded automatically as you progress in modules one, two, and four. Module three will be graded by library staff, and your grade will be sent to you.

Answer carefully! You will only have one opportunity to answer each question.

Module 1 THINK: How to use keywords	This will take approximately 20 minutes. There are **3 quiz questions**.
Module 2A FIND: How to find books	This will take approximately 10 minutes. There are **8 quiz questions**.
Module 2B FIND: How to find journal articles	This will take approximately 10 minutes. There are **8 quiz questions**.
Module 2C FIND: How to find newspaper articles	This will take approximately 10 minutes. There are **5 quiz questions**.
Module 3 EVALUATE: How to evaluate sources	This will take approximately 25 minutes. There are **3 quiz questions**.
Module 4 CITE: How to cite sources	This will take approximately 20 minutes. There are **7 quiz questions**.

Need Help? Come to the drop-in Research Center at the Information Literacy / Writing Center
Norlin E156; Monday - Thursday 2 - 5 pm; or email pwrhelp@colorado.edu.

support from PWR has increased to funding 0.75 FTE to assist with instruction, grading, and staffing in the research center.

Content

Five main learning objectives drive the First-Year Writing and Rhetoric classes, focused on writing, rhetorical sensitivity, proficient reading, research, and linguistic usage. The Libraries' online information literacy tutorial aims to meet the learning objective centered on research: "To develop strategies of research that will enable you to become an active investigator of your culture."[1] The First-Year Writing and Rhetoric textbook outlines how students will meet this objective. This outline and the ACRL Information Literacy Competency Standards drive the content of our online information literacy tutorial. The tutorial is divided into four main modules (figure 21.1). PWR instructors assign these modules at their discretion at the point of relevance in their individual courses.

Module One: Think

The Think module assists students in approaching their topic of research. This module's goals are derived from ACRL Standard One: "The information literate student determines the nature and extent of the information needed." To determine the nature of the information need, the tutorial asks students to consider the types of information sources that are required. Students are exposed to the difference between scholarly and popular sources, a concept new to many incoming freshman. The tutorial provides a definition of source types and a chart detailing the characteristics of both.

Next, the tutorial focuses on formulating the research question, problem, or inquiry. Specifically the tutorial introduces the concept of keywords by demonstrating an initial research question and then breaking it down into essential concepts and terms (figure 21.2). After modeling the effective construction of keywords from a research inquiry, the tutorial quizzes students on the concept. The quiz questions work to illustrate overly broad and overly narrow terms.

Module Two: Find

The Find module teaches students how to identify library tools appropriate for locating books, journal or magazine articles, and

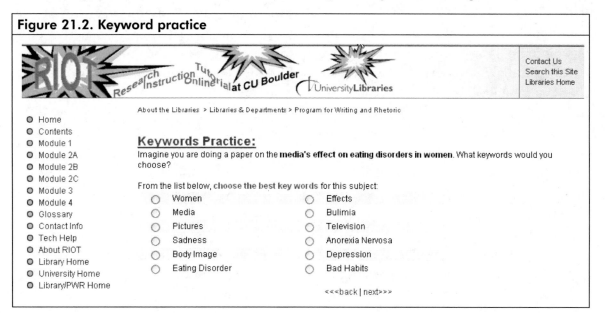

Figure 21.2. Keyword practice

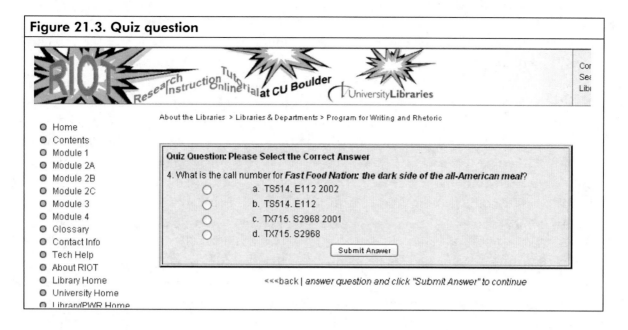

Figure 21.3. Quiz question

newspaper articles. The goals of this module are derived from ACRL Standard Two: "The information literate student accesses needed information effectively and efficiently." A large component of this standard involves comprehending and selecting appropriate information retrieval systems. Therefore, this module is divided into three sections focused on specific library tools: the online library catalog, Chinook; an interdisciplinary article database, Academic Search Premier; and a newspaper article database, LexisNexis.

Module Two, section A, begins by defining an online library catalog and what types of materials may be retrieved with it. Screenshots and sample searches of our catalog are provided. Keyword searching, title searching, and author searching are each illustrated for students. Additionally, the tutorial goes into depth about online catalog records and their components—call number, location, status, and the like.

Students are asked to apply this knowledge by searching the live online catalog and responding to various quiz questions (figure 21.3). The questions require students to se-

lect the appropriate search method (e.g., title or keyword) and to solve issues of stop words. Finally, the quiz questions emphasize the needed catalog record elements required for physical item location.

Module Two, section B, centers on finding journal and magazine articles. Students are taught how to access library databases, how to search the database, and how to retrieve full-text articles from the database. Additionally, the tutorial requires students to identify an article citation and its components. This section aims to clarify the need for article databases when searching for materials topically, and the use of the library catalog when working from a citation.

Module Two, section C, is much like section B. It details accessing LexisNexis, searching the database, and retrieving materials from it. The students are given further instruction on utilizing the search interface features. Sections B and C are not merely screenshots and instructions. Students are required to move interactively through a demonstrated search of the databases by selecting the appropriate features or entering search terms.

Module Three: Evaluate

The Evaluate module centers on ACRL Standard Three: "The information literate student evaluates information and its sources critically and incorporates selected information into his or her knowledge base and value system." At this stage in the research process, students have defined their information need and found appropriate sources. They are now ready to evaluate and synthesize the information found. The tutorial establishes three essential criteria for students to utilize in evaluating sources retrieved. The first, credibility is defined as the trustworthiness of the author (figure 21.4). The second, validity looks at the quality of research and the support of the work's argument. Finally, the tutorial teaches students to examine the relevance of a source for students' specific information needs. The tutorial provides model application of these criteria to sample articles before quizzing the students. The evaluation criteria are presented for both articles and websites.

Module Four: Cite

The Cite module focuses on the necessity of citing materials as well as the dangers of plagiarism. Specific goals of the module are derived from ACRL Standard Five: "The information literate student understands many of the economic, legal, and social issues surrounding the use of information and accesses and uses information ethically and legally." Students are taught why documentation matters, specifically in the context of CU Boulder's academic community. The requirements of the CU Honor Code are described in detail. The tutorial then examines and illustrates when citations are necessary;

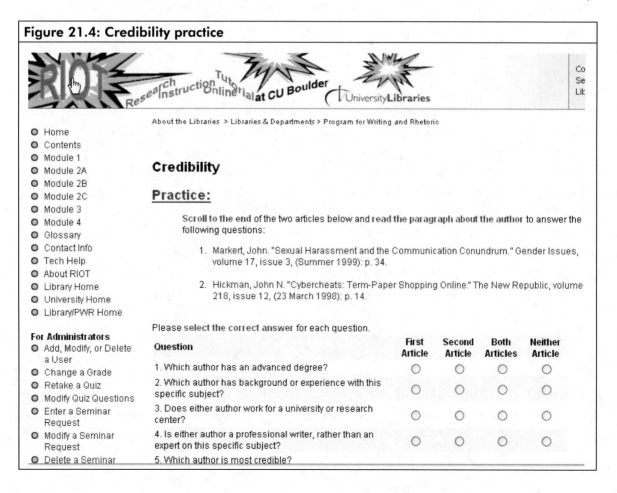

Figure 21.4: Credibility practice

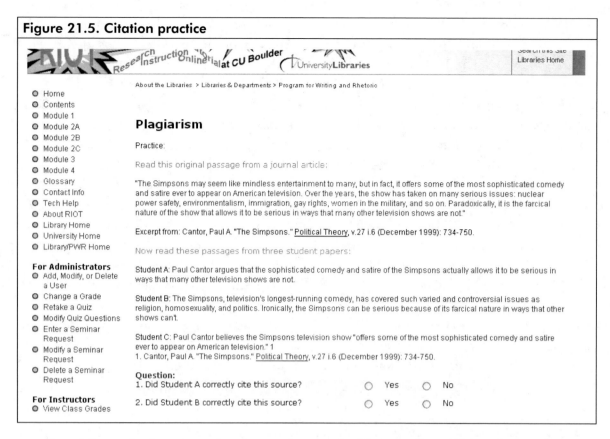

Figure 21.5. Citation practice

samples of direct citations, paraphrasing, and summarizing are each provided (figure 21.5). After introducing resources for style guides and methods, the tutorial finally suggests strategies for using information ethically and avoiding dangers of plagiarism.

Overall, the online information literacy tutorial works to introduce students to the essential aspects of information literacy: defining the information need, effectively forming a search strategy, locating information sources, evaluating information sources, incorporating the information retrieved, and using that information efficiently and effectively.

Instruction

Our information literacy program provides instruction through the online tutorial, which is then enhanced by a librarian-led seminar. The online tutorial establishes an introductory understanding of library research and

tools. The seminar allows the students to apply and transfer the tutorial's learning objectives to discipline-based sources for a real and personal research need.

The seminars provide guided search practice, demonstration of advanced searching, and individual research time with librarian assistance. The instruction team has generated a general lesson plan for the first-year writing seminars. The seminar begins with an introduction and welcome of any questions about the online tutorial. The students are led by the seminar librarian through a review of criteria for source evaluation, which are then applied to a few sample websites. The website evaluation leads into a discussion of library article indexes and databases and the advantages of using these tools. With librarian facilitation, the students take a sample inquiry and execute a search in a library database. During this practice, the librarian aims to prompt discussion about discipline resources. The librarian asks students to question where the conversation on their own topics might be occurring. Through the demonstration, the seminar reviews the transformation of a research question into an effective search strategy as well as illustrating the practical skills of using library resources. The seminar then shifts to students' application of the learned skills; students begin investigating their own topics as the librarian circulates, providing one-on-one assistance. During this portion of the seminar, the librarian works to help students select appropriate information retrieval tools, construct more sophisticated search strategies, and retrieve texts.

The general lesson plan provides a framework for the seminar but is often adapted to meet specific class needs. Prior to the seminar, the library requests details about the students' assignment and topics from the course instructor. Librarians are then able to adapt the seminar. This level of customization works to enhance student engagement and the perceived relevance of the seminar learning objectives. Additionally, because the tutorial may be completed throughout the semester as assigned by the course instructor, and because the seminar is scheduled according to individual course needs, students approach both the tutorial and seminar, ideally, at the point of need.

Together the tutorial and the seminar enforce models of well-constructed research methods and strategies. The seminar also provides a personal introduction to a librarian and the physical library. While in the seminar and pursuing individual research, students experience guidance and direction from a librarian with the often overwhelming volume of information retrieval tools and potential resources. Furthermore, students are physically introduced to the li-

brary, which serves to demystify a space that is not intuitive to many. After completing both tutorial and seminar, students should have the knowledge and tools for successful academic research as well as a familiarity with the help available to them through the library.

Throughout instruction, online and in-person, students enrolled in the first-year classes are provided with numerous support and communication mechanisms. For example, a dedicated e-mail address is made available to students throughout the tutorial. At any point, students may send e-mail with questions or concerns. The e-mail account is read and answered by graduate students employed by the library specifically to assist with the writing course. Furthermore, students are invited to visit the Research Center.

The Research Center is staffed throughout the semester and designed specifically for these first-year writing courses and students. Students receive instruction from the tutorial and the seminar; the Research Center is available for further instruction with any needs related to the tutorial, the seminar, or any step in the research process. With this service, students more comfortable with one-on-one instruction are served. The Research Center also aims to highlight areas unclear to students and to help avoid continued frustration. Conveniently, the Research Center is housed in the same location as PWR's Writing Center, which establishes a space devoted to enhancing student research and writing skills collaboratively.

PWR faculty are provided with recommendations on how to best incorporate the information literacy component into their courses. Continued collaboration and communication between librarians and the faculty is essential in maintaining the program.

When possible, changes are made on the basis of faculty suggestions, both in the online tutorial and through individual seminar customization. This collaboration and the shared space of the Research and Writing Centers serve to establish a sense of community around the program.

Program Assessment

The assessment of our program is an ongoing process aided by formal and informal assessment mechanisms. The online tutorial provides measurable assessment feedback in the form of students' quiz grades. The quizzes are graded and e-mailed to both the student and the course instructor. Students and instructors may also log in to the tutorial to view specific quiz questions and responses. Librarians are able to monitor overall student levels of comprehension throughout the semester, as well as by class and individual. Because students complete the tutorial prior to the seminar, librarians are able to adapt the seminar to emphasize areas of lesser or greater comprehension of the class as a whole. Additionally, librarians are able to monitor consistent trends in student performance and make changes accordingly. For example, in the two years (four semesters) of the tutorial, scores on module 2C (Find: finding newspaper articles in LexisNexis) were consistently very high, while scores on module 4 (Cite: citation and plagiarism) were consistently very low. Analysis on the part of the librarians suggested that module 2C required too little critical thinking, since most of the quiz questions were about specific interface usage rather than higher-order searching strategy. As a result, librarians modified 2C in a way that required students to give more thought to their research strategy for newspaper articles. Average scores for the section went from 89.4 percent to the mid

70s. Analysis also suggested that module 4 was not difficult enough to justify the poor scores students were receiving. At the time, the module focused almost exclusively on citation styles, such as APA, MLA, and Chicago. Students performed badly on these questions, despite the fact that they were not difficult, which led librarians to believe that the module did not demonstrate sufficient relevance to the students. As a result, the module was rewritten to focus much more on issues of plagiarism and the ethics, rather than the mechanics, of citation. Average scores have gone up, despite the fact that the content is more difficult, from 71.9 percent to the upper 70s.

When in the classroom with the students, librarians are able to do quick assessment by assigning tasks to the class and working with students individually. The effectiveness of having both the online and in-person components benefits us a great deal in this regard. With this structure, we are able to evaluate the success of the tutorial's learning objectives with definitive figures and observed experience.

We invite feedback from students and faculty via surveys and feedback forms (see appendices). These various forms and surveys focus on the tutorial, the seminar, and the research center individually. The responses provide insight to areas of the program needing more attention or enhancement based on faculty and student satisfaction. Informal feedback is also acquired through conversations between librarians and PWR faculty. A librarian maintains a seat on the PWR first-year committee, which also serves as an excellent avenue for feedback and continued development.

In the future, we would like to develop a more in-depth program assessment plan. The ability to see how students are actively applying the skills learned to their academic assignments would provide a great deal of insight. With the evaluation of students' conceptual understanding of information literacy skills and their application, we could more thoroughly evaluate the effectiveness of library instruction.

Lessons Learned

Major hindrances to the program development were both technical and pedagogical. Software built by a contracted programmer for the tutorial turned out to be flawed, and the tutorial had to be reprogrammed from scratch by our systems department. In the interim, the program was a complicated and sometimes frustrating hybrid of online and paper formats. These major programming flaws showed us that it would have been much better to spend a great deal more time planning before the first tutorial was built. We would have been better off to include more colleagues from the beginning, like our systems department, who helped us identify which campus players we needed to make our ideal tutorial a feasible project. The systems department also helped spot and avoid potential pitfalls that we would have otherwise discovered only in hindsight, such as the difficulties of maintaining a username and password database and the dangers of multiple users in Microsoft Access. These technological problems extended the time we had to use the frustrating hybrid of paper and online.

The vast majority of writing faculty welcomed the information literacy element of the course. They were teaching research in their course anyway, and most found it helpful to have research taught by the research experts. Some were skeptical upon hearing of this required element of the course, but almost all gave it good-faith effort in their

first semester. Though they initially struggled to integrate information literacy at the most appropriate time, after one semester and a deeper understanding of information literacy they saw the benefits of integrated information literacy both for their curriculum and for their students' learning.

Although the information literacy program was well received by most of the PWR faculty, some were resistant, creating a few barriers among the teaching faculty. Some saw the information literacy element as an invasion of their pedagogy, as a judgment of their ability to teach, or, worst of all, as a waste of time. This opinion was most frequently held by instructors who were accustomed to teaching literature-based writing classes that focused entirely on literary exegesis, and in which research was not only neglected but actually prohibited for any writing project. The writing department has, for the most part, reached an agreement that this style of writing course is not appropriate for a course required of all majors, and that particular style is now more commonly found at the upper-division level, where writing is designed to be taught in connection with a specific discipline.

One unexpected lesson was the importance of stressing to students the difference between good writing and good research. For example, one might argue that an article from *Atlantic Monthly*, while likely to be beautifully crafted writing, does not meet most standards for a scholarly source in an academic context. Initially, the information literacy component of the course heavily stressed the importance of author credibility and source validity, while at the same time writing instructors were primarily focused on writing quality, regardless of source. As a result, students were hearing from the library that some sources, such as opinion pieces and items written by non-expert authors, were less credible and less valid, while those same pieces were being taught as high-quality writing samples by the writing instructors. Students felt that they were receiving mixed messages. Once this contradiction became clear to the librarians and the teaching faculty, we added elements in the tutorial designed to stress the difference between good writing and good research. We emphasized that a beautifully written piece may lack both credibility and validity, and that a highly credible and valid scholarly article may be very poorly written indeed. Emphasizing this point seems to have cleared up the mixed message from the students' perspective.

Because the information literacy component was complex for brand new faculty to understand, the first semester or two of teaching this course was difficult for most incoming faculty. We attempted to give them maximum freedom as to when to incorporate the information literacy curriculum, asking them to assign the various elements not in a specific week of the course but rather when it was appropriate for their particular syllabus. Although this freedom is important for the long-term success of both information literacy instruction and our collaboration, it was sometimes confusing for faculty to try to identify the best time, since they were unfamiliar with the concept of information literacy and when it might best benefit their students. Librarians are consistently invited to new writing faculty orientations, but the orientations are heavily loaded, and faculty found it difficult to integrate everything they learned from the orientations into their syllabus in the short time between orientation and the beginning of the semester. Fortunately, some faculty would call us for assistance in setting up

timing, and others would figure out during their first semester a better timing for subsequent semesters.

Since the course was expanding rapidly, there were more than a dozen new faculty every year who all had to figure out the best way to integrate the information literacy component. In addition, since so many faculty were new and elements of the library component changed frequently in the beginning, there was minimal institutional knowledge for them to draw on among each other. The ongoing changes to the information literacy component exacerbated this confusion. The last-minute implosion of the first tutorial changed how they had to integrate information literacy. Later, the new tutorial again changed how they had to integrate it. But fortunately, since the initial deployment of RIOT, the changes have been minor. New faculty still come in, but the numbers are much smaller and they are able to draw much more easily on each other for help in appropriately integrating information literacy. Currently, most faculty find it helpful and are supportive of information literacy, as well as vocal to their students about its benefits, which helps their students place value on it as well. Ongoing open communication and collaboration have been key to overcoming all of these pedagogical barriers.

Conclusion

The University of Colorado at Boulder's information literacy instruction program, in collaboration with the Program for Writing and Rhetoric's required writing course, has proved to be an extremely successful integration of writing and research. The collaboration began with a librarian's involvement on the curriculum committee and has blossomed into a strong ongoing relationship between the library and the writing department. Information literacy instruction involves a four-module tutorial, an in-person seminar, and the availability of a drop-in research center. While some technical problems slowed initial development, the tutorial and seminar combination has proved very effective over time. The cross-campus collaboration of the writing department and the library can serve as a model for other institutions and has been a benefit to all involved: the librarians, the faculty, and, most of all, the students.

Appendix A.
Student Feedback Form in RIOT

1. What did you find most useful about this tutorial? Please be specific.

2. What did you find least useful about this tutorial? Please be specific.

For questions 3–12, please answer Yes or No.
3. After completing this tutorial, I understand the difference between a scholarly source and a popular source, and I know when it is appropriate to use each.

4. After completing this tutorial, I am more comfortable searching the library catalog for books.

5. After completing this tutorial, I am more comfortable searching for articles in an article database.

6. I understand the difference between credibility, validity, and relevance.

7. I know how to cite sources in APA, MLA, or Chicago style.

8. I can identify what is plagiarism and what isn't.

9. Completing this tutorial helped me find sources for a research project I was working on.

10. It was clear when I was taking the tutorial where I was supposed to go next.

11. When I had trouble with the tutorial, I could tell where I needed to go for help.

12. The quiz questions accurately reflected content of the tutorial.

13. Did you have technical trouble with the tutorial? If so, please explain what happened.

Appendix B.
Faculty Email Survey about Seminar

Hello X,

You and your students recently attended a seminar in the library as part of the information literacy component of your First Year Writing and Rhetoric course.

Please take a few moments to complete the evaluation below. Your responses will help us to improve our collaboration in the future.

Thank you,
Jennifer Knievel and Caroline Sinkinson

1. Who was/were your library seminar instructor(s)?

2. What do you consider the least effective part of the seminar?

3. What do you consider the most effective part of your seminar?

4. How would you characterize your students' reaction to the seminar?

5. Have you seen an increase in the quality or effectiveness of your students' research over the course of the semester?

6. What changes would you suggest for future seminars?

Appendix C.
Student Seminar Evaluation Form

SEMINAR FEEDBACK FORM   Students 2
Date: Course:

Please circle the one that best describes you:
Freshman   Sophomore   Junior   Senior   Graduate   Faculty/Staff   Other_____

Please circle the one that best describes your assignment:
Argumentative/Analytical Essay   Annotated Bibliography   Personal Narrative
Inquiry/ Research   Other :_____

1. Please list the most useful concepts/things you learned in this seminar.

2. How will you use what you have learned?

3. What do you wish was focused on more heavily?

4. What do you still want to learn about the library and research?

5. Other Comments:

Note

1.   Michelle Albert, Erik Ellis, Lonni Pearce, Caroline Sinkinson, and Tony Ruiz, eds., *Knowing Words: A Guide to First-year Writing and Rhetoric* (Plymouth, MI: Hayden McNeil, 2007), 15.

22. Connecting the Dots: An Inquiry-Based Approach to Information Literacy

K. Alix Hayden, Shauna Rutherford, and Paul R. Pival

Introduction

Librarians at the University of Calgary designed the Workshop on the Information Search Process for Research in the Library (WISPR) to change fundamentally our role as information literacy instructors. We realized that students were not developing transferable strategies and skills for doing research through "one-shot" sessions that focused primarily on the mechanics of database searching. They often did not recognize that (1) library research is an intellectual process, (2) library research is more than simply a matter of having computer skills, and (3) the information search process remains similar regardless of the discipline or the academic level of research. University trends towards supporting inquiry-based learning and the integration of online learning into face-to-face courses presented an opportunity for librarians to reconceptualize our approach to instruction through the Web-based workshop. We developed an online workshop that shows students how to "connect the dots," how to link their actions and strategies to specific components of the information search process, and how to understand the complex, iterative nature of information seeking.

Rationale

The trends shaping institutional priorities at the University of Calgary are the same as those influencing higher education throughout North America. Ernest Boyer's *Reinventing Undergraduate Education* recommends, among other things, introducing students to inquiry in their first year.[1] At the root of inquiry-based learning is the constructivist belief that students learn most effectively by building upon existing knowledge and interests to develop questions of personal significance. They explore widely the information surrounding questions to develop new (to them) knowledge, solutions, or perspectives on the issue at hand. Inherent in that understanding of inquiry is that students have the skills and strategies to develop sound questions, find relevant information, and interpret and evaluate the information in order to apply it. Librarians clearly recognize that information literacy is essential for students to succeed in an inquiry-based learning environment. We developed WISPR to respond to this need.

The university was facing space constraints, increasing student enrollment, and budget restraints. These factors along with the trend toward more technology-mediated instruction in all courses also drove the development of WISPR. As Blackboard became the campus standard course management system, more emphasis was placed on pedagogical applications of technology to make teaching more effective and not simply to use them as an add-on to the face-to-face components of the course. The challenge was to increase student learning through inquiry while also being responsive to cost implications. University administration felt that "blended learning" was the solution to the challenge. In 2001 a new

226

director was appointed to the University of Calgary's Teaching and Learning Centre (TLC). Dr. Randy Garrison came with a significant history of both research and practice in computer-mediated instruction, first in the context of distance education and, later, through blended learning involving onsite courses.

Garrison invited national and international speakers to present successful examples of technology positively influencing teaching and learning. One such speaker was Carol Twigg, executive director of the Center for Academic Transformation, which had received funding to implement the Pew Learning and Technology Program Initiative.[2] Twenty grants were given out to institutions to transform courses using technology. These projects were studied and analyzed and the findings demonstrated a remarkable cost saving as well as a distinct improvement in the quality of student learning. Like most universities, the University of Calgary has great interest in minimizing costs, maximizing the use of limited classroom space, and improving the student learning experience. Inspired by the results of the Pew course redesign project, campus administration sought ways to encourage similar projects on campus.

In fall 2004, an invitation to apply for an Inquiry and Blended Learning Course Development and Enhancement Pilot Project Grant was sent out to University of Calgary faculty. Although librarians do not offer a credit course in information literacy at the university, we submitted a proposal for an "Information Literacy syllabus" that could be meaningfully integrated into courses where inquiry-based and blended learning were employed. Our proposal was successful, and we received $10,000 to develop the "syllabus" that became WISPR.

Development
WISPR Framework

WISPR is founded on the theoretical work of Carol Collier Kuhlthau, whose longitudinal research demonstrates that people go through a specific process when searching for information.[3] She identified six stages of research: task initiation, topic selection, prefocus formulation, focus formulation, information collection, and search closure. Her model incorporates three realms: the physical (actions and strategies), the cognitive (thoughts), and the affective (feelings). These realms are common to each stage of the information search process (ISP).

Given that WISPR would be taught in either an online or blended learning environment, it was imperative that the framework encapsulate the iterative, intellectual, and complex nature of information seeking while being able to "stand alone" as a true graphic representation of the information search process. Often Kuhlthau's ISP model is depicted as a chart, full of detailed information related to the three realms within each stage. Such a linear, text-heavy depiction would not be meaningful or interesting to students. Fortunately, two colleagues (Vivian Steida and Lorraine Toews) developed a graphic, for a different purpose, which we acquired permission to use to represent the information search process (see figure 22.1).

Although the ISP is iterative, one must "connect the dots" when searching for information, that is, go through each phase prior to moving to the next without skipping a phase. This sequential nature is indicated by the arrows between each "dot" (phase). Although there is only one way to move forward through the process at any time, one may loop back to revisit a previous phase when necessary.

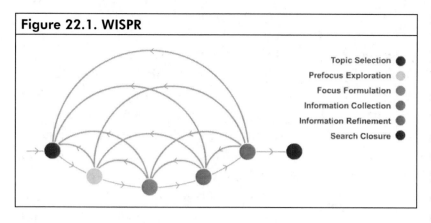

Figure 22.1. WISPR

The WISPR graphic drove the design for the workshop. Through consultation with a team of librarians and an instructional designer, programmers at the university's TLC created the framework for WISPR, designing standardized components for each phase. Color coding for each phase corresponds to the WISPR graphic. This standardized approach helps students become familiar with the framework quickly as well as providing a sense of cohesion throughout all phases. The programmers also included different navigation points to appeal to different expectations. Every screen shows a small WISPR graphic, indicating the phase currently under study and clearly indicating student progress through the ISP. Figure 22.2 illustrates an example of the layout used for every screen in all phases.

Instructional Designer

We spent our $10,000 grant exclusively on the technical programming of the WISPR framework. Because of the nature of the grant, we benefited from the expertise of an instructional designer without having to pay for his services. Our instructional designer, Norm Vaughan, was familiar with information literacy and libraries, so he was able to "talk our talk" and guide us to pedagogically sound instructional resources, materials, and

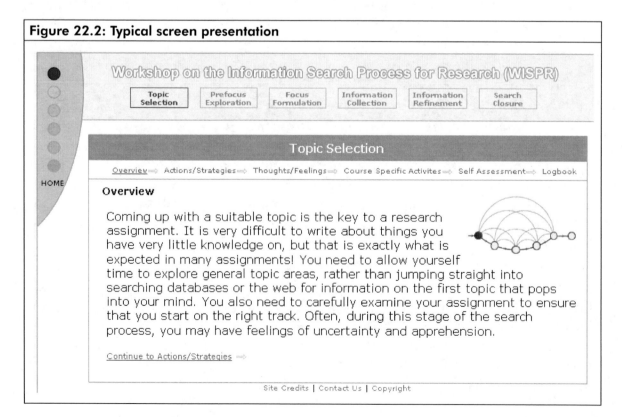

Figure 22.2: Typical screen presentation

technologies. He ensured that we were not dazzled by slick technologies but rather based our decision to implement a technology upon pedagogical purpose. He grounded us in appropriate activities for online learning, with a constant reminder of learning objectives for each activity and content area. In addition, Norm encouraged us to use a friendly, non-academic voice in all phases and associated activities.

Instructional Technology

We explored a variety of ways to engage our learners throughout WISPR. The instructional designer suggested that we address different learning styles (e.g., auditory and visual) and avoid the trap of many online tutorials that involve extensive reading of Web pages with little interactivity. As well, the principal of meaningful authentic learning through technology guided our decision making. Further, this learning had to work well in the online environment. For those components of WISPR that can be modified and adapted, we aimed, where possible, to use technology that was readily available (either free or inexpensive) and that would be fairly simple for other librarians to learn. Table 22.1 illustrates the different technologies used to create the various components of WISPR.

Content. All content in WISPR can be customized, adapted, and changed to reflect the teaching curriculum and meet course objectives. Specific course-related strategies and activities, meaningful integrated examples, assignment due dates, and links to specific resources and librarian contact information are all modified using a simple embedded WYSIWYG editor through WISPR's administrative interface. A WYSIWYG editor is essential so that librarians may easily change content without knowing HTML. We felt that this would assist librarians integrating WISPR into their various teaching activities and promoting it to their faculties and departments.

KWLF Chart. Macromedia Breeze is a software package that incorporates narration to Microsoft's PowerPoint slides and then converts the file to Flash. Breeze content and activities are easily delivered via the Web without requiring the student to download a plug-in. Further, a Breeze file plays automatically, providing the student with the opportunity to pause and rewind at will. The University of Calgary holds a site license for this software, so we were able to use it without any associated costs. The TLC provided training and support when required. Of benefit to new users of Breeze is that each slide's narration is a single recording. One does not need to redo the entire PowerPoint Presentation narration if a mishap occurs when speaking. Currently Breeze is used to introduce students to the KWLF Chart (What I Know, What I Want to Know, What I Learned, and Where I Found it). This chart would be tedious and very long if described

Table 22.1. Technology used for creating WISPR components		
WISPR Component	Technology	Responsibility
Content	TinyMCE WYSIWYG editor	Librarians
KWLF Chart	Macromedia Breeze	Librarians
Screencasts	ViewletBuilder Pro and Camtasia Studio	Librarians
Guided database tutorials	HTML, Boomer, Javascript (TILT)	Librarians
Self-assessment scenarios	Quandry 2.2	Librarians
Logbook	Jakarta Tapestry	Programmers

by text—and very likely skipped by students. Through Breeze, however, narration clearly describes the concept for each slide. Animation is also used to illustrate examples under each component of the chart. Breeze may be used for other instructional activities in WISPR in the future.

Screencasts. A screencast is a short recording, often incorporating audio, of a computer screen, showing all mouse movements, typing, screen changes, links, and the like. As well, some interactivity such as students answering a question or demonstrating knowledge by clicking on a portion of the screen before advancing may be included. We decided to use screencasts to provide orientations to tasks (e.g., authentication to access databases remotely), use of specific resources (e.g., Find It:SFX for full-text articles), and quick overviews of specific databases. A link is provided to a screencast, which is opened in a new window. We found that, particularly for databases, indicating the length of each screencast encouraged students to connect. Screencast software such as Camtasia does require a bit of time to learn. For more complex databases or search demonstrations, we determined that it is advantageous to have a script to read and guide you through the database rather than "winging it." Having a well-rehearsed script ensured a minimum of "takes" when recording a screencast. It is also advisable to review the script for library jargon, unexplained concepts, and missing steps in the search that may easily confuse the student who is working independently. Also, we learned to indicate that the student should turn on the computer's speakers for audio screencasts, something that was not readily apparent to many students.

Guided database tutorials. To enhance interactivity and student learning, we sought ways to provide guided searching experience in the online environment. It was important to allow students an opportunity to practice what they had learned but still provide guidance and structure, similar to a face-to-face hands-on session. The hands-on searching feature is accomplished through the presentation of a split screen using frames and JavaScript coding for interactivity provided by TILT (Texas Information Literacy Tutorial). Through a tool called Boomer, audio was added to each database tutorial. A short audio file is recorded as a WAV file, which Boomer then converts to Flash. The embedded Flash audio file plays as soon as the left frame loads. On the left side of the split screen, written and corresponding audio instructions guide students on the live database that appears on the right side of the screen. Given that the database is live, students may search anything they want; however, by following the guided instructions, all search features are explored, questions are embedded, and proper searching techniques are taught. These guided database tutorials require more expertise than the other instructional technologies used in WISPR. One librarian acted as the programmer and created the tutorials using content, examples, and scripts provided by a subject librarian. We hope that training will soon be provided to interested librarians so that we may expand our expertise in building guided database tutorials.

Self-assessment scenarios. WISPR encapsulates the information search process from a constructivist perspective. Therefore, it was deemed important to ensure that students were confident in their understanding and abilities for each phase prior to proceeding to the next phase. We determined that a simple checklist would not best serve our purposes nor be pedagogically appropriate for students. Instead we used Quandary, which is a decision-point tool, or "action maze." Through a self-assessment scenario at the end of each phase, students are presented with a situation (the phase) and a question focusing on actions and strategies related to the phase. Table 22.2 provides an example of a self-assessment question. The student selects either "yes" or "no." A "yes" response verifies the actions and strategies taken by the student. A "no" response results in suggestions for remedial work or links to previous portions of the phase for review. In both instances, a new question is posed, again with the yes/no option. The purpose of using an action maze is to provide students with assistance in areas that they have not completed or do not fully understand. In a sense, then, Quandary simulates the reference conversation between librarian and student in an online environment. Students are gently guided when they are missing information or lacking understanding of specific concepts based on the students' own self-assessment. Eventually, the student successfully completes the self-assessment action maze and is prompted to continue to the next phase.

Logbook. The electronic logbook is similar to a research diary or a scientific logbook and provides a means for students to chart their progress through the information search process. The logbook can be used by individuals or groups of students. It is submitted electronically to the professor or librarian. The questions for each phase ask students to record their actions and strategies and then encourage them to review their search process. Several courses have used the logbook as a course assignment; only students registered in such a course may access the associated logbook. The logbook was developed and programmed by the TLC and is currently not customizable because of complex programming issues. Further funding is sought to enhance the customization of the logbook as well as to make this process user friendly to librarians.

Content

Unlike many library tutorials, WISPR was not developed primarily as a means of teaching the skills required for electronic database searching. Rather, it was designed to provide students with a holistic framework with which to approach their research assignments. We wanted to teach them through a visual interface that information seeking is a complex

Table 22.2. Self-Assessment action maze example	
Self-Assessment Question	
I have thoroughly read through my assignment and am aware of all the criteria required.	
Action/Decision	Outcome
Yes, I understand my assignment and know what I need to do to in order to satisfy the assignment's criteria.	*New self-assessment question posed:* I'm starting to be on the "lookout" for an interesting topic.
No, I've only skimmed the assignment and many details are still hazy.	*Remedial guidance provided:* • Carefully read your assignment. • Being sure that you know all of the criteria for the assignment often results in less wasted time, and ultimately less frustration. Read your assignment to find out what types of materials are allowed (e.g., if no Internet sites, don't waste time searching the Internet), currency, topic may need to be approved, primary sources may need to be cited, citation style, etc. If you are unclear on any of the guidelines, speak to your professor or TA. • Continue to the next self-assessment question.

intellectual process. WISPR "connects the dots" for students. It teaches them the common phases of the information search process and provides guidance and strategies on how to progress through each phase. Several disciplines have incorporated WISPR into the curriculum including nursing, kinesiology, English, social work, psychology, general science, and science, technology and society. For the most part, WISPR is taught in first-year and second-year courses.

Phases

Phase 1. Topic selection instructs students to explore general topic areas as a first step in the research process (see figure 22.1). Most undergraduates do not have enough foundational knowledge of a subject area to select an appropriate research question for their assignments immediately. Students are encouraged to start their research early so that they have time to explore and discover. Often during this stage of the search process students may have feelings of uncertainty and apprehension. Reading the assignment carefully is a key element in this phase so that students do not start off under incorrect assumptions.

Phase 2. Prefocus formulation guides students to consider their topic in a more focused way. Often students need to expand their understanding of a topic, so they must investigate many aspects of a potential topic while considering what aspects are most interesting or promising to research. Students are encouraged to read to become informed about a topic, to take notes, and to be tolerant of inconsistencies. Often during this phase students feel that they are wasting their time, spinning their wheels, and get frustrated with searching.

Phase 3. Focus formulation is the phase when students must decide a fairly specific focus

to research. Four criteria for topic consideration are suggested: Interest—What do I find personally interesting/intriguing about this topic? Task—Will researching this aspect of the topic meet the requirements of my assignment? Information—Is there enough information out there on this aspect of my topic? and, Time—Do I have enough time to research this aspect of the topic? Students are often unaware of the considerable amount of time it takes to search for information, even in today's Internet age. Usually during this phase students' anxiety gives way to a sense of clarity and confidence.

Phase 4. Information collection teaches students how to search effectively for information. Once students have clearly defined the focus of their topic, they are best able to conduct a literature search for information that defines, extends, and supports their defined focus. It is in this phase that the guided database tutorials and screencasts are usually embedded. Students' confidence often builds as relevant literature is retrieved.

Phase 5. Information refinement suggests that students review the information retrieved. They need to identify missing gaps, areas not well defined, and irrelevant or off-track information. It is during this phase that students verify that they are meeting course guidelines, evaluate the information found, and review reference lists.

Phase 6. Search closure reminds students that they must eventually stop looking for information and start putting that information to use in order to complete their assignment. The decision to end a search may happen because the student found all the necessary information or because the deadline for the paper is near. During this phase students recheck information, confirm citations, and ensure that quotations are accurate. Depending on the entire search process, students may be relieved, satisfied, or dissatisfied. Students are encouraged to reflect on the entire process so that they may be better able to incorporate the suggestions and guidance in future research assignments.

Common Elements in Phases

Overview provides an orientation to the phase. A synopsis of the actions/strategies and thoughts/feelings for the phase are briefly described.

Actions/Strategies provides students with concrete suggestions and purposeful activities to help them progress through a specific phase.

Thoughts/Feelings is the affective realm of the ISP model. Many students do not realize that feeling frustrated, anxious, or overwhelmed is normal during certain phases. In other phases students feel relief or even resignation. The objective of this element is to confirm to students that there are feelings, both positive and negative, associated with information seeking, that these feelings change over the duration of the information search process, and that all the feelings are normal and to be expected.

Course Specific Activities relates directly to assignments, information resources, and concepts relevant to the teaching curriculum. Often course-specific activities are developed in collaboration with a faculty member. This is the component that is usually most customized. The KWLF Chart, guided database tutorials, and screencasts are presented in this component.

Self-Assessment. As noted previously, students are encouraged to complete the self-assessment prior to moving onto the next phase. If students answer "no" to any question, they are provided with suggestions and more activities to progress them toward the next phase.

Logbook, discussed above, is often used as a course assignment. It provides students with a means of tracking their progression through the search phases and promotes reflection on both the process and their feelings for each phase.

Instruction

WISPR is most often taught in a blended learning environment. During a one-shot instruction session (usually fifty minutes) the librarian introduces WISPR, focusing specifically on the theoretical perspective of the information search process. The lecture also discusses inquiry-based learning and its relationship to information literacy. The librarian demonstrates how students can connect to WISPR and provides an orientation to the workshop, including how to access the logbook. The point of this interaction with students is to set the tone for WISPR and to provide access instructions. In a purely online environment, the librarian develops a Breeze presentation covering similar content to that presented in a face-to-face session, which is embedded as a lecture in the Blackboard course. After the initial session librarians may work with students online, answering questions and clarifying any areas of concern through e-mail or Blackboard communication tools. In other courses, students may arrange more face-to-face meetings with the librarian to address specific concerns or issues with their particular question.

Student assessment is determined through collaboration with the faculty member. Some faculty have used the logbook, either for individuals or groups, as the deliverable for WISPR. Other faculty have encouraged multiple-choice or short-answer questions on midterm examinations, and still others have favored a reflective essay on the student's own information-seeking process in light of WISPR. Again, depending on the class and the instructor, the assignments or logbooks are marked by either the librarian or the professor. As much as 15 percent of the student's final grade has been assigned for the logbook.

Program Assessment

To date, WISPR has not been formally assessed, since research ethics approval is still in progress. But informal assessment clearly indicates that students have benefited from participating in WISPR. Student feedback from reflective assignments indicates that learning about the information search process, particularly the first three phases (topic selection, prefocus formulation, and focus formulation) has been worthwhile. Most students did not have appropriate strategies for coming to a well-formed, researchable topic. Students mentioned that they were not aware that they needed to spend time exploring their topic widely, following up on tangents, and then mindfully focusing the topic area. They thought that they must immediately sit down at a computer and start searching for answers and resources. By understanding that searching for information is an intellectual process, and that the process entails specific phases and strategies within each phase, students stated that they felt more comfortable approaching future research assignments.

Students also liked the fact that they could refer back to aspects that were confusing or unclear. Students, when unsure or confused, can easily return to WISPR. They can revisit the guided database tutorials until they are familiar with the search features and feel confident in their searching ability. This "point of need" aspect of Web-based tutorials is a clear benefit over face-to-face sessions.

As has been demonstrated by numerous researchers, students are more motivated to participate in information literacy instruction when there is a mandatory component such as an assignment, participation marks, or even pass/fail. Students whose professors made the logbook mandatory and worth a portion of their final grade were more likely to complete it, and to produce a more fulsome account of their information search process. For the future, it would be of benefit to be able to track student progress in WISPR, specifically, to analyze which students signed on and whether they went through every phase and all the associated actions and strategies as well as the course-specific activities. At the moment, we do not have a way to determine the paths taken or amount of time spent in WISPR by students. We can only determine, through Blackboard, whether a student connected to WISPR. By tracking student progression through WISPR, we hope to learn which components students spend the majority of their time with. We also want to determine whether students progress through WISPR linearly or jump to a specific phase immediately. This will help to shed light on students' information-seeking behavior.

Faculty members who have integrated WISPR into their courses have responded favorably. They appreciate that WISPR is customizable to be meaningful to the teaching curriculum and course objectives. One instructor, teaching an online academic writing course to second- and third-year students commented:

Here was an innovative Web-based tool [WISPR] that not only helped students to understand the research-writing process in general but also took them step by step through the stages of the process and introduced them in a hands-on way to online databases in their disciplines. For distance students, being able to point and click on the components of the tutorial was like having a virtual librarian on call 24 hours a day to help them through the information search process... . In short, the WISPR tutorial is grounded in relevant research, and students find its integrated and holistic perspective on research and writing to be not only instructive but reassuring as it validates the (often negative) feelings that they experience as they navigate the complex process of research-writing.

Because WISPR is Web-based, assignments may be linked to specific phases when required. Although collaboration with librarians is encouraged, teaching faculty may also revise content areas of WISPR to suit their course content.

Many online tutorials focus specifically on the mechanics of research (e.g., understanding Boolean operators, effective search strategies, manipulating specific databases). Though mechanical searching skills are important and are integrated into WISPR, students need to be provided with a more holistic approach that incorporates the intellectual aspects of searching.

Lessons Learned

The following points highlight some of the challenges we encountered:

Tight timelines. We had a little over four months from receipt of the grant to implementation of WISPR into a course. We would have liked time to pilot-test the framework with both undergraduate students and librarians. Further collaboration with librarians from different subject areas (e.g., the

sciences, business, and humanities) may have also been beneficial to provide a broader spectrum for actions and strategies within each phase. Given that WISPR is customizable, this shortcoming is easily overcome for courses in those disciplines.

Insufficient technical testing. Because of the short timelines, we were not able to test WISPR sufficiently prior to integration into a course. The majority of WISPR worked well, but we experienced significant problems with the logbook's functionality. Some students lost their input, and others were unable to sign in. We were fortunate that a programmer was on call to address these issues immediately, but students were less than satisfied with their first experience using WISPR.

No direct control over finances. Programmers from our TLC were paid to develop the framework and functionality, including the logbook, for WISPR. We were never provided with exact costs for enhancements and technical requests, so we ran out of money before developing an administrative module that would allow course creation and customization without the intervention of a programmer from the TLC. We might have reprioritized requests if we had been aware of costs. This also highlights that the $10,000 was insufficient to complete all components of WISPR, specifically an administrative interface needed to ensure that WISPR is self-sustaining within our library and by our librarians.

Lack of knowledge of programming. Although one of the librarians on our team is quite technologically oriented, we were unable to anticipate the difficulties related to developing the logbook because of our lack of programming experience. If we had had a greater understanding of the complexities, we might have chosen a less complex system for implementing an electronic logbook.

The following points briefly highlight what we feel worked well:

Collaboration with an instructional designer. Norm Vaughan was able to guide us toward developing a pedagogically sound online workshop that addressed different learning styles without using technology simply for technology's sake. He also liaised between us and the TLC programming staff.

Small core team of librarians. A small project team, each member with different strengths, ensured that the work was divided equitably and could be accomplished quickly.

Theoretical framework. We are confident in our approach to WISPR, based as it is on a theoretical model of information seeking that has been verified through numerous longitudinal studies with a variety of different populations. Although we did incorporate our collective wisdom, we were guided by Kuhlthau's model when developing the workshop.

Customizable content. We believe developing an online tutorial that easily incorporates course-specific assignments and content ensures ready implementation by both faculty and librarians. Of utmost importance is that students are learning about the information search process as it directly relates to their course content and is, therefore, meaningful and authentic.

Conclusion

Since its initial launch in fall 2005, WISPR has had a dramatic impact on information literacy instruction for those courses and disciplines where it has been used. Librarians' role is no longer simply as trainers whose only purpose is to demonstrate relevant databases. WISPR allows librarians to teach the entire process of information seeking, providing students with a greater understanding of the strategies and competencies involved. Although the specific content provided in a customized version of WISPR is tied to a particular course or discipline, the understanding students gain of the overarching framework and the information search process is entirely transferable to any other research situation. Evidence gathered from WISPR's implementation has demonstrated that this approach is more meaningful and rewarding to students, faculty, and librarians alike.

Notes

1. Boyer Commission on Educating Undergraduates in the Research University, *Reinventing Undergraduate Education: A Blueprint for America's Research Universities* (Stony Brook: State University of New York at Stony Brook for the Carnegie Foundation for the Advancement of Teaching, 1998). Available online at http://naples.cc.sunysb.edu/pres/boyer.nsf/.

2. Carol Twigg, "New Models for Online Learning," *Educause Review* 38, no. 5 (2003): 28–38. Available online at http://www.educause.edu/ir/library/pdf/erm0352.pdf.

3. Carol Collier Kuhlthau, *Seeking Meaning: A Process Approach to Library and Information Services,* 2d ed. (Westport, CT: Libraries Unlimited, 2004).

23. Sophisticated Simplicity in e-Learning: Online Instruction at UNC–Chapel Hill

Suchi Mohanty, Lisa Norberg, and Kim Vassiliadis

Introduction

As part of its mission, the University Library of the University of North Carolina at Chapel Hill (UNC–Chapel Hill) has for decades provided patrons with instruction in the use of the libraries, its search tools, and scholarly materials. In the mid-1990s, with the Web still in its infancy, the rate of technological change in libraries was unparalleled. Faculty, students, and librarians all struggled to keep pace. At the same time, the university was preparing to institute the Carolina Computing Initiative, a plan to require all incoming students to own a laptop. Campus-wide attention was focused on teaching and learning with technology, including the need for students to develop sophisticated information proficiencies.

In spring 1998, the university librarian convened a task force on information literacy to study the ways in which the library could bring its expertise to bear on both campus instructional needs and the growing interest in information literacy. As part of its work, the task force talked extensively with faculty, students, and librarians, inventoried the libraries' current instruction activities, and studied other college and university library models. The task force found that an integrated information literacy program would need to

- reach large numbers of students in an engaging, flexible, and timely fashion
- enhance the library's instructional services while preserving the many successful elements of the existing programs and practices
- emphasize the human interaction and personalization that are hallmarks of the library's reputation
- respond as needed to changing information needs, circumstances, priorities, and technologies
- develop from and be well integrated with the priorities and needs of the local university community.

Toward these ends, the task force developed a set of recommendations that addressed program design and implementation, human resources, and support and infrastructure. The task force's primary recommendation was for the library to develop an online instructional "toolkit" that would guide students in the use of library, electronic, and Internet resources. The intent was to close the gap with students who had not received formal library instruction, including students who test out of the English department's writing program (the libraries traditional outlet for first-year instruction), distance education students, and others.

Intended to support library instruction for the writing program, the first prototype was, at the time, a sophisticated online tutorial. It tracked students' progress as they advanced through a series of modules and included interactive elements that taught students how to read a call number and identify scholarly journals. From the library's perspective, it was an instructional marvel. In practice, however, it was anything but. The tutorial was rife with technical problems that required constant late-night programming to keep it functioning. With every new feature, the tutorial became more unstable. It crashed several times a semester, frustrating students and infuriating instructors. Finally, instructors had had enough and simply refused to assign the tutorial to their classes.

Humbled and ready to listen again, the library staff went back to the drawing board. We used a series of focus groups and informal interviews to talk to the faculty and instructors who taught in the writing program and the first-year students currently enrolled as well as those who had recently taken the courses, to understand their needs. They found that the original goals remained. The tutorial should supplement, not replace, classroom instruction; it should provide library instruction for those who do not have the opportunity to engage in traditional classroom instruction; but, more than anything, it should be stable. What emerged from this prototype was an introductory tutorial that would be the basis for more advanced and discipline-specific tutorials.

Content

In 2001 the Introduction to Library Research tutorial was created to provide first-year and transfer students with an overview of the campus library system and to introduce them to basic research concepts and search skills. The tutorial consisted of six separate modules—Introduction, Libraries and Services, Searching for Information, Finding Articles, Finding Books, Using Information—and a quiz.

The Introduction module provides an overview of the tutorial and presents students with its learning objectives. In the Libraries and Services module, students are presented with information about the three main libraries, the various branch libraries, and specialized collections. Because the libraries at UNC–Chapel Hill are dispersed across campus, it is important that students understand the extent of their services and collections. They also learn how they can use services such as reference, reserves, circulation, and interlibrary loan.

The third module, Searching for Information, begins to address research concepts and search strategies. Students learn about the information timeline and the difference between the free Web and subscription databases. Keyword searching, Boolean logic, truncation, and wildcards are explained, and examples of their proper use are presented for students to model. The Finding Articles module addresses fundamental research concepts and skills such as differentiating popular and scholarly material, selecting appropriate databases, and finding print and electronic articles when the full text is not immediately available. Finding Books, the fifth module, complements the content of the previous module, guiding the reader through UNC–Chapel Hill's online catalog and instructing students on how to construct effective author, title, and keyword searches. Because catalog records are sometimes difficult to decipher, notable parts of the record are diagramed and highlighted. Students also learn how to identify useful subject headings and how to read Library of Congress call numbers.

The final module of the tutorial promotes the responsible use of information. This section addresses the importance of evaluating information for accuracy and credibility, avoiding plagiarism, and citing correctly. The overarching goal of the Introduction to Library Research tutorial is to impart the most basic skills any researcher should understand. We expect that, as students progress through their courses, they will continue to build on these basic skills and master more advanced skills and concepts.

Students are instructed to enter their name if they have been assigned to take the quiz by their instructor. This ensures that at the completion of the tutorial the students will be able to print out and turn in a certificate with their name on it to their instructor. The quiz is made up of ten questions. Some are simple knowledge-based questions; others are skill based. The questions that require tasks to be completed in order to be answered have a "start here" button that opens a new browser window to the specific page where they need to perform the tasks. One such question asks students to locate the call number of a specific book. In order for a student to determine the call number, she first needs to search the catalog. The "start here" button opens the library's catalog in a new browser window. "Review Tutorial" links

are available for each question. These links allow students to go back into the tutorial to review a particular concept before they answer the question. Again, these links open to a specific page in a new browser window.

Students must earn a passing quiz score of 70 percent, though instructors have the option of setting a higher passing score of 100 percent. When they pass, students receive a certificate stating their name and score. The tutorial does not keep record of specific users, but students have the option of retaking the quiz to try to improve their score. The tutorial's simple, straightforward design was well received by both instructors and students.

Simple Instructional Design

Behind the content was a relatively simple instructional design created and coded by a team of instruction librarians and student assistants from UNC–Chapel Hill's School of Information and Library Science. A simple

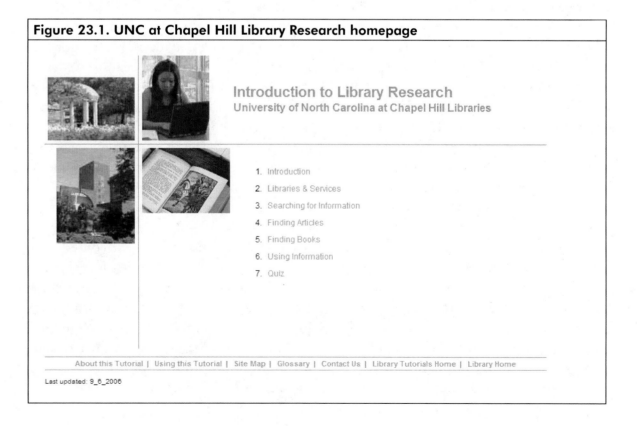

Figure 23.1. UNC at Chapel Hill Library Research homepage

Introduction to Library Research
University of North Carolina at Chapel Hill Libraries

1. Introduction
2. Libraries & Services
3. Searching for Information
4. Finding Articles
5. Finding Books
6. Using Information
7. Quiz

About this Tutorial | Using this Tutorial | Site Map | Glossary | Contact Us | Library Tutorials Home | Library Home

Last updated: 9_6_2006

Figure 23.2. Sample library research tutorial

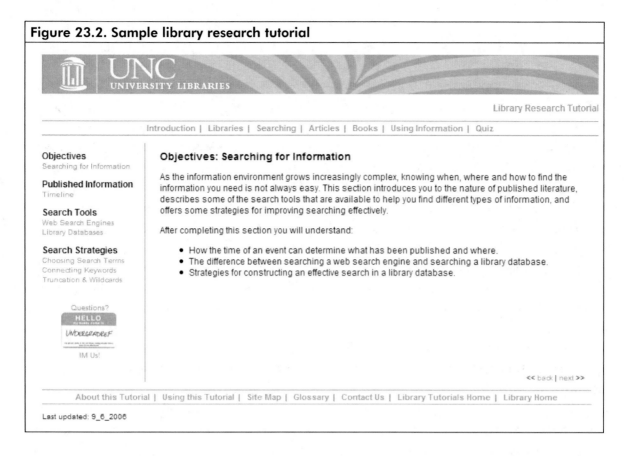

external cascading style sheet was employed to format the text, and the layout was created using HTML tables. A consistent navigation structure was visible on each page (figures 23.1 and 23.2). The module's titles were listed and hyperlinked along a horizontal navigation bar at the top of each page. Within each module were several related concepts, which were listed and hyperlinked on a vertical navigation bar on the left-hand side of each page. This allowed the user to access any part of the tutorial with just a few mouse clicks.

Although the tutorial was created with a linear structure, its modular design allows each section to be used alone or reused in subsequent tutorials. By breaking down the tutorial into sections, students can work through the contents from start to finish or skip to particular sections to familiarize themselves with a specific concept. One of the early decisions in the design was whether or not to have students log in with their student IDs so their progress could be tracked. We felt that such a login might deter students from using the tutorials for informal learning or reference. Because students do not need to sign into the tutorial, they can enter and exit it at any time. This approach gives them more control over how and when they view the tutorial. It allows them the freedom to complete the tutorial at their own pace.

Simple text and graphic elements, including screen captures, illustrations, and diagrams, are combined for the content. Although the onus is on the learner to read and comprehend the material presented, various support systems are incorporated into each tutorial. Each tutorial encourages the student to utilize reference services and includes a prominent graphic representing the instant messenger chat reference.

As with any online learning endeavor, building a sense of community among learners is important. Because students complete the tutorials individually, creating that sense of community can be a challenge. Sometimes this sense of community happens unintentionally; students bond when comparing their quiz scores in class. They are sometimes shocked that the quiz is so difficult. Because the tutorial is often assigned prior to a face-to-face instruction session, a truer sense of community occurs when the library instructor and students come together in the classroom. The shared experience of completing the tutorial provides a common ground for communication between instructors and students and provides the foundation upon which the subsequent instruction session can be built.

In traditional library sessions, it is evident which classes completed the tutorial and which did not. Librarians report that students who complete the tutorial have a better understanding of concepts such as Boolean logic and scholarly literature. They are able to follow the presentation and have fewer problems during worktime in the instruction lab. They are also more likely to assist their classmates and respond to the librarian's prompts.

For the students' own assessment of their understanding, "Quick Review Questions" are scattered throughout the tutorial. These questions are short multiple-choice questions based on the content just presented. They are not formally graded, but they allow students to immediately determine whether they grasped a particular concept. These questions are created using simple JavaScript. Depending on how a student answers a question, a small pop-up box opens and announces whether the answer is correct or not (figure 23.3). In either instances, an explanation of the answer is included.

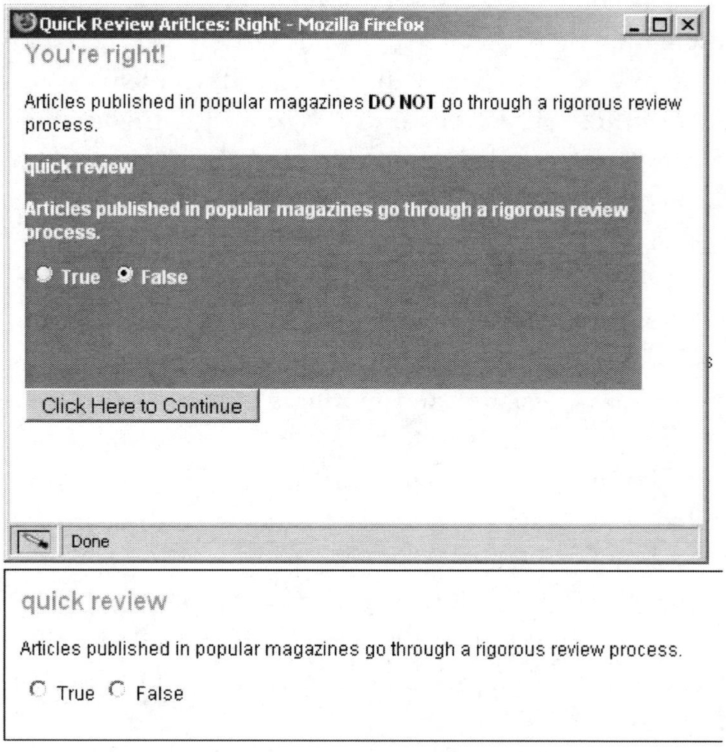

A more formal assessment tool comes in the form of a quiz that follows the final module.

Design Changes

Creating and maintaining an online tutorial is an intensive task for any librarian or department. Because of the success of the instruction program, the demand for more focused discipline-specific tutorials continues to grow. The library's services and research environment are in constant flux, and when a new library service or resource is introduced, each tutorial needs to be updated to reflect this change. To keep the tutorials fresh, specific

Figure 23.3. Sample Quick Review question and response

modules are often reorganized or removed while new modules are created. When this has occurred, the navigation links on each individual page had to be updated. As the range of online research tutorials grew, keeping them up to date became more difficult.

In an effort to streamline the tutorial creation and revision process, the table design was eliminated and a more robust cascading style sheet was employed to manage each tutorial's layout. Because all Web browsers interpret HTML differently, a style sheet allows the developer to make small modifications to create a design that is consistent across all browsers. Design changes can be updated once in the style sheet and be immediately reflected throughout the tutorial.

Although design changes could be streamlined using a cascading style sheet, the constant navigational updates on each page were still taxing. To solve this issue, the code that managed the library's banner and top navigation bar, the side navigation bar, and the footer links were stripped out of each individual page in the tutorial and instead placed into separate include files (.inc). Using PHP, these separate files could be called into each HTML page of the tutorial to handle all the navigation. With only one .inc file handling all of the vertical navigation for each module, new and deleted side navigation bar links have to be edited once only. The HTML pages within that module immediately reflect the changes. The same principal works for the top horizontal navigation bar and bottom footer navigation bar as well.

These changes in the tutorial's structure allow the content to be manipulated and updated easily. Developers can now customize the basic tutorial frame with .inc files and focus more time on the actual content. Once a tutorial's frame is created, tutorial developers with basic HTML skills are able to update and write new content. Creating tutorials has become an excellent learning tool for student assistants from the School of Information and Library Science. Most students have basic HTML skills, and after a short orientation to the page design they are able to build and update tutorials. With this new approach to tutorial management, the content from one tutorial can be revised and used in a new tutorial. This development in design has significantly streamlined the creation and customization of the tutorials.

As the library's traditional instruction program grew, so did the number of online tutorials. More discipline-specific tutorials were created to supplement or, in some cases, substitute for traditional face-to-face instruction. The Exercise and Sports Science Department requested an online tutorial to teach students how to search and evaluate health- and fitness-related Web sites. The Exercise and Sport Science: Using the Web tutorial was created using content from the main tutorial and examples based on health and exercise resources. It employed the same navigational structure as Introduction to Library Research. Although shorter in length, it utilized the same design elements and also included a quiz that could be assigned. Citing Information, Evaluating Information, and Information Ethics tutorials were later developed to expand on topics covered briefly in the main introductory tutorial.

In collaboration with subject librarians, faculty, and graduate students from different disciplines, new subject-specific tutorials were created for upper-division and graduate-level classes. Examples of these tutorials include ARTIFAQ: Researching Art and Artists, the Latin American Studies Tutorial, the Psychology Research Tutorial, Researching Congressional Legislation, and the Manuscripts Research Tutorial (http://www.lib.

unc.edu/instruct/tutorials.html). Each was tailored to meet a specific instructional objective, such as the introduction to the literature of a particular field or instructions on how to conduct a specific type of research. Broader use and application of the tutorials are always supported and encouraged.

The Manuscripts Research Tutorial is one of the most frequently used subject-specific tutorials. This tutorial was written and developed by the head of public services for the manuscripts department, with the assistance of students in the School of Information and Library Science. It is directed toward researchers who need assistance in understanding and using the manuscripts and archive collections at UNC–Chapel Hill, but the topics presented are also applicable at other institutions. The six modules of the tutorial are Introduction, Fundamentals of Library Research, Finding Manuscripts, Using Manuscripts, Collections in the Manuscripts Department, and Orientation

As in the Introduction to Library Research tutorial, the Introduction module presents the reader with the instructional objectives of the tutorial and an overview of the content. The Fundamentals of Library Research section defines and provides examples of primary sources, manuscripts, repositories, provenance, and arrangement of collections. This module also instructs students on using and interpreting finding aids and catalog records. The section closes with instructions on registering to use the collection and the proper handling of delicate materials. The Finding Manuscripts module addresses strategies to identify manuscript materials. Students learn how to conceptualize their topic and select appropriate search terms. This section also advises students on effective strategies for Googling and searching the OPAC as well as use of online and print finding aids. It

also recommends alternate local repositories and reference assistance if appropriate materials cannot be identified.

The Using Manuscripts module encourages researchers to investigate the context of the primary resource and to understand that history is the constant reinterpretation of past events. It encourages students to consider the type of document being examined, provides examples of handwriting and fragile document conditions, and acknowledges the evolution of language. This module even provides an example of a runaway slave poster and walks the reader through the process of questioning the content and context, and it prompts the researcher to evaluate each document carefully. This section closes with advice on citing manuscripts accurately and addresses issues of fair use and copyright.

The final two modules, Collections in the Manuscripts Department and Orientation, provide the reader with information about using collections in the manuscripts department at UNC–Chapel Hill. Collections in the Manuscripts Department describes the development of the manuscripts department; also included is information about the size and scope of the Southern Historical Collection, Southern Oral History Program, University Archives, and Southern Folklife Collection. The Orientation module provides information about the policies and procedures of the department, the physical orientation of the reading room, and the services available to researchers. As with Introduction to Library Research, the Manuscripts Research Tutorial closes with a quiz that instructors can assign to their classes.

Course-Integrated Resource Pages

There are situations in which tutorials do not meet the instructional need. More often we observe that students think in terms of assignment-based research, not discipline-based topics. In fall 2006 the library's online instruction program expanded to include integrated course pages designed to be incorporated into Blackboard sites. As Blackboard has evolved on our campus, the library has attempted to reach students in their online environments. Librarians have begun collaborating with faculty to create point-of-need library resources for their courses. These pages all include contact links for the subject liaison, the appropriate buddy name for instant messenger chat reference, links to the appropriate tutorials, the OPAC search box, and related databases. Depending on the requirements of the assignment, additional resources may include links to films, primary source material, reference sources, and Web sites. These course pages are particularly effective because they gather resources that are scattered across the library's Web site and list them on a centralized page to which students have easy access. Research tips and help guides are also embedded for students who need assistance but want to work independently.

Along with links to databases and Web pages, links are provided to examples of appropriate resources. If students are required to use scholarly books and articles for a research assignment, linked examples are included. These examples explain why the sources are appropriate and how to identify similar sources. Similarly, if students are encouraged or required to use primary manuscripts, the librarians link to specific examples of a primary resource along with the source of the document and provide hints for finding similar documents. By highlighting suitable resources, librarians are able to facilitate understated teachable moments. Students are able to learn what types of resources are required to conduct research

within that course, and they are able to learn this at their point of need. This streamlined approach enables students to find their course readings from one location and allows for seamless access to their course materials and the library's resources.

One of the most elaborate course guides the library has created was for an American Studies class, "No Place like Home: Material Culture of the American South." Library staff created a series of pages for the instruction— one corresponding to the general themes of the class, and four guides for each major assignment. In addition, staff compiled a list of southern films and Web sites addressing aspects of southern culture. Each assignment page provides access to material useful for that assignment. For example, students must write an essay on some aspect of material culture from *To Kill a Mockingbird* by Harper Lee. Instead of simply including the catalog search box, we provide suggested subject terms and sample keyword searches. In addition to including links to databases for researching the author, film, and novel, various help sheets are also included. Library staff included the Citing Information tutorial, "How Do I" guides, and longer research guides. At the instructor's request, we also included links to her book review guidelines, essay writing guide, and writing center guides.

As with the online tutorials, the key is simplicity. In an effort to create a reusable course page design that can be utilized for other classes and shared among staff, a simple three-column page was designed using a robust cascading style sheet (figure 23.4). The style sheet dictates the course page's look and feel and addresses the various browser issues so that the page looks consistent across browsers and screen resolutions. The flexible design allows the librarians to customize a course page. Anyone with mini-

---

Figure 23.4. Course page

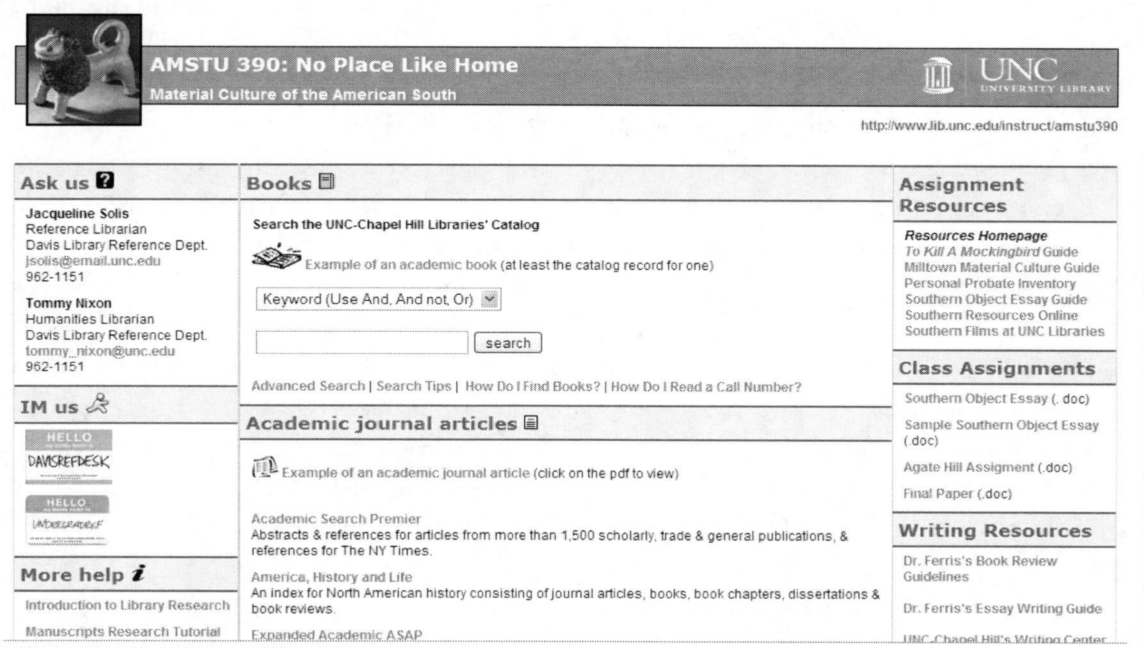

---

mal HTML skills should be able to add appropriate resources, change heading titles, and include personal contact information.

Program Assessment

Assessment of our online information literacy program has always been done in the context of our larger program. We rarely encourage the use of the tutorials as a stand-alone instruction option, except in cases where there is no alternative, such as distance education courses. Even then, we work with faculty to create additional online guides or course pages to emphasize further the right kinds of sources to use for a given assignment. We also make sure faculty know they can refer students to our virtual reference and instant messaging services for one-on-one instruction at any time.

Most of the time, we encourage faculty to pair our online tutorials and course pages with classroom instruction that includes hands-on problem solving. The tutorials are intended simply to familiarize students with basic in-

formation literacy concepts and terminology. Both the tutorials and the course pages are designed to provide that base level of information upon which students can build.

Our primary method of assessment is a Web survey sent to the instructors. The survey includes a series of questions that evaluate student learning outcomes. The information literate student should be able to do the following:

• Recognize that a need for information exists. Formulate a reasonable research question with appropriate focus and scope. Determine what information is needed.

• Understand how to make effective use of resources available within the library, through the library, and sometimes outside the library.

• Find the required information through identification and selection of appropriate resources.

• Evaluate the information found.

• Organize the information that is worthwhile.

• Communicate the resulting knowledge through oral or written means, or by direct or indirect application. Present the knowledge responsibly and effectively.

We also include questions specifically aimed at the tutorials, their use, and their effectiveness. Over the years, we have garnered useful suggestions for improvement such as including a section addressing plagiarism.

The University Library has also benefited enormously from its relationship with the UNC School of Information and Library Science and its students' interest in assessing online instruction tools. Over the years several studies have been conducted, and the results of these studies and others have guided the development of the tutorial series and our other online instruction offerings.[1] For instance, in 2006 a series of user tests was conducted on a series of prototype tutorials using Macromedia's Captivate software.[2] The study found that, although the Flash tutorials were easy to use and informative, students actually preferred the simpler control that a self-paced "clickable" tutorial provided over the movie-like stop, pause, and play interaction of a Flash tutorial. On the basis of this research, we postponed our use of more interactive "Flash-based" tutorials and continue to maintain the simple design.

Lessons Learned

Building the tutorials and resource pages has been an evolutionary process. Essential to this process are three principles that guide each online instructional tool.

Keep it simple. A simple design and coding structure allow staff to focus on content rather than the physical construction of the resource. Simplicity of design also facilitates collaboration among staff and lessens the learning curve in creating a tutorial.

Less is more. Building online learning tools is vastly different from creating print resources. The tutorials and course pages are meant to introduce library research, not cover every contingency that may arise. By focusing on a few key issues, we give students a foundation upon which they can build as they progress through their classes.

Reusability equals scalability. As an online instruction program grows, there must be a way to maintain the currency and accuracy of the information provided. By creating reusable modules, we have made it less intensive to maintain the content of the tutorials.

Notes

1. Lucy Holman, "A Comparison of Computer-Assisted Instruction and Classroom Bibliographic Instruction," *Reference and User Services Quarterly* 40, no. 1 (2000): 53; Anna M. Van Scoyoc, "Reducing Library Anxiety in First-Year Students," *Reference and User Services Quarterly* 42, no. 4 (2003): 329.

2. Joan A. Petit, "A Usability Study of Flash Tutorials for Library Instruction" (Master's thesis, University of North Carolina at Chapel Hill, 2006). Available online at http://etd.ils.unc.edu/dspace/bitstream/1901/300/1/petitjoan.pdf.

24. From B.I. to Wi-Fi: Evolution of an Online Information Literacy Program

Scott Rice, Kathryn M. Crowe, Amy Harris, and Lea Leininger

Introduction

The University of North Carolina at Greensboro (UNCG) is a doctoral-granting institution of 16,000 students with a Carnegie classification of "high research." The University Libraries supports the research needs of the university through an active course-integrated library instruction program at the undergraduate and graduate levels. This program has been in existence for several decades. Objectives for different levels of students were developed in the 1980s and updated more recently using ACRL's Information Literacy Competency Standards for Higher Education.

Using a fairly traditional approach, first-year students are reached through required courses such as English 101, Communication Studies 105, and freshman seminars. Many first-year students also receive an introduction to the library in a basic one-hour acculturation course, University Studies 101, and through a School of Business acculturation course, Business 105. Upper-level students are targeted in courses required for their major or in courses including a research assignment, and graduate students are usually reached in research methods courses.

During the 2005/6 academic year, the Reference and Instructional Services Department (RIS) provided 325 library instruction sessions for 6,335 students. Traditionally, our contact with students is via "one-shot" presentations in a computer lab in the library or another lab on campus. These sessions are supported by online course guides designed for each class. RIS also maintains subject guides, which include lists of appropriate databases, e-journals, online reference sources, new books, Web pages, and other useful information for each academic major at the university. Librarians work closely with teaching faculty to develop useful assignments and exercises to reinforce and apply the content taught in the instruction sessions.

The University Libraries and the library instruction program have long enjoyed support from the university community. Librarians have faculty status and serve on the Faculty Senate and on university-wide committees. In 2000, the university underwent a major curriculum revision. A librarian served on the commission that developed the new general education program and was successful in including information literacy skills in the structure of the new curriculum.

One of the five basic student learning goals of the general education program includes the "ability to locate, analyze, synthesize, and evaluate information." In addition, the program requires "proficiency level in information skills/research as required for the major" along with speaking, writing, and technology proficiencies. Each department must indicate how students in their major will gain required information skills. A librarian always sits on the undergraduate curriculum committee that reviews new courses and changes to existing courses, providing an opportunity to incorporate library instruction into new courses and programs at the ground level.

Because of its commitment to supporting the research needs of the university and the learning goals of its students, the University Libraries has extended its reach beyond the one-shot library instruction session and taken its information literacy program online. The program began several years ago with a simple online tutorial and has significantly expanded. Today, the information literacy program contains a general tutorial, F.I.R.S.T., tutorials specifically designed for nursing students, brief video tutorials designed to meet a specific information need, and an information literacy game.

Rationale

Although reference librarians considered the traditional instruction program successful, there were frustrations with inconsistencies, especially within the first-year instruction program, where librarians felt students should gain basic skills that could be built upon in their majors. Because of staff limitations, it was impossible to reach all sections of the basic first-year courses through the course-integrated approach. In addition, these courses were taught by a variety of teaching assistants and lecturers coordinated by a faculty member. The wide variety of student assignments that did not, as a rule, include research projects, and the transient nature of teaching assistants and lecturers created difficulties for librarians with regards to establishing and maintaining relationships with this group.

At the same time, distance learning was expanding, and librarians needed to reach off-campus students. The Web had emerged as a learning platform and tool, and this new technology was particularly appealing to our traditional-age students. Some libraries, most notably the University of Texas with

TILT, were experimenting with online tutorials to teach library skills. RIS decided an online tutorial was a perfect way to use new technology to address students' needs and help meet both the libraries' instruction objectives and the goals of the university's general education program.

Development

First Steps/F.I.R.S.T. Tutorial

RIS recruited a first-year instruction coordinator in 1999 to focus on working with the freshman-level courses and developing an online library instruction tutorial. The online tutorial, First Steps: An Explorer's Guide to Research, was launched in August 2000 (figure 24.1). It included six chapters that took students through the steps of the research process. To be appealing and effective, it was imperative that the tutorial be interactive and not just content read on the Web.

The tutorial provided several opportunities for interactivity including quizzes at the end of each chapter and certificates that could be presented to teaching faculty. The quizzes allowed the students multiple opportunities to answer each question while providing feedback until a correct answer was given. In addition, a chapter on navigating and using the library's online catalog included the opportunity for students to complete sample searches in a simulated version of the catalog. Students were given a topic and asked to perform a search that led to actual results in the catalog.

Not long after the tutorial was created, the need to keep it up to date with technology became apparent. Millennial students, who comprise the majority of UNCG's undergraduate population, are used to sophisticated games and devices. The first-year instruction coordinator recruited the help of the networked information services librarian to improve and expand the technology supporting the tutorial.

In 2005 the tutorial's programming was upgraded with an emphasis on improving the usability and operability of the interface. Several improvements were implemented, such as rewriting the coding of the page to make it more compliant with the Americans with Disabilities Act. Tables used for formatting on the page were removed and cascading style sheets were used for positioning and appearance of elements. Images were coded so that users with screen readers are better able to understand the content of a page or skip the navigation if desired. The appearance was changed to match the rest of the libraries' Web site, and the name was changed to "F.I.R.S.T.: Finding It! A Research Skills Tutorial" (figure 24.2, and visit at http://library.uncg.edu/depts/ref/tutorial/).

Other improvements included the addition of an improved menu system that allows users to navigate to any part of the tutorial easily. The previous incarnation of the tutorial allowed for navigation only to the beginning pages of chapters, whereas the new navigation shows the student the full range of topics within the current chapter. The quizzes were updated, dropping the use of pop-up windows and the Perl programming, which made the tutorial unusable in Blackboard, the university's widely used course management system. The quizzes were also coded to allow e-mail notification of chapter completion to instructors. The content was edited and rewritten to make it more succinct and easily understandable.

Nursing and Health Resources Tutorial

With the growth and success of one tutorial, demand arose for others. In 2005 the coordina-

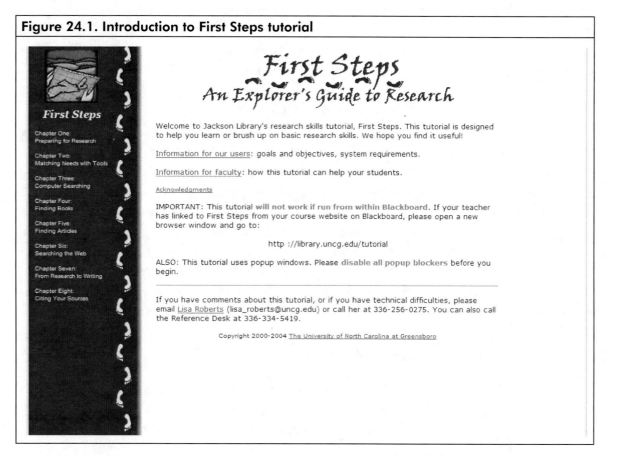

Figure 24.1. Introduction to First Steps tutorial

First Steps

Chapter One:
Preparing for Research

Chapter Two:
Matching Needs with Tools

Chapter Three:
Computer Searching

Chapter Four:
Finding Books

Chapter Five:
Finding Articles

Chapter Six:
Searching the Web

Chapter Seven:
From Research to Writing

Chapter Eight:
Citing Your Sources

First Steps
An Explorer's Guide to Research

Welcome to Jackson Library's research skills tutorial, First Steps. This tutorial is designed to help you learn or brush up on basic research skills. We hope you find it useful!

Information for our users: goals and objectives, system requirements.

Information for faculty: how this tutorial can help your students.

Acknowledgments

IMPORTANT: This tutorial will not work if run from within Blackboard. If your teacher has linked to First Steps from your course website on Blackboard, please open a new browser window and go to:

http ://library.uncg.edu/tutorial

ALSO: This tutorial uses popup windows. Please disable all popup blockers before you begin.

If you have comments about this tutorial, or if you have technical difficulties, please email Lisa Roberts (lisa_roberts@uncg.edu) or call her at 336-256-0275. You can also call the Reference Desk at 336-334-5419.

Copyright 2000-2004 The University of North Carolina at Greensboro

Figure 24.2. Introduction to the F.I.R.S.T. tutorial

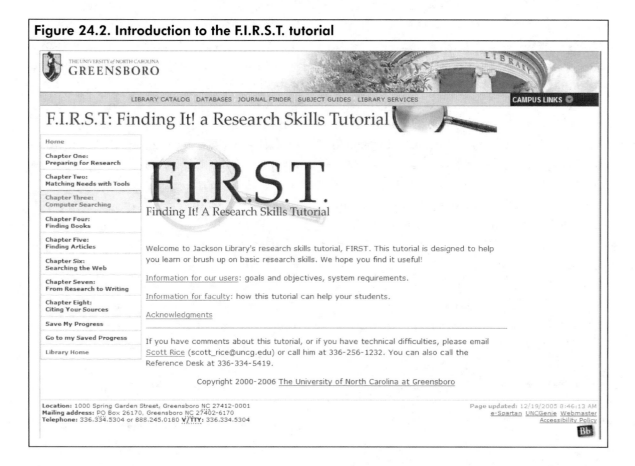

tor of Nursing 210, a course for sophomores entering UNCG's Bachelor of Science in Nursing program, requested an online tutorial to help students find reliable, authoritative health care information that would meet the demands of the Nursing 210 research assignment.

The newly appointed life sciences librarian set about creating a subject-specific counterpart to the popular First Steps tutorial. Her first step was to determine the information needs of the students by talking with faculty and analyzing assignments and map out tutorial content that could realistically meet these needs. Then she recruited the networked information services librarian to provide technology and instructional design assistance. Over the course of the summer, the Nursing and Health Resources Tutorial emerged (access from http://library.uncg.edu/depts/ref/bibs/nur/nur620/index.asp).

In August 2005 the coordinator for the distance education program assigned her master's-level nurse education students to take the tutorial and suggest improvements. Once these suggestions were implemented, the Nursing and Health Resources Tutorial was officially launched in December. This tutorial was intended to be modular, beginning with a few obvious, stand-alone topics to which others could be added in the future. It included three chapters that guided students from topic development to searching CINAHL, then using the library's journal linking system to retrieve the full-text of the article.

Users navigated the nursing tutorial by using a menu similar to F.I.R.S.T. Viewlets, small Flash movies demonstrating a specific task, made their first appearance in the Nursing and Health Resources Tutorial.

The ability to see the actual interface of a database such as CINAHL and follow along with demonstrations of searches and exploration of database features is invaluable to students. This tutorial was seen as the first step in a push to decentralize online instruction, making it more subject-specific and responsive to a wider range of needs.

Brief Video Tutorials

Early in 2006 the head of the Department of Community Practice within the UNCG School of Nursing requested that the library provide even more specific tutorial content. Master of Science in Nursing students in a law and policy course were being asked to find a dizzying array of information sources entirely new to them (recent court cases, bills, and laws at the federal and state levels). The students needed readily available reinforcement in addition to traditional face-to-face library instruction. Nursing faculty requested a video of a full-length library instruction session with animated searches. Creating such a large chunk of content posed several challenges:

Technology. The life sciences librarian had to obtain the technological expertise and production tools to create a video. The new tutorial would need to be constructed with commonly known technology and inexpensive, easy-to-use tools. Given the use of Viewlets in adding brief videos to the earlier Nursing and Health Resources Tutorial, this software seemed an ideal choice.

Student attention span. Feedback from students regarding the long Nursing and Health Resources Tutorial convinced the librarian that an hour-plus video would not keep student attention.

Updates. Appearance and features of online search tools change frequently. One semiannual change to a search platform can render a long, time-consuming video tutorial obsolete.

For these reasons, the life sciences librarian decided not to create one large tutorial to address the various search tools and techniques needed by the students. Librarians at that time were discussing the conversion of long, animated online tutorials into brief video segments. At the spring 2006 meeting of the Association of North Carolina Health and Science Libraries, a panel discussion included best practices for creating inexpensive tutorials using software such as Camtasia and ViewletBuilder.

Armed with this information, the life sciences librarian arranged access to ViewletBuilder software and a microphone and began planning brief video segments. First she created an outline with a storyboard showing the most appropriate screenshots. Next came the script. She chose to work from a bulleted list of ideas to cover rather than an exact script. At this point the librarian used ViewletBuilder software to capture screenshots and put them together into a video with narration and graphic highlights. A few viewings of the file within the Viewlets software allowed the librarian to cut unnecessary content before the final video file was posted online. This process was used to create two initial videos demonstrating the searches most needed by the nursing students: "Find a Court Case (LexisNexis Academic)" and "Find a Law (LexisNexis Congressional)."

Online Information Literacy Game

Although F.I.R.S.T., Nursing and Health Resources, and the brief video tutorials have been successful, the librarians knew there were other ways to help students learn information literacy concepts. One new approach that broadened the appeal of information literacy to students was the addition of the

Information Literacy Game (http://library. uncg.edu/game/)—a question-and-answer game and allows two to four students to play against each other by answering questions about information literacy topics in four different categories (e.g., Choose your Resource, Avoiding Plagiarism, and Searching and Using Databases). The game also has a one-player version in which students provide timed responses to questions. The game was created with AJAX (a combination of Javascript and XML) and intended to be adapted easily by other libraries. Other libraries immediately showed interest in creating their own versions of the game.

One of the innovative additions to the game is evaluative exercises designed to get students to think about information literacy concepts in a concrete manner. When landing on special squares placed around the board, students are asked to evaluate either one or two Web sites. Exercises in which students evaluate one Web site ask the student to find specific information, such as a company's physical address or contact information. Other exercises ask students to look at two Web sites and decide which one best fits specified criteria. For example, one exercise asks students to figure out which Web site has more accurate information, the library's Web site or The Onion (www.theonion.com). The addition of evaluation of actual Web sites reflects the growing role of the Web in the lives of students and reflects the need for librarians to address the importance of evaluating Web sites.

Content

F.I.R.S.T. Tutorial

The original content of the F.I.R.S.T. tutorial followed the research process from choosing a topic through finding the best books, articles, and Web sites. Six chapters (see

below) took students through these steps. Each chapter took around twenty minutes to complete. Faculty could assign the whole tutorial or specific chapters that were most relevant to the sources needed:

Chapter 1. Planning for Research
  Designing a search strategy
  Finding background information
  Developing a topic
Chapter 2. Matching Needs with Tools
  Choosing the best sources (books, articles, web resources) for the topic
  Choosing the best tool (OPAC, database, etc.)
Chapter 3. Computer Searching
  Choosing appropriate keywords
  Constructing a search using Boolean operators
  Activity in which students find keywords and choose Boolean operators to execute a search
Chapter 4. Finding Books
  Using the OPAC
  Locating the books in the library
  Activity using the catalog to find books by author, title, keyword
Chapter 5. Finding Articles
  Finding articles online or in print
  Using a database to locate articles
Chapter 6. Searching the Web
  Locating and evaluating Web resources

The language and content were focused primarily toward first-year students. Care was taken to avoid library jargon so that the tutorial was understandable to students with little or no library experience, such as using the phrase "search connectors" instead of "Boolean operators." Students may not know what Boolean logic is, but they can easily understand that search connectors are words used to connect terms when doing a search. Where jargon cannot be avoided, as with words such as "periodical" and "database," it is carefully explained: "Back in Chapter Two, you learned that magazines, journals and newspapers are all types of periodicals, so called because they are published *periodically* (every day or every week, for example). You also learned that the tools you use to get access to the contents of periodicals are called periodical databases."

In addition to removing library jargon, a story was added to engage students and maintain interest. Each chapter builds upon the story, a conversation between two students who have a research assignment due and the frustrations they face in completing it. The skills discussed in each chapter are those needed by the fictional students at that point in the story. For example, the chapter on using computers to find information begins with this conversation:

Bryan: You know, I'm kind of concerned about my psych paper.
Julie: Yeah? What's on your mind?
Bryan: It's the research. Have you been in that library? It's huge! And the computer thing freaks me out.
Julie: It's kind of scary at first. But you'll get over it.
Bryan: I dunno. I just feel like I don't know what I'm doing.
Julie: Bryan, what happened the first time you rode a bike?
Bryan: Heh, I fell off! Screamed bloody murder, too.
Julie: And then what?
Bryan: My dad helped me out. He held the bike for me until I got it going. And then I was OK.
Julie: Well, this is kind of the same thing. The librarians can help you get going with the computers. And then you'll be doing it on your own. You're going to do fine!

Questions to consider:

In what ways is a large university library like Jackson Library similar to other libraries you have used? How is it different?

Do you have a library card for your hometown public library?

The tutorial's focus on remaining approachable to a wide audience was essential to its success, but it was also important for the tutorial to grow in response to campus needs. Plagiarism and citing sources properly were major issues for faculty. In response, two new chapters were added in 2003. Chapter 7, "From Research to Writing," provides information on the appropriate use of sources and plagiarism. Students are given several scenarios and asked if the situation is plagiarism or not and then given pointers on paraphrasing and quoting. Chapter 8, "Citing Your Sources," walks students through the process of using APA and MLA styles with interactive exercises.

The librarian in charge of the tutorial consulted extensively with the campus Writing Center on both of these chapters. The dean of students office also provided feedback on the concepts covered in Chapter 7 as well as information about the university's academic integrity policy. As a result of the relationships forged during the creation of these chapters, librarians have been asked to participate in workshops for students on academic integrity, which has provided a good opportunity to increase outreach activity beyond the classroom.

Nursing and Health Resources Tutorial

Nursing faculty were interested in a tutorial that would address the needs of the current Nursing 210 research assignment. Students were assigned one of the following topics: variations of time orientation, space orientation, biology, environmental control, or communication within a particular population (African American, Vietnamese American, American Indian, Afghan, etc.). Acceptable sources were articles published in American or Canadian peer-reviewed nursing journals in the previous five years. Although the difficulty of the assignment justified any additional help that could be made available to students, creating a full-length tutorial designed around a single assignment seemed inappropriate. The content would be relevant only to a small proportion of nursing students, some information literacy skills might be emphasized at the expense of others, and complete rewrites would be needed with each assignment revision.

These considerations led the life sciences librarian to design a tutorial for Nursing 210 students that might also be used by other undergraduate nursing students. She reviewed several sources to determine student information needs: surveys administered during the first round of Nursing 210 library instruction (especially the two questions "What is the most valuable thing that you learned today?" and "What was presented that you already knew?"); self-created assessment notes made immediately after these library instruction sessions; and notes from consultations with Nursing 210 and other undergraduate nursing students. As a result of this examination, a picture of information needs began to emerge. Students needed to know how to

- convert a topic into a search query
- perform a basic search in CINAHL using keywords, Boolean operators, and appropriate search limits
- adapt search strategies to gain more or fewer results
- use the CINAHL guide to subject headings (in CINAHL EBSCO*host,* using the guide to subject headings is often essential to an effective search)

- determine whether results were entire articles or simply citations
- use Journal Finder, the local serials linking system, to get full text for article citations

These needs became the main topics of the tutorial. To make the content manageable for students with different information needs, it was divided into three chapters: "Getting Starting," "Using CINAHL," and "Getting Full Text." Once a student clicks the sidebar link for the chapter, the navigation links for subtopics appear under the chapter title. "Getting Started" includes a page on each of these topics: read instructions, know the library tools, choose a topic, choose keywords, expand a topic, narrow a topic, and review. "Using CINAHL" includes a page on each of these topics: what is CINAHL?, getting to CINAHL, anatomy of CINAHL, keyword search with limits, evaluating results, CINAHL headings, reading citations, printing, e-mailing, and saving citations, and review. "Getting Full Text" includes a page on each of these topics: recognizing full text, introduction to Journal Finder (the library's journal linking system), Journal Finder search, when you're stuck, and a review.

Brief Video Tutorials

Nursing students in the Master of Science program were being asked to find a recent bill, a recent law, and a recent court case, all at federal and state levels. Previous library instruction had presented the students with an impressive array of search tools (library subscription databases and Web sites) for each of these information needs. Although nursing faculty requested a full-length video demonstrating searches in several sources for each of these information needs, the life sciences librarian adopted a "one need, one tool" approach. She approached these needs with a series of brief videos, each demonstrating how to use a single search tool to satisfy a single information need. The initial result was two brief videos: "Find a Court Case (LexisNexis Academic)" running approximately two minutes, and "Find a Law (LexisNexis Congressional)," running approximately four minutes.

Each was a narrated, point-and-click video that recreated a search leading from the library homepage through e-mailing a successful search result. The videos included running commentary describing login requirements, the types of results to expect, how one could increase results, and the meanings behind the legal/legislative citations at the top of each result.

Instruction

The F.I.R.S.T. tutorial has been used in three main ways: as a stand-alone instruction instead of an instruction session, a required assignment before attending a library instruction session, or a refresher or update suggested by librarians or faculty. The tutorial provides the flexibility to meet the needs of students and faculty in all three situations.

Some teaching faculty are unwilling to use a class session to bring students to the library for library instruction. Also, limited teaching space within the library and insufficient staff made reaching all first-year students impossible. With the creation of the online tutorial, professors could assign all or part of the tutorial to their students to teach them basic research skills without using classtime. Once the tutorial was updated to allow students to e-mail results, professors could easily monitor students' completion of the tutorial.

Librarians often found that students who had completed some or all of the tutorial be-

fore an instruction session were much better prepared and able to accomplish more during the class period. Several English 101 instructors require their students to complete the "Citing Your Sources" chapter before their in-person library instruction session. An introductory recreation course requires students to find relevant Web sites. Students were asked to complete the class "Searching the Web" before the library instruction class. The chapters "From Research to Writing" and "Citing Your Sources" have also been extremely popular with faculty and used campus-wide by the dean of students, Learning Assistance Center, and Writing Center.

The nursing tutorials (Nursing and Health Resources Tutorial as well as the brief videos) have mainly been used as reinforcement and additional content for library instruction sessions. Some students have a large number of information needs, but best practices research indicates that library instruction sessions should allow opportunities for discussion and hands-on activities. So the nursing tutorials are often recommended during the sessions as reviews and guides to more advanced searching. The brief videos demonstrating LexisNexis searches for court cases, bills, and laws are integrated into a static Web page that includes other resources recommended for nurses doing legal research. All of the nursing tutorials are also listed on a Nursing Tutorials and Guides page (http://library.uncg.edu/depts/ref/bibs/nur/nur_tutorials.asp).

Program Assessment

Although some assessment of our online information literacy program has taken place, it is an area that needs further development. An evaluation form was included with the original First Steps tutorial, and the feedback was quite positive. During the first year, eighty evaluations were submitted by students, with more than 80 percent responding that they learned "very much" or "quite a bit." F.I.R.S.T. was also well received in the library community. In 2001 another university in the University of North Carolina system asked to use it in their instruction program. In 2002 it was accepted into ACRL's Internet Education Project.

The Nursing and Health Resources Tutorial has been assessed in several ways. First it was submitted to librarians and faculty outside the library. Then master's students on the nurse educator track were asked to read and evaluate the tutorial. Most of the feedback centered on the brief videos embedded within the tutorial:

I thought the tutorial was very useful in learning techniques on how to search. For instance, using the asterisk to search for word variations.

The CINAHL tutorial was very helpful with learning how to use the database. I loved the areas where you were able to click on the computer screen image and it took you through the process of the different things you can do in CINAHL (that was great for those of us who are visual learners).

I found your tutorial to be extremely informative and user-friendly. I especially like the links to the step-by-step instruction on how to navigate or carry out specific functions. It did take me a minute to realize that the illustration [video] was at the bottom of the screen.

For those of us learning to navigate on the computer, this is GREAT!!!!!

The Show Me links [to videos] were great for visual learners…. The only negative I have about this tutorial is that when you click on the "show me" link, the next screen is completely blank, and if you don't realize that by scrolling you can see the next page, you miss it.

In response to student feedback, the entry points of the videos were made more obvious. Instead of a link titled "Show Me" leading to a page with the video located at the bottom of the page, an image of the video was incorporated directly into the text of the tutorial. Other changes included content editing and minor navigation improvements. The most prominent point made by the student evaluators was the usefulness of the brief videos.

To assess the impact the Information Literacy Game was having on students, a brief three-question survey with additional room for open comments was added. The survey was optional and was presented as a link from the final screen of the game, which shows the results after a winner (or loser, in the case of solo games) has been determined. Feedback from the evaluation form has been quite positive:

Great game!"

Thanks for the effort. Definitely more fun than a lot of lessons.

Fun way to learn the facts! I'll have to tell the librarian at my college about this!

Campus assessment measures indicate that adding the tutorial raised the profile of the instruction program. Every other year,

UNCG's Office of Institutional Research conducts a survey of all sophomores that includes a question on library training. Between 2000 and 2002 (after the tutorial had been available for two years), the proportion of students rating their library training as "excellent" rose 5 percent and those rating it as "good" rose 3 percent.

In addition to assessing its own information literacy program, UNCG has participated in standardized assessment programs to look at the information literacy skills of students. In 2005 the University Libraries participated in ARL's Project SAILS. The results indicated that UNCG students performed at about the same level as the average student from other institutions that administered SAILS. During the academic year 2007/8, the UNCG Libraries will be participating in ARL's Effective, Practical and Sustainable Assessment project. A major component of this effort will be to assess student learning of information literacy skills.

Lessons Learned

Each of the new parts of the online information literacy program created in the University Libraries has inspired valuable instructional design lessons and provided valuable lessons on improving existing products. Collaboration seems to be the key to each lesson learned, from technology to updates and maintenance to marketing. Involving librarians from various departments and with various strengths leads the librarians of the University Libraries to create a higher-quality final product.

The first online information literacy project, First Steps, brought many technology-related frustrations. One obstacle was the fact that students could not e-mail their completion certificates to their instructor. Another was that the tutorial could not be accessed via Blackboard. As course management software became the preferred communication tool between faculty and students, this conflict became more of an issue. It became apparent that librarians must listen and respond quickly to student and faculty feedback, or these groups would stop using the products. Including contact information for someone who is able to provide help quickly is a simple but vital part of having a successful online tutorial. The lessons on technology and feedback from First Steps made the subsequent projects work more smoothly. For instance, not all of the Nursing and Health Resources Tutorial content was being used by all students. Because students reported that the brief videos were the most useful portions, these parts of the tutorial were emphasized. When another full-length nursing tutorial was requested, it was produced in the format that had been most useful to the students—a set of brief videos.

In addition to remaining committed to receiving feedback and fixing technological problems, it is also important to keep a tutorial's technology and content up to date. Technology is constantly improving, and our students are becoming more technologically savvy. In order for a tutorial to remain relevant and continue being used by students, it must be continuously evaluated and updated as necessary. Since the content of the F.I.R.S.T. tutorial has not been updated since the final two chapters were added in 2003, and the technology has not been updated since 2005, it is time to do a major overhaul to make it more interactive and less text-centered. The need to incorporate new technology into the online information literacy program led to creation of the online Information Literacy Game.

Another important lesson learned is the need for marketing. An online tutorial cannot help students learn information literacy concepts if they do not know about it. At UNCG, a link to the tutorial was placed on the navigation bar that appears on the library's homepage and most of the library's other Web sites. A logo for the tutorial was created and placed on course guide Web pages to give the tutorial a recognizable brand. Librarians leading first-year library instruction sessions often point to the tutorial as a way to learn research skills at a student's own pace.

The nursing tutorials Nursing and Health Resources, Find a Law (LexisNexis Congressional), and Find a Court Case (LexisNexis Academic) are much less familiar to students because marketing has been limited to library instruction announcements and links. Recently these tutorials have been marketed through e-mail and subject portal links targeting not only nursing but other disciplines of interest, such as political science. Marketing these products in tandem with the First Steps tutorial can be tricky. It is confusing for students to be faced with a set of tutorials that use different technologies to address sometimes slightly different objectives. It is hoped that the future plans for the tutorial will resolve this issue.

Future Plans

To remain relevant, tutorials must continue to evolve to reflect user needs and improved technology. The planning for the new incarnation of F.I.R.S.T. is under way, with an emphasis on ease of use, gaming, and interaction. Ease of use and ADA compliance will be maintained and improved by testing the tutorial in the library's usability lab. The content will be broken down into smaller thematic segments to provide more targeted assistance throughout the library's Web site and reduce the tutorial's linearity in favor of a more topic-driven approach. This approach

will also involve changing the navigation of the tutorial and abandoning the use of the word "chapter' for "module" or "topic."

In addition, the programming of the tutorial will be changed dramatically, to an AJAX format that allows subject librarians to offer different examples and databases as content. A user of the tutorial will be able to select from several choices of subject matter and receive content tailored to that particular interest and receive content for a specific skill level. For instance, a business student might receive examples connected with gathering company intelligence or researching stocks, with Viewlets guiding him through business databases such as EBSCO's Business Source Premier. Nursing and other interested students will have a larger array of videos demonstrating how to use freely available resources to search for North Carolina bills and laws and how to find regional health statistics. It is hoped that this will simplify the logistics of fulfilling requests for subject tutorials as well as maintaining and marketing these resources.

F.I.R.S.T. will be updated to include more interactivity in order to engage the students who are its demographic target. The interactivity of the new tutorial will include the addition of many links to cross-referenced content and the ability to delve further into a topic by clicking on "Tell Me More" links. Mini-games will be included along with quizzes within each module to enhance learning and retention of concepts. The current information literacy game will be augmented with other games to provide engagement with student learners on many levels.

The addition of Wi-Fi in the library and the laptop initiative at UNCG (which requires all new students to have laptops) will also allow further enhancements to library instruction, both online and in-person.

Classes can become mobile and the tutorial can go along with them, leading to a greater integration of in-person and online information literacy instruction.

Conclusion

The online content of UNCG's information literacy program has proved, both by design and by circumstance, to be an organic, dynamic, and necessary component of the University Libraries' mission to provide library instruction. From its beginning as a six-chapter tutorial through its foreseen change into a loosely connected collection of targeted content, examples, games, and quizzes, the tutorial has evolved with the needs of the students and faculty. Every aspect of the tutorial has changed in some manner, including the content, the technology, the target audiences, and the look and feel. As technology changes and improves, so too will the online information literacy program.

25. Wartburg College: Planful Deployment

Gillian Gremmels and Kimberly Babcock Mashek

Introduction

Wartburg College, a liberal arts college of 1,800 students located in Waverly, Iowa, is known for its extensive, course-integrated, across-the-curriculum information literacy program. One of ten academic institutions of all sizes and types chosen for the 2002 Best Practices in Information Literacy Invitational Conference, Wartburg College takes advantage of its small size and dedicated staff to ensure that each student receives several in-class information literacy sessions taught by librarians. The college's general education program mandates multiple lessons and scaffolded information literacy strands that build upon prior instruction through all majors. The typical impetus for online library instruction—too many students, not enough librarians—is absent, and the college does not offer distance education, yet Wartburg College has a nascent online instruction program. The "why" and the "how" are the subjects of this chapter.

Rationale

Building on Wartburg's strong program of face-to-face instruction, the information literacy librarians determined early on that the rationale for online instruction would be to reinforce, not replace, in-class instruction. Online instruction, it was believed, would facilitate:

• extending instruction beyond class-time, allowing students to prepare ahead of time for their information literacy lessons and follow up after class

• targeting instruction to multiple learning styles, making information literacy lessons more accessible to some learners

• teaching tools, saving classtime for higher-order concepts

• providing opportunities for students to practice new skills

Vogel Library's stated mission is to educate information-literate lifelong learners. With a small staff (9.5 FTE in eleven people), every initiative and activity must serve that mission. The staff believes that "we can do anything, but we probably can't do everything" and chooses carefully where to invest scarce personnel resources. A second key rationale for the method with which the library developed its online instruction program was to maximize the work of the responsible librarian by planful deployment. As Nancy Dewald cautioned, "Librarians may be tempted to place pages on the Web simply because they can, but they need to determine what the pedagogical reasons are for doing so and how best to do it."[1]

Development

The library's Web site has been based on instruction practices at Wartburg College since its creation in 1997/98 (figure 25.1). The early design was organized like a search strategy; users accessed online tools by selecting the appropriate type of source: "overview" (encyclopedic), "finding" (bibliographic databases), or "fact" (dictionaries, statistical sources). This forced choice served to reinforce in-class instruction. Search strategy is taught in the required English composition course, and the Web site reminded students of that lesson every time they used an online resource. The Web site, developed by student Webmasters under the direction of an information literacy librarian, was tweaked intermittently for several years. Additional instructional content included class handouts in electronic form and interactive information-seeking logs, which were basically step-by-step online forms with the search strategy outlined. These tools provided basic information for students in the online environment. They also helped the librarians provide point-of-need instruction at the reference desk.

In summer 2005, the time came for a major redesign of the library's Web site that would complement the college's marketing and branding standards. Although that impetus was not strictly instructional, the librarians took advantage of the opportunity to change the library's presence on the Web and how users interact with the site. Now led by an information literacy librarian whose charge was focused on virtual instruction, librarians codified their belief in the instructional nature of the Web in a Web site mission statement: to educate, inform, and facilitate access to lifelong learners. The statement was created to give focus and direction to the Web site during the redesign of the site's look and content. Since the mission is educationally focused, instructional content is given a priority, with location on the front main page and subsequent pages. In addition, the main headings chosen to organize content are meant to be intuitive and instruction-focused (figure 25.2).

With the Web site providing stealth instruction, the librarians decided to develop tutorials strategically for more overt instruction. The library's first tutorial rolled out in September 2005 and was a basic instruction tool teaching students, faculty, and staff how to create an online interlibrary loan account

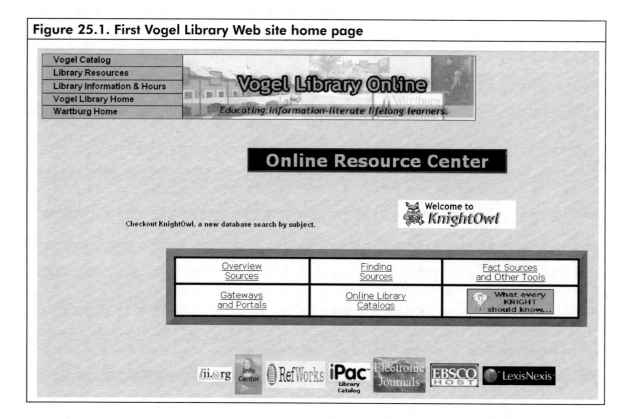

Figure 25.1. First Vogel Library Web site home page

Figure 25.2. New Vogel Library Web site homepage

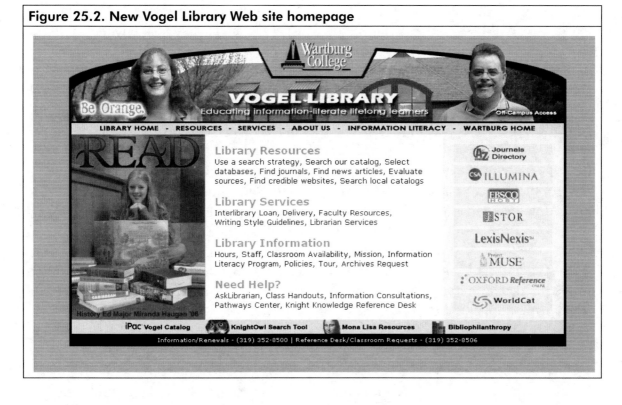

in ILLiad. The tutorial was intended to be a fairly simple pilot tutorial, although one with relevance and utility, to produce a useable product as well as give the users an opportunity to learn and practice.

After this tutorial was launched, the librarians felt that tutorials could enhance the instruction program. The librarians discussed what departments could benefit from the use of tutorials and determined that maximum benefit could be achieved by targeting departments that generated numerous reference inquiries, represented significant parts of the general education requirement, or produced high numbers of majors. This led to the creation of two tutorials: one for the oral communication class and the other for Biology 151, the introductory course for majors. Both of these classes have high enrollment and are tied to general education requirements. The biology course can satisfy a general education category, and the oral communication class is required of all students. A third tutorial, cur-

rently under development, teaches students to find and interpret biblical commentaries, a component of the Literature of the Old and New Testaments religion course that almost all students take.

With the classroom faculty members who coordinated these courses, the librarians determined a purpose for each course tutorial, created learning objectives using Bloom's taxonomy, and storyboarded content. For the storyboarding activity, a librarian and the faculty member considered the concepts and objectives, brainstormed content suggestions, and mapped out specific pages. Many times, the tutorials contained ideas and activities that were previously developed in handouts or worksheets for in-class instruction.

It was deemed important in developing the tutorials to incorporate the diverse learning styles of today's learners. In the storyboarding, efforts were made to have activities for Kolb's four learning styles: accommodating, diverging, assimilating, and converging.[2] Sometimes this was accomplished, and at other times it was determined that a learning style could better be incorporated into the classroom lesson paired with the tutorial. For example, it was hard to incorporate a reflective learning activity tied to discussion in an asynchronous tutorial without having the technical capabilities on campus for an online discussion forum. (The college uses an off-brand course management system that does not support this learning function.) Therefore, reflective and discussion activities are part of the in-class learning. Another goal was not to overload the student with content, and the tutorials combined sound and graphics for visual and auditory learners.

After the storyboarding was complete, a script was written for the audio component. The tutorial was then created using Macromedia Captivate. This software was chosen because the college had purchased a site license for Macromedia software, but its ease of use in screen capture and adding audio and text later to the screencasts were appealing features. Despite the relative user-friend-

liness of the software, the development of tutorials in Captivate continues to be a very organic, time-consuming process. The average tutorial takes almost fifteen hours to complete in Captivate alone. The in-depth class-based tutorials contain two or more screencasts with narration, animation, and audio. Most tutorials are not completed in one setting but over the span of several days.

When the screencasts were completed, they were incorporated into an HTML-based tutorial template created with Macromedia Dreamweaver. A standardized Web tutorial template was created for ease of development and speed of incorporating the multimedia segments. All the tutorials have a standard subtitle of "Information Gathering Tutorial" with the tutorial segments on the left-hand side (figure 25.3). Tutorials are also segmented into parts that do not rely on other segments. This way, a tutorial can be completed in sequence or in parts chosen by the learner in response to questions or needs. After the tutorial is fully completed, it is placed on the test Web server in order to find glitches and identify where improvements could be made.

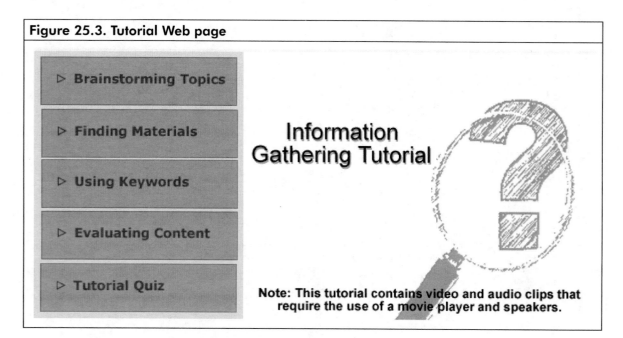

Figure 25.3. Tutorial Web page

▷ Brainstorming Topics

▷ Finding Materials

▷ Using Keywords

▷ Evaluating Content

▷ Tutorial Quiz

Information Gathering Tutorial

Note: This tutorial contains video and audio clips that require the use of a movie player and speakers.

Content

At present, the library's online instruction "program" includes an intentionally instructional Web design, several online tutorials, and information-seeking logs that can be filled out online. The Web site section that is most relevant to instruction is the first Web page, Library Resources (www.wartburg. edu/library/resources.html), where students are invited to

- use a search strategy
- search our catalog
- select databases
- find journals
- find news articles
- evaluate sources
- find credible Web sites
- search local catalogs

Clicking on any of the options reveals links to selected sources along with brief commentary that provides reinforcement for those who have had in-class instruction and an "advance look" for those who have not yet learned the material from a librarian. For example, the text in the "Use a search strategy" link states, "You'll learn more about this in EN 112 [the required composition course], but here's an advance look at a strategy and resources that will be useful in your information-seeking" and reminds students that "Overview Sources clarify unfamiliar terms or ideas, and usually provide a list or bibliography of other recommended sources. They help to narrow a big topic or give you topic ideas" (figure 25.4).

Figure 25.4. Library Resources Web page

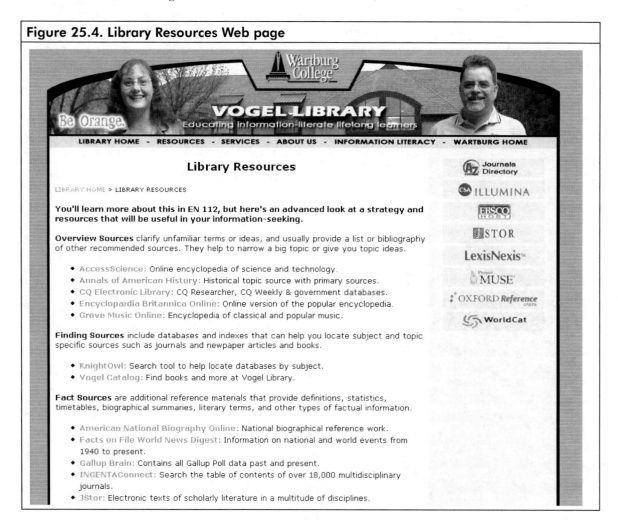

Online tutorials are found via the Class Handouts link under the Need Help section of the Web site (www.wartburg.edu/library/handouts.html). A brief description of each and objectives are as follows:

BI 151: Information Gathering Tutorial. This tutorial is a preinstruction tutorial introducing first-year biology majors to the resources the library provides. After completing the tutorial, the student should be able to search science-specific databases, find books and journals in the library, find science-specific information on the Internet, and evaluate content for scholarly worth.

Students work through the tutorial before coming to a lab session in the library. At the library session, the students work in their lab groups to complete a detailed worksheet on applying the universally recommended search strategy to biology. Students are required to use proper format when citing sources in the worksheet, and the worksheet is handed in to the librarian for grading based on a prepared rubric. The library session is a starting-off point for research for the group's final group poster.

CA 112: Information Gathering Tutorial. This tutorial introduces students to library resources that help them find materials for basic speech topics, most commonly topics for their informative and persuasive speeches. The student learning outcomes of the tutorial are to use brainstorming tools to determine and investigate a potential topic, find materials in the library, generate keywords for searching in databases, and evaluate content for scholarly worth.

Oral communication is a half-credit course, and it is not part of the Information Literacy Across the Curriculum plan, so this tutorial stands alone. The information literacy learning it reinforces is from the composition course's search strategy lesson and the first-year seminar lesson on evaluating information.

RE 101: Information Gathering Tutorial. This tutorial teaches students how to find biblical commentaries. Upon completion of the tutorial, the student should be able to find book-length commentaries using the library catalog, find journal article commentaries using a religion-specific database, and use keywords and truncation.

Instruction

As stated earlier, an important caveat for online instruction at Wartburg College was not to create tools for which there was no clear need or place in the curriculum. With each tutorial costing almost a full week of work for the one librarian in charge of virtual instruction, the library cannot afford to create comprehensive module-based tutorials like CLUE (http://clue.library.wisc.edu) or TILT (http://tilt.lib.utsystem.edu). Both the biology and oral communication tutorials are required course activities, and students are graded for their participation. When the biblical commentaries tutorial is completed, it will be shared first with the faculty teaching the course in hope that they, too, will insist that their students take part. If not, it will certainly help librarians with their teaching at the reference desk, where commentary questions are a frequent occurrence.

Program Assessment

Wartburg's librarians were early campus adopters of assessment, and the information literacy program has long relied on data about student performance for insight into what works and what needs improvement. The team believes assessment is best when it is direct (measures students' ability actually to do the desired outcome) and authentic (measured in a real-life application). Indirect assessment (reflects students' reactions to their learning experience) has proved much less useful.

When collaborating with faculty members on the development of these tutorials, the librarians wanted to build in useful assessment. Authentic assessment is difficult to incorporate into online tutorials, but quizzes can readily be programmed in, so the goal of direct assessment can be achieved. Cooperation with classroom faculty members and the campus instructional technology department led to the development of quizzes that tested students on the content and skills taught in the tutorial (figure 25.5). Each student's quiz results are then e-mailed either to the librarian who is facilitating the classroom lesson for the instruction session or to the faculty member teaching the class. In the case of the oral communication tutorial, the quiz is sent to the faculty member, who grades the student's completed quiz. In addition to quiz results, instructors have reported much improvement in the quality of sources used in students' speeches because of the tutorial, and they are fielding fewer questions about topic selection because of the resources outlined in the tutorial.

Figure 25.5. Sample tutorial quiz

The BI 151: Information Gathering Tutorial also has a quiz component, but the results are e-mailed to a librarian and the quiz completion is one requirement of students' in-class instruction activity. The results of the quiz showed that students understood how to use the catalog and databases but had trouble creating keywords for database searching and determining proper citation format. After seeing the mistakes students made in the tutorial quiz, the librarian plans to make revisions to the online tutorial and in-class activity to address and reinforce these important concepts.

An opportunity for authentic assessment may exist with the Finding Biblical Commentaries and Journal Articles tutorial. Students currently are asked to use commentaries for class assignments without any prior instruction. If classroom faculty and librarians can collaborate on some kind of instrument evaluating students' use of these sources, then compare before and after tutorial completion, it may show not only the effectiveness of the tutorial but students' ability to transfer skills learned online to the real-world library environment.

Usability testing can be seen as another type of assessment. Here the library has not been as proactive. A few student workers have been asked to complete the tutorials and offer feedback before they are released to the general public, but there has not been a systematic testing process. Currently, all tutorials may not be readily accessible to those who have visual or hearing impairments. In the future, the tutorials will be subjected to more strenuous usability testing, including focus groups and observational task activity with users to detect tutorial problems.

Lessons Learned

Online instruction is like other modalities: one begins with desired outcomes and meets the students where they are. Although Mestre has said that "most online situations best serve students who function well in a logical, text-based, passive environment"[3] (much like other library interfaces), the Web provides opportunities to meet many more students with varied learning styles. As with all teaching, it is important to plan the instruction carefully, but the online element adds the challenge of mastering the technology, creating additional time demands. In addition, it is important to conduct usability testing for Web sites and tutorials to make sure users understand the instruction and can find their needed information.

We would advise small libraries without armies of programmers and Web designers to define clear learning objectives, start small, and assess. All instruction team members should be involved in planning instruction—even if just one will do the technical work—to increase buy-in and to diversify the learning styles that program architects bring to the enterprise. It is also important to involve the institution's information technology staff in the process and ask them questions about the computers on campus: do they all have sound capabilities or have Macromedia Flash installed so videos can be viewed? The Wartburg College librarians made the unwelcome discovery midsemester that most tutorials were being viewed with graphics alone because the main computer lab on campus did not have audio capability. IT staff can also give insight on graphics and technical glitches that may occur. By aiming to do a few things well and taking advantage of local expertise, any library can benefit from online instruction.

Notes

1.   Nancy H. Dewald, "Web-Based Library Instruction: What Is Good Pedagogy?" *Information Technology and Libraries* 18, no. 1 (1999): 26.

2.   David A. Kolb, *Experiential Learning: Experience as the Source of Learning and Development* (Upper Saddle River, NJ: Prentice Hall, 1984).

3.   Lori Mestre, "Accommodating Diverse Learning Styles in an Online Environment," *Reference and User Services Quarterly* 46, no. 2 (2006): 30.

Contributors

Editors

Alice Daugherty is Information Literacy Librarian at Louisiana State University's Middleton Library, where she teaches Library Research Methods and Materials using online and face-to-face formats. She is actively involved in the ALA, currently holding chair positions within the ACRL Distance Learning Section and New Members Round Table. E-mail: adaugher@lsu.edu.

Michael F. Russo received his MLIS from Louisiana State University in 2000. That same year, he was hired by LSU Libraries as an instruction librarian, a position he held until 2002, when he was made Instruction Coordinator. While still an instructor, he fronted as the instructor-of-record for LSU Libraries' first online course. In the intervening years, the library system's online instruction course has expanded to the point of accommodating as many students as the classroom version. To its growing suite of online instructional resources, the LSU Libraries has recently added TigerTAIL, an adaptation of the Texas Information Literacy Tutorial. E-mail: mrusso1@lsu.edu.

Authors

Norma Allenbach Schmidt has been Instruction and Reference Librarian at Prince George's Community College in Largo, Maryland, since 1996. As a part of Instruction and Reference, she began offering the online information literacy program in 2003 and has assumed the duties of Distance Learning Librarian. Prior to that, she was Adult Services Librarian in the areas of collection development and reference at the Amherst Public Libraries in Erie County, New York. Her MLS is from the State University of New York at Buffalo. E-mail: NSchmidt@pgcc.edu.

Kristina Appelt worked in the libraries of several small liberal arts colleges before deciding to pursue her master's degree. She received her MSIS from the University of Texas at Austin in 2004. She is the library liaison to the College of Nursing and College of Pharmacy and serves as Education Coordinator for the Library of the Health Sciences at the University of Illinois at Chicago. E-mail: khoward2@uic.edu.

William Badke has been teaching credit information literacy courses since 1985. Since 1988, he has been Associate Librarian of Trinity Western University for Associated Canadian Theological Schools and Information Literacy, teaching one-credit graduate research courses and a three-credit undergraduate course on research in the information age. He is the author of *Research Strategies: Finding Your Way through the Information Fog* (2d ed., 2004) and *Beyond the Answer Sheet: Academic Success for International Students* (2003). E-mail: badke@twu.ca.

Julie Chapman is Instructional Services Librarian at the University of Illinois at Springfield.

Before returning to the Midwest, she worked for six years at Valdosta State University as Outreach Services Librarian. She has taught credit courses using WebCT and Blackboard and developed multimedia instructional modules. E-mail: jchap2@uis.edu.

Nancy Wootton Colborn is Associate Librarian and Coordinator of Library Instruction and Staff Development at Schurz Library, Indiana University–South Bend. She was one of the team leaders in the development of the online course in 2001/3 and taught the first section of the online course in 2003. E-mail: ncolborn@iusb.edu.

Kathryn M. Crowe is Associate Director for Public Services at the University Libraries, University of North Carolina at Greensboro. E-mail: kmcrowe@uncg.edu.

Lara Ursin Cummings is Instruction Librarian at Washington State University Libraries. Her interests include undergraduate teaching and learning, working with distance students, and campus collaboration. She graduated from the University of South Carolina's College of Library and Information Science in 2001. E-mail: lursin@wsu.edu.

Barbara J. D'Angelo is Lecturer in the Multimedia Writing and Technical Communication Program at Arizona State University at the Polytechnic Campus. Ms. D'Angelo received her MSLIS from the University of Illinois in Urbana-Champaign and is currently working toward her PhD in the online doctoral program in Technical Communication and Rhetoric at Texas Tech University. Prior to becoming a lecturer, she worked as a reference and instruction librarian at Southeastern Louisiana University, Arizona State University West, and Arizona State University

Polytechnic. Her experience in information literacy includes teaching both single sessions and for-credit library instruction courses, collaborating with faculty to incorporate information literacy standards into courses and assignments, and assessment. E-mail: bdangelo@asu.edu.

Denise D. Green is Instructional Services Librarian and Coordinator of Reference at the University of Illinois at Springfield. Before coming to UIS in January 1995, she was Reference Coordinator at the Ohio Wesleyan University Beeghly Library and Bibliographic Instruction Librarian at the University of Toledo Carlson Library. She has taught credit courses at UIS in Women's Studies as well as Library Research Methods since 1996. She is an alumna of John Carroll University, Kent State University, and the University of Illinois at Springfield. E-mail: Green.Denise@uis.edu.

Louise Greenfield has been a librarian at the University of Arizona for twenty-five years. Her career emphasis has been on developing user information literacy skills and she views herself as a teacher/librarian. Louise has served on a variety of state and national library committees and has given presentations at state and national conferences. She graduated from Drexel University in Philadelphia with an MS in Library Science and also has a background in education. E-mail: greenfieldl@u.library.arizona.edu.

Gillian Gremmels, Library Director at Davidson College, Davidson, North Carolina, was College Librarian at Wartburg College from 1994 to 2007. A longtime proponent of information literacy, she holds an MLS from the University of Maryland. E-mail: jigremmels@davidson.edu.

Amy Harris is Reference Librarian and First-Year Instruction Coordinator at the University of North Carolina at Greensboro. She is involved in coordinating and teaching first-year instruction sessions, creating online guides and tutorials, marketing, and virtual reference. E-mail: a_harri2@uncg.edu.

K. Alix Hayden has more than fourteen years' experience as a liaison librarian in academic libraries and is currently Liaison Librarian for Nursing and Kinesiology at the University of Calgary. She received her MLIS and MSc from the University of Alberta and completed her PhD in 2003 from the University of Calgary. Her doctoral work, supported by an SSHRC Doctoral Fellowship, investigated undergraduate students' lived experience of information seeking. Her current research interests focus on merging the theoretical aspects of information seeking into the everyday practice of academic librarianship. E-mail: ahayden@ucalgary.ca.

Christy Hightower is Biology and Biomolecular Engineering Librarian at the University of California, Santa Cruz, Science and Engineering Library, having joined the UCSC staff in 2000. Formerly Engineering Librarian at the University of California, San Diego (a position she held for eleven years), she has written scholarly publications and presented at national conferences on the topics of metasearching, Web site development, and evaluation of online engineering resources. She was the 2003 recipient of the Homer I. Bernhardt Distinguished Service Award from the Engineering Libraries Division of the American Society for Engineering Education—the division's highest honor. E-mail: christyh@ucsc.edu.

Beth Hill is Library Manager at Kootenai Medical Center in Coeur d'Alene, Idaho, and is interested in information literacy instruction in healthcare settings. E-mail: bhill@kmc.org.

Ben Hunter received his MS in Library Science from the University of North Carolina at Chapel Hill in 2005. He is currently Reference and Instruction Librarian and Social Sciences Bibliographer at the University of Idaho Library. E-mail: bhunter@uidaho.edu.

Kathryn Kennedy holds an MLIS from the Florida State University College of Information. She is currently Engineering Outreach Librarian at the University of Florida, responsible for selecting materials for and providing library instruction and reference assistance to biomedical engineering, mechanical and aerospace engineering, and nuclear and radiological engineering students. In addition to her on-campus responsibilities, she provides library assistance to UF EDGE (Electronic Delivery of Graduate Engineering), the distance learning engineering program. She is currently pursuing her PhD in Educational Technology at the UF College of Education. E-mail: katkenn@uflib.ufl.edu.

Jim Kinnie is Humanities Reference Librarian at the University of Rhode Island and teaches one face-to-face section of Introduction to Information Literacy each semester and an online section during summer sessions. He coordinates library instruction for the URI College Writing Program and is a member of the campus-wide Online Learning Committee. Since 2002 he has participated as member and chair of Librarians on Online Course Information (LOCI), a special interest group of the ACRL New England chapter. E-mail: jkinnie@uri.edu.

Jennifer Knievel is Humanities Reference and Instruction Librarian and Assistant Professor in the Reference and Instructional Services Department at the University of Colorado at Boulder. Instruction for the Program for Writing and Rhetoric has been one of her primary responsibilities since 2000, and she has shepherded this element of the information literacy program from its infancy of worksheets through its current iteration of a tutorial combined with seminars and the research center. E-mail: jennifer.knievel@colorado.edu.

Cliff Landis is Reference Facilitator at Valdosta State University. Valdosta, Georgia. He has developed and taught undergraduate and graduate information literacy courses as well collaborating to integrate library services into online courses. E-mail: jclandis@valdosta.edu.

Shirley O. Lankford was Head of Instructional Services at the University of West Georgia Ingram Library from 1999 to 2007. She earned an MLS from Clark Atlanta and MED from the University of West Georgia and has been an academic librarian for more than twenty years, with experience in circulation, cataloging, and instructional services. Ms. Lankford developed the original online library research class at Ingram Library. E-mail: slankfor@westga.edu.

Lea Leininger is Life Sciences Reference Librarian at University of North Carolina at Greensboro. She is involved in library instruction, creating online guides and tutorials, collection management, and creating Web pages and other supporting materials. E-mail: laleinin@uncg.edu.

Elizabeth Blakesley Lindsay is Assistant Dean for Public Services and Outreach at the Washington State University Libraries. She was previously Head of Library Instruction at the same institution and has also worked in public services at Indiana State University and the University of Massachusetts–Dartmouth. She earned an MLS and an MA in comparative literature at Indiana University–Bloomington. E-mail: elindsay@wsu.edu.

Ken Lyons is a generalist reference librarian and Reference Unit Training Coordinator at McHenry Library, University of California, Santa Cruz. An academic librarian since 2001, he also has experience in public librarianship. Ken currently cochairs the UCSC Library's Web Coordinating Group and serves as the Library's publication officer. E-mail: kbplyons@ucsc.edu.

Kimberly Babcock Mashek is Information Literacy Librarian at Wartburg College, Waverly, Iowa, and the coordinator of virtual instruction. She received her MA in library and information studies from the University of Wisconsin–Madison. E-mail: kim.babcock@wartburg.edu.

Kelly Rhodes McBride is Instruction Librarian and Assistant Professor in Belk Library and Information Commons at Appalachian State University in Boone, North Carolina. Her primary responsibilities are to provide library instruction and support for the departments of Art, Theatre and Dance, and Communication. Her research interests include information literacy and assessment design. E-mail: mcbridekr@appstate.edu.

Mark McManus was Associate Director of Libraries at the University of West Georgia from 1993 to 2007. He earned an MLS from the University of Tennessee–Knoxville and an MA from Auburn University and did postgraduate study at the University of Maryland. Mark has been an academic librarian for nearly thirty years; although his early experience was in technical services, library systems, and collection management, he also has expertise in administration, personnel, and planning issues in academe. For the past several years his major areas of interest or inquiry have been information literacy and the changing architecture of scholarly information. E-mail: markmcmanus@mindspring.com.

Suchi Mohanty is Reference and Instruction Librarian/Coordinator of Instruction for the R. B. House Undergraduate Library and Adjunct Professor of Practice at the University of North Carolina School of Information and Library Science. She received a BA from the University of Mary Washington and an MSLS from the University of North Carolina at Chapel Hill. Suchi is active in LAUNCH-CH, NCLA, ALA, and ACRL and has presented on the use of Instant Messenger chat as a virtual reference and outreach tool and instruction and outreach efforts for first-year students. E-mail: smohanty@e-mail.unc.edu.

Deborah A. Murphy has been Reference Librarian at the University of California, Santa Cruz, McHenry Library, since 1987, where she has coordinated computer and instructional services and currently heads the NetTrail tutorial development team. Deborah was formerly a librarian at Stanford University, where, as a member of the Faculty Software Developer's Program, she authored BiblioMania, one of the first interactive library instruction programs for the Macintosh computer. She has contributed scholarly publications and spoken at national conferences on instructional software design and development of online teaching resources. At UCSC, she continues developing instructional and information literacy resources, integrating new technolo-

gies. She and the team continue development of the nationally recognized UCSC NetTrail, an interactive Web-based information literacy course. E-mail: damurphy@ucsc.edu.

Lisa Norberg is Director of Public Services for the University of North Carolina's University Library and Adjunct Professor of Practice at UNC's School of Information and Library Science. She received her BS from the University of Wyoming and MLS from Indiana University. Before coming to UNC, she held positions at George Mason University and Pennsylvania State University at Harrisburg. She is active in ALA, ACRL, and NCLA and has published and presented papers on digital library usability, reusable learning objects, and library instructional design. E-mail: lnorberg@e-mail.unc.edu.

Megan Oakleaf is Assistant Professor in the School of Information Studies at Syracuse University. She previously served as Librarian for Instruction and Undergraduate Research at North Carolina State University. In this role, she trained fellow librarians in instructional theory and methods. She also provided library instruction for the First-Year Writing Program, First-Year College, and Department of Communication. Her research interests focus on information literacy, outcomes-based assessment, evidence-based decision making, user education, information services, and digital librarianship. E-mail: moakleaf@syr.edu.

Cleo Pappas, a former private piano teacher and high school English teacher, has been a professional librarian since receiving her MLIS from Dominican University in 1998 and served in public libraries and in a hospital setting before becoming Assistant Information Services Librarian and Assistant Professor at the University of Illinois at Chicago. She appreciates the intellectual challenge that evidence-based medicine represents and particularly enjoys interacting with medical residents, medical students, and their mentoring physicians. E-mail: cleop76@uic.edu.

Kimberly Pendell earned her MSIS from the University of Texas at Austin in May 2005. She is the liaison to the College of Dentistry and the residency programs at the Library of the Health Sciences at Chicago. E-mail: kpendell@uic.edu.

Paul R. Pival, MLS, has been Distance Education Librarian at the University of Calgary since July 2001. Prior to his arrival in Canada, he supported distance students through the library at Nova Southeastern University in Ft. Lauderdale, Florida. Paul has been an early adopter of technology to train and teach students at a distance and is the author of the blog *The Distant Librarian.* E-mail: ppival@ucalgary.ca.

Diane Prorak is Associate Professor and Reference Librarian at the University of Idaho Library, where she coordinates the library's information literacy instruction program. She has worked closely with the UI Library's freshman composition orientation sessions since pre-Internet days, designing numerous successive instructional programs that taught students to use the information resources of the times—print indexes, CD-ROM databases, and then the changing world of Web-based resources. E-mail: prorak@uidaho.edu.

Eric Resnis has been Engineering and Environmental Sciences Librarian at Miami University since 2004. He works closely with the departments of library instruction, collection development, and outreach to engineering and environmental sciences students. He cocreated Smart Searching, a series of handouts and workshops that help students easily grasp literature searching techniques. He also teaches Introduction to Information Studies in the Digital Age, a semester-long course in locating and creating information in a variety of digital formats. E-mail: resnisew@muohio.edu.

Scott Rice is Networked Information Services Librarian at the University of North Carolina at Greensboro. He is involved with distance education, e-books, proxy software, and online tutorials and games. E-mail: serice2@uncg.edu.

Peggy Ridlen is Assistant Professor and Reference/Instruction Librarian at Fontbonne University in St. Louis, Missouri, with an MA in library science from the University of Missouri. As a former secondary and elementary school librarian, she has many years of experience as an educator. She has offered workshops on information literacy and currently serves on several committees at both the local and national levels. Peggy has been teaching information literacy since her arrival at Fontbonne University in 2004. E-mail: pridlen@fontbonne.edu.

Shauna Rutherford, MLIS, is Information Literacy Coordinator at the University of Calgary. Developing effective and innovative means of teaching students how to find and use information has been the focus of Shauna's career since she began working at the University of Calgary in 1997. Since that time, she has worked with professors and students in the faculties of Communication and Culture, Social Sciences, Environmental Design, and Social Work. E-mail: srutherf@ucalgary.ca.

Pamela M. Salela is Instructional Services Librarian at the University of Illinois at Springfield. Before coming to UIS in spring 2005, she was Reference Librarian in the Learning Resources and Technology Services as well as faculty instructor in the Center for Information Media at St. Cloud State University. For fifteen years she has taught a variety of credit courses at UIS, St. Cloud State University, Miami University, and the University of Illinois at Urbana Champaign. E-mail: psale2@uis.edu.

B. Jane Scales is Distance Learning Librarian at the Washington State University Libraries. She earned an MA in German from Ohio State University and an MLIS from the University of Kentucky. E-mail: scales@wsu.edu.

Feng Shan is Assistant Librarian and Head of Electronic Resources at Schurz Library, Indiana University–South Bend. He was the library Webmaster and technical programming librarian for the development of the online course at IUSB. E-mail: fshan@iusb.edu.

Caroline Sinkinson is Instruction Coordinator and Undergraduate Services Librarian in the Reference and Instructional Services Department at the University of Colorado at Boulder. She has been responsible for coordinating library instruction for the libraries, including instruction for the Program for Writing and Rhetoric, since 2005. She continues active support of the information literacy program through collaboration, revision, and management. E-mail: caroline.sinkinson@colorado.edu.

Shilo Smith is Outreach Services Librarian at Valdosta State University, Valdosta, Georgia. She has taught a three-credit graduate level course in WebCT and consulted with her colleagues on the development of additional WebCT courses. E-mail: shismith@valdosta.edu.

Leslie Sult began her professional career as a high school librarian in Chino Valley, Arizona. In spring 2001, she completed her graduate studies in Library and Information Science at the University of North Carolina at Chapel Hill. She has worked at the University of Arizona Library since 2003 and currently serves as the Library's Instructional Design Librarian. E-mail: sultl@u.library.arizona.edu.

Jane Theissen has been Assistant Professor and Reference/Electronic Resource Librarian at Fontbonne University in St. Louis, Missouri, since 2004. Teaching information literacy is among her many responsibilities. She received her MLIS from the University of Missouri–Columbia. As a trainer for a major library software vendor, Jane traveled extensively before coming to Fontbonne University, where she is currently involved in many committees on both the state and local levels. E-mail: JTheissen@fontbonne.edu.

Kim Vassiliadis is Instructional Design and Technology librarian and Assistant Department Head for Instructional Services at the University of North Carolina at Chapel Hill's University Library. She received her BA from Flagler College and her MLIS from the University of Texas at Austin. Before coming to UNC, she served as Instruction Librarian for Christian Brothers University. She is actively involved in ALA, ACRL, RUSA, LITA, and NCLA and has published and presented on a wide variety of topics including library Web site usability, reusable learning objects, and the changing roles of librarians. E-mail: kimv@e-mail.unc.edu.

Lisa Wallis is Web Resources Librarian at Ronald Williams Library, Northeastern Illinois University, Chicago, Illinois. She was formerly Assistant Information Services Librarian and liaison to the College of Medicine, University of Illinois at Chicago. E-mail: lisacwallis@gmail.com.

Red Wassenich has been Reference Librarian at Austin Community College since 1984 and has chaired or cochaired the library's instruction program for much of that time. He has given a presentation and poster session at ACRL national conferences. Austin Community College Library Services won the 2001 ACRL Excellence in Academic Libraries Award and was selected to participate in ACRL's Best Practices in Information Literacy conference in 2002. E-mail: redwass@austincc.edu.

Jen-chien Yu has been Electronic Information Services Librarian/Data Specialist at Miami University Libraries since 2001. She develops Web-based services and applications, with a focus on applications for numeric data users and instructional outreach to first-year students. She is involved in the development of E-learn, a Web-based instruction for first-year students funded by an Ohio Board of Regents Grant. She also teaches Introduction to Information Studies in the Digital Age. She recently cowrote a book chapter titled "Introducing Undergraduates to Data Literacy: How to Find, Use, & Evaluate Numeric Data" for D. Cook and T. Cooper (eds.), *Teaching Information Literacy Skills to Education and Social Sciences Students and Practitioners: a Second Casebook of Applications.* E-mail: yuj@muohio.edu.